FOUNDATION PRESS

EDUCATION LAW STORIES

Edited By

MICHAEL A. OLIVAS
William B. Bates Distinguished Chair in Law
University of Houston Law Center

RONNA GREFF SCHNEIDER
Professor of Law
University of Cincinnati College of Law

FOUNDATION PRESS
75TH ANNIVERSARY

Cover Design: Keith Stout

395 Hudson Street
New York, NY 10014
Phone Toll Free 1–877–888–1330
Fax (212) 367–6799
foundation–press.com
Printed in the United States of America

ISBN 978–1–59941–032–6

I dedicate this book, as I do all my work, to Dr. Augustina H. Reyes, who has taught me for twenty five years. She makes all my accomplishments possible and worthwhile.

MAO

To my husband John and my children, Sam, Ben, and Julia, who are the best chapters of my life.

RGS

*

EDUCATION LAW STORIES

FOUNDATION PRESS

EDUCATION LAW STORIES

*

1

Education Law Stories: Law and Society in the Classroom

Michael A. Olivas and Ronna Greff Schneider

Schools and colleges are the major organizational mechanisms for personal achievement and social stability, so it is little wonder that they are also the staging grounds for the major social battles and disagreements of our time. As a consequence, legal issues involving education have greatly proliferated in recent times. The Supreme Court has addressed at least one issue affecting education virtually every term in the last thirty years. Even as the Supreme Court docket has generally shrunk, education related cases have remained on the docket, as the Court's last term clearly indicates. There does not appear to be any abatement in the near future in either the number or complexity of legal issues arising in the education context. In the October, 2006 term alone, the Supreme Court demonstrated its continuing interest in legal issues in the school context by deciding two cases involving freedom of expression in the school context,[1] two cases involving voluntary school district efforts to use race in student assignment plans,[2] one case involving disabilities in the education context,[3] and one case involving educational funding.[4]

The dozen cases selected for inclusion in this book span a half century and address most of the significant social topics of our time. Because of the importance of education and, in the K–12 level, its mandatory nature, it is inevitable that some of society's most important civil rights issues are litigated within the school context. These include equality of opportunity, affirmative action, race, gender, language and disability discrimination, freedom of expression, loyalty oaths, the constitutionally permissible scope of religion in the public sphere, and the constitutional limits on search and seizure. This book is centered around these themes.

The human drama behind these pivotal cases clearly resonates within the chapters in this book. The telling of these stories demonstrates the courage often shown by those who become the "names" of the cases, reveals the development of the litigation strategies of the advocates, and underscores the legacies left by the impact of these important Supreme Court decisions.

The decisions from the Court's October 2006 term indicate that it is strongly divided over some of the most important civil rights issues of our day, including several covered by the stories in this book. These most recent decisions from the Court also reinforce the continuing relevancy of the stories we have chosen to tell. These older decisions provide a useful reference point for measuring the direction of the current Court with regard to educational issues.

Perhaps the most famous case involving education is *Brown v. Board of Education*.[5] While much has been written about *Brown*, especially in its fiftieth anniversary year, Professor Leland Ware, a co-author of a behind-the-scenes book on the decision,[6] offers an important perspective of the case. He focuses not only on the Supreme Court decision itself, but on the development of litigation strategy in the lower court cases that paved the road to *Brown*. In so doing, Professor Ware highlights not only the meaning of the Supreme Court decision, but the extraordinary roles played by Charles H. Houston and Thurgood Marshall in the struggle for equality of educational opportunity for African–Americans. He looks at the very personal ways in which the two men became involved in this struggle and their role in the training and inspiration of students and other lawyers, sharing insightful biographical information about both Houston and Marshall. He examines the choice of education as a battleground for the civil rights movement and the development of necessary strategies to accomplish critical goals—from Houston's initial equalization challenges to subsequent direct attacks on segregation laws. Professor Ware discusses the development in the lower courts of the "*Brown* cases," the six school desegregation cases that would be consolidated for two rounds of hearing in the Supreme Court. He captures the detailed preparation for the second argument in the Supreme Court—necessitated by the unexpected death of Chief Justice Fred Vinson—in a way that makes the reader almost feel a part of that historical moment.

Professor Ware provides a perceptive evaluation of the Supreme Court's decision and its legal aftermath. He rejects the conclusion that *Brown* was wrongly decided. He thus takes issue with the argument that the *Brown* decision was too weak, or the assertion that segregation would have ended in a more gradual fashion without *Brown*, avoiding the radicalization, resistance, and violence generated among whites by the decision. He also disagrees with the assertion that African–American students would have benefited more from a strategy that required southern states to equalize black and white schools rather than to impose desegregation. Offering his own thoughtful assessment of the *Brown* legacy, Professor Ware observes that divisions along class lines within the African-American community as well as the continuing impact of housing segregation serve as significant barriers to achieving the kind of quality education envisioned by the litigants in *Brown*.

While *Brown* addressed the question of *de jure* race discrimination in education, it left unanswered many other questions regarding educational opportunity. In looking at the story underlying the Supreme Court's decision in *San Antonio Independent School District v. Rodriguez*,[7] Professor Michael Heise examines the twin issues of determining whether there is any federal constitutionally protected right to an education and whether there are any federal constitutional requirements regarding the sufficiency of the funding of such education. His scholarship often is empirical, especially with regard to school finance issues, and he brings this extensive knowledge of school finance to his storytelling.

The *Rodriguez* Court rejected the federal constitutional challenge to the manner in which Texas—and many states—fund public education, despite the resultant vast disparities between the amounts of funds available to rich and poor school districts. In all likelihood, *Rodriguez* has foreclosed the use of the federal constitution as a vehicle for affecting any dramatic change in the funding structure of public education by its holding that there was no fundamental right to a quality public education under the federal constitution and that poverty was not a suspect class. *Rodriguez* signaled the end of federal litigation on these important issues, pushing educational funding challenges into the state courts where remedies would be sought under state constitutions. Therefore, while the *Rodriguez* story unfolds in the federal court arena with a focus on the scope of federal constitutional rights, its legacy may well be the development of a greater reliance on state constitutional law, at least with regard to some civil rights issues in the education context.

Juxtaposed to both *Brown* and *Rodriguez* is the more recent *Grutter v. Bollinger*[8] decision in which the Supreme Court examined a more contemporary aspect of the issue of educational opportunity, namely that of the constitutionality of affirmative action in admissions at the University of Michigan. Professor Wendy Parker, a former litigator in the Department of Justice, has used that experience as a base for her scholarship in the area of race and education. She has written eloquently on desegregation cases and their complex civil procedure. In her story on the law school admissions case in *Grutter*, Professor Parker also comments upon the companion University of Michigan undergraduate admissions case, *Gratz v. Bollinger*.[9] In November, 2006, Michigan voters weighed in on a state constitutional ballot measure[10] that leaves the use of race in affirmative action unclear, but it is certain that the last chapter of this complex issue has not yet been written. The ballot measure enacted into law in Michigan in 2006 amends the state constitution and contains the following language:

> (1) The University of Michigan, Michigan State University, Wayne State University, and any other public college or university, community college, or school district shall not discriminate against, or grant preferential treatment to, any individual or group on the basis of race, sex, color, ethnicity, or national origin in the operation of public employment, public education or public contracting.
>
> (2) The state shall not discriminate against, or grant preferential treatment to, any individual or group on the basis of race, sex, color, ethnicity, or national origin in the operation of public employment, public education, or public contracting.
>
> (3) For the purposes of this section 'state' includes, but is not necessarily limited to, the state itself, any city, county, any public college, university, or community college, school district, or other political subdivision or governmental instrumentality of or within the State of Michigan not included in sub-section 1.[11]

It has not yet been determined whether the ballot measure precludes consideration of the racially disparate impact of governmental action or just disparate treatment based on the prohibited criteria. For example, would the increased use of the SAT, with its demonstrable racial effects,[12] violate the prohibition against the use of race as proscribed in the ballot measure? The *Grutter* and *Gratz* cases revealed that the University of Michigan, a public institution, awarded "legacy credit," or special points for the children of alumni.[13] Would the continued use of alumni legacy preferences by the University of Michigan, where more legacies are white than persons of color, trigger this racial proscription?[14] The practice was not struck down, as it was considered to have minimal impact.[15] Such use, if subsequent analysis indicates greater disparate impact, could arguably render such a formal practice a racial advantage, one that could trigger this ballot provision.

The Supreme Court addressed the constitutionality of the voluntary plans of two different school districts—Seattle and Louisville—in using race in the assignment of students to schools in the K–12 context in June, 2007. In a bitterly divided decision, *Parents Involved in Community Schools v. Seattle School District No. 1*,[16] the Court struck down the plans of both districts, holding that they violated the Equal Protection Clause. The Court reasoned that the plans, in one school district that had never been found to be legally segregated (Seattle) and in one that had been declared "unitary" (Louisville), were not sufficiently narrowly tailored to meet the Court's constitutional test that would have enabled the educators to use race in school assignments. The decision offered the

Court the first opportunity to examine issues touching on the voluntary use of race to achieve or maintain some racial diversity in education since the Court's decisions in *Grutter* and *Gratz*. Chief Justice Roberts, writing for the Court, stated that "[i]n design and operation, the plans are directed only to racial balance, pure and simple, an objective this Court has repeatedly condemned as illegitimate."[17] Justice Breyer vehemently dissented:

> We have approved of 'narrowly tailored' plans that are no less race-conscious than the plans before us. And we have understood that the Constitution *permits* local communities to adopt desegregation plans even where it does not *require* them to do so. The plurality pays inadequate attention to this law, to past opinions' rationales, their language, and the contexts in which they arise. As a result, it reverses course and reaches the wrong conclusion.[18]

In a separate opinion, concurring in part and concurring in the judgment, Justice Kennedy wrote what may well turn out to be the pivotal opinion in the case:

> Governmental classifications that command persons to march in different directions based upon racial typologies can cause a new divisiveness. The practice can lead to corrosive discourse, where race serves not as an element of our diverse heritage but instead as a bargaining chip in the political process. On the other hand, race conscious measures that do not rely upon differential treatment based on individual classifications present these problems to a lesser degree.
>
> The idea that if race is the problem, race is the instrument with which to solve it cannot be accepted as an analytic leap forward. And if this is a frustrating duality of the Equal Protection Clause it simply reflects the duality of our history and our attempts to promote freedom in a world that sometimes seems set against it.[19]

The specific nature of the various steps that may be taken by public school districts remains to be seen—as we enter an era of great uncertainty with regard to the proper scope of those remedies that may meet the approval of Justice Kennedy. Some passage of time and further examination of the issues in various factual contexts will be needed before there is a fuller understanding of the meaning and significance of these various opinions.

Grutter and *Gratz* involved higher education and thus merit selection, which was not at issue in either the Seattle or Louisville programs. The full extent to which such a distinction is important in the K–12 context, including public K–12 schools that have special admissions criteria based at least in part on merit selection, of course remains to be seen. However, both the plurality opinion and the dissents set out the *Grutter* test as an individualized and narrowly-tailored approach to college admissions, suggesting that the use of race in college admissions lives to see another day. Chief Justice Roberts, for example, held that "[t]he entire gist of the analysis in *Grutter* was that the admissions program at issue there focused on each applicant as an individual, and not simply as a member of a particular racial group."

In her telling of the story behind *Lau v. Nichols*,[20] Professor Rachel Moran brings her longstanding expertise in education law and experience as the co-author of an education law casebook[21] to bear upon this important case. *Lau* held that a public school district's failure to provide English language instruction to non-English speaking students of Chinese ancestry denied them a meaningful opportunity to participate in an educational program that received federal financial assistance in violation of Title VI of the Civil Rights Act of 1964.[22]

Professor Moran finds the decision to be a most unusual but important case for a host of reasons: the lead protagonist has largely declined to comment publicly beyond what is in the decision itself for fear of being misunderstood; the case was not fully developed and school administrators received no guidance on remedies from the opinion; language instruction is a complex issue and is not well-understood, then or now; and there is a growing school population of children for whom English is not the first or the home language. The basis of the *Lau* decision, Title VI, bans "national origin" and "race" discrimination, and has thus always seemed an odd vehicle for a successful claim on behalf of linguistic minority children, and Professor Moran finds it so here. It is also the rare equity case where, as in *Lau*, the plaintiffs urged no specific remedy, and appeared to want the issue remanded back to the offending Board of Education. The Supreme Court did remand the case, although to the courts. In fact, Judge Burke of the Northern District of California oversaw the development of a remedy on remand. This was a challenge for the plaintiffs' allies, who sought to circumvent him as well as unsympathetic school personnel by forcing the school district to collaborate with community representatives in formulating a remedy. The United States played an integral role in shepherding this process to a successful conclusion.

As with so many of these cases, the real game afoot is the implementation, once a case has resolved itself, with winners and losers. As noted by Professor Ware in his recounting of *Brown*, it was *Brown I* in 1954 that resolved the theoretical principles, only to have the next year's *Brown II* wink at the Southern judiciary ("with all deliberate speed") and, in effect, slow the implementation of desegregation. *Lau* did directly lead to Office for Civil Rights (OCR) guidelines, but as Professor Moran notes, these "*Lau* remedies" never did resolve the issue satisfactorily, and as her chapter and her casebook reveal, this issue has often foundered on research, politics, and efficacy.[23]

While *Brown, Rodriguez, Grutter*, and *Lau* all focused on educational opportunity with regard to race, ethnicity or language, *United States v. Virginia*[24] focused on the issue of gender discrimination in the higher education context. Professor Rosemary Salomone recounts the fascinating way in which this case was developed, and the important advocacy efforts that forced this matter to its inevitable resolution. After other postsecondary sex discrimination issues had been litigated in the Supreme Court decision in *Mississippi University for Women v. Hogan*[25] (a case brought by a male nursing school applicant) and in a similar fashion in the Fourth Circuit decision in the Citadel case, *Faulkner v. Jones* (woman applicant to all-male public college),[26] this case showed the unusual congruence of gender discrimination, college law, and military instruction. Particularly devastating was the Court's likening the alternative Mary Baldwin College program for women cadets to the substandard basement, evening law school offered by the University of Texas in 1950 for African–American law school applicants, prohibited in *Sweatt v. Painter*.[27] Today, when female undergraduates outnumber male undergraduates,[28]—particularly men of color,[29] the significance of these cases may be underappreciated.

Laura Rothstein, who has written a disabilities law treatise[30] and casebook,[31] examines *Southeastern Community College v. Davis*,[32] the lead higher education case in this developing area, but one with surprisingly little scholarship on its provenance and background. Professor Rothstein takes a very clever and innovative approach to elucidating *Southeastern Community College*, by showing how disability law has played out in today's pervasive cultural conduit, television, especially the long-running prime-time evening show ER. Such shows have mainstreamed many of the disability issues in a way that most Supreme Court cases could use. (Contrast "all deliberate speed" and "*Lau* remedies" with television's treatment of penile implants, transsexual surgery, ADD, dysfunctional doctors, and other socio-medical issues.) Even so, a number of cultural stereotypes affect the admission and schooling of college students with disabilities, and she notes that there are many miles to go before we sleep.

The Supreme Court continued to address issues involving disabilities in the education context this past term when it decided *Winkelman v. Parma City School District*.[33] In *Winkelman*, the Court held that parents of children with disabilities have their own independent, enforceable rights under the Individuals with Disabilities Education Act (IDEA) and thus could represent themselves in court. Unlike *Southeastern Community College*, *Winkelman* involved the K–12 context. However, *Winkelman* does reinforce *Southeastern Community College*, in that it recognizes the importance of federal statutory protection in the disabilities area. While we have chosen to tell the story of a nursing student who was singled out on the basis of her disability at the higher education level, the holding in *Winkelman* demonstrates that these cases will continue to arise in schools and colleges.

The Supreme Court, as well as the academic community itself, has often recognized the importance of freedom of expression in the education context. Our book looks at this important issue from three different perspectives—that of school-sponsored speech in the secondary school context; that involving the imposition of mandatory student fees in the university setting; and that of loyalty oaths for public employees.

In analyzing *Hazelwood School District v. Kuhlmeier*,[34] Professor Anne Proffitt Dupre examines a challenge brought by public high school student journalists[35] to a principal's deletion of two stories from the school paper, the *Spectrum*. One article dealt with the impact of divorce on students, including negative comments made by named and unnamed students, and one recounted the experiences of three pregnant students, who were not expressly named. With the richness of her scholarship in the children's rights field[36] and student speech,[37] Professor Dupre recounts the tale of what has become one of the most important school speech cases of the twentieth century. She looks at the roles of various participants in shaping the case—from the faculty newspaper advisor who resigned shortly before the articles in question were to be published to the principal concerned with any harm that could result from publication, including potential school tort liability. In providing excerpts from the actual content of the articles in question, Professor Dupre ensures that her reader understands the dilemma faced by the school principal in deciding whether to allow the publication of the articles in question. With generous use of the Supreme Court transcript of the arguments in the case, Professor Dupre is able to highlight the tension between the value of freedom of expression in school and school authorities' concern for denying students a school-sponsored platform for expressing ideas viewed as antithetical to the educational mission.

As other storytellers in this volume have done, she notes the importance of the way in which courts or litigants frame the issue to be decided—and the importance of the way in which evidence presented in support of a particular position is characterized. In her analysis of the Supreme Court's decision, Professor Dupre ponders what to make of Justice Stevens' unanticipated switch from a student speech supporter[38] to a silent member of the *Hazelwood* Court's majority[39] upholding the school's restriction of speech. Professor Dupre examines the immediate as well as long range aftermath of *Hazelwood* and the reactions of constitutional scholars, educators, journalists, lower courts, legislators and voters. Finally, she addresses the question whether *Hazelwood* could or should apply to the university setting, an issue not yet decided by the Supreme Court.

As already noted, the Supreme Court decided two school speech cases this past term. In the first of these speech cases, *Tennessee Secondary School Athletic Association v. Brentwood Academy*,[40] the Supreme Court rejected the argument that a state athletic association's rule that prohibited school coaches from recruiting middle school athletes violated the First Amendment. While *Brentwood* is valuable for examining the scope of any constitutional limitations on recruitment restrictions, it probably does not have the potentially extensive ramifications for free speech doctrine in the school setting as does the second case decided by the Supreme Court during this same term, *Morse v. Frederick*.[41]

In *Morse*, the Court held a student's free speech rights were not violated when a school suspended the student for unfurling a banner during an off-campus, but "school-sanctioned and school- supervised"[42] activity occurring during school hours, that expressed what the school could reasonably construe to be a message advocating the use of illegal drugs. The Court's reasoning focused on the authority of the school to take action against the student for his behavior at the activity off-campus and the reasonableness of school officials in so interpreting the student's remark, "Bong Hits 4 Jesus." The school's interpretation was deemed reasonable, despite the student's assertion that "the words were just nonsense meant to attract television cameras."[43] The Court's recent decision in *Morse* stated that the Court's earlier decision in *Hazelwood*[44] was not controlling, because *Hazelwood* applies to school-sponsored speech, which was not at issue in *Morse*. Nevertheless, the *Morse* Court reiterated that the earlier *Hazelwood* decision set forth two basic principles that continue to be valid and relevant even to the Court's decision in *Morse*.[45] The first principle is that "schools may regulate some speech even though the government could not censor similar speech outside the school."[46] The second principle is that there is more than one "basis for restricting student speech."[47] *Morse* therefore reinforced the importance of *Hazelwood*, even as it expressly stated that that earlier decision was not applicable to the one currently before the Court. For this reason and because of the large number of speech cases that inevitably involve school-sponsored speech, we chose to tell the tale of *Hazelwood*.

Professor Linda Greene also examines the issue of freedom of expression—this time with regard to the imposition of mandatory university student activity fees. Money may talk—but as far as the federal Constitution is concerned, the critical question is—what does that money say? Professor Greene offers her own insider knowledge of the University of Wisconsin's involvement in the case of *Board of Regents v. Southworth*,[48] and readers are better for it. Student fee cases can be very vexing, as they are like tax cases, where taxpayers do not want to contribute to government programs with which they disagree, but the common weal requires we all pay into the fisc. Given the many hundreds of student organizations that any comprehensive campus houses, it is hard to imagine an organization that does not have precepts with which another student disagrees or abhors.[49]

Southworth seems to be a natural outgrowth of the Supreme Court's decision in *Widmar v. Vincent*,[50] which struck down a state university's ban on the use of university facilities by a student religious organization where such use by nonreligious student groups was permitted. Content neutral action under the Free Speech Clause may thus seem to trump Establishment Clause concerns under such circumstances.[51]

This analysis pervades other public forum-type cases where a college or other educational entity can not exclude certain speech, such as religious speech or expressive activity, on the basis of content or viewpoint once it has opened itself up to student groups and their activities.[52] Such claims against educational institutions may well proliferate. Limits or exclusions of student groups or activities may also raise questions under the Equal Protection Clause and various anti-discrimination laws as well when a group's membership or leadership criteria are considered to be discriminatory.

Professor Robert O'Neil, one of the country's senior college law scholars, was also the last public college employee in New York State to be asked to swear to the loyalty oath, and his actions ensured that the stake was driven through the heart of this requirement. He examines *Keyishian v. Board of Regents*,[53] one of a number of higher education cases that have arisen out of mergers between public and private systems, or that have reflected the complex issues that result from the state taking over a formerly-private or municipal institution. A generational divide has developed as today's students seem unaware of loyalty oath requirements, remnants of the anti-Communist era, and they often fail to appreciate the divisiveness and public debate over their existence. But Professor O'Neil's account makes the controversy fresh and relevant to the larger issue of free expression, and the depredations of September 11 provide the backdrop for discussions of national security in contemporary classrooms. Both the *Southworth* and *Keyishian* chapters bristle with behind-the-scenes details and previously-unpublished information, all of which brings these cases to life.

Perhaps no issue is more contentious in the school context than determining the constitutionally permissible scope of religious expression or religious observance in public schools, and the extent to which religious belief may impact upon the curriculum. Litigation often results from the potential clashes involving a school's inculcation of values or the development of critical thinking skills that may conflict with individual or parental religious beliefs, the teaching of religiously influenced ideas in the curriculum, as well as efforts to allow religious expression or observance in school or during school-sponsored activities. Two of our stories explore such issues—one in the context of the public school curriculum and one in the context of public school activities.

Professor Leslie Griffin, a scholar of law and religion,[54] examines the intersection of constitutional questions involving public school curricular policy based on the religious beliefs of some and the concept of academic freedom as she brings to life the case of *Aguillard v. Edwards.*[55] In *Aguillard,* the Supreme Court considered the constitutionality of a Louisiana law that required public schools to give "balanced treatment to [the teaching of] creation-science and evolution-science."[56] The Court struck down the law on the basis that it did not have a secular purpose. In contrast, the dissent accepted the state's argument that requiring such balanced treatment was a matter of academic freedom that must be constitutionally respected.

Professor Griffin explores both lower court decisions in *Aguillard* as well as a lower court decision challenging a similar Arkansas statute. Based on her interviews gathering the personal recollections of the lawyers on both sides of the issue, she highlights the strategic considerations underlying the debate as to whether the *Aguillard* challenge should be decided on the basis of a summary judgment or a jury verdict. The answer revolved around the resolution of what she describes as the "simple yet complex question" that permeates the entire narrative—how to determine the difference between religion and science—as well as the critical follow-up question of whether courts are capable of such a task.

Professor Griffin also examines the newest controversy in this area—whether teaching Intelligent Design (ID) in the public schools violates the Establishment Clause. The answer from at least one district court has been a resounding yes.[57] The court characterized ID as "a mere re-labeling of creationism."[58] Professor Griffin concludes with an exploration of the recent alternative argument that evolution is itself a religion and its teaching is therefore a violation of the Establishment Clause.

Professor Erwin Chemerinsky, a renowned constitutional scholar as well as Supreme Court advocate, examines the issue of prayer under the lights of Friday night football in Texas in *Santa Fe Independent School Dist. v. Doe.*[59] *Santa Fe* is the Supreme Court's most recent decision addressing the issue of prayer or moment of silence in the public schools.[60] The case involved a challenge to the school-sponsored recitation of prayer during the course of activities beyond the ordinary school day. Through the extensive use of newspaper accounts as well as interviews, Professor Chemerinsky sets the stage for the development of the school policy in question as well as the litigation challenging it. He even describes the actions taken by a group of Congressmen in passing a resolution that called upon the Supreme Court to uphold the school policy permitting the football game prayer. The case discusses the various approaches the Supreme Court has used during the last three and a half decades as well as examines the relationship between the prohibitions of the Establishment Clause and the protections of the Free Speech Clause with regard to religious expression. He concludes with recognition of the deep division within both the Court and the country on the proper constitutional limits on religion in the public sphere.

Finally, our book looks at the ongoing debate surrounding the scope of protection for students under the Fourth Amendment. In his chapter on the Supreme Court's decision in *Pottawatomie County v. Lindsay Earls*,[61] Professor Robert Bloom looks at the Court's latest attempt to determine the proper scope of student drug testing. His story is told primarily from the perspective of Lindsay Earls, the high school student who challenged her school's policy requiring drug testing for participants in extra-curricular activities. Professor Bloom examines her objections to the drug testing policy as a high school student and then examines her response to the Supreme Court's decision from her perspective as a young college student when the case was actually decided. Professor Bloom's story of *Earls* is clearly one of admiration for the young woman who showed great personal courage in standing up to the gossip and the challenges to her own integrity for a principle in which she believed. After detailed analysis of the opinions in the *Earls* decision, Professor Bloom explores all sides of the debate about high school drug testing—from both policy and constitutional vantage points. He observes that future cases, with a newly constituted Supreme Court, will have to decide whether the *Earls* decision may be extended to all students at school and whether, and to what extent, there will need be a specific showing of a drug abuse problem in a particular school before testing is permitted. He notes that those on both sides of this controversy acknowledge that there have been few organized empirical studies of the efficacy of drug testing as a way of combating drug abuse. In conclusion, Professor Bloom ponders how the use of state constitutions and decisions may impact upon the drug testing controversy. It remains to be seen whether, as in *Rodriguez*, students will look to the states and their constitutions for greater protection of their civil liberties than that provided under the federal Bill of Rights.

We have structured this book so that it may serve as a supplemental text for law school classes addressing issues involving K–12, higher education or both. Thus, cases from both levels of education are represented in our selections. The book is also designed to serve as a supplemental or a primary text outside the law school arena, such as colleges of education or schools of public policy. These stories may be helpful to today's educators who must be able to identify those issues that could potentially develop into problems with major legal implications.

Virtually all readers possess a certain degree of expertise in identifying and appreciating the implications of legal issues in the education context because everyone has experienced the education process. The narratives presented in this book offer an opportunity to use that personal expertise to assess the Supreme Court's analysis of the important issues presented in this collection of landmark cases. This experience in the educational process also provides us with an understanding of the scope of unanswered legal questions that remain as challenges for the educational decisions of the future. We hope that the narratives in this book will serve as a platform for a discussion of those issues as well.

Endnotes

1. Tennessee Secondary School Athletic Association v. Brentwood Academy, 127 S.Ct. 2489 (2007); Morse v. Frederick, 127 S.Ct. 2618 (2007). The Court also decided Davenport v. Washington Education Association, 127 S.Ct. 2372 (2007), which addresses First Amendment concerns in the context of requiring affirmative consent before spending a nonmember's agency-shop fees for election-related purposes. While the decision involves the Washington Education Association, neither the holding nor the reasoning underlying it is unique to the education context.

2. There were two cases, Parents Involved in Cmty. Sch. v. Seattle Sch. Dist. No. 1, 426 F.3d 1162 (9th Cir. 2005) (en banc), cert. granted, 126 S.Ct. 2351 (2006) and McFarland v. Jefferson County Pub. Schs., 416 F.3d 513 (6th Cir. 2005) (per curiam), cert. granted, Meredith v. Jefferson County Bd. of Educ., 126 S.Ct. 2351 (2006), that were decided in a single decision, Parents Involved in Cmty. Sch. v. Seattle Sch. Dist. No. 1, ___ U.S. ___, 127 S.Ct. 2738 (2007).

3. Winkelman v. Parma City School District, 127 S.Ct. 1994 (2007).

4. Zuni Public School District No. 89 v. Department of Education, 127 S.Ct. 1534 (2007) (Department of Education's technical definitions of school funds distribution formulae were not unreasonable construction of complex statute).

5. 347 U.S. 483 (1954).

6. Robert Cottrol, Ray Diamond and Leland Ware, Brown v. Board of Education: Caste, Culture and the Constitution (2003).

7. 411 U.S. 1 (1973).

8. 539 U.S. 306 (2003).

9. 539 U.S. 244 (2003).

10. *See* Paul Schmidt, *Michigan Overwhelmingly Adopts Ban on Affirmative–Action Preferences; Foes of the ballot measure vow to keep fighting while supporters eye new fronts*, Chron. of Higher Educ., November 17, 2006, at A23.

11. Mich. Const. art. I, § 26.

12. William C. Kidder and Jay Rosner, *How the SAT Creates "Built-in Headwinds": An Educational and Legal Analysis of Disparate Impact*, 43 Santa Clara Law Review 131 (2002) (critique of racial impact of admissions testing).

13. *Grutter*, 539 U.S at 368 (Justice Thomas, with whom Justice Scalia joins as to Parts I–VII, concurring in part and dissenting in part); *Gratz*, 539 U.S. at 255 (points accorded for "alumni relationship"); 539 at 257 n.9 (affirming lower court finding that previous criteria did not constitute "discrimination").

14. *See generally* John Lamb, *The Real Affirmative Action Babies: Legacy Preferences in Harvard and Yale*, 26 Col. J. L. & Soc. Prob. 491 (1993) (reviewing legacy admissions at elite private colleges, showing alumni preference children are admitted at more than twice the rate of all applicants). *See also* Thomas J. Espenshade and Chang Y. Chung, *"The Opportunity Cost of Admission Preferences at Elite Universities,"* 86 Social Science Quarterly 293 (2005) (noting how alumni preference program give disproportionate advantages to less-well qualified applicants, the vast majority of whom are white); Daniel Golden, *The Price of Admission: How America's Ruling Class Buys Its Way into Elite Colleges—and Who Gets Left Outside the Gates* (2006).

15. 539 U.S at 368.

16. ___ U.S. ___, 127 S.Ct. 2738 (2007).

17. ___ U.S. ___, 127 S.Ct. 2738, 2755 (2007).

18. ___ U.S. ___, 127 S. Ct. 2738, 2800 (2007) (Breyer, J., dissenting).

19. ___ U.S. ___, 127 S.Ct. 2738, 2797 (2007) (Kennedy, J., concurring in part and concurring in the judgment).

20. 414 U.S. 563 (1974).

21. Mark G. Yudof, David L. Kirp, Betsy Levin, and Rachel F. Moran, Educational Policy and the Law (4th ed. 2002).

22. 42 U.S.C. § 2000d.

23. Yudof et al., *supra* note 15, at 649–667.

24. 518 U.S. 515 (1996).

25. 458 U.S. 718 (1982).

26. 51 F.3d 440 (4th Cir. 1995).

27. Sweatt v. Painter, 339 U.S. 629 (1950).

28. Robin Wilson, *The New Gender Divide; Data show that more women than men now enroll in college, but is there really a "boy crisis"?* Chron. of Higher Educ., January 26, 2007, at A36.

29. *Id.* at A36–37. ("more men than women are forgoing higher education. But those men are primarily from low-income and minority groups, making the gap more about class and race than about gender. The number of men attending college is still increasing, those analysts point out, just not as fast as the number of women.")

30. Laura Rothstein and Julia Rothstein, Disabilities and the Law (3rd ed. 2006).

31. Laura F. Rothstein, Disability Law: Cases, Materials, Problems (4th ed. 2006).

32. 442 U.S. 397 (1979).

33. ___ U.S. ___, 127 S.Ct. 1994 (2007).

34. 484 U.S. 260 (1988).

35. The students would graduate before the trial in the district court.

36. Anne Proffitt Dupre, *Children and the Law* (2d ed. 2006).

37. Anne Proffitt Dupre, *School Speech* (Harvard University Press forthcoming).

38. Justice Stevens dissented two years earlier in the Court's previous decision upholding school authorities' right to punish a student for the delivery of a speech to other students through the use of sexual innuendo *See* Bethel School Dist. v. Fraser, 478 U.S. 675, 691 (1986) (Stevens, J., dissenting).

39. Only eight Justices decided the *Hazelwood* case. Justice Powell had resigned and Justice Kennedy would be sworn in until the month following the decision.

40. 127 S.Ct. 2489 (2007).

41. 127 S.Ct. 2618 (2007).

42. *Id.* at 2622.

43. *Id.* at 2624 (citing the Ninth Circuit opinion in the case, 439 F.3d 1114, 1117–1118 (9th Cir. 2006)).

44. The Court in Morse v. Frederick actually refers to Hazelwood School Dist. v. Kuhlmeier, 484 U.S. 260 (1988) as *Kuhlmeier* rather than *Hazelwood*.

45. The *Morse* Court stated that the two principles were "distill[ed]" from the Court's earlier opinion in Bethel School District No. 403 v. Fraser, 478 U.S. 675 (1986) and that *Hazelwood* (as already noted, the Court referred to the opinion as *Kuhlmeier*) "confirms both principles." 127 S.Ct. 2618, 2626, 2627 (2007).

46. *Id.* at 2627.

47. *Id.* The *Morse* Court stated that the Supreme Court's earlier opinion in Bethel School District No. 403 v. Fraser, 478 U.S. 675 (1986) made clear that "the mode of analysis set forth in" the Court's previous decision in Tinker v. Des Mones Independent Community School Dist., 393 U.S. 503 (1969) "is not absolute." *Id.* Justice Thomas,' concurring opinion in *Morse* would have preferred to "dispense with *Tinker* altogether." *Id.* at 2636 (Thomas, J., concurring). But see also the concurring opinion of Justice Alito, joined by Justice Kennedy, stating that

> [t]he Court is also correct in noting that *Tinker*, which permits the regulation of student speech that threatens a concrete and substantial disruption ... does not set out the only ground on which in-school student speech may be regulated by state actors in a way that would not be constitutional in other settings.
>
> But I do not read the opinion to mean that there are necessarily any grounds for such regulation that are not already recognized in the holdings of this Court ... I join the opinion of the Court on the understanding that the opinion does not hold that the special characteristics of the public schools necessarily justify any other speech restrictions.

Id. at 2637 (Alito, J., concurring). Justice Alito also emphasized that he joined the Court's opinion on the understanding that "it provides no support for any restriction of speech that can plausible be interpreted as commenting on any political or social issue ..." *Id.* at 2636 (Alito, J., concurring). See also the dissent of Justice Stevens, joined by Justices Souter and Ginsburg. *Id.* at 2644 (Stevens, J., dissenting) ("the First Amendment protects student speech if the message itself neither violates a permissible rule nor expressly advocates conduct that is illegal and harmful to students").

48. 529 U.S. 217 (2000).

49. In Rosenberger v. University of Virginia, as just one example, the University of Virginia was shown to have had 343 such student organizations in 1990. 515 U.S. 819, 825 (1995).

50. 454 U.S. 263 (1981).

51. The Court stated that "the forum is available to a broad class of nonreligious as well as religious speakers ... The provision of benefits to so broad a spectrum of groups is an important index of secular effect ... At least in the absence of empirical evidence that religious groups will dominate ... [the university's] open forum, we agree with the Court of Appeals that the advancement of religion would not be the forum's 'primary effect.' " *Id.* at 277. *See also*, Thomas Bartlett, *Southern Ill. Settles With Christian Group*, Chron. of Higher Educ., June 1, 2007, at A28 (reporting on settlement to allow Christian Legal Society to operate as registered campus organization, notwithstanding violation of campus anti-discrimination policy).

52. This analysis pertains even more forcefully to K–12 schools, as in Board of Education v. Mergens, 496 U.S. 226 (1990). *See, e.g.*, Nicole B. Casarez, Public Forums, Selective Subsidies: Shifting Standards of Viewpoint discrimination, 64 Alb. L. Rev. 501 (2000).

53. 385 U.S. 589 (1967).

54. Law and Religion: Cases and Materials (2007).

55. 482 U.S. 578 (1987). This case is the second time in which the Supreme Court has looked at some aspect of the debate surrounding the teaching of evolution in public schools. In the first case, Epperson v. Arkansas, 393 U.S. 97 (1968), the Supreme Court struck down a state law that prohibited the teaching of evolution in the public schools.

56. 482 U.S. at 598 (quoting § 17:286.4(A) (West 1982) as well as other parts of the Balanced Treatment for Creation–Science and Evolution–Science Act, La.Rev.Stat.Ann. § 17:286.1 *et seq.* (West 1982)).

57. Kitzmiller v. Dover Area Sch. Dist., 400 F.Supp.2d 707 (M.D. Pa. 2005).

58. *Id.* at 726 ("The overwhelming evidence at trial established that ID is a religious view, a mere re-labeling of creationism, and not a scientific theory. The overwhelming evidence at trial established that ID is a religious view, a mere re-labeling of creationism, and not a scientific theory.").

59. 530 U.S. 290 (2000).

60. *See* Engel v. Vitale, 370 U.S. 421 (1962); School Dist. of Abington Tp., Pa. v. Schempp, 374 U.S. 203 (1963); Wallace v. Jaffree, 472 U.S. 38 (1985); and Lee v. Weisman, 505 U.S. 577 (1992).

61. 536 U.S. 822 (2002).

*

2

The Story of *Brown v. Board of Education*: The Long Road to Racial Equality

Leland Ware[1]

Introduction

In 1892, Homer A. Plessy, a 30–year–old New Orleans shoemaker, was arrested after refusing to leave a railroad car reserved for white passengers. Plessy was acting on a plan organized by a group of Louisiana residents who had decided to orchestrate a challenge to a New Orleans' "separate car law," which required racial segregation on public transportation. Plessy, a light-complexioned New Orleans Creole, was chosen to execute the plan because he was "white enough to gain access to the train and black enough to be arrested for doing so."[2]

In the ensuing criminal prosecution, Plessy's lawyers argued that the segregation law violated the Fourteenth and Thirteenth Amendments of the U.S. Constitution because it treated African–Americans differently and less favorably than similarly situated whites. In 1896, however, the Supreme Court ruled in *Plessy v. Ferguson*[3] that the segregation laws did not violate the Constitution if the facilities provided for blacks were equal to those reserved for whites. After *Plessy*, a regime of white supremacy was imposed. The Fourteenth and Fifteenth Amendments[4] were all but nullified in the South. African–Americans were disenfranchised, confined to substandard housing in segregated neighborhoods, and excluded from all but the lowest paying, least desirable occupations. Separate, but never equal.

In the years following *Plessy*, African–Americans reacted by establishing organizations that promoted their equality rights, most notably the National Association for the Advancement of Colored People. Despite the NAACP's efforts, segregation became an all-encompassing aspect of the lives of African–Americans. In the early 1930s, however, the NAACP decided to alter its direction from lobbying and ad hoc litigation. It hired Charles H. Houston to lead a campaign that would challenge segregation in the courts. Houston was, at the time, the dean of Howard University's

School of Law, where he inspired the generation of African–American lawyers who led the legal battle against segregation.

To avoid an affirmation of *Plessy* in the conservative legal climate of the 1930s, Houston proposed a gradual and indirect approach, the "equalization strategy." When the plan was implemented, cases would be filed arguing that states operating segregated schools were in violation of the Fourteenth Amendment based on the inadequate facilities and inequitable distribution of resources for black students. Houston calculated that if the equality aspect of *Plessy's* "separate but equal" doctrine were enforced, states would be compelled to make black schools physically and otherwise equal to the white institutions. The resulting burden and expense would be too much for the southern states to bear. Under the pressure of litigation, segregation would eventually collapse under its own weight.

Southern states had established segregated colleges for African–American students, but none of them provided instruction beyond the undergraduate level. As a result, graduate and professional schools were targeted as the focus of the equalization cases. The first of these involved a black student's efforts to be admitted to the University of Maryland School of Law. As Maryland had not established a law school for African–Americans, the Court ordered the university to admit the applicant to the entering class the following semester. Another case was filed against the University of Missouri in which a similar challenge was mounted. When that case reached the Supreme Court, it ordered the black student's admission to Missouri's School of Law.

In 1946, the NAACP filed a suit against the University of Oklahoma. When that case reached the Supreme Court, it held that Oklahoma was obligated to provide legal instruction to black students. A similar case was filed in Texas and a second case was commenced against Oklahoma. The Supreme Court issued decisions in both cases on the same day in 1950. In opinions that went beyond equalizing school buildings, the Supreme Court acknowledged the stigmatic and other intangible injuries that segregation caused. It ruled in the NAACP's favor, but it stopped short of reversing *Plessy*.

After the rulings in the Texas and Oklahoma cases, the direct challenge to *Plessy* was commenced. Eventually, six cases were filed in five jurisdictions: Kansas, South Carolina, Virginia, Washington, D.C., and Delaware. The cases were consolidated in the Supreme Court. The unanimous opinion in *Brown v. Board of Education*, announced on May 17, 1954, held that "[s]eparate educational facilities are inherently unequal."[5]

Brown was a turning point for all Americans. No other Supreme Court decision has had such lasting significance. A few months after the

Brown decision was issued, historic events unfolded in Montgomery, Alabama. Rosa Parks sat down, Martin Luther King stood up, and the Civil Rights Movement was launched. After a decade of marches, boycotts, and protest activities throughout the South, Congress enacted civil rights laws that ended the official regime of white supremacy. This would not have happened without the courage, perseverance, and vision of the lawyers who waged the legal battles that culminated with *Brown*.

This chapter examines the long-range, carefully orchestrated legal strategy that culminated with *Brown*. It also contains an analysis of official resistance to desegregation efforts in the South during the era of "massive resistance" and in the North where segregated housing patterns hampered integration. The discussion includes an analysis of the Supreme Court's "resegregation" decisions in the 1990s, which led to the end of busing and the return to neighborhood schools. The final section evaluates the continuing significance of *Brown's* legacy.

The NAACP's Legal Campaign

Not long after it was organized in 1909, the NAACP established a steering committee that supported legal actions on behalf of African-Americans victimized by discrimination. Throughout the years, several cases were brought on behalf of individuals, but litigation was not the focus of the organization's efforts. The organization relied primarily on public education, lobbying, marches, and public demonstrations to advance its cause. Responding to the violence and intimidation regularly inflicted on African-Americans, repeated, but ultimately unsuccessful, efforts were made to persuade Congress to enact federal anti-lynching legislation. An event that would alter the NAACP's direction occurred in 1922 when Charles Garland, the son of a Boston millionaire, donated $800,000 to establish a fund to support radical causes. What became known as the "Garland Fund" was administered by a committee comprised of liberal activists that included James Weldon Johnson, the executive secretary of the NAACP; Roger Baldwin, the founder of the American Civil Liberties Union, and others.

The committee drafted a proposal recommending that the Garland Fund award a grant to the NAACP to carry out large-scale legal campaigns to enforce the constitutional rights of African-Americans in the South. The grant announcement stated that it would assist in areas such as unequal apportionment of school funds, barring African-Americans from juries, residential segregation, disenfranchisement, and civil liberties defense. The NAACP stated that it would find a "very able lawyer" to review the relevant legal authorities, develop an overall strategy, and supervise the cases that would be filed. Nathan Margold, a recent graduate of Harvard Law School, was hired in 1930 to prepare a report.

Margold prepared a comprehensive report that analyzed the constitutional foundations of *Plessy's* separate but equal doctrine and recommended a strategy to attack segregation.[6] The Margold Report contained a comprehensive analysis of laws and applicable legal precedents beginning with *Plessy*. After analyzing the turn-of-the-century decisions, the report worked its way through the laws governing segregation up to 1931. Margold's main conclusion was that segregation as practiced was unconstitutional even if the *Plessy* rationale were accepted. In the key conclusion of his report, Margold argued "segregation coupled with discrimination resulting from administrative action . . . is just as much a denial of equal protection of the laws as is segregation coupled with discrimination required by express statutory enactment."[7]

Margold submitted his report to the NAACP's Board of Directors in 1931. Nearly four years passed before the organization could act on Margold's suggestions. By that time the prospects of receiving the $100,000 from the Garland Fund had evaporated in the stock market crash of 1929 and the depression of the 1930s. Margold accepted a position as an assistant solicitor at the Department of the Interior. This departure left vacant the anticipated position for a full-time attorney to direct the litigation campaign. Walter White, the new executive secretary of the NAACP, settled on Charles H. Houston as the ideal person for the position.

Training Civil Rights Lawyers

"A lawyer's either a social engineer or he's a parasite on society."[8]

—Charles H. Houston

Charles Hamilton Houston was the architect of the NAACP's legal strategy; Howard University School of Law was his laboratory. Houston was born in Washington, D.C., in 1895. His father, William Houston, was a lawyer who obtained his degree while working for the federal government and attending Howard University at night. Charles Houston attended public schools in Washington, D.C. After graduating, he was admitted to Amherst College in Massachusetts, where he enrolled in 1911. At Amherst, Houston was elected to Phi Beta Kappa during his senior year. After graduating in 1915, Houston returned to Washington.[9]

After America's entry into World War I in 1917, Houston entered the Army's Negro officers' training corps at Des Moines, Iowa. During World War I, black soldiers were the victims of racism. In a 1940 article, Houston recalled a particularly dangerous encounter that occurred when he and a companion stumbled on a confrontation between a black serviceman and a group of white soldiers. Houston and his friend found themselves surrounded by an angry mob of white Americans. The tense episode ended only after a military police officer intervened. Years later he recalled: "I made up my mind that I would never get caught again without knowing something about my rights; that if luck was with me, and I got through this war, I would study law and use my time fighting for men who could not strike back."[10]

In 1919, Houston enrolled in Harvard Law School. During his first year, Houston served on the staff of the *Harvard Law Review*. Houston's academic record during his second year and his *Law Review* performance resulted in his elevation to its Editorial Board. He was the first African–American to serve in this capacity. In 1922, Houston graduated cum laude. In the following fall, he enrolled in the program for the advanced degree of Doctor of Juridical Science. After receiving the S.J.D. degree in 1923, Houston was awarded a Sheldon Traveling Fellowship, which he used to study law at the University of Madrid during 1923 and 1924.[11]

In 1924, Houston returned to Washington and joined his father's law firm. A few months later Houston joined the faculty at Howard University School of Law. The university's administration was concerned about the law school's academic standing. In 1920, Howard's Board of Trustees voted "that steps be taken to so advance the School of Law that it may become eligible for membership in the American Association of Law Schools."[12] A bout with tuberculosis forced Houston to take a leave of absence during the 1928–29 academic year. When he returned, "the Board appointed Charles Hamilton Houston Resident Vice–Dean in charge of the three-year Day School along with general supervision of the Law School Library, beginning July 1, 1929."[13]

Houston began almost immediately to upgrade the quality of instruction at Howard. The night school was closed, new professors were hired, and substantial additions were made to the law library's collection. Some of the alumni complained that Houston was attempting to "Harvardize" Howard. The accrediting authorities reacted favorably to these accomplishments. Following a 1930 inspection, the law school was accredited by the American Bar Association, and on December 28, 1931, it was elected to the American Association of Law Schools. Houston's goal involved more than upgrading Howard's academic standing. He trained the generation of African–American lawyers who led the fight against segregation. Years later Judge Robert Carter, a Howard graduate, explained

> [t]he overriding theory of legal education at Howard during those years was that the United States Constitution—in particular, the Civil War Amendments—was a powerful force heretofore virtually untapped, that should be used for social engineering in race relations ... A principal objective of the faculty at Howard was to produce lawyers capable of structuring and litigating test cases that

would provide effective implementation of these guarantees on behalf of the black community.[14]

Houston's Equalization Strategy

The NAACP confronted formidable obstacles in the South where segregation was firmly entrenched. Schools, restaurants, hotels, theaters, public transportation, and waiting rooms were segregated as were elevators, parks, public restrooms, hospitals, drinking fountains, prisons, and places of worship. The system was all encompassing. Whites and blacks were born in separate hospitals, educated in separate schools, and buried in segregated graveyards. Segregation was codified in state and local laws and enforced by intimidation and violence. There were, in effect, two criminal justice systems: one for whites and another for blacks. When the color line was breached, violence was unleashed against offenders by the Ku Klux Klan and local whites; often in concert with local law enforcement officials. Lynching and other forms of racial violence and intimidation were routine.

Prior to joining the NAACP's staff in 1935, Houston prepared a memorandum in which he outlined what became the equalization strategy. As a result of losses during the stock market crash of 1929, the funds available from the Garland grant were diminished. As a consequence, the Joint Committee that had been established to administer the grant lowered its sights to legal challenges against discrimination in education and public transportation. After considering what the campaign would entail, Houston recommended a still narrower focus. In a memorandum to the Joint Committee, Houston wrote

> [o]n a budget of $10,000.00 it is exceedingly difficult to execute an effective program on a national scale on two issues as large as discrimination in education and discrimination in transportation. Isolated suits mean little unless the communities and persons affected believe there is an unexpended reserve available to sustain a persistent struggle.[15]

Houston's memorandum presented two proposals. One was based on the premise that the entire effort would focus on education cases. The second budget proposed an equal division of the funds between education and transportation litigation. Houston believed that the education proposal should be given priority because of the potential benefits for African–American students while the campaign was still in progress. He recommended a two-pronged attack: one against unequal allocation of school funds and the other against differentials in teacher salaries. Houston explained his goals were: "(1) to arouse and strengthen the will of the local communities to demand and fight for their rights; (2) to work out model procedures through actual tests in court which can be used by local communities in similar cases brought by them on their own initiative and resources."[16]

This strategy would be carried out over the next several years in hundreds of cases and ultimately result in the reversal of the *Plessy* doctrine. Margold's legal analysis was sound, and his suggestion of a direct challenge to segregation laws would be adopted by the NAACP's lawyers several years later. However, Houston believed that the Supreme Court was not prepared to respond favorably to a direct challenge to *Plessy*. Under Houston's direction a different strategy was devised. Focusing on education, Houston proposed a series of lawsuits demanding that states comply with *Plessy* by providing equal allocations of financial and other resources for black students in segregated schools. This would be followed by a second series of suits demanding equal salaries for black teachers. Judge Robert Carter explained some years later that

> underlying this strategy was the belief that the segregation system would eventually implode—in other words, that the financial burden of having to duplicate educational systems for blacks and whites in the various professions would become so great that the states would be forced to abandon segregation all together at the graduate and professional school level.[17]

Houston applied for a leave of absence from Howard and made preparations to move to New York. He arrived there on July 11, 1935, and found a room at the Harlem Branch of the YMCA. On the next day he reported to work at the NAACP headquarters at 69 Fifth Avenue.

Murray v. The University of Maryland

Shortly after Houston assumed his new position, events that would lead to his first case began to unfold in Baltimore, Maryland. Donald Gaines Murray applied for admission to the University of Maryland School of Law in 1935. Although two African-Americans had graduated from the law school before the Maryland's laws were modified, in 1920 the state enacted legislation that required segregated schools. As in other states that practiced segregation, the resources provided for the black students of Maryland were not the same as those provided for whites.

Despite the restrictions imposed by segregation laws, the number of African-American students attending institutions of higher learning rose steadily during the 1920s. Houston's activities at Howard produced dozens of young African-American lawyers who were anxious to apply Houston's theories to actual cases. None was more eager than Thurgood Marshall, one of Houston's former students. Marshall graduated at the top of his class in 1933 and established a busy, though far-from-lucrative practice in Baltimore, Maryland.

Alpha Phi Alpha, a black fraternal organization, began to organize an effort to force the desegregation of the University of Maryland. This effort was led by Belford Lawson, a Washington, D.C., attorney who was counsel to the fraternity. Lawson enlisted the aid of the Washington Branch of the NAACP and another organization, the New Negro Alliance to assist him. After Marshall became aware of Lawson's activities, he wrote Houston in New York to inquire whether the NAACP's national office would be interested in backing the litigation. Houston did not immediately respond.

In November 1934, Lawson invited Marshall and William Gosnell, another Baltimore attorney, to a meeting of supporters of the desegregation effort. Marshall contacted Houston who replied with a telegram instructing Marshall to attend the meeting but cautioning him to avoid making any commitments. At the meeting Lawson outlined his plans and asked whether Gosnell or Marshall knew of any potential plaintiffs. A few weeks later Gosnell suggested Donald Gaines Murray. A 1934 graduate of Amherst College, Murray was an ideal plaintiff. He was articulate and had a pleasant appearance and impeccable educational credentials. Houston agreed to represent him.

The Joint Committee passed a formal resolution that authorized Houston to "proceed at once with the case against the University of Maryland."[18] With this action, the NAACP embarked on what would become a decades-long campaign to eliminate formal segregation. After receiving the Joint Committee's approval, Houston filed a civil action in Baltimore City Court against the University of Maryland. The case was tried before Judge Eugene O'Dunne in June 1935.

Houston began with an opening argument on Murray's behalf. Summarizing the facts, Houston explained that Murray had applied for admission to the University of Maryland School of Law and that he satisfied the prerequisites for admission, but his application had been denied solely on the basis of his race. These actions, Houston asserted, violated Murray's rights under the Fourteenth Amendment of the United States Constitution.

After the conclusion of the opening statements, Houston called the plaintiff as his first witness. Murray took the stand and testified about his life-long residency in Maryland, his desire to attend law school within the state, and his unsuccessful efforts to secure admission to the state university. Houston called as his next witness Dr. Raymond A. Pearson, president of the university. Pearson spent an uncomfortable hour and a half on the witness stand. His evasive statements could not stand up to Houston's withering questioning.

Houston used the testimony of Pearson and other university officials to establish all of his major points. First, Houston forced Pearson to confirm that Murray's application had gone through the proper channels. Maryland and other states with segregated schools had established out-of-state scholarships, which subsidized the tuition expenses of African–American students who attended graduate schools elsewhere. Houston compelled Pearson to admit that the out-of-state scholarships were not available at the time Murray's application was rejected. During subsequent questions, Pearson conceded that appropriations voted by the legislature were insufficient to satisfy the demands of the numerous scholarship applicants. After Pearson claimed that the state had made adequate provisions for black students at Princess Ann Academy, Houston led him through a step-by-step comparison of the two facilities. It became clear to everyone present that the facilities for African–American students were grossly inferior to the resources available to whites. The examination of other witnesses proceeded along the same lines.

Houston and Marshall shared the closing argument. Carefully remaining within the confines of *Plessy*, Marshall argued that the state had a constitutional obligation to provide equal educational opportunities for students of all races. Houston concluded the argument by emphasizing that state laws did not bar black students from attending publicly funded institutions. Houston emphasized that *Plessy* obligated the state to make equal educational opportunities available to students of both races. Maryland violated its constitutional duty by failing to do so.

At the conclusion of the hearing, the trial judge issued a ruling from the bench. He found the university had a legal obligation to offer the same educational opportunities for black students as those provided to whites. Because the state had failed to fulfill its constitutional duty, the judge issued a *writ of mandamus* compelling the university to admit Murray to the class that was scheduled to enter in the fall.[19]

After the trial court entered its decision, Maryland's attorneys filed an appeal. The court of appeals decision was issued on January 15, 1936.[20] Because the state did not have a law school for black students, "the main question in this case [was] whether the separation can be maintained, and negroes excluded from the present school, by reason of equality of treatment furnished the latter in scholarships for studying outside the state."[21] The scholarships, the court found, could not provide the basis for a defense because they were not available at the time Murray's application was rejected.

The court held that the "slender chance for any one applicant an opportunity to attend an outside law school at increased expense, falls short of providing for students of the colored race facilities substantially equal to those furnished to the whites in the law school maintained at Baltimore."[22] After holding that Murray had been denied equal protection of the law, the court considered the question of relief. It found that "the erection of a separate school [was] not an available alternative remedy."[23] As a consequence, it affirmed the trial court's order requiring Murray's admission to the University of Maryland.

Murray represented a solid victory for Houston, Marshall and the NAACP. In their first major case after launching the litigation campaign, the NAACP's lawyers won a judgment that broke through the racial barriers erected by *Plessy*. The Maryland Court recognized that the mere provision of some facilities for African-American students did not satisfy the requirements of the Equal Protection Clause of the Fourteenth Amendment.

For Thurgood Marshall, the victory in *Murray* had a personal significance. He was prevented from attending Maryland's law school based on its policy of excluding African-Americans. Maryland's law school was located in Baltimore where Thurgood Marshall resided. To obtain his legal education, Marshall had to rise in the early hours of each morning to travel from his home in Baltimore to attend classes at Howard University in Washington, D.C. He returned each day to his home in Baltimore, usually arriving late at night. Marshall endured this inconvenience for three years; *Murray* was his means of extracting revenge for this indignity.[24]

Gaines v. Missouri

A few days after the conclusion of the *Murray* trial, the NAACP convened its 1935 annual meeting in St. Louis, Missouri. Houston was unable to attend, so he submitted a written report of his activities to the conference. He advised the association that a possible hearing in the *Murray* appeal prevented him from appearing in person, but that the NAACP had won "a significant victory in the [Maryland] trial court, which if it can be held all the way to the United States Supreme Court will mean the opening up, in one form or another, of professional and graduate education for Negroes in all the States."[25] Houston also reported "the favorable Court decision in [*Murray*] will encourage similar suits in other states. Already Sidney R. Redmond, Esq., of St. Louis, Missouri, is investigating discrimination and exclusion at the University of Missouri."[26]

Lloyd Gaines was a 1935 graduate of Lincoln University, Missouri's segregated college for black students. He applied to the University of Missouri's School of Law.[27] After his application was denied, a civil action was filed on his behalf. Sidney R. Redmond and Henry D. Espy of St. Louis and Charles Houston represented Gaines. Houston traveled to St. Louis to complete the final preparations a few days prior to the trial.

The case was tried in Columbia, a town in central Missouri where the University of Missouri was located. Dozens of farmers were in town to visit officials at the county relief agencies located in the courthouse. Several of the farmers wandered into the courtroom to watch the *Gaines* proceedings. Nearly a hundred students who were attending a summer session at the University of Missouri also crowded into the courtroom. Before long the courtroom was filled to capacity. The opposing counsel shook hands cordially, and they all shared a single table, an arrangement "odd to us," Houston reported later.[28]

In a memorandum to his office, Houston explained "[a]ll during the trial we looked down one another's throats. For private conferences at the table we almost had to go into a football huddle."[29] Although the courtroom was filled with spectators, there were no displays of overt hostility during the trial. Furthermore, unlike many courthouses during that period, the one in Boone County was not segregated. Houston noted that during the recess, some of the farmers "looked a little strange at us drinking out of the same fountain and using the same lavatories with them, but they did not say anything."[30]

Houston reported that the university's lawyers, practitioners from a Kansas City firm, were "driving and dramatic"[31] in their opening presentation. They argued that Gaines's remedy lay with the officials of Lincoln University; he should have requested that Lincoln establish a law school. During the trial, university officials admitted that Gaines was otherwise qualified for admission and was denied admission solely on the basis of his race. The trial judge was not receptive to Houston's arguments. In the memorandum to his office, Houston concluded that "it is beyond expectation that the court will decide in our favor, so we had just as well get ready for the appeal."[32] As Houston expected, the trial judge entered a judgment for the university. The case was appealed to the Supreme Court of Missouri, which affirmed the trial court's ruling.[33]

Gaines was appealed to the United States Supreme Court.[34] On the day before the oral arguments, Houston rehearsed at a gathering of students and professors at Howard University School of Law. This was one of the first practice sessions conducted at Howard. On the following day, Missouri's lawyers argued that Gaines was not entitled to a writ of mandamus because if he had applied to the curators of Lincoln University they would have been obligated to establish a law school. The Supreme Court found no such obligation because the state law on which the university relied left "to the judgment of the curators to decide when it will be necessary and practicable to establish a law school."[35]

The Court found "the fact remains that instruction in law for Negroes is not now afforded by the State, either at Lincoln University or elsewhere within the State."[36] Based on these findings, the Court reasoned that the critical issue was "the question [of] whether the provision for the legal education in other States of [negro] residents in Missouri is sufficient to satisfy the constitutional requirement of equal protection."[37]

The Court found that each state had an independent constitutional obligation to provide equal educational opportunities and that this requirement could not be shifted by one state to another. The Court also concluded that the right to equal protection is a "personal one."[38] As a consequence, "the State was bound to furnish [Gaines] within its borders facilities for legal education substantially equal to those which the State there afforded for persons of the white race."[39] Because Missouri had failed to establish a law school for African–American students, Gaines was entitled to admission to the state-supported law school.

Gaines was a significant victory for the NAACP. The Maryland Court's reasoning in *Murray* had been adopted by the United States Supreme Court. This meant that *Gaines* had nationwide applicability as a binding legal precedent. *Murray* was a significant decision, but a victory in the Supreme Court carried far more weight. Houston's "equalization" strategy prevailed for a second time.

One of the strangest episodes of the legal campaign involved the ultimate disposition of the *Gaines* litigation. After the case was remanded to the trial court, the university scheduled a deposition of Gaines. After repeated efforts by Houston and others to contact him, it became apparent that he had disappeared. He was last seen leaving an Alpha Phi Alpha fraternity house in Chicago, but was never seen again. Various theories exist as to what happened to Gaines, but all that is actually known is that he was never heard from again.[40]

By the middle of 1936, Houston found himself almost overwhelmed with his duties at the NAACP. He was serving not only as director of the NAACP's litigation campaign but also as general counsel, fund-raiser, public speaker, and legal advisor to Walter White, the head of the NAACP. At the same time, Marshall's work in Baltimore caused the financial aspects of his practice to suffer. In one of his frequent letters to Houston, Marshall wrote in desperation about his financial straits. Houston replied that Marshall should consider joining the staff of the NAACP on a full-time basis. Marshall eagerly accepted Houston's proposal. In mid-October 1936, Marshall moved to New York to serve as Houston's assistant.

A year later, Houston moved to Washington, where he rejoined his father's law firm, but continued to serve as special counsel to the NAACP. The reasons for Houston's departure are not entirely clear, but a mixture of personal and professional reasons probably prompted the move. Houston suffered occasional bouts with tuberculosis, which he had contracted during World War I. He was suffering from extreme exhaustion when he returned to Washington. Other changes occurred in Houston's personal life. He divorced and remarried during the time he lived in New York, having separated from his first wife when he moved to New York in 1935. In a letter to his father written in 1938, Houston expressed his sentiments about the move, "I have had the feeling all along that I am much more of an outside man than an inside man ... I usually break down under too much routine." Houston continued, "Certainly, for the present, I will grow much faster and be much more of service if I keep free to hit and fight wherever the circumstances call for action."[41]

The Post–War Cases

During the early to mid–1940s, the NAACP filed numerous actions against local school districts in teacher salary cases, but the pace of the university cases declined. America was preoccupied with World War II. The NAACP turned much of its attention to discrimination in the military, and it responded to requests for assistance in cases raising other issues.

After the War concluded in 1945, the NAACP returned to the graduate school cases. When thousands of World War II veterans returned with government benefits that subsidized academic study, the NAACP recognized that there was an increased demand for higher education. With Thurgood Marshall at the helm of the legal department, the NAACP renewed its campaign to eliminate the barriers that prevented black students from attending state-supported institutions. In the post-war cases, several innovative approaches were introduced. One involved a move from state courts to federal courts. This expedited cases by eliminating several steps in the appeals process. Instead of appealing from a trial court to an intermediate appellate or a state supreme court, the lawyers took advantage of a procedure that allowed constitutional challenges to state statutes to be heard by special three-judge panels in federal district courts. Judgments entered by these tribunals could be reviewed directly by the Supreme Court.[42]

Another development involved the strategic use of expert testimony. NAACP lawyers began to employ the testimony of educational and other experts to demonstrate the psychological harm that enforced segregation inflicted on black students. Focusing carefully on the intricacies of the educational process, the lawyers also used experts to prove that several intangible features of the educational experience could not be duplicated in a segregated setting even if the physical facilities were equalized.

The final graduate school cases represented a transition from the holdings in the early equalization cases to the final decisions involving primary and secondary schools. The post-war cases went beyond a demand for physical equality to a showing that equal facilities could not remedy the deprivations caused by racial segregation.

Sipuel v. Oklahoma

The first of the post-war cases was filed against the University of Oklahoma in April 1946. Roscoe Dundee, an attorney and publisher of a black newspaper, was one of the leaders of the Oklahoma Chapter of the NAACP. Like Missouri and Maryland, Oklahoma established separate schools for black students but made no provisions for graduate school training. After months of publicizing the inequities of the Oklahoma system, Dundee identified several potential plaintiffs. From a pool of several candidates, the NAACP selected Ada Louise Sipuel.

Sipuel was an honor student at the State College for Negroes in Langston, Oklahoma. She applied for admission to the University of Oklahoma's College of Law, but was denied on the grounds that the school did not admit black students. The lawsuit was filed in an Oklahoma trial court. In July, the trial court dismissed Sipuel's case. On appeal the Oklahoma Supreme Court held that Sipuel's failure to demand a law school for black students precluded her from seeking admission to the school established for whites. The court found Oklahoma was not obligated to establish a black law school until demand justified the expenditure of funds. The court ruled that Sipuel had "wholly failed to establish any violation of the Fourteenth Amendment of the Federal Constitution."[43]

The NAACP sought review of the Oklahoma court's decision in the United States Supreme Court. At the time the petition for a writ of *certiorari* was filed, Marshall was reluctant to proceed because the facts of the case had been stipulated. This meant that the evidentiary record was not as fully developed as he would have preferred. Despite Marshall's reservations, the appeal was pursued and the case was argued in the Supreme Court during the first week of 1948. In a surprise move, the Court issued a decision four days later that reversed the Oklahoma Supreme Court.[44] In a brief, per curiam opinion, the Court noted first that Sipuel's "application for admission was denied, solely because of her color."[45] The Court held that

> [t]he petitioner is entitled to secure legal education afforded by a state institution. To this time, it has been denied her although during the same period many white applicants have been afforded legal education by the State. The State must provide it for her in conformity with the equal protection clause of the Fourteenth

> Amendment and provide it as soon as it does for applicants of any other group.[46]

On January 17, 1948, the Oklahoma Supreme Court ordered the Board of Regents to allow Sipuel to attend law school as soon as it accorded that opportunity to any other student. On the basis of that decision, the Oklahoma trial court issued an order that enjoined the state from enrolling any students at the university's law school until a separate school for black students was established and ready to function. Unwilling to retreat from its policy of racial segregation, the Board of Regents responded by roping off an area in the state capitol, designating it as the "Negro law school," and hiring three black lawyers to serve as faculty. Marshall was so outraged that he took the extraordinary step of returning to the United States Supreme Court with a request that it find that the State of Oklahoma had not complied with the Court's decision. To Marshall's disappointment, the Supreme Court ruled in Oklahoma's favor.[47]

Sweatt v. Painter *and* McLaurin v. Oklahoma

At the same time that the NAACP battled Oklahoma, an identical suit was filed on behalf of a student in Texas. In 1946, Hemon Marion Sweatt, a letter carrier for the United States Post Office, applied for admission to the University of Texas School of Law. Sweatt's application was denied on the grounds of his race even though Texas had not established a separate law school for black students. On May 14, 1946, the suit was filed in state court. In June, the trial court held a hearing and issued an order giving the state six months to establish a law school for African-American students.

The state responded by renting a few rooms in Houston and hiring two black lawyers to serve as faculty for what it designated as the newly established branch of Prairie View University, the state college for black students. At a status conference in December 1946, the trial court found that the facilities at Houston were "substantially equal" to the law school at the Austin campus.

Marshall appealed the trial court's ruling. While the appeal was pending, Texas took steps to bolster the trial court's finding of substantial equality. The location of the "Negro" law school was transferred to Austin, pending the construction of a permanent facility in Houston. Three rooms in a building across the street from the state capitol were set aside to house the temporary law school. The students were given access to the law library located at the state capitol. Professors from the University of Texas were assigned to provide instruction. The Texas legislature appropriated $3 million to upgrade Prairie View and designated $100,000 for the creation of a law school. Because of the change in circumstances, the case was remanded to the trial court for an evidentiary hearing.

Faced with a weakened case on the issue of physical inequality, Marshall chose a different tack. He presented an array of expert witnesses who testified that segregation had no scientific basis in public schools. Other experts testified about the relative learning abilities of black and white students. The dean of the law school at the University of Pennsylvania testified about the importance of interaction among students in the learning process. A professor, he explained, however well qualified, could not provide the elements of the educational experience that are derived from interaction among students. Another witness, Robert Redenfield, who held doctorates in anthropology and law, testified that there was no scientific basis for assumptions concerning the intellectual inferiority of black students.[48]

The university's attorneys attacked Sweatt's motives for filing the lawsuit and attempted to prove that the case was actually initiated by the NAACP. They also contended that Sweatt's refusal to enroll in the black law school demonstrated bad faith. Approximately one month after the trial ended, the trial court entered a judgment for defendants. The case was appealed to the Texas Court of Civil Appeals. On February 25, 1948, that court issued a decision affirming the trial court's ruling.[49]

The last graduate school case involved a sixty-eight-year-old black professor at Langston University, George W. McLaurin, who applied in 1948 to the Graduate School of Education at the University of Oklahoma to obtain an advanced degree. After his application was denied, the NAACP filed a suit on his behalf.[50] This time Marshall pursued an approach that the NAACP and other public interest lawyers would follow in later years. Charles Houston had preferred to file suits in state courts based on his multi-purpose strategy of winning cases for individual plaintiffs, creating precedents that could be applied later, and generating broad-based support for the NAACP's mission within African-American communities. Marshall decided to expedite the process by eliminating the intermediate appellate review. *McLaurin* was heard by a three-judge panel in the federal district court.[51] After the trial court entered a judgment for the university, a petition for a writ of *certiorari* was filed in the Supreme Court.

Sweatt and *McLaurin* reached the Supreme Court at the same time. *McLaurin* was argued on April 3 and 4, 1950, and *Sweatt* was presented on April 4, 1950. The decisions in both cases were issued on June 5, 1950. The Court declined to reconsider *Plessy*, but it came close to acknowledging the inequities inherent in state-sponsored segregation. In *Sweatt*, the Court found that the facilities available at the newly established law school were not equal in quantity or quality to those available at the law school in Austin. "In terms of number of the faculty, variety of courses and opportunity for specialization, size of the student body, scope of the library, availability of law review and similar activities, the University of Texas Law School is superior."[52]

The Court did not limit its analysis to a comparison of physical resources. It went on to conclude that the quality of educational instruction was diminished by isolation. The Court found

> [t]he University of Texas Law School possesses to a far greater degree those qualities which are incapable of objective measurement but which make for greatness in a law school. Such qualities, to name a few, include reputation of the faculty, experience of the administration, position and influence of the alumni, standing in the community, traditions and prestige. It is difficult to believe that one who had a free choice between these law schools would consider the question close.[53]

The Court reached a similar conclusion in *McLaurin*.[54] The Oklahoma case was different from *Sweatt*. After denying his admission, the state modified its position and allowed McLaurin access to the same instruction as whites, except on a racially segregated basis. Thus, in *McLaurin*, the Court considered whether segregation within a university violated the Fourteenth Amendment. As the opinion explained, McLaurin was required to sit apart at a designated desk in an anteroom adjoining the classroom; to sit at a designated desk on the mezzanine floor of the library, but not to use the desks in the regular reading room; and to sit at a designated table and to eat at a different time from the other students in the school cafeteria. While the case was pending, some modifications were made in the arrangements to accommodate McLaurin. The Court observed that

> [f]or some time, the section of the classroom in which [McLaurin] sat was surrounded by a rail on which there was a sign stating, "Reserved For Colored," but these have been removed. He is now assigned to a seat in the classroom in a row specified for colored students; he is assigned to a table in the library on the main floor; and he is permitted to eat at the same time in the cafeteria as other students, although here again he is assigned to a special table.[55]

These actions, the Court found, "handicapped [McLaurin] in his pursuit of effective graduate instruction. Such restrictions impair and inhibit his ability to study, to engage in discussions and exchange views with other students and, in general, to learn his profession."[56]

With these decisions, the stage was set for a direct challenge to *Plessy*. In *Sipuel*, *Sweatt*, and *McLaurin*, the Court did not directly address the constitutionality of state-enforced segregation, but it is clear from the analysis of these decisions that the *Plessy* doctrine had been considerably undermined. As the Court recognized in earlier cases, the states failed to provide educational facilities for black students that were equivalent to those established for white students. This legal recognition meant that the states could not continue to allocate generous resources to white schools while they maintained inadequate and poorly financed facilities for black students. Responding to the NAACP's expert testimony, the Court recognized in *Sweatt* that there was more to education than bricks and mortar. Much of the process involved interaction among students and the exchange of diverse ideas through discussions. Exchanges of this sort could not occur in a system in which African–American students were cut off from contact with other students.

The final and, in many ways, most compelling case was made by the State of Oklahoma's actions in *McLaurin*. Because *McLaurin* was allowed to sit in a classroom and receive the same instruction as white students, the isolation rationale of *Sweatt* did not apply. Yet, by separating McLaurin in a "colored-only" section in the classroom and setting aside separate tables in the library and cafeteria, the state graphically demonstrated the stigmatizing effects of segregation far better than any expert testimony ever could. While the case was pending, a photograph of Professor McLaurin appeared in newspapers and magazines across the country. Sitting in a corner of the classroom McLaurin is shown leaning forward, peering into the classroom, apparently straining to hear the discussion. The photograph showed just how demeaning segregation was in actual practice. In both cases the Court ordered the admission of the African–American applicants.

When the NAACP proceeded with the primary school cases, the defenses raised by segregation's supporters had been completely undermined. The separate facilities were not equal, and there was never any pretense of equivalence in any place where segregated education was practiced. The legal fiction on which segregation was premised had never been a reality. The expert testimony in *McLaurin* and *Sweatt* focused the courts attention on the devastating psychological effects of segregation and on the impact these practices had on the learning process. Each of the graduate school cases struck a decisive blow to the legal foundation on which segregation rested. By 1950, the infrastructure was crumbling. All that was needed was a final strike.

The Brown *Cases*

After the decisions in *Sweatt* and *McLaurin*, the NAACP lawyers decided that the foundation for a challenge to *Plessy* had been established. In 1950, the NAACP held a conference of the lawyers and consultants who were working on desegregation cases. During that meeting the conferees adopted a formal resolution that in all future cases the relief sought would be "aimed at obtaining an education on a non-segregated basis."[57] The school desegregation cases consisted of six consolidated cases involving five separate jurisdictions: *Brown v. Board of Education of Topeka*[58] arose in Kansas. *Briggs v. Elliott*[59] involved schools in South Carolina. There was a Virginia case, *Davis v. County School Board of Prince Edward County.*[60] *Bolling v. Sharpe*[61] was filed in the District of Columbia. There were two Delaware cases, *Belton v. Gebhart* and *Bulah v. Gebhart.*[62]

The expert testimony in the *Brown* cases was a critical component of the evidence. In the "doll tests," psychologists Kenneth and Mamie Clark used dolls that were identical except for their color; some were white, others were brown. The Clarks showed the dolls to black children between the ages of three and seven and asked them a series of questions such as "Show me the doll you like?" and "Which doll looks like you?" Almost all of the children showed a marked preference for the white dolls. The Clarks also showed the children outline drawings of a boy and girl and asked them to color the images the same color as themselves. Many of the children with dark complexions colored the figures white or irrelevant colors such as yellow or green. The Clarks concluded that these experiments showed that discrimination and segregation inculcated low self-esteem in young African-Americans.[63]

The Clarks' research was controversial in and outside of the NAACP and remains so decades after *Brown*. Some challenged the methodology. Others questioned the Clarks' interpretation of their data. What is lost in the methodological debates is the significance of Robert Carter's legal stratagem. The tests were evidence that vividly conveyed the pernicious effects of discrimination. The experiments showed young African-American children rejecting their racial identity by preferring white dolls. This was compelling evidence of the adverse effects of segregation that had a profound impact at the intellectual and emotional levels.[64]

Under a procedure that allowed a direct appeal to the Supreme Court, a special three-judge panel presided at the trial in the South Carolina case, *Briggs v. Elliott*. At the outset of the proceedings, South Carolina's attorneys made a dramatic concession: they admitted that the black schools were inferior, but would soon be equalized. This was calculated to forestall the NAACP's challenge as the southern states believed that the only remedy available was an order equalizing school facilities. Unfazed, Thurgood Marshall responded that the State's concession did not matter as they were challenging segregation itself. The case proceeded.

During the trial, Marshall's evidence established that the black schools were physically unequal. Kenneth Clark testified that segregation inflicted severe psychological damage on black students. On June 23, 1952, relying on *Plessy*, the court ruled that segregation in public schools was permissible as long as the facilities provided were equal. The court found that the plaintiffs were entitled to an order declaring the state's obligation to equalize its schools, but could not prevail on the challenge to segregation itself. That decision was appealed.

While the South Carolina case was pending in the trial court, another controversy was brewing in Virginia. In April 1952, a group of black students who attended a high school in Prince Edward County, Virginia, organized a strike to protest the deplorable condition of their school; they eventually contacted the NAACP. Oliver Hill and Spottswood Robinson, Richmond-based NAACP lawyers, responded to the students' pleas for assistance. The students wanted the school board to construct a new building. Hill and Robinson agreed to aid them if they would serve as plaintiffs in a lawsuit that would seek to desegregate, rather than equalize, the county's schools. A suit, which proceeded along the same lines as the South Carolina case, was eventually filed. During the trial, witnesses testified about the physical condition of the black high school. Psychologists described the detrimental effect that segregation had on black students.

The decision in *Davis v. County Board of Prince Edward County* was issued in 1952. The three-judge panel found that controlling legal precedent amply supported segregated schools. It stated further that segregation was a way of life in Virginia. "Separation of white and colored children in the public schools of Virginia has for generations been part of the mores of her people. To have separate schools has been their use and wont."[65]

The District of Columbia case, *Bolling v. Sharpe*,[66] was filed on behalf of a group of black parents, led by Gardner Bishop, a Washington, D.C., barber. The group initially sought only to equalize the public school facilities in Washington. Charles Houston agreed to represent them. By the time the case began, Houston's health was failing, so he persuaded the group to ask James Nabrit to represent them. Nabrit undertook the group's representation after they agreed to a direct challenge to segregation. *Bolling* was different from the other cases in one significant aspect: as a federal territory, the District of Columbia was not subject to the Fourteenth Amendment, which applies only to state actions. All of the other cases challenged segregation as a violation of the Equal Protection Clause of the Fourteenth Amendment. In *Bolling v. Sharpe*, however, the legal challenge was based entirely on alleged violations of the Due Process Clause of the Fifth Amendment.

In 1948, the Topeka, Kansas, branch of the NAACP petitioned the local school board to desegregate the public schools. After two years of inaction, the group contacted the NAACP's headquarters in New York and requested assistance in filing a lawsuit. There were several plaintiffs in the Kansas case, but in what reflected the then prevailing views of gender, the group felt that a male should be the lead plaintiff. As a result, Oliver Brown became one of the best-known names in twentieth-century legal history. On February 14, 1951, *Brown v. Board of Education of Topeka* was filed in the federal district court in Kansas.

The racial disparities in Topeka's schools were not as extreme as they were in other localities. For tactical reasons, Robert Carter, Thurgood Marshall's deputy and the lead counsel in *Brown*, chose not to focus on physical comparisons. He relied almost entirely on evidence relating to the psychological injuries that segregation inflicted on black students. The court ruled in the Kansas case that the qualifications of the teachers and the quality of instruction available at the black schools in Topeka were not inferior to what was provided to white students. However, the court went on to rule

> [s]egregation of white and colored children in public schools has a detrimental effect upon the colored children. The impact is greater when it has a sanction of law, for the policy of separating the races is usually interpreted as denoting the inferiority of the Negro group. A sense of inferiority affects the motivation of a child to learn. Segregation with the sanction of law, therefore, has a tendency to restrain the education and mental development of Negro children and to deprive them of the benefits they would receive in a racially integrated school system.[67]

Despite this important factual finding, the court concluded that it was bound by *Plessy's* separate but equal doctrine to rule against the plaintiffs. However, the decision was structured in a way that virtually invited the Supreme Court to re-examine *Plessy*.

There were two cases in Delaware, *Belton v. Gebhart* and *Bulah v. Gebhart*.[68] In 1950 there was only one public high school in the entire state of Delaware for black students. Howard High School was located in a black neighborhood in Wilmington. Its aging physical plant stood in marked contrast to the modern, well-equipped school in the town of Claymont, which is located just north of Wilmington. Meanwhile, in Hockessin, which was then a rural village not far from Wilmington, Sarah Bulah was required to drive her adopted child past the white students' school to a dilapidated, one-room schoolhouse that served black children.

Louis Redding and Jack Greenberg represented the plaintiffs in the Delaware proceedings. The Delaware cases were originally filed in federal court but the Attorney General removed them to state court. This meant that the cases would be heard by Collins Seitz, a judge in Delaware's Court of Chancery, who had ruled in Louis Redding's favor in *Parker v. University of Delaware*,[69] which ordered the desegregation of the University of Delaware. As he had in the university case, Seitz personally visited the schools to compare them. At the trial of the two cases, extensive expert testimony was presented concerning the negative effects of segregation; other evidence confirmed the physical disparities.

Seitz ruled in favor of Redding and Greenberg. He concluded that he lacked the authority to overturn *Plessy*, but he ruled that the black schools were inferior and, unlike the trial judges in the other cases, Seitz ordered the admission of the black students to the white schools. This was the only case in which the plaintiffs prevailed at the trial court level.[70]

The Supreme Court Proceedings

On December 9, 1952, at 1:35 p.m., the Supreme Court arguments commenced in the six consolidated school desegregation cases.[71] Separate arguments were presented in each case by lawyers representing the various parties. After two and a half exhausting days, the arguments concluded on December 11, 1952, at 3:50 p.m. A few months later, the Supreme Court issued an order that set the cases over to the next term for re-argument. The Court directed the parties to submit briefs addressing a series of questions concerning Congress's intent when it adopted the Fourteenth Amendment. Additionally, the Court questioned the way in which a desegregation order might be implemented if one were issued.[72]

The order setting down a second argument was an unusual event. Some of the NAACP lawyers took the order as a positive sign, while others believed that it was an ominous signal. In the end, there was nothing they could do except respond to the court's questions. To research the original intent question Marshall enlisted John A. Davis, a professor of political science at Lincoln University in Pennsylvania. Davis obtained the assistance of Horace Mann Bond who was, at that time, the president of Lincoln University. C. Vann Woodward, who later became one of the leading authorities on the Reconstruction period, and John Hope Franklin, a distinguished African-American historian, also assisted with the research. William Coleman, a young African-American lawyer, who had graduated first in his class at Harvard and clerked for Supreme Court Justice Felix Frankfurter, agreed to coordinate research in the various states.[73]

During the next several months, the lawyers, historians, law professors, and others assisting the NAACP lawyers grappled with the research concerning the intent of the framers of the Fourteenth Amendment. Records in state archives were examined. There were many long days and nights of exhaustive work. In the end, the researchers were unable to find any unequivocal evidence that directly addressed the court's questions. Eventually, the lawyers settled on an argument that the Fourteenth Amendment was intended to prohibit state-sponsored segregation. They would argue that *Plessy* rested on a false premise. Segregation was intended to perpetuate racial subordination rather than some form of separate equality. The separate but equal doctrine was a pernicious legal fiction used to enforce a regime of white supremacy.

John W. Davis and the other lawyers defending the southern school boards reached an entirely different conclusion, relying on, among other things, evidence of segregated schools in the District of Columbia when the Fourteenth Amendment was ratified. They were encouraged by the court's decision to order re-argument. They believed that the historical record and applicable legal precedent amply supported their position.

The Justices were divided after the initial round of arguments. On the night of September 8, 1953, Chief Justice Vinson, who reportedly opposed reversing *Plessy*, died after suffering a massive heart attack. Justice Felix Frankfurter, who supported reversing *Plessy*, reportedly said, "This is the first indication I have ever had that there is a God."[74] Less than three weeks later, President Dwight Eisenhower nominated Earl Warren, the Republican governor of California, to replace Vinson.

On December 7, 1953, the three days of re-argument commenced. This was a dramatic moment in the Supreme Court's history. Spectators filled the courtroom. The crowd flowed onto the steps outside of the Supreme Court building. Reporters, lawyers, students, and ordinary citizens wanted to witness what everyone knew would be a historic event. Segregation itself was on trial. The proceedings commenced at 1:05 p.m. with the *Briggs* case. Over the next two days the Court heard arguments from the lawyers representing the parties. The Court recessed on December 9, 1953, at 2:40 p.m.

After reviewing the briefs and listening to the oral argument, Warren was convinced segregation was unconstitutional. During the months that followed, he persuaded the reluctant holdouts to agree to a unanimous ruling striking down segregation in schools. The decision in *Brown* was announced on May 17, 1954, to a packed courtroom by Chief Justice Warren. In an opinion notable for its brevity and simplicity, the Court framed the issue as whether "segregation of children in public schools solely on the basis of race ... deprives the children of the minority group of equal educational opportunities." The Court found that it did, concluding that "[t]o separate [black] children from others of similar age and qualifications generates a feeling of inferiority as to their status in the community that may affect their hearts and minds in ways unlikely ever to be undone." In its most significant conclusion, the Court held that "[s]eparate educational facilities are inherently unequal."[75]

Too Much Deliberation and Not Enough Speed

The Supreme Court's 1954 decision in *Brown* did not address the remedy. The cases were held over and reargued in 1955 to determine the manner in which the Court's decision should be implemented. In the *Brown II* decision, the Court remanded the cases to the trial courts and ordered the school boards to proceed with "all deliberate speed," to develop desegregation plans under the supervision of the local federal courts.[76] Chief Justice Earl Warren decided to follow Justice Felix Frankfurter's suggestion to use the deliberately ambiguous phrase, "all deliberate speed" as the timetable for accomplishing integration.[77] The Justices anticipated resistance but underestimated the reaction to their decision.

The white South's response to *Brown* was swift and severe. On March 12, 1956, *The Southern Manifesto* was read into the Congressional Record. This document contained 96 signatures, 19 from the U.S. Senate and 77 from the House of Representatives. The *Manifesto* proclaimed, "the Supreme Court of the United States, with no legal basis for such action, undertook to exercise their naked judicial power and substituted their personal political and social ideas for the established law of the land." It also alleged "outside agitators are threatening immediate and revolutionary changes in our public school systems. If done, this is certain to destroy the system of public education in some of the states." The *Manifesto* concluded with a pledge to "use all lawful means to bring about a reversal of the [*Brown*] decision, which is contrary to the Constitution and to prevent the use of force in its implementation."[78]

The *Manifesto* set the stage for the South's response to *Brown*: the era of "massive resistance" commenced. School boards and elected officials engaged in tactics that ranged from delay and passive resistance to violent defiance. The 1950s and '60s were the years in which the Civil Rights Movement reached its apex, but very little progress was made toward school desegregation. Ten years after the *Brown* decision, only 1.2 percent of black students in the South attended schools with whites. In five states, Alabama, Mississippi, South Carolina, Florida, and Georgia, there were no black students attending white schools.

In the late 1960s, the Supreme Court issued decisions that were intended to put an end to the South's massive resistance. In *Griffin v. County School Board of Prince Edward County*,[79] a case in which the school district involved in the original *Brown* cases had closed all of its schools to avoid desegregation, Justice Hugo Black concluded, "[t]here has been entirely too much deliberation and not enough speed in enforcing the constitutional rights which we held in *Brown*."[80] Prince Edward County was ordered to reopen its schools. In *Alexander v. Holmes County Board of Education*,[81] the Court ruled that the "continued operation of segregated schools under a standard allowing 'all deliberate speed' for desegregation is no longer constitutionally permissible . . . the obligation of every school district is to terminate dual school systems at once and operate now and hereafter only unitary schools."[82]

In *Green v. County School Board of New Kent County*,[83] the Court held that states that maintained segregated schools had an affirmative duty to eradicate all vestiges of the formerly segregated system "root and branch," and that school boards were obligated to bear the burden of proving compliance with the new standard.[84] In *Swann v. Charlotte-Mecklenburg Board of Education*,[85] the Supreme Court endorsed busing as a means of achieving racial balance in schools.

Housing Discrimination and School Desegregation

In the South, school desegregation finally commenced after *Green*. In rural districts where there were only one or two high schools, the white and black high schools simply merged with all students attending a single, racially integrated school. In urban areas, however, demographic patterns made school desegregation far more difficult. In the years during and after World War I, African-Americans migrated, in large numbers, from rural areas in the South to urban communities in the North and Midwest. From 1910 to 1970, 6.5 million African-Americans relocated from the South to the North.[86] They were attracted by employment opportunities in factories that paid far more than they could earn as sharecroppers and farm laborers in the South. African-Americans were also seeking to escape the oppressive conditions that existed in the South where violence, lynching, and other forms of racial intimidation were commonplace.[87]

In cities in the North, however, African-Americans were confined to segregated neighborhoods by redlining, racially restrictive covenants, and other discriminatory practices. The impact of residential segregation on school desegregation was the focus of *Milliken v. Bradley*,[88] a case involving schools in Detroit, Michigan. The plaintiffs in *Milliken* attempted to address residential segregation by including the suburban school districts surrounding Detroit in a metropolitan desegregation plan. As a consequence of racially segregated housing patterns and "white flight" to suburban communities, the schools in Detroit were rapidly shifting to predominately black populations. At the same time, enrollments in suburban districts were nearly all white. Based on these circumstances, the plaintiffs in *Milliken* argued that racial balance could not be achieved without including the suburban districts in the desegregation plan.

The Supreme Court held that suburban school districts could not be required to participate in court-ordered desegregation plans unless it could be proven that their actions contributed to segregation in the jurisdiction in which the case arose.[89] There could be no busing across district lines without a showing of an inter-district violation. After the decision in *Milliken*, suburban districts were effectively insulated from the desegregation process.

Throughout the following two decades, school desegregation proceeded slowly with courts relying heavily on intra-district busing to achieve racial balance. During the same period, residential segregation in inner city areas increased substantially despite the anti-discrimination provisions of the Fair Housing Act of 1968.[90] In the early 1990s, the Supreme Court's desegregation jurisprudence took a dramatic shift. The decisions in *Board of Education of Oklahoma City v. Dowell*,[91] *Freeman v. Pitts*,[92] and *Missouri v. Jenkins*[93] created a much lower standard for finding that a school system had achieved "unitary status," the ultimate goal of desegregation efforts.

Under *Green*, school districts had been required to completely eradicate all remnants of the segregated system "root and branch." Now, they need only show good faith compliance with the original desegregation decree and the elimination of most, but not necessarily all, lingering vestiges. If student populations reflect segregated housing patterns, school officials will not be held responsible. The new standard requires courts to hold that the desegregation obligation has been satisfied, even though most urban school enrollments are largely black and Latino as a result of the persistence of segregated housing patterns.[94] Under this new standard school districts have been declared unitary and are returning to neighborhood school assignments.

Brown's *Continuing Significance*

Recently, a number of scholars have reassessed the efficacy of *Brown* and questioned its contribution to equality rights of African–Americans. Although the *Brown* decision is still praised as the decisive blow to American Jim Crow, Professor Charles Ogletree and other scholars have criticized *Brown II* as a weak decision that set no meaningful timetable for desegregation.[95] In *From Jim Crow to Civil Rights*,[96] Professor Michael Klarman argued that *Brown* radicalized the social and political climate in the South, which led to years of sometimes violent resistance orchestrated by segregationist leaders. Klarman contended that segregation would have ended without *Brown* in a more gradual manner that would have had broader support among southern whites.

In *Silent Covenants*,[97] Professor Derrick Bell, who has long been a critic of the post-*Brown* school desegregation tactics, contended that the case was wrongly decided. Bell argued provocatively that African–American students would have fared better had the Supreme Court ordered the southern states to equalize black and white schools. Had the Court done so, black students would have attended schools that were physically and otherwise equal to white schools; parents would have participated in educational leadership by serving on school boards. Bell believes that competent and caring instruction in an all-black environment would have been preferable to the obstacles encountered by many black students attending racially mixed schools in the years following the *Brown* decision.

Contrary to these assertions, *Brown* was not wrongly decided. Professor Bell's pessimism may be justified in light of the conditions in most urban schools, but his separatist arguments reflect a nostalgic view of a time when black teachers in segregated schools nurtured their students, stressed academic excellence, and performed admirably with the limited resources. Pre–*Brown* enclaves of African–American excellence, such as the District of Columbia's Dunbar High School, were rare and would not have been replicated in a segregated South. Moreover, an interview of students or teachers at the best of such schools would have revealed how anxiously they awaited a release from racial isolation.

Professor Klarman's naively optimistic view of the racial attitudes of southern whites disregards decades of history and reality. As Leon Litwak, Eric Foner, and many other distinguished historians have documented,[98] lynching, violence, and other forms of intimidation were routinely inflicted on African–Americans throughout the first half of the twentieth century. These atrocities did not escalate in reaction to *Brown*. What changed was the attention they received. The intense media coverage of school desegregation efforts and the emergence of television broadcasting brought the horrors of southern racism to the attention of a much wider audience. Without *Brown* the Jim Crow system of racial segregation would have persisted far longer than Klarman suggests.

There have been many difficulties with school desegregation beginning with the era of massive resistance and continuing into the present with housing patterns that create segregated schools. But these problems cannot fairly be attributed to the opinions in *Brown*. When *Brown* was decided, neighborhoods were already highly segregated as a result of decades of redlining,[99] restrictive covenants, and other discriminatory practices. During the post-World War II era, population distributions were in the midst of a dramatic shift as white families were rapidly relocating to suburban communities.[100] This was facilitated by a prosperous, post-war economy and federal subsidy programs such as Veterans Administration and Federal Housing Authority loans.

The suburban communities that became a staple of the American landscape were developed during this period. However, black families who were ready, willing, and able to purchase suburban homes were excluded by discriminatory practices, many of which were imposed by the federal government, which required restrictive covenants on government insured mortgage loans.[101] The result was that African-Americans were locked out of suburban communities.[102]

In 1968, Congress enacted the Fair Housing Act,[103] which prohibited discrimination in housing transactions. After the law was adopted, African-American families with the resources to do so began to move away from inner-city communities. However, of all the civil rights laws enacted in the 1960s and afterward, the Fair Housing Act proved to be the least effective. Reports periodically produced by the U.S. Department of Housing and Urban Development and other organizations document widespread discriminatory practices in the nation's housing markets.[104]

Researchers analyzing the 2000 Census found that high levels of residential segregation persist. The data shows that 33 of the top 50 metropolitan areas in the United States are highly segregated. The remaining 17 are moderately segregated. None of the 50 was within the range that social scientists would consider integrated.[105] Commenting on this phenomenon, sociologist Loïc Wacquant concluded that whites accepted integration "in principle," but "in practice they strove to maintain an unbridgeable social and symbolic gulf with their compatriots of African descent. They abandoned public schools, shunned public space, and fled to the suburbs in their millions to avoid mixing and ward off the spectre of 'social equality' in the city."[106]

Conclusion

Conditions for most African-Americans are considerably better than they were in the pre-*Brown* era. Family income, educational attainment levels, employment opportunities, and other conditions have improved to an extent that was unimaginable during the Jim Crow era. These advances are the direct result of *Brown* and the Civil Rights Movement that it inspired. Unfortunately, the benefits have not been shared by all African-Americans. The African-American community is now segmented economically, geographically, and ideologically along class lines.[107]

One-fourth of the African-American population still resides in high-poverty, inner-city communities. Living the dark side of the American dream, these families experience unique, and often devastating, disadvantages resulting from the interaction of race and class. The return to neighborhood schools means that inner-city schools will be as segregated and impoverished as the communities in which they are located. Conditions in such schools make it extremely difficult for educators to maintain a nurturing, stable, and intellectually stimulating environment. African-American students in many inner-city neighborhoods are as isolated now as their grandparents were in the pre-*Brown* era. Given the persistence of segregated neighborhoods in urban communities, it is unlikely that this trend will change in the foreseeable future.

Endnotes

1. Portions of this chapter are based in part on *Setting the Stage for Brown: The Development and Implementation of the NAACP's School Desegregation Campaign, 1930–1950*, 52 Mercer L. Rev. 631 (2001).

2. Keith Medley, *We as Freemen: Plessy v. Ferguson* (2003).

3. 163 U.S. 537 (1896).

4. The Thirteenth Amendment abolished slavery stating "[n]either slavery nor involuntary servitude, except as a punishment for crime whereof the party shall have been duly convicted, shall exist within the United States, or any place subject to their jurisdiction." The Fourteenth Amendment provides that "[n]o state shall ... deny to any person within its jurisdiction the equal protection of the laws." The Fifteenth Amendment states that "[t]he right of citizens of the United States to vote shall not be denied or abridged by the United States or by any state on account of race, color, or previous condition of servitude."

5. 347 U.S. 483, 484 (1954).

6. Margold Report, Papers of the NAACP, Part 3: The Campaign for Educational Equality, 1913, 1950, Series A. Reel 4, Frames 560–772.

7. *Id.* at Frame 648.

8. Genna Rae McNeil, *Groundwork*; *Charles Hamilton Houston and the Struggle for Civil Rights* at 84 (1983), quoting Charles Hamilton Houston.

9. McNeil, *Groundwork*, *supra* note 8, at 88–89.

10. Charles Hamilton Houston, *Saving The World For Democracy*, Pittsburgh Courier, Aug. 24, 1940.

11. McNeil, *Groundwork*, *supra* note 8 at 21, 24 (1983).

12. Rayford W. Logan, *Howard University: The First Hundred Years, 1867–1967*, 225 (1969). (The American Bar Association and the American Association of Law Schools are the principal accrediting bodies for law schools).

13. *Id.*

14. Robert Carter, *A Tribute to Thurgood Marshall*, 105 Harvard L. Rev. 33, 36–37 (1991). (Judge Carter served as Thurgood Marshall's Deputy at the NAACP during the NAACP's litigation campaign and argued the Kansas case, *Brown v. Board of Education of Topeka.*).

15. Committee Report, May 28, 1930, Papers of the NAACP Part 3: The Campaign for Educational Equality, 1913–1950, Series A–Reel 1.

16. *Id.*

17. Carter, *A Tribute to Thurgood Marshall*, *supra* note 14, at 36–37.

18. Minutes of AFPS/NAACP Joint Committee Meeting, March 21, 1935, Papers of the NAACP, Part 3: The Campaign for Educational Equality, 1913–1950, Series A. Reel 4, Frame 00008.

19. Pearson v. Murray, 182 A. 590 (Md. 1936).

20. *Pearson*, 182 A. at 590.

21. *Id.*

22. *Id.* at 593.

23. *Id.*

24. Juan Williams, *Thurgood Marshall: American Revolutionary* (1998).

25. Houston's Report to the Officers and Delegates of the 26th Annual Conference of the NAACP, June 25, 1935, Papers of the NAACP, Part I, Reel 9.

26. *Id.*

27. Richard Kluger, *Simple Justice*, 203–04 (1975); McNeil, *supra* note 8 at 143–44. *See also* Lucille Bluford, *The Lloyd Gaines Story*, 232 J. Educ. Soc. 243 (1959). Larry Grothaus, *The Inevitable Mr. Gaines*, 26 Arizona and the West 21 (1984). University of Missouri Case Won, Crisis, Jan. 1939, at 10–11.

28. Kluger, *supra* note 27, at 203.

29. *Id.*

30. *Id.*

31. *Id.* at 204.

32. *Id.*

33. Missouri ex rel. Gaines v. Canada, 113 S.W.2d 783, 785 (Mo. 1938).

34. Missouri ex rel. Gaines v. Canada, 305 U.S. 580 (1938).

35. *Id.* at 347.

36. *Id.* at 345.

37. *Id.* at 348.

38. *Id.* at 351.

39. *Id.*

40. Walter White, *A Man Called White* (1948).

41. McNeil, *supra* note 8, at 149. *See also* Mark Tushnet, *Making Civil Rights Law: Thurgood Marshall and the Supreme Court*, 1936–1961 (1994).

42. Under 28 U.S.C. §§ 2281 and 2284, a three-judge district court could hear and determine cases involving injunctions against the enforcement of state statutes based on allegations of unconstitutionality; 28 U.S.C. § 1253 allowed decisions of such tribunals to be appealed directly to the Supreme Court.

43. Sipuel v. Board of Regents of the Univ. of Okla., 180 P.2d 135, 141–44 (Okla. 1947).

44. Sipuel v. Board of Regents of the Univ. of Okla., 332 U.S. 631 (1948).

45. *Id. See also* Crisis, Nov. 1947, at 343–44.

46. *Sipuel*, 332 U.S. at 632.

47. Fisher v. Hurst, 333 U.S. 147 (1948).

48. *See Segregation and the Equal Protection Clause: Brief of the Committee of Law Teachers Against Segregated Legal Education*, 34 Minn. L. Rev. 289 (1950). *See also* Mark Tushnet, *The NAACP's Legal Strategy Against Segregated Education 1925–1950* (1987).

49. Sweatt v. Painter, 210 S.W.2d 442, 443 (Tex. Civ. App. 1948).

50. Crisis, Sept. 1948, at 274.

51. 87 F.Supp. 528 (W.D. Okla 1949).

52. *Sweatt*, 339 U.S. 633–634.

53. *Id.* at 634.

54. McLaurin v. Oklahoma State Regents for Higher Educ., 339 U.S. 637, 640 (1950).

55. *Id.* at 640.

56. *Id.* at 641.

57. Crisis, Nov. 1950, at 650.

58. 98 F.Supp. 797 (D. Kan. 1951).

59. Briggs v. Elliott, 103 F.Supp. 920 (E.D.S.C. 1952).

60. Davis v. County School Board of Prince Edward County, 103 F.Supp. 337 (E.D. Va. 1952).

61. In *Bolling* the final decree of the United States District Court for the District of Columbia was not reported.

62. Belton v. Gebhart; Bulah v. Gebhart, 87 A.2d 862 (Del. Ch. 1952).

63. K.B. Clark, *Effect of Prejudice and Discrimination on Personality Development* (Midcentury White House Conference on Children and Youth, 1950).

64. Robert L. Carter, *A Matter of Law: A Memoir of Struggle in the Cause of Equal Rights*, 94–96 (2005).

65. Davis v. County Board of Prince Edward County, 103 F.Supp. 337, 339 (E.D. Va. 1952).

66. 347 U.S. 497 (1954).

67. *Brown*, 98 F.Supp. at 798.

68. 87 A.2d 862, 865 (Del. Ch. 1952).

69. 75 A.2d 225 (Del. 1950). The University of Delaware case generated some controversy. Redding and Greenberg did not want to jeopardize Seitz' pending re-appointment as Chancellor by the Delaware legislature so they filed the school desegregation cases in federal court. Delaware's Attorney General filed a motion asking the federal court to abstain from hearing the case to give the state court an opportunity to consider the constitutional issues. After deciding not to oppose the abstention motion, Redding and Greenberg filed the Delaware cases in state court. Jack Greenberg, *Crusaders in the Courts: How a Dedicated Band of Lawyers Fought for the Civil Rights Revolution* 136 (1994).

70. 91 A.2d 137.

71. A transcript of the arguments in *Brown* can be found in *Argument: The Oral Argument before the Supreme Court in Brown vs. Board of Education of Topeka*, Leon Friedman Ed. (1969).

72. Brown v. Board of Education of Topeka, 345 U.S. 972 (1953).

73. Kluger, *Simple Justice*, *supra* note 27, at 618–646. Greenberg, *supra* note 68, at 177–189. *See also* Robert Cottrol, Raymond Diamond, and Leland Ware, *Brown v. Board of Education: Caste, Culture and the Constitution* (2003).

74. Morton J. Horowitz, *The Warren Court and the Pursuit of Justice* (1999).

75. Brown v. Board of Education, 347 U.S. 483, 494 (1954). A separate decision was entered in *Bolling v. Sharpe*, the District of Columbia case. As the Fourteenth Amendment does not apply to the District of Columbia, which is a federal territory, the Court relied on liberty interests protected by the Fifth Amendment to conclude "[s]egregation in public education is not reasonably related to any proper governmental objective, and thus it imposes on Negro children of the District of Columbia a burden that constitutes an arbitrary deprivation of their liberty in violation of the Due Process Clause." 347 U.S. 497 (1954).

76. 349 U.S. 294 (1955).

77. Charles Ogletree, *All Deliberate Speed: Reflections on the First Half-Century of Brown v. Board of Education* 10–11 (2004).

78. 102 Cong. Rec. 4693 (1956).

79. 377 U.S. 218 (1964).

80. *Id.* at 229.

81. 396 U.S. 19 (1969).

82. *Id.* at 20.

83. 391 U.S. 430 (1968).

84. *Id.*

85. 402 U.S. 1 (1971).

86. Nicholas Lemann, *The Promised Land: The Great Migration and How it Changed America*, 6 (1991).

87. Leon F. Litwak, *Trouble in Mind: Black Southerners in the Age of Jim Crow* (1999).

88. 418 U.S. 717 (1974).

89. *Id.* at 746.

90. Douglas S. Massey and Nancy A. Denton, *American Apartheid: Segregation and the Making of the Underclass* (1993).

91. 498 U.S. 237 (1991).

92. 503 U.S. 467 (1992).

93. 515 U.S. 70 (1994).

94. *Ethnic Diversity Grows, Neighborhood Integration Lags Behind* (Lewis Mumford Center, December 18, 2001).

95. Ogletree, *All Deliberate Speed*, *supra* note 76.

96. Michael Klarman, *From Jim Crow to Civil Rights: The Supreme Court and the Struggle for Racial Equality* (2004).

97. Derrick Bell, *Silent Covenants: Brown v. Board of Education and the Unfulfilled Hopes for Racial Reform* (2004).

98. Litwak, *supra* note 86; Eric Foner, *Reconstruction: America's Unfinished Revolution*, 1863–1877 (1988); John Hope Franklin and Alfred A. Moss, Jr., *From Slavery to Freedom: A History of African Americans* (8th ed. 2000).

99. Massey and Denton, *supra* note 84.

100. Massey and Denton *supra* note 84, at 74–78.

101. Melvin L. Oliver and Thomas M. Shapiro, *Black Wealth/White Wealth: A New Perspective on Racial Inequality* 18 (1995).

102. *Id.*

103. 42 U.S.C. § 3601 *et seq.*

104. *See generally* John Yinger, U.S. Dep't of Housing and Urban Development, Housing Discrimination Study, *Incidence of Discrimination and Variations in Discriminatory Behavior* ix, 1 (1991); John Yinger, *Closed Doors, Opportunities Lost: The Continuing Costs of Housing Discrimination* 51–52, 121 (1995); Discrimination in Metropolitan Housing Markets: National Results from Phase 1 of the Housing Discrimination Study (2000) *available at* http://www.huduser.org/publications/hsgfin/phase1.html.

105. Lewis Mumford Center, University at Albany, *available at* http://mumford1.dyndns.org/cen2000/WholePop/WPreport/page2.html.

106. Loïc Wacquant, *From Slavery to Mass Incarceration: Rethinking the "Race Question" in the U.S.*, 13 New Left Review 41, 47 (Jan. Feb. 2002).

107. Massey and Denton, *supra* note 84.

3

The Story of *San Antonio Independent School Dist. v. Rodriguez*: School Finance, Local Control, and Constitutional Limits

Michael Heise

The story of *San Antonio Independent School Dist. v. Rodriguez*[1] is comprised of many different stories deriving from many different perspectives. For Demetrio Rodriguez (and the other plaintiffs), the *Rodriguez* decision meant that the federal courts were not going to assist in a drive to secure greater school resources and increase equity among school districts in Texas. For the state of Texas (and, indeed, almost every other state), the decision prevented a dismantling of the basic architecture of the state's school finance system which relies heavily on local property taxes. As a consequence, per pupil spending in most states, including Texas, remains acutely sensitive to variations in local property tax receipts. For school finance reformers, the 5–4 defeat in *Rodriguez* precluded a single federal resolution to persisting school finance fights. To be sure, the *Rodriguez* decision did not end the school finance debate in Texas or elsewhere. Instead, the decision redirected reformers and their legal claims to state courts and constitutions across the country. For constitutionalists, the *Rodriguez* decision made clear (once again) that education is not a fundamental right, wealth is not a suspect classification, and the Constitution's reach has limits. So long as rationality tethers a state's school finance system to a legitimate end, *Rodriguez* insulates states from federal courts. Finally, for institutionalists, the *Rodriguez* litigation forced the Court to confront judicial capacity issues anew. Already humbled by the challenges incident to the federal courts' effort to dismantle *de jure* and *de facto* school segregation, the *Rodriguez* decision evidences reluctance by some of the Justices to become ensnarled in an effort to dismantle school finance systems in way that would affect an overwhelming majority of the nation's public schools. By side-stepping such a confrontation, *Rodriguez* implicitly reveals important aspects about the federal courts and, in particular, how the Justices view their role in our federal system and the Court's ability as an institution to achieve sought-after policy goals. These various stories and perspectives, separately and collectively, enrich, fuel, and complicate *Rodriguez*'s enduring and evolving legacy.

This Chapter seeks to convey the richness of the many stories and perspectives that collectively comprise *Rodriguez*. I first describe the major parties as well as the initial lawsuit in federal district court. I then turn to the judicial opinions generated by the district court and U.S. Supreme Court. A comparison of the two opinions reveals decidedly different approaches to such issues as judicial capacity, fundamental rights, and federalism. I also consider the opinions' practical consequences and place them into the broader legal context, especially with respect to the concurrent school desegregation litigation. I conclude with a brief review of the school finance setting in Texas today, including in the Edgewood and Alamo Heights districts, which illustrates that while *Rodriguez* may have answered some questions, it raised others and deflected school finance battles from the federal government to state governments.

Demetrio Rodriguez and the Edgewood School District

Demetrio Rodriguez, then six years old, moved in 1931 with his migrant farming family from a small Texas farming town near the Rio Grande to San Antonio in search of better public schools. In 1957, Demetrio, by then a U.S. Navy and Air Force veteran as well as a husband and father, moved his family to the Edgewood area, a "sprawling Hispanic barrio" on San Antonio's southwest side and close to an air force base where Demetrio worked as a sheet-metal welder.[2]

In 1968, public schools in the San Antonio area varied tremendously in numerous ways. The Edgewood school district, one of seven in the San Antonio area, enrolled approximately 22,000 students in its twenty-five elementary and secondary schools.[3] Edgewood schools served predominately minority children (over 90 percent Hispanic and 6 percent African-American) from low-income households ($4,686 median family income).[4] The schooling situation was quite different in the nearby Alamo Heights school district, San Antonio's most affluent school district. Alamo Heights schools served students from wealthier households (median family income exceeded $8,000) which were far more likely to be white (only 18 percent Hispanic and less than 1 percent African-American).[5]

Beyond potentially dry Census data on the two school districts, Edgewood and Alamo Heights differed in other important ways. For example, parental education levels varied dramatically between the two districts. While in Alamo Heights 75 percent of the residents had completed high school, fewer than one in ten of the Edgewood residents had earned high school diplomas.[6] These stark differences in education attainment levels correlated with other predictable differences, including employment outcomes. The Alamo Heights district teemed with lawyers, doctors, and bankers—professionals with college (and beyond) training. In 1970, for example, more than 50 percent of male workers in Alamo Heights held executive or professional titles. In Edgewood, however, only four percent of the males enjoyed similar success in the workforce.[7]

Although only a few miles separate the Alamo Heights and Edgewood school districts, from an educational perspective the two districts could not have been farther apart. Although it is seductively easy to become lost in the highly technical, arcane, and formulaic world of school finance, what typically lurks behind most discussions of mill levies, equalized tax rates, and assessed valuations is one profoundly simple yet forceful observation—education resources distribute unevenly across districts within a state. In 1968, the distribution of school resources in Texas followed a pattern typical for that era. Per pupil spending in Edgewood, an overwhelmingly poor and minority school district, was $356,[8] while per pupil spending in the predominately white and affluent neighboring Alamo Heights district was $594,[9] or two-thirds more. Although a per pupil spending difference of $238 does not sound like much by today's school spending standards, in today's (2006) dollars the difference amounts to $1,435 per pupil.[10]

Making matters worse was that the per pupil spending disparity arose even though Edgewood residents taxed themselves at a rate higher than the Alamo Heights residents.[11] To completely off-set the stark difference in property values between Edgewood and Alamo Heights and generate equal per pupil spending, the tax rate in Edgewood would have to had been twenty times greater than the Alamo Heights tax rate.[12] Adding further insult to injury was a Texas law that imposed a property tax ceiling which in effect precluded equal per pupil spending in Edgewood and Alamo Heights. Demetrio Rodriguez and other parents in the Edgewood school district confronted a vexing dilemma. Texas school finance law, specifically its reliance on local property tax revenues, generated considerable differences in per pupil spending and Texas tax law prevented equalization. Recognition of this dilemma, however, did little to ameliorate conditions in Demetrio Rodriguez's children's dilapidated Edgewood schools.

The Complaint

About the same time Demetrio Rodriguz and other parents began focusing on school funding disparities with an eye toward possible litigation, two developments emerged. First, parents and activists in

California were focusing in a similar—though distinct—way. One distinction in particular was critical. In their complaint in the *Serrano* litigation, the plaintiffs in California alleged state (as well as federal) constitutional violations in state court,[13] claims that ultimately prevailed in the California Supreme Court.[14] Second, emerging academic research (part of which stimulated and shaped the *Serrano* litigation in California) began to sketch the contours of a federal legal challenge to state school finance systems.

Frustrated with Texas lawmakers' disinterest in equalizing school spending, dispirited by their under-resourced schools, and buoyed by similar (though distinct) litigation in California, Rodriguez and other parents sought redress in the courts. Unlike their counterparts in California, however, Rodriguez turned to the federal constitution and federal courts. In 1968, with his children attending Edgewood schools, the forty-two year-old Demetrio (along with six other parents) filed a class action lawsuit in federal district court that fundamentally challenged the way Texas funded its public schools.

The complaint filed in *Rodriguez* is important for the arguments and theories it advanced as well as for those it did not. The lead attorney, Arthur Gochman, developed two principal claims. First, he asserted that low-income households, clustered in low-spending school districts like Edgewood, constituted a suspect class, thereby triggering strict judicial scrutiny of Texas' school finance system. Second, he argued that education was a fundamental right and, under the Fourteenth Amendment, Texas was obligated to provide it on an equal basis. Gochman asserted that the per pupil spending disparities between Edgewood and Alamo Heights districts, as well as similar disparities between and among other school districts across Texas, evidenced unconstitutionally unequal treatment.

Gochman's focus on poverty as a suspect classification warranting strict judicial scrutiny was not without legal precedent, albeit tangential to and non-binding in the education context. In *Griffin v. Illinois*,[15] the United States Supreme Court struck down state laws that prevented an indigent criminal defendant from access to a trial transcript. The state fee requirements were held to discriminate against low-income defendants who were otherwise financially unable to access trail transcripts. Similarly, in *Douglas v. California*,[16] the Court established an indigent defendant's right to court-appointed (and funded) counsel for those defendants with no other way to gain access to an attorney. Finally, in *Bullock v. Carter*,[17] the Court invalidated a Texas filing-fee requirement for candidates seeking to compete in primary elections. Under the fee system, potential candidates without the financial ability to pay the filing fee were unable to compete for public office. The litigants in *Rodriguez* set out to leverage the comparative poverty in the Edgewood district and extend suspect class status—recognized by the Court in non-education contexts—to include the school setting.

Although direct legal support for Gochman's argument that the per pupil spending gap between Edgewood and Alamo Heights students violated the federal Equal Protection Clause was lacking, potentially analogous case law existed. One decision, *Hobson v. Hansen*,[18] involved per pupil spending variations within a single district—the District of Columbia public schools. Gochman sought to extend *Hobson*'s logic to variation across districts within Texas. As well, the now-substantial intellectual and scholarly attention to school finance today[19] was only emerging at the time Gochman crafted the *Rodriguez* complaint and, as a consequence, Gochman had comparatively fewer scholarly assets to leverage.[20]

Interestingly (especially so in the shadow of the concurrent school desegregation litigation), the *Rodriguez* complaint did not pursue racial (or ethnic) discrimination theories. Indeed, Gochman assiduously avoided casting the *Rodriguez* case as a "race" case. He ignored the racial and ethnic dimensions even though the Edgewood district was overwhelmingly Hispanic and the Alamo Heights district predominately white. Nevertheless, *Rodriguez* was consciously framed as a finance case and the attorneys in *Rodriguez* emphasized the Edgewood district's poverty rather than the district's overwhelmingly non-white citizenry.

What might explain the strategic decision to cast *Rodriguez* in financial rather than racial or ethnic terms? After all, racial discrimination was the dominant theme of the quickly maturing school desegregation jurisprudence. The absence of perfect correlation between ethnicity and geography might have deterred Gochman. (If so, his intuition was vindicated by the Court's reliance on a study by Professor Burke documenting something less than a perfect correlation between a school district's percentage of minority students and per pupil spending levels.[21]) Although Edgewood was overwhelmingly Hispanic, it was not *exclusively* so. Similarly, while Alamo Heights was predominately white, *some*—albeit few—residents were either Hispanic or non-white. Another possibility is that the predominately Hispanic Edgewood residents were simply more interested in increasing resources for their schools than in increasing racial and ethnic integration levels. Regardless of the reason, it is difficult to overstate the strategic importance of the decision to frame *Rodriguez* in terms of poverty and education rather than in terms of race and ethnicity.[22]

By the time the district court decided the *Rodriguez* case the relevant legal terrain had evolved in important ways as the school finance litigation movement had begun in earnest. In *Serrano v. Priest*,[23] the California Supreme Court concluded that within state per pupil spending variations violated the Fourteenth Amendment as well as state law. In *Van Dusartz v. Hatfield*,[24] the court reached a similar conclusion and made the more subtle point that the wealth variations (specifically, per pupil spending differences) were created by state policy. Although unavailable at the time Gochman crafted the legal complaint, the district court opinion in *Rodriguez* made good use of these new cases.

District Court Decision

Although the district court heard arguments in the *Rodriguez* case in 1968, its opinion was not issued until late 1971, more than three years after the lawsuit was filed. Because the case challenged state (Texas) law on federal grounds (Fourteenth Amendment), the case was argued to a three-judge district court panel.[25] The district court panel initially wrestled with the standard of review question. The state of Texas urged the court to apply the less onerous rational basis test, while the plaintiffs urged strict scrutiny as the appropriate standard of judicial review. The district court concluded that because the Texas school finance system was based upon wealth—a suspect classification—and, in addition, implicated a fundamental interest—education—strict judicial scrutiny was warranted.[26] To survive strict judicial scrutiny, the court noted that Texas must demonstrate that a compelling governmental interest supporting its use of a property tax-based school finance regime that generated uneven per pupil spending among districts across the state.

Texas' central argument, that its property tax-based school funding system enhanced local control and autonomy by giving local taxpayers a significant voice in deciding how much to spend on their local public schools,[27] did not persuade the district court. Instead, the district court felt that Texas' school finance system, combined with state property tax caps, had the effect of *reducing* local district autonomy,[28] thereby turning Texas' critical argument on its head. Because "Texas discriminates on the basis of wealth by permitting citizens of affluent districts to provide a higher quality education for their children, while paying lower taxes," the district court concluded the plaintiffs had been denied equal protection afforded by the Fourteenth Amendment.[29]

In addition to concluding that Texas failed to articulate and support a compelling governmental interest, the court went on to reach the far more provocative conclusion that Texas' school finance plan failed the far less onerous rational relation test. The federal district court felt that the purported relation between Texas' property tax-based school finance system was not rationally related to any legitimate governmental end such as local autonomy or control over local school spending.[30]

Setting aside formal legal reasoning, the palpable differences between the Edgewood and Alamo Heights schools likely were not lost on the three-judge panel hearing the case. One of the three, Judge Spears, appointed to the federal bench by President Kennedy, lived in Alamo Heights. According to one commentator, "[Judge] Spears knew very well the disparities between schools in Edgewood and Alamo Heights."[31]

Two key themes emerge from the district court opinion that continue to resonate throughout many aspects of education law in general and school finance litigation in particular. First, the court opinion implicitly equated "higher quality education" with higher per pupil spending. Second, the opinion conveyed some trepidation owing to separation of powers concerns.

School Spending and Quality

Embedded within the plaintiffs' complaint and the district court opinion is the assumption that the quality of education offered in Alamo Heights is superior to the education offered in Edgewood and that this quality difference is a function of per pupil spending. Such an assumption risks conflating education quality (and related reform efforts designed to enhance and more broadly distribute quality), school spending, and student academic achievement.[32] By accepting such an assumption, the court presumed causal simplicity and clarity where reality is anything but simple and clear. If anything, debates over whether money "matters," especially as it relates to student academic achievement, are noted for their technical complexities and endurance.[33] Explanations for and theories on why some students perform well and others perform poorly are endlessly debated in the literature.[34]

Two major studies, both by Professor Coleman,[35] sparked public and academic debates about the relation between school spending and student achievement. In 1966, Coleman (and colleagues) released a large and controversial report on the nation's schools, which emphasized the influence of family and the socioeconomic status of a student's classmates on academic achievement.[36] The study found that, from the perspective of influencing student academic achievement, school spending mattered very little and that a student's socioeconomic status mattered a great deal.[37] Although the question about the relation between school spending and student academic achievement remains hotly contested,[38] the assertion that students' socioeconomic status matters a great deal has withstood the test of time.[39] Numerous subsequent studies find that "the social composition of the student body is more highly related to achievement, independent of the student's own social background, than is any other school factor."[40] Notably, education commentators of every political stripe acknowledge the robustness and consistency of these findings.[41] Simply put, "[i]f there is one thing that is more related to a child's academic achievement than coming from a poor household, it is going to school with children from other poor households."[42]

In addition to exploring the larger question of whether money "matters" in terms of student achievement, scholars have compared results from schools that spend different amounts on similar types of students. Again, research by Professor Coleman resides at the heart of this ongoing debate.[43] Professor Coleman (and colleagues) published the first major quantitative study exploring differences in student achievement between public and private (principally Catholic) schools and found that students in private schools performed slightly better, after controlling for student race and socioeconomic background.[44] What makes the comparison especially important for the school finance debate in general and the *Rodriguez* case in particular is that many of the higher performing inner-city private schools spent less on a per pupil basis than their public school counterparts.[45]

Separation of Powers and Judicial Remedies

A second important theme developed in the district court opinion involves the court's sensitivity to separation of powers concerns. Mindful that it is not a "super-legislature,"[46] the district court's order evidenced some degree of tentativeness when it ordered relief that was prospective and became effective only if, after two years, the Texas Legislature did not modify the school finance system in a manner that addressed the court's concerns.[47]

What to make of the prospective relief awarded by the district court? Some view it as an abdication of the court's responsibility.[48] After all, from a remedies' perspective the court effectively turned to the very institution that created the unconstitutional school finance system in the first place—the Texas General Assembly—for a resolution. Some wondered whether the court's approach to the remedy reflected a misapprehension of the lessons learned in *Brown v. Board of Education (Brown II)*[49] and from the "with all deliberate speed" experiment.[50] After all, one decade after *Brown II*, the Supreme Court itself remarked that the implementation of the desegregation remedy resulted in "entirely too much deliberation and not enough speed."[51]

The district court's prospective relief may also have reflected a necessary (if regrettable) judicial bow to reality. First, if the federal courts learned anything from the debate surrounding the "all deliberate speed" remedy articulated in *Brown II* they learned something about judicial capacity. In the school finance context, empirical evidence on the ability of court decisions to influence education spending is mixed, at best, and some suggest that courts in some states may have overestimated their comparative institutional strength.[52] Second, with something as technically complex as school finance, institutional capacity and comparative expertise suggest some role for state lawmakers and policymakers in fashioning a remedy.

Third, it is likely that political context cannot be ignored without peril. Indeed, Professor Gewirtz,[53] among others, argues that "remedies must take account of resistance from the world they hope to transform and that in some cases courts may properly make compromises and limit remedies because of this resistance."[54] Many governors and state lawmakers do not appreciate the perceived (or real) "end-run" around the legislative process to the courthouse in an effort to garner increased educational resources. Resistance to judicially-mandated or initiated school finance reform, both formal and informal, hinders many successful lawsuits that rely on legislators and governors for implementation at the remedial stage. Of course, such an argument risks collapsing into tautology. After all, one reason why successful school finance lawsuits, such as *Rodriguez*, may not generate the sought-after increased per pupil spending equity is precisely *because* courts may be reluctant to vigorously impose judicial sanctions owing to either real or theoretical separation of powers concerns.

The benefit of a two-year window to generate a legislative fix to the school finance problems the district court identified did not placate Texas lawmakers. Given the novel legal theories pushed in the *Rodriguez* complaint, Texas lawmakers were publicly (and privately) confident that the district court would see the situation their way and would not disrupt the Texas school finance system. Clearly, officials in Texas were caught off guard by the district court's decision.[55] Not surprisingly, the defendants swiftly decided to appeal the ruling. Because of the case's unusual procedural posture, a direct appeal to the Supreme Court was possible and, indeed, successfully pursued by the defendants.

Supreme Court Opinion

The various parts of the Supreme Court's *Rodriguez* opinion consume 137 pages in the U. S. Reports and include concurring and dissenting opinions. Justice Powell, a Nixon appointee (and former Chair of the Richmond (Virginia) School Board),[56] structured the opinion around three central tasks. First, the opinion distinguished the class of low-income members challenging Texas' school finance system from other low-income individuals who successfully established poverty as a suspect class in other cases.[57] Second, once establishing that the Edgewood schoolchildren did not constitute a suspect class,[58] the Court concluded that public education was not a fundamental right under the U.S. Constitution.[59] Third, without the benefit of a suspect class or a fundamental right, the Court left Rodriguez with only the argument that the Texas school finance system did not rationally relate to various state interests, including local control. The Court concluded that Texas' school finance system was not irrationally related to such legitimate governmental ends (such as local control), reversed the district court's holding, and upheld Texas' school finance system.

The Court's decision had two immediate practical consequences for Demetrio Rodriguez in particular and the then-nascent school finance movement more generally. First, the opinion contributed significant momentum to the proposition that education was not a fundamental right under the federal constitution. During the second half of the twentieth century the Supreme Court had at least two separate and prime opportunities to deem education as a fundamental constitutional right. On both occasions, in *Brown v. Board of Education (Brown I)*[60] and *Rodriguez*, the Court declined to make such a finding. In *Rodriguez*, the Court hinted at the hypothetical possibility of some federal constitutional right to education when it noted: "Even if it were conceded that some quantifiable quantum of education is a constitutionally protected prerequisite to the meaningful exercise of either right, we have no indication that the present levels of educational expenditures in Texas provide an education that falls short."[61] While entertaining the possibility that the federal constitution might substantively require that Texas provide some level of education, the Court assiduously declined to articulate the federal threshold, save to remark that Texas already exceeded it.[62]

A second immediate consequence of the *Rodriguez* decision was to fundamentally redirect the school finance litigation movement. Although the decision shut the federal door on school finance litigation in federal court, the *Rodriguez* opinion did not end the school finance litigation movement. Instead, the decision redirected the litigation to state courts and state constitutions. Despite this abrupt change in fora as well as the source of a potential right, the school finance litigation movement survived the *Rodriguez* decision. Indeed, school finance activists did not have to wait long for success in the state courts. Just thirteen days following the *Rodriguez* decision, the New Jersey Supreme Court declared that its school finance system violated the New Jersey Constitution's promise for a "thorough and efficient education."[63]

The Dissents

Even if *Rodriguez* was not a 5–4 decision, the dissenting opinions warrant careful consideration. The dissenting Justices pursued two main points. Justice White's dissent conceded rational relation as the appropriate standard for judicial review but (echoing the district court opinion) argued that the Texas school finance system nonetheless failed to meet the "rational" threshold. Justice Marshall's dissent, in contrast, argued that because education was a fundamental right the Texas school finance system warranted strict judicial scrutiny which, Marshall argued, it failed to survive.

Justice White, joined by Justices Douglas and Brennan, began his dissent by conceding the critical role played by local control and decision making in our democratic system of government. Nevertheless, Justice White went on to point out that to satisfy the rational relation test, the Texas school finance system must satisfy two elements. First, it must pursue a valid, rational, legislative end (enhancing local control). Second, the "means chosen by the State must also be rationally related to the end sought to be achieved."[64]

Justice White's dissent dwelled on the second element and construed the magnitude of the per pupil spending difference between the Edgewood and Alamo Heights districts as evidence that Texas' reliance on property-based tax revenues paradoxically *undermined* the state's articulated goal of enhancing local control. This paradox emerged because disparities in property valuations interacted with local taxing power incident to the Texas school funding system in a way that made it "impossible" for Edgewood residents to generate "comparable school revenues."[65] And this impossibility, according to Justice White, makes Texas' school finance system constitutionally irrational because it turned Texas' purported rational for its desired legislative end—a school finance system that enhanced local control—on its head.

In contrast to Justice White, Justice Marshall continued to argue that education was a fundamental right. Justice Marshall's prior inability to persuade the Court to declare education as a fundamental right in *Brown* (as an advocate for the plaintiffs) did not deter him from revisiting the issue now that he sat on the Court. After categorizing Court pronouncements of education's importance, Justice Marshall developed the argument that education "directly affects" a child's ability to enjoy other core rights clearly articulated by the Constitution and deemed fundamental by the Court, such as speech.[66] Justice Marshall argued that the nexus between education and the engagement in the political process was sufficiently robust that, according to Marshall, the former was fundamental as a matter of constitutional law and, as such, triggered strict judicial scrutiny of Texas' school finance system. Recognizing that some students in property-poor schools academically out performed their counterparts attending property-rich schools[67] helped prompt Marshall to shift his analytic focus of the Equal Protection Clause from student achievement (outputs) to education inputs (per pupil spending and taxing efforts).[68]

Fundamental Rights and Limiting Principles

In *Brown*, although the Court famously noted education's importance to citizens and society,[69] the Court declined to construe education as a fundamental right. The plaintiffs in *Rodriguez* invited the Court to re-think the issue. Although the Court again concluded that education was important,[70] it affirmatively and unambiguously declined to construe the right to education as fundamental.[71] Indeed, one decade later in *Plyler v. Doe*,[72] the Court reiterated this theme when it once again acknowledged that education, while not constitutionally fundamental, nonetheless occupied a "fundamental role in maintaining the fabric of our society."[73]

Why has the Court for more than one-half century self-consciously declined to construe education as a fundamental right under the federal constitution? Or, more to the point, why did the Court in *Rodriguez* decline to extend the logic in *Brown* and deem education a fundamental right? For plaintiffs like Demetrio Rodriguez and, more importantly, his (and other) children attending Edgewood schools, the stakes were, of course, enormous. Were the Court to deem education fundamental, encroachments against education rights would trigger strict judicial scrutiny.

Ironically, some of the leading reasons offered to support education's status as a fundamental right help explain the Court's reluctance to embrace the argument. In *Rodriguez*, for example, the petitioners argued that education deserved elevated constitutional stature partly because of its nexus with other Court-recognized fundamental rights, notably those involving speech and voting.[74] Such an argument is not without legal foundation. Prior to *Rodriguez*, the Court in *Harper v. Virginia Board of Elections*[75] determined that a citizen's right to vote was fundamental because it is "preservative of other basic civil and political rights,"[76] such as political expression.[77]

From the Court's perspective in *Rodriguez*, however, such an argument proved too much and logically took the Court into uncomfortable terrain. The Court noted that such an argument lacked a limiting principle that would enable the Justices to clearly demark a boundary separating fundamental from non-fundamental interests. The Court wondered how one might distinguish education from hunger, clothing, or shelter in relation to the First Amendment or rights to meaningful political participation. And if a logically coherent line could not distinguish education from other such interests, the result would conflict with existing Court precedent (unchallenged by *Rodriguez*).[78]

That said, the *Rodriguez* Court conceded some analytic ground, if only rhetorically. Specifically, the Court held open the possibility that "some identifiable quantum of education" may, in fact, be fundamental as it might be required to protect other constitutional rights.[79] Having raised the theoretical specter of education as a fundamental right, the Court then quickly dismissed the issue's relevance in *Rodriguez* by noting that whatever amount of education is required by the federal constitution, Texas met that minimal burden. Thus, the Court hinted at the conceptual possibility of a fundamental right in education without meaningfully defining that threshold, aside from a nod to Texas' efforts.[80]

The Persistently Uneasy Relations Among Race, Resources, and Student Achievement in School Reform Litigation

An important vein in the debate about the relation between school spending and educational opportunity involves the equally complex relation between school spending and race. The arguments advanced in *Rodriguez,* when combined with many arguments advanced in numerous school desegregation cases of that era, uncover a critical struggle to coherently synthesize the influences of race and resources on student academic achievement. The juxtaposition between the standard school desegregation case, moored in racial equality, and the nascent school finance cases, principally pivoting on economic disparity, could not have been more stark to the Justices on October 12, 1972, as on that day, both the *Rodriguez* and *Keyes v. School District No. 1*[81] cases were argued.

In *Keyes*, the Court confronted the first major test of the *de jure/de facto* desegregation distinction. Two years earlier, in *Swann v. Charlotte-Mecklenberg Board of Education,*[82] the Court articulated a rebuttable presumption of segregative intent where schools were "substantially disproportionate in their racial composition."[83] In *Swann*, the Court imputed the racially isolated schools to the district's prior *de jure* segregation policies. In *Keyes*, in contrast, Denver's school district never operated *de jure* school segregation policies. Nevertheless, due to complex interactions among such variables as population shifts, school district student assignment policies, and demographic trends, racially identifiable (and thus, under *Swann*, presumptively unconstitutional) schools emerged. Embedded within school desegregation litigation efforts that sought to redistribute students within a district owing to race was an implicit assumption about disparities in school quality.

While *Keyes* understood equal educational opportunity (and thus, to some degree, school quality) in terms of race, *Rodriguez,* in contrast, eschewed that approach and instead operationalized educational opportunity in terms of school resources *independent* of race. Having embarked upon an argument that the low-income families in Edgewood were denied equal educational opportunity, the *Rodriguez* litigants claimed that, because of Texas' school finance system the Edgewood district was consigned to an inferior education (as compared to families in high-income districts). Although educational quality was operationalized largely in terms of traditional inputs—teacher turnover rates, teacher quality and experience, and school facilities—such outputs as student achievement and high school completion rates were also folded into the argument.[84]

Judicial remedies isolated problems flowing from competing conceptions of equal educational opportunity promoted in school desegregation and finance cases. As Professor Liu observes,[85] while both *Keyes* and *Rodriguez* pushed the equal educational opportunity doctrine, the two cases differed in a critical assumption incident to the requested remedies.[86] The *Keyes* litigation embodied an assumption that increased educational resources—absent integration—were ineffectual. The *Rodriquez* litigation, by contrast, implicitly assumed that increased educational resources were necessary to enhance equal educational opportunity even in intensely racially isolated schools. Unlike the district court's embrace of the asserted relation between school spending and quality,[87] the Supreme Court's opinion conveyed discomfort with even entertaining what it characterized as a controversial assertion.[88] No doubt owing to the complexity and uncertainty surrounding these issues, courts since *Rodriguez* remain split over their understanding of the relation between school funding and student achievement.[89] Perhaps even more startling is the confidence expressed by some courts in reaching a firm conclusion on this issue, especially in light of the acknowledged uncertainty within the social science community.[90]

Race, Resources, Rodriguez, *and Hindsight*

Although the evolution of the equal educational opportunity doctrine includes a transition from a focus on race to a focus on resources and thereby cements a link between race and resources,[91] the plaintiffs in *Rodriguez* took great pains to frame their lawsuit in terms of wealth disparity rather than race. This strategic decision was pursued despite palpable racial and ethnic dimensions that separated the Edgewood and Alamo Heights school districts. Whatever the strategy's merits were in the late 1960s, conventional litigation wisdom today is to conflate—and not separate—school finance and race and ethnicity.[92]

Efforts to separate wealth from race and ethnicity in the school context risk running against intellectual currents propelled by the *Brown* decision. While litigation aimed at eliminating school segregation on the basis of race descend directly from *Brown*, leading school finance litigants argue that school finance litigation resides within a "progressive legal dynamic" created by the *Brown* decision.[93] Moreover, school finance and desegregation litigation persist as integral parts of a larger project seeking enhanced educational opportunity.[94]

Even if it made sense to divorce wealth from race and ethnicity in the school context during the late 1960s, as evidenced by *Rodriguez*'s framing, from a practical standpoint it makes less strategic sense today.

Indeed, the two litigation efforts complement each other. As Professor Ryan notes,[95] it is easy to contemplate how school desegregation and finance litigation efforts could have coalesced in a way beneficial to poor and minority students by "ensuring that the fate of disadvantaged students was tied to the fate of their more advantaged peers."[96] In addition, the prospect for school finance reform is far higher where its beneficiaries are not of one race, and desegregation is more palatable to more where all schools are already amply resourced.[97] To some, then, the *Sheff v. O'Neill*[98] litigation in Connecticut, which conspicuously conflated race and school finance, addressed a task side-stepped by the Supreme Court in *Rodriguez*: synthesizing school finance and desegregation theory in a manner that advances a broader understanding of equal educational opportunity.[99]

The Lure of Local Control

Presaging one key rationale supporting the outcome in *Milliken v. Bradley*,[100] decided one year later, the *Rodriguez* opinion placed great analytic weight on the notion of local control and articulated fidelity to principles of federalism and separation of powers. The Court's comfort with local control in the education setting has increased over time. In *Rodriguez*, the Court concluded that local control was important and that Texas's reliance on local property taxes was not irrational. One year later (1974) in *Milliken* the Court more forcefully defended local control and declared: "No single tradition in public education is more deeply rooted than local control over the operation of schools; local autonomy has long been thought essential both to the maintenance of community concern and support for public schools and to the quality of the educational process."[101] Indeed, the *Milliken* opinion cites to *Rodriguez* for support for the proposition that local control over education policy fuels citizen participation and education quality.[102]

A fidelity to local control over education policy continues to occupy an exalted place in American lore and exerts significant sway over many citizens.[103] Moreover, the education sector evidences a consistent desire to decentralize educational policymaking authority, especially as it relates to elementary and secondary education. In all states but Hawaii, for example, legislatures have delegated substantial policymaking authority to local school districts, governed by local school boards.[104] The structural allocation of educational policymaking authority itself implies a belief that states and local school boards are comparatively better positioned to set desirable education policy and to do so in a manner that better reflects local conditions and preferences.[105] Finally, key federal actors and institutions have long understood that education—particularly elementary and secondary education—resides at the core of state and local, not federal, responsibility.[106]

The Court's fidelity to local control, however, rests increasingly uneasy in today's education setting. Stylized notions about local control over America's school policy, however powerful, have not accurately described the allocation of American education policy for decades.[107] The influence of local school authorities on school policy has waned due to legislative assertions by states and the federal government. Thus, the Court displayed increased confidence in local control over school policymaking (including fiscal policy) as state and federal lawmakers encroached upon local autonomy.[108] Since the 1970s the trend toward greater centralization of education policymaking authority has, if anything, accelerated and broadened.

State lawmakers started asserting greater policy control beginning the mid–1980s, as states assumed a greater absolute and relative share of local school funding responsibility. In some states the emergence of increased state control was in response to successful (or threatened or even unsuccessful) school finance litigation efforts. Also, governors, increasingly held politically responsible for school reform results, demanded greater policy control. Finally, in response to *A Nation At Risk* report in 1983[109] and the explosion of legislative responses the report fueled,[110] policymakers in many states began the task of reviewing and, in some instances, articulating for the first time goals for student education outcomes. All these factors inevitably led to a greater concentration of policy authority at the state level and a concurrent diminution of local control.

Ironically, state efforts to develop and implement standards and assessment regimes better enabled the federal government to enter the education policymaking field with greater force which had the practical effect of further blurring federalism lines and diluting local control.[111] Federal involvement with K–12 education policy increased in dramatic fashion with the No Child Left Behind Act 2001[112] ("NCLB"). At its core, NCLB leverages state-created standards and assessments, increases transparency by disseminating data on progress, and imposes consequences on local districts and schools for insufficient progress. States desiring NCLB funds must establish school accountability systems that moor annual student proficiency to math and reading assessments for grades three through eight.[113] States must also gather, report, and disseminate results for all students as well as for various student subgroups that contain a minimum number of students.[114] Although state standards must be "challenging,"[115] NCLB essentially leaves it to the states to establish their own standards and assessments, as well as proficiency thresholds.[116] A sliding scale of consequences befalls schools that do not achieve adequate yearly progress.[117] In exchange for federal education dollars, districts and states must now submit to increasingly onerous federal education laws. One inevitable consequence of school reform initiatives at the state and federal levels (as well as increased state and federal education spending) has been a further dilution of local control over school policy.

The Court as a "Super Legislature" and Practical Concerns

Embedded within the *Rodriguez* opinion are logical dilemmas and practical concerns. For example, the Court points to federalism, fear of unintended consequences, and practical concerns as reasons for declining the plaintiffs' invitation to restructure much of the nation's school finance system. According to the Court, "consideration and initiation of fundamental [school finance] reforms" are issues properly "reserved for the legislative processes of the various States."[118] More specifically, proposed solutions to school finance problems "must come from the lawmakers and from the democratic pressures of those who elect them."[119] By deferring to Texas lawmakers, the Court noted, "we [the Court] do no violence to the values of federalism and separation of powers by staying our hand."[120] The Court left unanswered, however, whether striking down the Texas law would also violate federalism principles.[121]

The Court noted its concerns about the possible consequences (unintended or intentional) and the potential political backlash that striking down Texas' school finance system might unleash. The concerns ranged from political resistance to calls for significant increases in education spending[122] to exacerbating spending gaps between urban and suburban districts.[123] Some—but not all—of the Court's concerns were well-founded. The decades of judicial engagement with school finance reform since *Rodriguez* reveal that the Court's prediction about political resistance to calls for significant spending increases proved far more prescient than the Court's prediction about exacerbating gaps between urban and suburban districts.

Practical concerns also informed the Court's analysis in *Rodriguez.* At the institutional level, the opinion conveys a presumption of judicial incompetence, at least when it comes to the practical nuances of school finance. The opinion notes that "the Justices of this Court lack both the expertise and familiarity with local problems necessary to the making of wise decisions with respect to the raising and disposition of public revenues."[124]

Finally, the majority opinion in *Rodriguez* breaks with tradition by closing with a "cautionary postscript"[125] that develops two general practical points. First, the Court characterizes Rodriguez's request as one that would involve billions of new tax dollars,[126] "massive change," and "completely uprooting the existing (education) system."[127] Although noting that such predictions about the future consequences of upholding the district court ruling were little more than mere guesses, the Court clearly conveyed its unwillingness to risk such consequences. Having noted such "practical considerations," in an almost self-conscious gesture, the Court went on to explain that such considerations, "of course, play no role in the adjudication of the constitutional issues presented here."[128]

Second, even though the Court concluded that Texas' school finance system passed constitutional muster, the Court also made clear its view that school finance reform was needed.[129] The *Rodriguez* opinion specifically encouraged further attention from scholars.[130] Despite suggesting that change was necessary, the Court's opinion closed on its most salient theme. That is, despite the necessity of reform, the *Rodriguez* opinion returned to a central theme that, as a matter of constitutional law, reform must flow from the legislature or executive rather than the judiciary.[131]

The Influence of Student Research

The *Rodriguez* lawsuit underscored student research's potential to influence litigation and judicial opinions. In 1965—three years before the *Rodriguez* complaint was filed—while pursuing a Ph.D. at the University of Chicago, Arthur Wise published an article that contemplated federal Equal Protection Clause dimensions flowing from per pupil funding disparities.[132] Wise's full argument emerged two years later in his dissertation,[133] which elicited a published response from one of his professors,[134] and culminated in the 1968 publication of his influential book, Rich Schools, Poor Schools: The Promise of Equal Educational Opportunity.[135]

Elements of the *Rodriguez* complaint reveal the influence of Art Wise's work conducted while he was in graduate school. As early as 1965, Wise identified poverty's potential Fourteenth Amendment salience and argued that, from the perspective of school finance litigation, the criminal and education contexts were similar.[136] The potential federal constitutional implications posed by intrastate variations in per pupil spending, such as what existed in Texas when *Rodriguez* was filed, were novel and a distinct break from *Serrano*'s focus on the California constitution. By arguing that poverty constituted a suspect classification and triggered strict judicial scrutiny in the school setting, Wise articulated one of the *Rodriguez* lawsuit's two fundamental analytic pillars.[137]

Although graduate student work informed the structure of the *Rodriguez* lawsuit, law student research informed the *Rodriguez* opinion.[138] One of the plaintiffs' central arguments was that low-income families clustered in the poorest property school districts and that Texas' school finance system discriminated against low-income students. That per pupil spending in the less affluent Edgewood schools was less than that in the more affluent Alamo Heights district evidenced the discrimination. The argument—critical to Rodriguez's case—necessarily assumed a relation between low-income households and low per pupil spending school districts, an assumption the district court accepted.[139]

A law student undertook a clever study which assessed whether poor families in fact clustered in the poorest property districts. The study analyzed data from the 130 largest towns in Connecticut, which accounted for 95 percent of the state population and 96 percent of the state's total property values. Although the author analyzed three separate—though related—premises critical to school finance litigation, the Court's *Rodriguez* opinion focused on the first premise: that individual wealth corresponded with [school] district wealth.

The law student considered three different ways to assess individual family wealth and six alternatives for school district wealth. Partial correlations analysis[140] of the various combinations of family and school district wealth revealed several interesting outcomes. First, when poverty was construed to mean "percent of population living below the poverty line," no statistically significant correlation existed between families in poverty and total per pupil spending.[141] Second, when district wealth was construed more narrowly and only in terms of residential property value, a statistically significant relation emerged between district wealth and family poverty.[142] Third, ironically, when district wealth was defined in terms of business wealth, a *positive* correlation emerged with family poverty. That is, poor families tended to cluster in wealthier areas, where wealth was construed in terms of commercial and industrial property value.[143] The authors noted that, at best, the statistical relation between families living in poverty and school district wealth was unclear. In terms of business and industrial wealth, however, low-income families were more likely to live in wealthier districts. Thus, the author concluded that "the popular belief that the 'poor' live in 'poor' [school] districts is clearly mistaken."[144]

Although the study's methodology might be viewed as somewhat crude by today's standards, it was not at the time the work was published (1972). In terms of its probative value to the *Rodriguez* case, however, the study possessed important limitations. First, the study used cross-sectional (1970) data from one state (Connecticut). Whether findings from Connecticut could properly be generalized to Texas (or any other state) remained unclear. Indeed, the Court wondered whether the statistical findings in Connecticut "would be discovered in Texas."[145]

What to do with such uncertainty, however, was a separate question. General scholarly norms, especially in the empirical social sciences, place the burden of such uncertainty on the shoulders of those seeking to expand the scope of research findings. Thus, professional prudence would counsel against social scientists drawing inferences for Texas from Connecticut's findings absent persuasive evidence that the two states were similar in salient respects. The Court (composed of jurists rather than formally trained social scientists), however, drew just such an inference. More specifically, because the plaintiffs in *Rodriguez* did *not* factually establish that poor families cluster in poor spending school districts in Texas, the Court implicitly assumed that the findings from the Connecticut study (finding no such clustering) were informative and, thus, rejected an assumption critical to the plaintiff's case in *Rodriguez*.[146] In so doing, the Court effectively flipped the traditional social scientific burden placement.

Rodriguez's *Aftermath in San Antonio and Elsewhere*

To be sure, Demetrio Rodriguez (and others in the plaintiff class) lost in the United States Supreme Court. The loss all but foreclosed a single, national judicial solution to a persistent school finance dilemma. And losses in court, even 5–4 losses such as *Rodriguez*, resist sugar-coating efforts. Unlike many litigation losses, the outcome in *Rodriguez* was the end of one story and the beginning of many others, including protracted state court litigation and political squabbles in Texas.[147] In 1991, reflecting on decades of school finance litigation and reform, then-Dean Mark Yudof predicted a "long and tedious" tussle between Texas courts and lawmakers and further observed that: "The story is beginning to resemble War and Peace, though it is likely to be less amusing. One can only hope that its conclusion will be less catastrophic."[148] Although it is abundantly clear that the story in Texas is already long, it is far from clear whether anything resembling a conclusion is in sight more than three decades since the *Rodriguez* decision.

Edgewood v. Kirby

Just over one decade following the *Rodriguez* decision, another lawsuit was filed, this time in Texas state court. Unlike the initial lawsuit, in the state litigation the Mexican American Legal Defense and Education Fund (MALDEF) took the litigation lead and argued that Texas' school finance system violated the state's equal protection[149] and education clauses.[150] In 1989 the Texas Supreme Court sided with the school district and ordered state lawmakers to fix its school finance system in time for the 1990–91 school year.[151] The 1989 decision unleashed a series of legislative efforts and successive litigation, culminating in Texas Senate Bill 7.[152] Passed in 1993, Senate Bill 7 had the effect of reducing per pupil spending disparities by redistributing funds generated in wealthy districts to their less wealthy counterparts.[153] A hold-harmless provision provides wealthy districts with some redistributive relief. Notwithstanding Senate Bill 7, funding disparities persisted and fueled subsequent litigation. Incident to litigation, the Texas Supreme Court concluded in 1995 (however reluctantly) that Texas' Senate Bill 7 passed constitutional muster.[154]

Neeley v. West-Orange Cove Consolidated Schools

School finance controversy in Texas did not end in 1995, however, with the final *Edgewood* litigation and the passage of Senate Bill 7. Senate Bill 7, which re-structured school finance, did so in a manner that created a state property tax, which is prohibited by the Texas Constitution.[155] Indeed, the Texas Supreme Court noted as much and warned that Senate Bill 7, if ignored over time, would likely create additional legal problems sometime in the future. That future arrived in 2001 when Texas school districts initiated yet another round of litigation challenging the Texas school finance system for precisely the reasons the court warned of years earlier.[156]

The Texas courts' most recent activity will likely ensure even more litigation in the future, but, perhaps, on slightly narrower grounds. As expected, the Texas court concluded that the state's control over local taxation for education amounted to a *de facto* state property tax that violated the Texas Constitution.[157] The 2005 court decision requires Texas lawmakers, once again, to take up the issue of school finance.[158] If history is any guide, further litigation will arise regardless of what Texas lawmakers do.

The subsequent litigation, which will assuredly follow, will likely be somewhat more focused owing to the court's conclusion that Texas school finance system's deficiencies—including, notably, the substantial unequal access to education revenue—do *not* render the school finance system constitutionally inadequate or inefficient.[159] Given its historic prominence in the Texas school finance battles, it is not surprising that the Edgewood District, once again, led the charge.[160] What is particularly ominous to Edgewood's prospects for litigation success in the future, however, was the Texas Supreme Court's finding that: "While the end-product of public education is related to the resources available for its use, . . . more money does not guarantee better schools or more educated students."[161] Whether the Texas high court's recent decision in *Neeley* signals the Court's desire to wind down judicial engagement or, rather, merely a narrowing of the terrain in which the Court will engage remains to be seen.

The Twenty-First Century and an Emerging National Trend Toward Increased Judicial Reluctance

The recent developments in Texas' multi-decade school finance litigation saga, ignited decades ago by Demetrio Rodriguez, are consistent with a potential nation-wide trend toward increased judicial modesty in the school finance setting. Specifically, courts have pulled back a bit in a few states where lawmakers and executives acted incident to litigation.[162] Even where legislatures and executives acted in ways designed to address school finance challenges, follow-up litigation frequently ensues and asserts that constitutional violations persist. This follow-up litigation invites the judicial branch not only to re-engage with school finance policy but also to assume even broader and deeper roles in reshaping school finance systems.

It is at this precise point where school finance litigation enters a critical stage. On the one hand, such litigation can follow the "New Jersey" path and risk a multi-decade struggle among the executive, legislative, and judicial branches over the school finance turf.[163] On the other hand, recent experiences in others states differ and hint at a potential trend. During the 1990s state supreme court decisions in Alabama, Ohio, and Massachusetts were cited by school finance reform activists as evidence of a litigation strategy's efficaciousness. Subsequent decisions in all three states, however, suggest something of a judicial retreat. In 1993, an Alabama court boldly announced that the state was obligated to provide an adequate education to its citizens.[164] The court order was especially particular in what it meant by an adequate education.[165] More recently, however, the Alabama Supreme Court dismissed further proceedings, pointing to separation of powers concerns.[166] Likewise, after protracted litigation in Ohio, in 2003 the Ohio Supreme Court terminated a trial court's jurisdiction over a school finance case and effectively brought to a close multi-decade litigation in Ohio.[167]

A similar court response emerged in Massachusetts. In 1993, Massachusetts' Supreme Judicial Court ruled in *McDuffy v. Secretary of the Executive Office of Education*[168] that the state failed to fulfill its state constitutional obligation and noted in particular the deleterious consequences of the state's overwhelming reliance on local property tax revenues. Three days after the *McDuffy* opinion was announced Massachusetts lawmakers passed the Education Reform Act of 1993.[169] The Act radically restructured education in Massachusetts, especially as it related to school funding, student goals and performance, and school and school district accountability provisions. After another round of school finance litigation challenging the state's Education Reform Act, the Massachusetts high court concluded that the state had taken reasonable and appropriate steps in a timely manner to address school funding and student achievement disparities.[170] The decision brought to a close twenty-seven years of litigation and twelve years of state court supervision over school finance matters in Massachusetts.[171]

Conclusion: Assessing Rodriguez's *Legacy*

Demetrio Rodriguez noted as recently as 2005 that the school finance fight he helped launch in 1968 is one that "you never get finished with."[172] From Demetrio's perspective, while the struggle has yielded some progress, "the state doesn't really want to give every child in Texas a fair share of the state's wealth."[173] Although emerging school finance litigation trends contribute to a broader understanding of *Rodriguez* and Demetrio's perspective, *Rodriguez*'s full legacy is not yet understood, even though almost four decades have passed since the *Rodriguez* complaint was filed in federal district court.

On the one hand, the *Rodriguez* litigation may represent a mis-step that cost the Edgewood schools and residents six important years in terms of their quest for greater school finance justice. On the other hand—regardless of the loss at the U.S. Supreme Court—*Rodriguez* might be better understood as a necessary step. Once school finance reform activists learned that the U.S. Constitution would not construe education as a fundamental right or poverty as a suspect classification, the school finance movement understood precisely where it needed to fight its battles—in state courts and legislatures.

A responsible account of *Rodriguez* cannot run away from the decidedly mixed school finance litigation movement that *Rodriguez* both informed and helped inspire. Setting aside disputes about the efficacy of successful school finance lawsuits in generating sought after increases in educational spending, two large themes endure that almost crowd out technical academic debates. First, despite multiple decades of school finance litigation, it remains abundantly clear—indeed, painfully obvious—that far too many schools persistently fail their duty to competently educate. This is true in Texas as well as in every other state in the Union. Worse still, these failures remain hauntingly easy to predict. As Professor Howard Gardner[174] notes:

> Tell me the zip code of a child and I will predict her chances of college completion and probable income; add the elements of family support (parental, grandparental, ethnic and religious values) and few degrees of freedom remain, at least in our country.[175]

The notion that geography is educational destiny for children is precisely what *Rodriguez* endeavored to eradicate. To be sure, the plaintiffs consigned to the Edgewood district zip code lost in *Rodriguez*. But more than thirty years of *Rodriguez*-inspired school finance litigation has taken place, and plaintiff victories, while not assured, have increased over time. Despite such victories, however, the empirically demonstrable correlations Professor Gardner describes—correlations easily replicated by most second-year graduate students—persist. And their persistence drives a stake through the heart of what *Rodriguez* sought to accomplish. Although reasonable observers may differ on how to best understand what equal educational opportunity means in any given context, reasonable observers should agree that if equal education means anything, at the very least, it must mean that geography should no longer predict a child's educational future. The link between the happenstance of geography and education quality is precisely what *Rodriguez* and the school finance litigation movement it contributed to sought to sever. Nevertheless, the link persists. It remains critical to understand why.

The two zip codes at issue in *Rodriguez*—78237 and 78209—while close numerically remain far apart in terms of education futures. The former is the zip code for Edgewood schools; the latter for Alamo Heights schools. Although the magnitude of the gaps has lessened, differences in educational resources persist. Edgewood schools spend approximately $7,238 per pupil and benefit from a 17:1 student-teacher ratio.[176] For Alamo Heights schools, the figures are $7,852 and 14:1, respectively.[177] Setting aside nettlesome and complicated questions about causation, the Edgewood students continue to struggle despite decades of litigation. In 2004, 41 percent of Edgewood's tenth-graders and 71 percent of its third-graders passed various statewide standardized math and reading tests.[178] Even though Edgewood students evidence progress, they still lag behind state averages (64 and 86 percent, respectively). As well, in 2003 Edgewood SAT takers averaged a combined score of 791 (out of 1600) compared with the state average of 989.

What to make of current data is far from clear. What is clear, however, is that *Rodriguez*'s legacy remains mixed and it continues to mean different things to different people. Although the school finance reform movement—including its litigation prong—has long moved beyond the *Rodriguez* opinion, important challenges remain. While perhaps of little solace to Demetrio Rodriguez and the many children struggling to learn in Edgewood's comparatively under-resourced schools, the Supreme Court's deference to federalism in *Rodriguez* generated at least one unexpected result. By effectively closing federal courts to the school finance litigants in *Rodriguez,* the Court redirected the school finance reform movement to the nation's state legislatures, courts, and state constitutional text. In so doing, the school finance experience helped bring to life Justice William Brennan's plea for state supreme courts to continue the Warren Court's rights revolution under the auspices of state constitutional interpretation.[179] Although the results have been mixed in the school finance context, school finance litigation serves as a powerful reminder to all about limits to the federal Constitution as well as the potential breadth, scope, and promise of state constitutions.

Endnotes

1. 411 U.S. 1 (1973).

2. Peter Irons, *The Courage of Their Convictions* 283 (1988).

3. *Rodriguez*, 411 U.S. at 11–12.

4. *Id.* at 12.

5. *Id.* at 12–13.

6. Irons, *supra* note 2, at 286–87.

7. *Id.* at 287.

8. *Id.*

9. *Id.*

10. To convert 1967 to current (2006) dollars I used the Bureau of Labor Statistics inflation adjuster which is based on the Consumer Price Index. *See* Bureau of Labor Statistics Inflation Adjuster, *at* http://www.bls.gov/bls/inflation.htm (last visited June 5, 2006).

11. Irons, *supra* note 2, at 287.

12. *Id.*

13. Serrano v. Priest, No. C 938254 (Super. Ct. Los Angeles County 1969), *rev'd*, 487 P.2d 1241 (Cal. 1971).

14. Serrano v. Priest, 487 P.2d 1241 (Cal. 1971).

15. 351 U.S. 12 (1956).

16. 372 U.S. 353 (1963).

17. 405 U.S. 134 (1972).

18. 269 F.Supp. 401 (D.D.C. 1967), *aff'd en banc sub. nom.* Smuck v. Hobson, 408 F.2d 175 (D.C. Cir. 1969).

19. Indicia of intellectual and scholarly attention to school finance and school finance litigation are wide and varied. They include significant law review symposium attention, *e.g.*, *Symposium: Investing in our Children's Future: School Finance Reform in the '90s*, 28 Harvard Journal on Legislation (1991); peer-reviewed journals devoted to school finance scholarship, *e.g.*, *Educ. Fin. & Pol'y*, *J. of Educ. Fin.*; and an academic society, American Education Finance Association.

20. *See, e.g.*, John E. Coons et al., *Private Wealth and Public Education* (1970).

21. *See Rodriguez*, 411 U.S. at 16 n.38.

22. *See generally* Goodwin Liu, *The Parted Paths of School Desegregation and School Finance Litigation*, 24 Law & Ineq. 81 (2006) (discussing the strategic and conceptual issues flowing from the plaintiff's decision to push *Rodriguez* as a poverty rather than a race case).

23. 487 P.2d 1241 (1971).

24. 334 F.Supp. 870 (D.Minn. 1971). It is important to note that the *Van Dusartz* opinion involved a summary judgment motion ruling and not a decision on the full merits.

25. If filed today, federal statute would preclude *Rodriguez* from a three-judge federal district court panel. *See* 42 U.S.C. § 2284(a) (limiting three-judge federal panels to apportionment cases as well as any other case required by Congress).

26. Rodriguez v. San Antonio Indep. Sch. Dist., 337 F.Supp. 280, 282–23 (W.D. Tex. 1971), *rev'd*, 411 U.S. 1 (1973).

27. For a more formal and theoretical version of this argument, see Charles Tiebout, *A Pure Theory of Local Expenditures*, 64 J. Pol. Econ. 416 (1956).

28. *Rodriguez*, 337 F.Supp. at 284 ("Hence, the present system does not serve to promote one of the very interests which defendants [State of Texas] assert.").

29. *Id.* at 285. The court also identified various aspects of the Texas Constitution and Texas Education Code that contributed to plaintiffs' harm.

30. *Id.* at 284 ("Not only are defendants unable to demonstrate compelling state interests for their classifications based upon wealth, they fail even to establish a reasonable basis for these classification.").

31. Irons, *supra* note 2, at 286.

32. *See e.g.*, Henry M. Levin, *Educational Vouchers: Effectiveness, Choice, and Costs*, 17 J. Pol'y Analysis & Mgmt. 373, 374 (1998) ("Because student achievement is considered to be a universal goal of schools, it has become the sine qua non for evaluating school reforms.").

33. For articles generally skeptical of a correlation between educational spending and educational opportunity, *see* Eric A. Hanushek et al., *Making Schools Work: Improving Performance and Controlling Costs* (1994); Clayton P. Gillette, *Opting Out of Public Provision*, 73 Den. U. L. Rev. 1185, 1213–14 (1996); Eric A. Hanushek, *Money Might Matter Somewhere: A Response to Hedges, Laine, and Greenwald*, 23 Educ. Researcher 5 (1994); Allan R. Odden & Lawrence O. Picus, *School Finance: A Policy Perspective* 277–81 (1992); Eric A. Hanushek, *When School Finance "Reform" May Not Be Good Policy*, 28 Harv. J. on Legis. 423 (1991); Eric A. Hanushek, *The Impact of Differential Expenditures on School Performance*, 18 Educ. Researcher 45 (1989); Eric A. Hanushek, *Throwing Money at Schools*, 1 J. Pol'y Analysis & Mgmt. 19 (1981). For articles generally supportive of a correlation between expenditures and educational opportunity, see Larry V. Hedges et al., *Does Money Matter? A Meta-Analysis of Studies of the Effects of Differential School Inputs on Student Outcomes*, 23 Educ. Researcher 5 (1994); Ronald F. Ferguson, *Paying for Public Education: New Evidence on How and Why Money Matters*, 28 Harv. J. on Legis. 293 (1991); Christopher F. Edley, Jr., *Lawyers and Education Reform*, 28 Harv. J. on Legis. 457 (1991).

34. *See, e.g.*, James S. Coleman, et al. U.S. Dep't of Health, Educ. & Welfare, *Equality of Educational Opportunity* 304 (1966) (hereinafter "Coleman Report") (finding that "student body characteristics" account for an impressive percent of variance in student achievement, and that "[c]hildren from a given family background, when put in schools of different social compositions, will achieve at quite different levels"). Scores of subsequent studies have confirmed Coleman's conclusion. For citations to the literature, see Richard D. Kahlenberg, *All Together Now: Creating Middle-Class Schools Through Public School Choice* 26–28, 86–69 (2001); James E. Ryan, *Schools, Race, and Money*, 109 Yale L.J. 249, 287 n.167 (1999).

35. James Coleman, one of the nation's leading and most prominent sociologists, taught at Johns Hopkins University and the University of Chicago. Much of his work profoundly influenced public policy, especially education policy.

36. *See* Coleman Report, *supra* note 34, at 298–305.

37. *See id.* at 21–22, 296–97, 312–16.

38. *See supra* note 33 and accompanying text.

39. *See* Gary Orfield & Susan Eaton, *Dismantling Desegregation: The Quiet Reversal of* Brown v. Board of Education 53 (1996) (stating that the powerful influence of the socioeconomic status of peers on student achievement is "one of the most consistent findings in research on education").

40. James S. Coleman, *Toward Open Schools*, 9 Pub. Int. 20–21 (Fall 1967) (summarizing findings of Coleman Report). For discussion of the numerous studies confirming this point, see Kahlenberg, *All Together Now*, *supra* note 34, at 26–28.

41. *See* Richard D. Kahlenberg, *Learning From James Coleman*, 144 Pub. Int. 54 (2001). *See also* Chester E. Finn, Jr., *Education That Works*: *Make the Schools Compete*, 65 Harv. Bus. Rev. 64 (1987) (acknowledging that "disadvantaged children [tend] to learn more when they attend[] school with middle-class youngsters"); Interview by Ted Koppel with Jonathan Kozol, *Nightline* (ABC television broadcast Sept. 17, 1992), (stating that "money is not the only issue that determines inequality. A more important factor, I am convinced, is the makeup of the student enrollment, who is sitting next to you in class"), *quoted in* Kahlenberg, *All Together Now*, *supra* note 34, at 37.

42. Trine Tsouderos, *Kids in City's Poor Schools Get Worse Scores*, Tennessean, Dec. 27, 1998, at 2A (quoting James Guthrie).

43. For a helpful summary of Professor Coleman's thirty-five years of research in the education policy area, see Kahlenberg, *Learning*, *supra* note 41.

44. *See* James S. Coleman, Thomas Hoffer & Sally Kilgore, *High School Achievement: Public, Catholic, and Private Schools* (1982).

45. Thomas C. Berg, *Anti-Catholicism and Modern Church–State Relations*, 33 Loy. U. Chi. L. Rev. 121, 165 (2001).

46. *Rodriguez*, 337 F.Supp. at 285.

47. *Id.* at 286.

48. *Rodriguez*, 411 U.S. at 71 (Marshall, J., dissenting) (arguing that it is insufficient to remit school finance plaintiffs "to the vagaries of the political process which . . . has proved singularly unsuited to the task of providing a remedy for this discrimination"); J. Ely, Democracy and Distrust 84 (1980) ("[E]ven the technically represented can find themselves functionally powerless. . . ."). *See generally* Note, *Unfulfilled Promises: School Finance Remedies and State Courts* 104 Harv. L. Rev. 1072 (1991) (arguing against judicial reliance on the legislative and executive branches in the school finance reform context in state courts).

49. 349 U.S. 294 (1955).

50. *See, e.g.*, Doug Rendleman, Brown II*'s "All Deliberate Speed" at Fifty: A Golden Anniversary or a Mid-Life Crisis for the Constitutional Injunction as a School Desegregation Remedy?*, 41 San Diego L. Rev. 1575 (2004).

51. Griffin v. County Sch. Bd., 377 U.S. 218, 229 (1964).

52. *See, e.g.*, Michael Heise, *Preliminary Thoughts on the Virtues of Passive Dialogue*, 34 Akron L. Rev. 73 (2000) (discussing New Jersey's four-decade school finance saga).

53. Paul Gewirtz, a law professor at Yale, is an expert on federal courts and jurisdiction.

54. Paul Gewirtz, *Remedies and Resistance*, 92 Yale L.J. 585, 674 (1983).

55. Irons, *supra* note 2, at 288.

56. Justice Powell was appointed to the Richmond (Virginia) School Board in 1950, and served as the Board Chair from 1952–60. *See* John C. Jeffries, Jr., *Justice Lewis F. Powell, Jr.* 124, 131–82 (1994).

57. *Rodriguez*, 411 U.S. at 18–25.

58. *Id.* at 29.

59. *Id.* at 35 ("Education, of course, is not among the rights afforded explicit protection under our Federal Constitution. Nor do we find any basis for saying it is implicitly so protected.").

60. 347 U.S. 483 (1954).

61. *Id.* at 36.

62. *Id.* at 37.

63. Robinson v. Cahill (*Robinson I*), 303 A.2d 273, 291–92 (N.J. 1973); N.J. Const. art. VIII, § 4, par. 1.

64. *Rodriguez*, 411 U.S. at 67 (White, J., dissenting).

65. *Id.* at 70.

66. *Id.* at 112 (Marshall, J. dissenting).

67. *Id.* at 83–84.

68. *Id.* at 84 ("Discrimination in the opportunity to learn that is afforded a child must be our standard.").

69. The Court noted:

> [E]ducation is perhaps the most important function of state and local governments. Compulsory school attendance laws and the great expenditures for education both demonstrate our recognition of the importance education to our democratic society. It is required in the performance of our most basic public responsibilities, even service in the armed forces. It is the very foundation of good citizenship. Today, it is a principal instrument in awakening the child to cultural values, in preparing him for later professional training, and in helping him to adjust normally to his environment. In these days, it is doubtful that any child may reasonably be expected to succeed in life if he is denied the opportunity of an education. Such an opportunity, where the state has undertaken to provide it, is a right which must be made available to all on equal terms.

Brown v. Board of Educ. (*Brown I*), 347 U.S. 483, 493 (1954).

70. *Rodriguez*, 411 U.S. at 36.

71. *Id.* at 35.

72. 457 U.S. 202 (1982).

73. *Id.* at 221.

74. *Rodriguez*, 411 U.S. at 35–36.

75. 383 U.S. 663 (1966).

76. *Id.* at 667 (quoting Reynolds v. Sims, 377 U.S. 533, 561–62 (1964)).

77. *See id.*

78. *See, e.g.*, Dandridge v. Williams, 397 U.S. 471 (1970); Lindsey v. Normet, 405 U.S. 56 (1972).

79. *Rodriguez*, 411 U.S. at 36.

80. *Id.* at 37. For a discussion, see, e.g., Susan H. Bitensky, *Theoretical Foundations for a Right to Education Under the U.S. Constitution: A Beginning to the End of the National Education Crisis*, 86 Nw. U. L. Rev. 550 (1992); Brooke Wilkins, *Should Public Education be a Federal Fundamental Right?*, 2005 BYU Educ. & L.J. 261 (2005).

81. 413 U.S. 189 (1973).

82. 402 U.S. 1 (1971).

83. *Id.* at 26.

84. *See* Brief for the Appellees at 20–22, San Antonio Indep. Sch. Dist. v. Rodriguez, 411 U.S. 1 (1973) (No. 71-1332). While the approach in *Rodriguez* failed, the approach has been refined since then and adopted by leading school finance advocacy groups with mixed success. *See, e.g.*, Campaign for Fiscal Equity v. New York, 801 N.E.2d 326, 333–40 (N.Y. 2003) (construing adequate education in terms of both traditional inputs and outputs).

85. Professor Goodwin Liu teaches law at the University of California, Berkeley.

86. Liu, *supra* note 22.

87. *Rodriguez*, 337 F.Supp. at 285.

88. *Rodriguez*, 411 U.S. at 43.

89. *See, e.g.*, John Dayton, *Correlating Expenditures and Educational Opportunity in School Funding Litigation: The Judicial Perspective*, 19 J. Educ. Fin. 167, 178 (1993) (describing state court responses to an asserted positive correlation between educational funding and opportunity).

90. For a fuller treatment of this point, see Michael Heise, *Schoolhouses, Courthouses and Statehouses: Educational Finance, Constitutional Structure, and the Separation of Powers Doctrine*, 33 Land & Water L. Rev. 281, 291–93 (1998).

91. For a discussion, *see, e.g.*, Rachel F. Moran, Brown*'s Legacy: The Evolution of Education Equity*, 66 U. Pitt. L. Rev. 155, 157 (2004); Michael Heise, *Equal Educational Opportunity By the Numbers: The Warren Court's Empirical Legacy*, 59 Wash. & Lee L. Rev. 1309, 1324–25 (2002); Ryan, *Schools, supra* note 34, at 259–60.

92. *See generally* Sheff v. O'Neill, 678 A.2d 1267 (Conn. 1996) (demonstrating plaintiffs' decision to combine racial and poverty issues in a lawsuit against the state of Connecticut).

93. *See, e.g.*, Michael Rebell, *Adequacy Litigations: A New Path to Equity, in* Bringing Equity Back: Research for a New Era in American Education Policy 291, 192 (Janice Petrovich & Amy Stuart Wells eds., 2005).

94. For a discussion of how the equal education opportunity doctrine has evolved over time, see Michael Heise, *Litigated Learning and the Limits of Law*, 57 Vand. L. Rev. 2417 (2004).

95. Professor James Ryan, a leading education law scholar, teaches law at the University of Virginia.

96. Ryan, *Schools, supra* note 34, at 259.

97. *See, e.g.*, James E. Ryan, *The Influence of Race on School Finance Reform*, 98 Mich. L. Rev. 432 (1999).

98. 678 A.2d 1267 (Conn. 1996). *See also supra* note 92.

99. Liu, *supra* note 22, at 105.

100. 418 U.S. 717 (1974).

101. Milliken v. Bradley, 418 U.S. 717, 741–42 (1974) (citing Wright v. Council of Emporia, 407 U.S. 451, 469 (1972)).

102. *Id.* at 742 (citing *Rodriguez*, 411 U.S. at 50).

103. Mary Frase Williams, *American Education and Federalism, in* GOVERNMENT IN THE CLASSROOM: DOLLARS AND POWER IN EDUCATION 1 (Mary Frase Williams ed., 1978).

104. Hawaii Department of Education, About Us, *at* http://doe.k12.hi.us/about/index.htm (last visited June 1, 2006) (noting Hawaii has "a single, statewide [school] district with 285 schools").

105. *See Rodriguez*, 411 U.S. at 42–43.

106. *See, e.g.*, Brown v. Board of Education, 347 U.S. 483, 493 (1954) (noting education's importance to state and local governments).

107. *See generally* Denis P. Doyle & Chester E. Finn, Jr., *American Schools and the Future of Local Control*, 77 Pub. Int. 77 (1984) (noting the diminution of local control over school policy over time).

108. For a discussion of the federalism consequences in education policymaking authority shifts among local, state, and federal governments, see generally Michael Heise, *The Political Economy of Education Federalism*, 56 Emory L.J. 125 (2006).

109. *See* Nat'l Comm'n on Excellence in Educ., *A Nation at Risk: The Imperative for Educational Excellence* (1983). *See also* Karen MacPherson, *A Nation Still at Educational Risk: Two Decades Later Reports Still Focusing on the Mediocrity of U.S. Education*, Pittsburgh Post–Gazette, Aug. 31, 2003, at A11 (discussing *A Nation At Risk* report).

110. MacPherson, *supra* note 109.

111. *See* R. Craig Wood & Bruce D. Baker, *An Examination and Analysis of the Equity And Adequacy Concepts of Constitutional Challenges to State Education Finance Distribution Formulas*, 27 U. Ark. Little Rock L. Rev. 125, 158–60 (2004).

112. Pub. L. No. 107–110, 115 Stat. 1425 (codified in scattered sections of 20 U.S.C.).

113. 20 U.S.C. § 6311(b)(3)(C)(vii) (Supp. II 2002).

114. *Id.* at § 6311(h).

115. *Id.* at § 6311(b)(1).

116. *Id.* at § 6311(b)(2).

117. *Id.* at § 6316(b)(5), (8).

118. *Rodriguez*, 411 U.S. at 58.

119. *Id.* at 59.

120. *Id.*

121. *Id.* at 49–53.

122. *Id.* at 58 n.111.

123. *Id.* at 57–58.

124. *Id.* at 41.

125. *Id.* at 56–57.

126. *Id.* at 58 n.11 (noting that approximately $2.4 billion of additional new tax funds would be needed to bring Texas' lower-spending districts up to its highest spending counterparts).

127. *Id.* at 56.

128. *Id.* at 58.

129. *See id.* at 58 ("The need is apparent for reform in tax systems which may well have relied too long and too heavily on the local property tax.").

130. *See Id.* at 58–59.

131. *See id.* at 59.

132. Arthur E. Wise, *Is Denial of Equal Educational Opportunity Constitutional?*, 13 Admin. Notebook 1 (1965).

133. Arthur E. Wise, The Constitution and Equality: Wealth, Geography, and Educational Opportunity (1968) (unpublished Ph.D. dissertation, University of Chicago) (on file with the University of Chicago).

134. Phillip Kurland, *Equal Educational Opportunity: The Limits of Constitutional Jurisprudence Undefined*, 35 U. Chi. L. Rev. 583 (1968).

135. Arthur Wise, *Rich Schools, Poor Schools: The Promise of Equal Educational Opportunity* (1968). In fairness, it is important to recognize that while Wise was researching and writing, the general issue was emerging among scholars. *See, e.g.*, Harold W. Horwitz, *Unseparate But Unequal: The Emerging Fourteenth Amendment Issue in Public School Education*, 13 U.C.L.A. L. Rev. 1147 (1966).

136. Wise, *Denial*, *supra* note 132, at 3–4.

137. The other pillar—undeveloped in Wise's 1965 essay—was education as a fundamental right under the U.S. Constitution.

138. Note, *A Statistical Analysis of the School Finance Decisions: On Winning Battles and Losing Wars*, 81 Yale L.J. 1303 (1972).

139. *Rodriguez*, 337 F.Supp. at 282.

140. Note, *Wars*, *supra* note 138, at 1326, 1330 n.114.

141. *Id.* at 1327.

142. *Id.* at 1328.

143. *Id.*

144. *Id.* at 1327.

145. *Rodriguez*, 411 U.S. at 23.

146. *Rodriguez*, 411 U.S. at 23 (concluding there was no reason to assume that poor families in Texas cluster in poor spending school districts).

147. The school finance saga in Texas has been a multi-year drama. For a fuller description *see e.g.*, J. Steven Farr & Mark Trachtenberg, *The* Edgewood *Drama: An Epic Quest for Education Equity*, 17 Yale L. & Pol'y Rev. 607 (1999).

148. Mark G. Yudof, *School Finance Reform in Texas: The* Edgewood *Saga*, 28 Harv. J. on Legis. 499, 505 (1991).

149. Tex. Const. art. I, § 3.

150. Tex. Const. art. VII, § 1.

151. Edgewood Indep. Sch. Dist. v. Kirby (*Edgewood I*), 777 S.W.2d 391, 399 (Tex. 1989).

152. Act of May 28, 1993, ch. 347, 1993 Tex. Gen. Laws 1479. Now codified in title 2, subtitle 1 of the Texas Education Code. Tex. Educ. Code Ann. Title 2.

153. For a discussion *see e.g.*, Maurice Dyson, *The Death of Robin Hood?: Proposals for Overhauling Public School Finance*, 11 Geo. J. on Poverty L. and Pol'y 1, 11–12, 51 (2004).

154. Edgewood Indep. Sch. Dist. v. Kirby (*Edgewood IV*), 917 S.W.2d 717 (Tex. 1995).

155. Tex. Const. art. VIII, § 1–e.

156. Neeley v. West–Orange–Cove Consol. Indep. Sch. Dist., 176 S.W.3d 746, 754 (Tex. 2005) (noting that the Texas Supreme Court warned about this prospect ten years earlier), rehearing denied (Dec. 16, 2005).

157. *Id.* (concluding that the local ad valorem taxes have become a de facto state property tax in violation of the Texas Constitution, art. VIII, § 1–e).

158. The state had until June 1, 2006, to respond to the court's concerns before injunctive relief becomes effective. *Id.* at 799. After three special legislative sessions, Texas lawmakers passed tax legislation that provided additional resources for Texas schools. The plaintiffs agreed only that the special legislative activity provided fiscal "breathing room" for the 2006–07 school year. As a consequence, both parties to the litigation agreed to a motion that confirmed the dissolution of the court's pending injunction. The district court judge John Dietz granted the motion on May 26, 2006.

159. *Id.* at 754 (concluding that the Texas school finance system does not violate the "efficient system of public free schools" requirement in the Texas Constitution, art. VII, § 1).

160. *Id.* at 751.

161. *Id.* at 788.

162. *See, e.g., Ex Parte* James, 836 So.2d 813 (Ala. 2002); State of Ohio v. Lewis, 789 N.E.2d 195 (Ohio 2003).

163. *See, e.g.*, Alexandra Greif, *Politics, Practicalities, and Priorities: New Jersey's Experience Implementing the Abbott V Mandate*, 22 Yale L. & Pol'y Rev. 615, 68–52 (2004).

164. Opinion of the Justices, 624 So.2d 107 (Ala. 1993).

165. *Id.* at 165–66 (noting the essential parts of a "liberal system of public schools").

166. Opinion of the Justices, 624 So.2d 107 (Ala. 1993).

167. State of Ohio v. Lewis, 789 N.E.2d 195 (Ohio 2003).

168. 615 N.E.2d 516 (Mass. 1993).

169. Mass. Ann. Laws ch. 69 (2002).

170. Hancock v. Commissioner of Educ., 822 N.E.2d 1134 (Mass. 2005).

171. *Id.* at 1137–46 (summarizing school finance litigation in Massachusetts).

172. Jan J. Russell, *The Equity Myth*, Tex. Monthly, Sept. 2005, at 154.

173. *Id.*

174. Howard Gardner teaches at Harvard University's Graduate School of Education.

175. Howard Gardner, *Paroxysms of Choice*, N.Y. Rev. of Books, Oct. 19, 2000, at 44, 49.

176. For current publicly available district-level data from the U.S. Department of Education, see National Center for Education Statistics, *available at* http://nces.ed.gov/ccd/districtsearch/.

177. *Id.*

178. *Id.*

179. William J. Brennan, Jr., *State Constitutions and the Protection of Individual Rights*, 90 Harv. L. Rev. 489 (1977).

4

The Story of *Grutter v. Bollinger*: Affirmative Action Wins

Wendy Parker[1]

In 1996, at the age of forty-three, Barbara Grutter decided a career change was in order. She applied to a nearby law school, the University of Michigan Law School, with the hopes of becoming a health care attorney. A white woman, she had graduated from Michigan State University eighteen years before with a 3.81 grade point average. She was raising two sons (then seven and ten) and running her own small business as a health care information technology consultant in Plymouth, Michigan.[2] She had recently scored a 161 on the LSAT, placing her in the 86th percentile. Grutter made it onto the Michigan waiting list, but not its classrooms. The rejection initially surprised her, but her surprise turned to "dismay" when she recalled a recent article in a Detroit newspaper.[3] The article indicated that minorities admitted to Michigan had lower test scores and grades than admitted whites. Believing Michigan Law School had discriminated against her on the basis of her race, she eventually agreed to become the name plaintiff in a suit brought by the Center for Individual Rights ("CIR") against the law school's race conscious admission policies.

CIR was engaged in a well-financed litigation strategy to have Justice Lewis Powell's opinion in *Regents of University of California v. Bakke* declared legally wrong.[4] That opinion had endorsed diversity as a reason for states to engage in racial preferences in university admissions. When CIR filed suit on behalf of Grutter, its goal seemed in sight. It had already won a significant victory in a similar case filed on behalf of Cheryl Hopwood, a white woman denied admission to The University of Texas School of Law. CIR had also recently filed two other similar suits on behalf of other white women: Katuria Smith's suit against the University of Washington Law School and Jennifer Gratz's suit against the University of Michigan College of Literature, Science, and the Arts.

Public opinion appeared to favor CIR's goal as well. In November 1996 voters in California had passed Proposition 209, which broadly prohibited race conscious activity by the state. Two years later, voters in Washington would pass a similar measure. CIR seemed unstoppable: both the judiciary and voters appeared on its side. Affirmative action supporters were clearly losing at the ballot box and in the courts.

Yet, the tide came to favor affirmative action in the courts. In *Grutter v. Bollinger*, the Supreme Court affirmed that diversity could be a legally legitimate rationale for affirmative action, and validated Michigan's approach to deciding who is admitted to the law school.[5] Michigan voters responded by passing their own version of Proposition 209. Here I tell the story of what ended up stopping CIR and how and why affirmative action survived as an option—at least for now. The story takes us not just to why Grutter never attended law school, but also to the students who benefitted from race-conscious admissions. On a larger scale, the story is one of diversity gathering public support, and the Supreme Court constitutionalizing that public acceptance and allowing voluntary integration. Yet, the story also raises the possibility that diversity's survival will prove transitory.

Race-Based Affirmative Action in Higher Education: The Beginnings

College admissions has rarely been just about meeting objective qualifications.[6] Harvard, for example, adopted in 1905 the College Entrance Examination Board to open admissions beyond those attending Eastern prep schools. By 1922 Harvard alumni and administrators feared, however, that admissions had gotten too open for one group in particular—Jews. The objective test had given Jews more than a fifth of the seats in Harvard's freshman class, and Harvard, like Yale and Princeton, feared a "Hebrew Invasion." Harvard President A. Lawrence Lowell tried, unsuccessfully, to limit Jews to 15% of the enrollment through an explicit quota. Instead, the three colleges decided to define merit as more than a test score and turned to test the "character" of applicants. Now personal essays and interviews were required, and applicants were asked about " 'Race and Color,' 'Religious Preference,' 'Maiden Name of Mother,' 'Birthplace of Father,' and 'What change, if any, has been made since birth in your own name or that of your father? (Explain fully).' "[7] These very effective anti-Jewish policies eventually gave way at the Ivy Leagues in the 1960s.

What remained, however, was the notion that admission could mean more than test scores. Some schools, but not all, used that idea in the 1960s to expand their student body to groups historically under-represented. Schools began an explicit quest to increase their enrollment of African Americans and, to a lesser extent, Asian Americans, Latinos, and Native Americans. To admit students from these groups, the schools decreased the importance of test scores, prep school attendance, and financial need—thereby allowing minority students to gain admission. The colleges opened up admissions mainly in the name of increasing "Negro leadership," but also to compensate for past, societal injustices to the groups and to foster institutional diversity.[8] The methods were relatively successful. Only around 200 African Americans enrolled in historically white law schools in 1964; that number increased to 1,700 by 1973.[9]

Other schools at the time, particularly Southern ones, took a quite different approach to minority enrollment: they admitted African American students only under court order. For example, rather than enrolling both African American and white school children in the same school, Prince Edwards County, Virginia ordered its schools closed. The schools remained closed for five years, until the Supreme Court ordered them reopened.[10] Matters were equally problematic at the college level. It took not only a court order but 23,000 soldiers (three times the population of Oxford), including the Marines and Air Force, to enroll James Meredith at Ole Miss—and at a cost of two lives.[11] The school was far from pleased with the order to admit Meredith, and responded with racially neutral admission standards designed to forestall minority enrollment.[12]

These two different approaches to minority enrollment—one struggling against it, the other struggling for it—were legally connected by the Fourteenth Amendment and the Civil Rights Act of 1964, both of which prohibit discrimination on the basis of race and ethnicity. If schools could not refuse admission because of the race of the student—a principle of *Brown v. Board of Education*—could the schools consider race to admit a minority student into a historically white institution? In other words, did *Brown*'s principles also mean that voluntary affirmative action plans to increase minority enrollment were as unconstitutional as schools reserved solely for white students?

In 1974 Allan Bakke prominently brought that issue to the courts. He sued the University of California Medical School at Davis ("Davis") in state court, after he was twice rejected and a sympathetic admissions officer told him of a special admissions program for minority students. Davis specifically set aside 16 of its 100 admissions slots for African Americans, Asian Americans, Latinos, and Native Americans, a set aside percentage that mirrored California's minority population. The thirty-four-year-old white man of Norwegian ancestry initially won his lawsuit in the California state courts. The Supreme Court took the case and attracted national attention and a then recording breaking number of 57 amici briefs. The overwhelming majority were on the side of Davis.

The Supreme Court Justices had a harder time reaching a majority. Justice Powell announced the judgment of the Court, but he wrote only for himself. Justice Powell concurred with four justices that Bakke should be admitted and that Davis' practices were an unconstitutional quota. Yet, he also agreed with four other justices that race could be a factor in admissions. Four justices of the Court's liberal wing (Justices Blackmun, Brennan, Marshall, and White) concluded that race can be considered to redress the societal discrimination that had depressed the number of minority doctors. Justice Powell rejected, with almost no analysis, that societal discrimination could legally justify any race conscious activity. Instead, Justice Powell concluded that race could be a factor if the school was seeking diversity to improve educational learning.[13] As an example, he pointed to the Harvard College Admissions Program, which allowed race to be a factor in a system with individual review and no racial set aside of admission slots.

Most colleges were relieved with *Bakke*'s holding that race could be a factor in admissions, even in the absence of a majority opinion explaining when race could be considered. The question became on what basis, and most went with Justice Powell's diversity justification. Thus began what Professor Sanford Levinson has called a game of "Simon Says," where colleges and universities would take into account race in deciding who got admitted and who didn't and would claim diversity as their legal justification.[14] In doing so, affirmative action continued, but it became disconnected from any notion of rectifying societal discrimination or the history of racial discrimination.[15] Affirmative action's focused on benefitting the historically white institution instead.

Michigan's Affirmative Action History

Michigan Law School has a history of enrolling African–Americans and has never excluded them from admission. Its first African American student enrolled in 1868; its first Mexican American, 1894. In 1966, it joined other schools seeking to increase its African American enrollment. It was soon second only to Harvard in number of African American law students. In 1991, however, newly appointed Dean Lee Bollinger recognized that the law school's practices made it legally vulnerable. He appointed a faculty committee to devise an affirmative action policy consistent with Justice Powell's *Bakke* opinion. Committee members included Ted Shaw, a faculty member with substantial civil rights experience as a former lawyer with the NAACP Legal and Educational Fund ("LDF").

In 1992, the law school faculty unanimously approved the committee's proposal. The law school receives around 3,500 applications for approximately 350 slots, with about 1,300 offers extended each year. The policy stated that only qualified students could be admitted, but left a great deal of flexibility in admissions decisions. Each application would get individual review, with LSAT and undergraduate GPAs the general measure of expected student success. The policy emphasized a commitment to all types of diversity, but specifically emphasized "the inclusion of students from groups which have been historically discriminated against, like African-Americans, Hispanics and Native Americans, who without this commitment might not be represented in our student body in meaningful numbers."[16] It did not grant preference to other minority groups such as Asian-Americans or those of Middle-Eastern descent. For the purposes of simplicity, this chapter refers to the minority applicants benefitting from the policy as "minority applicants."

The policy asserted that diversity would improve learning for all students. Students from a variety of backgrounds, including underrepresented racial and ethnic identities, the policy explained, "are particularly likely to have experiences and perspectives of special importance to our mission."[17] To achieve this, the law school sought to enroll "a 'critical mass' of minority students."[18] The law school omitted, at the instance of Shaw, any reference to a prior written commitment to a minority enrollment of 10–12%, and ended a separate "special admissions program" to increase minority enrollment. In sum, the law school's policy mirrored the approach of Justice Powell in *Bakke*. The policy emphasized not societal concerns but classroom learning; the school used no numerical goal; and applicants all received the same individual review.

CIR's Bakke *Quest*

With time, Justice Powell's *Bakke* solo opinion grew more vulnerable. The Supreme Court in the late 1980s and early 1990s issued a series of opinions restricting governments' authority to consider race for the purpose of benefitting minorities.[19] Justice Sandra Day O'Connor, for example, wrote for the majority that race conscious activity is " 'simply too pernicious to permit any but the most exact connection between justification and classification.' "[20]

The most prominent group litigating the legality of race conscious admission in schools was CIR.[21] Starting in 1989, CIR sought to limit governmental interference with individual rights. Its telephone message declared it was "bringing lawsuits for a better America."[22] Foundations lined up with money, including Richard Mellon Scaife's Carthage Fund, Lynde and Harry Bradley Fund, Smith Richardson Foundation, and John M. Olin Foundation. Corporations provided money as well, including Archer-Daniels-Midland Co., Chevron USA Inc., Pfizer Inc., and Philip Morris Co.

CIR chose its cases well, and it won a series of challenges, particularly in *Hopwood v. Texas*. On behalf of Cheryl J. Hopwood, CIR sued The University of Texas School of Law for the school's race-based admissions practices. In 1996 a Fifth Circuit panel held that race could never be a factor in admissions decisions and that Justice Powell's *Bakke* opinion had been effectively overruled by subsequent Supreme Court precedent. The opinion was sweeping in its analysis, going so far as to declare that considering race "is no more rational on its own terms than would be choices based upon the physical size or blood type of applicants."[23] With the en banc Fifth Circuit and Supreme Court refusing to review the decision, the opinion bound the states of Louisiana, Mississippi, and Texas to race neutral admissions. Georgia voluntarily abided by *Hopwood*. CIR co-founder Michael Greve predicted that within ten years or so "*Hopwood* will be remembered as the beginning of the end of affirmative action higher education."[24]

Mere months after the panel decision in *Hopwood*, California voters passed Proposition 209, the California Civil Rights Initiative, with 54% of the vote. Proposition 209 declared that the State of California "shall not discriminate against, or grant preferential treatment to, any individual or group on the basis of race, sex, color, ethnicity, or national origin."[25] This followed an earlier vote of the Board of Regents of the University of California to prohibit the consideration of race, religion, sex, color, ethnicity, or national origin in university admissions.

Proposition 209 and *Hopwood* were just a beginning. Washington state citizens passed their own Civil Rights Initiative in 1998, which mirrored the language of Proposition 209, with 58% of the vote. A similar attempt was made in Houston in 1997; yet, the Houston City Council changed the language of the initiative to be pro-affirmative action. Fifty-five percent of the voters rejected it. Florida Governor Jeb Bush pre-empted an attempt for an anti-affirmative action ballot initiative on the November 2000 ballot with the One Florida Initiative. Its Talented 20 Plan guaranteed college admission to students graduating in the top 20% of their high school class and eliminated race-based college admissions. (California and Texas had already implemented similar percent plans for their public undergraduate programs after the states were prohibited from race-based admissions.)

On the litigation front, the strength of the *Hopwood* victory generated much interest in—and telephone calls to—CIR. University of Michigan philosophy professor Carl Cohen, a civil libertarian and former head of the local ACLU chapter, was particularly interested in *Hopwood*. In 1995, he had written a ten-page report titled "Racial Discrimination in Admissions at The University of Michigan" on undergraduate admissions. Cohen published the report in *Commentary*, a monthly magazine of the American Jewish Committee, and Michigan newspapers publicized his findings. He had also testified before a state legislative subcommittee on a bill to end affirmative action in Michigan.

After *Hopwood*, Michigan state representatives contacted CIR about Cohen's report. The lawmakers promised to find potential plaintiffs if

CIR would sue the University of Michigan over its race conscious admissions practices. CIR expressed interest, and the state representatives issued an open call on May 1, 1997 for people who believed they were denied admission or a scholarship at Michigan because of a racial preference.

CIR co-founder Michael McDonald and Minneapolis attorney Kirk Kolbo interviewed six of the 200 people who responded at a hotel near the Detroit airport. Barbara Grutter was one of the six, and fit one criterion—that the named plaintiffs include white women so the case wouldn't just be about " 'angry white men' "[26] Grutter had also been accepted at Wayne State University Law School in Detroit (where she had been offered an unsolicited scholarship), but she found the school to be a poor fit with her desire to be a health law lawyer. She had not attended law school, and felt a strong responsibility to challenge the law school's use of racial preferences because of her earlier experiences with sexist behavior and her values as a parent.[27]

She certainly had diversity factors: "She is one of nine children, the daughter of an itinerant, financially struggling Protestant minister. She worked in an inner-city clinic for two years to save money for community college. She didn't have a college counselor in high school, hadn't heard of such things as SAT prep classes—or even the SAT college-admissions test."[28] Although she eventually made her way into a four-year college and a 3.81 GPA, she was also one of the few women graduating with a Bachelor of Science in 1978.[29] Since then she had had significant corporate and small business experience. Michigan General Counsel Marvin Krislov later admitted that those qualities "absolutely qualif[y] for consideration in bringing diversity attributes," but that Grutter's application omitted many of them.[30] Grutter explains later that she "did not think it would be appropriate, 18 years later, to build my law school application around whining about those difficulties; the facts were indeed there for anyone to see."[31] CIR took the case against the law school, and Grutter was chosen as the sole named plaintiff.

The Intervenors' Claims

Michigan had decided to mount a vigorous, multi-faceted defense of its admissions policy. The university turned not only to top notch legal talent (both internally and externally), but also undertook studies to substantiate the educational benefits of diversity and sought widespread support outside Ann Arbor, as discussed *infra*. The intervenors' claims expanded the defense even further.

Shaw, now back with LDF after his stint as a Michigan law professor, represented proposed intervenors in the undergraduate lawsuit. He planned to argue in the undergraduate suit that the affirmative action programs could be legally supported as an attempt to redress past discrimination by the University of Michigan. For example, the school had a history of intentionally segregating dorms. Not surprisingly, the defendants themselves were not planning on making this argument, and Shaw knew that the strict limits on this justification for race conscious activity would severely limit its chances of success. Yet, the history of discrimination would provide a necessary context, he believed, for the university's program.

The judge was unlikely to let more than one group intervene on the defendants' side in the undergraduate case, and Shaw could probably not represent anyone in the law school case given his participation in the drafting of the law school policy. That left the law school case open for intervention. Miranda Massie, a recent graduate from New York University Law School and an attorney with a small civil rights firm in Detroit, saw the lawsuits as an avenue to start a "new" civil rights movement seeking equality. Shanta Driver—co-chair of BAMN, a pro-affirmative action activist group[32]—gave Massie the idea of seeking intervention in *Grutter*, a topic Massie had not studied in law school.[33]

Massie decided to pursue intervention, but in two ways different from Shaw. First, Massie sought a broader range of intervenors than Shaw, who represented seventeen African American and Latino high school students from Michigan and a nonprofit group of prospective Michigan students and their families in his intervention motion. Massie and Driver found forty-one African American and white students from both high schools and colleges in California, Michigan, and Texas. Massie filed a motion to intervene on behalf of these individuals and three pro-affirmative action student organizations, including BAMN. Second, Massie wanted to do more than make legal arguments in a court of law. The case was for more than that, for "inspiring, galvanizing, and mobilizing a new generation of civil rights activists and leaders"[34] Her goals for the lawsuit were ambitious: "We sought to make this case a referendum on racism and race in American, on racial equality and inequality in America."[35]

One *Grutter* intervenor was Agnes Aleobua. She was attending a downtown Detroit magnet high school, Cass Technical, as a high school junior when Massie visited her school for potential intervenors. Aleobua was in the top fifth of her class, with extracurricular activities and student leadership roles, and a 26 ACT score.

Intervention had been denied in *Hopwood*, but was allowed in *Gratz* and *Grutter*, by order of a divided Sixth Circuit panel.[36] By definition, the granting of intervention expanded the suits beyond a debate about diversity. Validity of test scores, current racial disparities, and the history of discrimination were now at issue. The suits, already expensive, became more costly and time consuming to both sides.

The District Courts: The First Split Double Header

Gratz and *Grutter* were assigned to different judges, despite an attempt by the *Grutter* defendants to switch to the *Gratz* judge.[37] The undergraduate suit was heard by Judge Patrick Duggan, nominated by President Ronald Reagan and a 1958 graduate of the University of Detroit Law School. District Court Judge Bernard Friedman decided the *Grutter* case. Also nominated to the bench by President Reagan, Friedman was a Detroit native and 1968 graduate of Detroit College of Law.

The undergraduate system was heard first. Starting in 1999, Michigan's undergraduate program, for which it received over 13,000 applications for about 4,000 slots, had admitted freshman under a 150-point system. One hundred points guaranteed admission, but admissions counselors could "flag" for additional review certain applications. Applicants scored twenty points for being a member of an under-represented racial/ethnic minority, but also could receive points for being a legacy or graduating from a high school with high average SAT scores. Ruling on a summary judgment motion in *Gratz*, Judge Duggan upheld the 1999 system under Justice Powell's opinion in *Bakke*.[38] He subsequently rejected the *Gratz* intervenors' claim that remedying past discrimination could legally justify the defendants' affirmative action plan.

The law school case took more time. Judge Friedman set an evidentiary hearing after summary judgment arguments. Minneapolis attorney Kolbo tried the case for CIR. He was a close law school friend of CIR co-founder McDonald, and Michigan attorneys willing to take on University of Michigan had proven difficult to find. Kolbo carefully focused his case. He did not take a position on whether or how to use the LSAT, and he presented no testimony on the value of diversity. Instead he attacked Michigan's use of diversity as being "so broad, so undefined, so amorphous that it simply cannot ... ever be a compelling governmental interest."[39] He likened the law school's use of diversity as effectively operating as a quota because it permitted double standards. He called three witnesses. Allan Stillwagon, a former Michigan law school admissions director, testified that the faculty had set a 10–12% goal for minority enrollment in an earlier affirmative action policy. Current admissions director Erica Munzel testified that race was a factor in admissions.

Lastly, Kinley Larntz, a University of Minnesota emeritus professor, presented statistical evidence that the district court found particularly persuasive. Larntz testified that minority applicants had a large advantage in admissions when comparing LSAT scores and undergraduate

GPAs. He put together two primary types of evidence to demonstrate that benefit. One was a series of graphs detailing the rates of applications and admissions rates by LSAT and undergraduate GPAs and by race. That evidence indicated, for example, that for those with Grutter's scores—undergraduate GPAs of 3.75 and above, and LSATs of 161–163—the 1995 admission rate for minority applicants was 100%: three out of three, while the rate for other applicants was 9%: 13 out of 138. The second were the relative odds of acceptance, which measured the likelihood particular racial groups would be admitted given a particular LSAT and undergraduate GPA as compared to whites with similar scores. The analysis also indicated that minority groups had much higher chances of admission, given similar scores, than did white applicants. From this, Larntz testified that race was more than a factor, but effectively operated as a quota. This placed the law school's program outside of *Bakke*, argued Kolbo. While fully prepared to testify,[40] Grutter did not do so. No Michigan law school professor had offered to testify for plaintiff either.

John Payton, an attorney with an elite Washington, DC law firm and impeccable credentials, represented the law school. He focused on the value of diversity in the classroom. He presented four witnesses on the value of diversity in the classroom: Bollinger, former law school dean and then university president; Michigan law professor Richard Lempert, the chairman of the committee that drafted the policy; Jeff Lehman, then dean of the law school; and Kent Syverud, a former Michigan law school professor and then dean of Vanderbilt Law School. On cross-examination, Kolko attempted to elicit a precise percentage that would reflect the "critical mass" of minority enrollment that the law school sought with its admissions policies, but no law school witness would do so.

Payton also presented statistical evidence by Stephen Raudenbush, a professor of education at the University of Michigan. Raudenbush testified that plaintiff's expert Larntz erred in his conclusions. For example, Raudenbush explained that in many categories of scores race had no impact, as all or none of the applicants were admitted. Only in the close cases, where Larntz focused, did race matter. The statistician agreed with Larntz that race does make a difference—that is the intended result of the affirmative action program—but disagreed as to its degree. Raudenbush also concluded that a race-blind system would reduce minority enrollment considerably, from 14.5% to 4%.

With eight days of evidence, Massie's presentation of the intervenors' case took more than half of the trial time. Four minority students recounted at length their personal experiences with racism and segregated education. Experts testified on the history of segregation, the continuing significance of racism, the racial biases in LSAT, and the causes of the achievement gap between minority and white students. Noted historian John Hope Franklin was the most famous trial witness. His five-hour testimony chronicled the history of American racism, including his own personal experiences, but his support of affirmative action was mixed.[41]

In response, Judge Friedman issued a ninety-page opinion rejecting all of the university's and intervenors' respective cases and adopting the plaintiff's analysis of the law school's policies. He characterized the law school as "plac[ing] a very heavy emphasis" on race and having a target range of 10–17% minority enrollment.[42] In addition, he agreed with the Fifth Circuit in *Hopwood* that Justice Powell's *Bakke* opinion was not the prevailing standard. He faulted diversity on its terms, reasoning that racial diversity differs from the viewpoint diversity the law school's policy heralds. He recognized the societal and educational benefits of diversity, but concluded that they fell short of a legal justification. Further, even if diversity could be a compelling governmental interest, the law school's program was not narrowly tailored. Judge Friedman held the intervenors' evidence on past and continuing societal discrimination legally unpersuasive as well.

In sum, the district courts were, to use Justice Scalia's phrase, the first "split double header."[43] Judge Duggan had declared the undergraduate admissions policies constitutional and Justice Powell's *Bakke* opinion good law, with Judge Friedman taking the opposite positions in the law school case.

A Seventh Inning Stretch: The Sixth Circuit Weighs In

The Michigan cases next made their way to the Sixth Circuit. Since the Fifth Circuit's opinion in *Hopwood*, a circuit split had developed. The Ninth Circuit in the University of Washington case had deemed diversity a legally legitimate goal, but one now prohibited in Washington by its Civil Rights Initiative.[44] The Eleventh Circuit, in a non-CIR case, assumed the legitimacy of diversity for the purposes of the opinion, but held the University of Georgia's admissions policies at the undergraduate school not narrowly tailored.[45] The First and Fourth Circuits, in cases involving K–12 education, had taken similar approaches as the Eleventh Circuit—assuming the legal validity of diversity, but holding a lack of narrow tailoring.[46]

The Sixth Circuit granted petitions for initial *en banc* hearings in *Grutter* and *Gratz*, thus foregoing a panel decision.[47] In *Grutter*, the Sixth Circuit split on a five-to-four vote, upholding the law school's program and reversing the district court. The majority, per Chief Judge Boyce F. Martin, held Justice Powell's opinion in *Bakke* to be good law until the Supreme Court instructed otherwise, and the law school's practices to be akin to the Justice Powell-approved Harvard Plan. The majority allowed that race and ethnicity are " 'plus' factors, [which] play an important role in some admissions decisions."[48] Given that the law school had admitted to no fixed enrollment goal and that minorities and non-minorities were evaluated under the same system, the majority held that the school's practices were narrowly tailored as well.

Judge Boggs wrote the primary dissent. He found the case far from close: "the constitutional justifications offered for this practice would not pass even the slightest scrutiny."[49] He faulted diversity as a general manner (arguing that "the Law School grants preference to race, not as a proxy for a unique set of experiences, but as *a proxy for race itself*"),[50] and the law school's use of race specifically (deeming the impact of race in admissions decisions as "shocking").[51] One dissenter, Judge Gilman, did not join Judge Boggs' dissent, writing instead on his own why the law school's program was not narrowly tailored and not reaching the legality of pursuing diversity.

The Sixth Circuit largely ignored the intervenors' arguments of societal discrimination and of bias in LSAT and undergraduate GPA scores. Nor did any judge have anything to say about Massie's 50,000 petition signatures, including Michigan President Bollinger's and some members of Congress, affirming a commitment to *Brown v. Board of Education*, which she had presented at the beginning of her oral argument.

In the undergraduate case, the Sixth Circuit held an initial en banc hearing, but no opinion was ever forthcoming. Reportedly, the Sixth Circuit had voted five-to-four to uphold the undergraduate program as well, but Chief Judge Martin, who assigned himself the majority opinion, eventually came to doubt its legality.[52] He never circulated a draft to the members of the court.

CIR had already appealed the law school case, and both sides agreed to ask the Supreme Court to grant *certiorari* before judgment in the undergraduate case (Michigan's request was conditioned, however, on *certiorari* being granted in the law school case). Supreme Court granted petitions for *certiorari* from plaintiffs and defendants, although not the separate petition from the *Gratz* intervenors. (The *Grutter* intervenors did not separately petition the Sixth Circuit's decision for review—the appellate court having upheld the law school's practices—but still supported the defendants' conditional petition for *certiorari*). Although the intervenors could file papers with the Supreme Court as a party, they were afforded no argument time. The Court was interested solely in the diversity justification.

The Amici Mascots

For the Michigan defendants, litigating the case was much more than a contest of legal arguments, but also a search for public support.[53] In 1997, while awaiting the expected filing of the *Grutter* complaint, Michigan President Bollinger hosted a conference call with more than a dozen corporate and university leaders, asking them to publicize their commitment to affirmative action. Until the university secured the public backing of one its most famous graduates, former President Gerald R. Ford, however, that aid was slow in coming.

Bollinger approached President Ford, a 1935 B.A. Michigan graduate and Wolverine football player in 1998. Ford agreed to write an op-ed piece for the Sunday *New York Times*. The article, entitled "Inclusive America, Under Attack," was firm in its support of affirmative action in general and the school's affirmative action program in particular. He told the story of when Georgia Tech refused to play the Michigan Wolverines if Michigan player Willis Ward, an African American, took the field. Ward sat out the game, although his teammates had offered to refuse to suit-up without him. Reflecting on this event, Ford advised: "I don't want future college students to suffer the cultural and social impoverishment that afflicted my generation . . . [D]o we really want to risk turning back the clock to an era when the Willis Wards were penalized for the color of their skin, their economic standing or national ancestry?"[54] For President Ford, affirmative action expressed racial and ethnic justice.

The next year, General Motors ("GM"), headquartered in Detroit, also offered its public support to the university, after intense Michigan lobbying. Harry Pearce, GM's vice chairman, thought affirmative action reflected moral and good business sense given the company's increasingly diverse customer base. After a meeting with Bollinger and Michigan General Counsel Krislov, he agreed to file an amicus brief with the district court and recruit other companies to file a separate Fortune 500 brief.

President Ford and GM were just the beginning. By the time the Supreme Court had accepted review of the case, the *Grutter* defendants had secured a record number of amicus briefs submitted on one side—eighty-three amici on behalf of over three hundred organizations. Almost a hundred colleges, universities, and educational associations filed briefs supporting Michigan, as did one hundred and twenty-four members of the House, thirteen senators, and twenty-three states. The Fortune 500 Supreme Court amicus brief included sixty-five companies, with GM submitting its own brief. In addition, seventeen media companies, the AFL–CIO, eleven Indian Tribes, and eight Jewish groups (including the American Jewish Committee, which had opposed the Davis program challenged in *Bakke*) filed amici briefs. Law students numbering 13,922 submitted their own eight-page brief.

Only nineteen amicus briefs supported CIR, and none by any educational institution, major business, or member of Congress. Only one State—Florida—filed on the side of plaintiffs, but even that brief accepted the value of diversity. As noted by Professor Neal Devins, "when compared to other controversial social issues (abortion or religion in the schools), the absence of important, powerful voices on one side of the issue seems especially stark."[55]

Two briefs stand out as particularly important. One was the brief of retired military officers. That brief came about after a meeting between Bollinger and Jim Cannon, chairman of the U.S. Naval Academy's Board of Visitors. The Naval Academy had long sought a racially diverse class for the purposes of producing better leaders and improving enlisted morale and discipline. The military had refused to file a brief supporting affirmative action, but Cannon and others were able to secure the support of retired military officers on an amicus brief on Michigan's side in *Gratz* and *Grutter*. (President Ford, as former commander-in-chief, refused to sign.) Using public records, the brief contended that the Air Force Academy, the Naval Academy, and West Point all used race-conscious policies, with numerical targets for enrollments documented for the Naval Academy and West Point. The retired officers defined such practices as a "military necessity."[56] They validated the need for diversity and argued that only race conscious activity would do: "Today, there is no race-neutral alternative that will fulfill the military's, and thus the nation's, compelling national security need for a cohesive military led by a diverse officer corps of highest quality to serve and protect the country."[57]

The second was that filed by the Bush Justice Department. The United States, which had filed nothing before the Sixth Circuit, had little choice but to voice an opinion before the Supreme Court. (The Clinton Justice Department had filed a brief supporting the University's position at the district court level.) Solicitor General Theodore B. Olson had helped CIR in *Hopwood*, most notably by successfully arguing the plaintiffs' case before the Fifth Circuit. His draft of the United States' briefs in *Gratz* and *Grutter* mirrored that of the Fifth Circuit in *Hopwood* and CIR's position in *Gratz* and *Grutter*: race should never be considered and Justice Powell's *Bakke* opinion was not controlling. The White House rejected the proposed briefs, and instead took a compromise position. White House Counsel Alberto Gonzales, Secretary of State Colin Powell, and National Security Adviser Condoleezza Rice were instrumental in getting the Bush administration to offer some support for affirmative action.[58] Ironically, Trent Lott also had a role in getting the Bush Administration to a compromise position. Senate Majority

Leader Lott had made racially insensitive remarks in December 2002 to great public outcry, and a month later when *amicus* filings were due, "there was little question that the Lott imbroglio helped push the administration towards its middle ground position."[59]

Critically, the United States' brief recognized the value of diversity, although it did not conclude whether diversity was a compelling governmental interest.[60] It relegated to a footnote Justice Powell's *Bakke* opinion, offering that the Supreme Court need not decide whether the opinion was still good law.[61] Instead it argued that the law school and undergraduate programs were both unconstitutional quotas and would fail narrow tailoring. Diversity, it argued, could be achieved through race neutral approaches such as the percent plans operating in California, Florida, and Texas. (The brief neglected to mention how the percent plans could be applied to a post-baccalaureate program such as a law school, and failed to mention that the plans had been used only for state undergraduate programs.) As the Supreme Court prepared for oral arguments, it was presented with almost universal acclaim for diversity itself, from the White House, Congress, retired military officers, states, schools, media, and big business. Diversity was the status quo, and no prominent voice disagreed with its value.

Final Score: Diversity Wins 6–2 and 5–4

As was true with the Sixth Circuit argument, affirmative action supporters held marches and rallies the day of the Supreme Court argument. BAMN's Driver organized and personally help finance the buses that brought thousands to march and rally in favor of affirmative action. Inside the Supreme Court courtroom, one brief in particular garnered intense questioning—that by the retired military officers. The United States had begun Operation Iraqi Freedom just days before oral argument, and the Justices asked about the military brief at length.[62]

The Michigan defendants and their *amici* were not disappointed by the Supreme Court's opinion in *Grutter*. Diversity won in theory and in practice: a majority of Justices held diversity to be a compelling governmental interest and the law school's use of diversity to be constitutional. In *Grutter*, six Justices deemed diversity a compelling governmental interest, and only two (Justices Thomas and Scalia) specifically disagreed. Surprisingly, Chief Justice Rehnquist voiced no view on whether diversity could ever be a compelling governmental interest. On the fundamental legal question, Michigan won, with a vote of six to two in diversity's favor.

Five justices validated the law school's practices to create diversity, and four strongly disapproved them. That outcome narrows diversity's utility, as did the undergraduate case, which held the undergraduate point system unconstitutional. Justices Breyer and O'Connor, who had voted to uphold the law school's practices, joined the six-to-three majority in *Gratz* to declare the undergraduate system unconstitutional. *Grutter* still leaves, however, ample room for other educators to consider race in higher education and stay within constitutional boundaries.

Diversity in Theory: Compelling Governmental Interest

Justice O'Connor authored the majority opinion in *Grutter*; it was her first time to vote in favor of race conscious activity. Justices Breyer, Ginsburg, Stevens, and Souter joined her opinion. She began in *Grutter* by noting her respect for the law school. Her first sentence states the issue of the case, mentioning the law school, but not Barbara Grutter. Her second sentence tells her readers that "[t]he Law School ranks among the Nation's top law schools."[63] How a school's ranking is relevant to the plight of Grutter or to the constitutionality of race conscious decision making is far from clear. But the beginning signals the tenor of the opinion: one of esteem for Michigan Law School, and ultimately one of cooperation rather than oversight. Tellingly, Barbara Grutter is mentioned by name only once in the majority opinion. Thereafter, she is called "Petitioner," with the Michigan defendants almost always referenced as the "Law School."[64]

Rather than finding a technical validity to Justice Powell's *Bakke* opinion, the majority analyzes the issue anew and makes an explicit endorsement of racial diversity. In declaring diversity a compelling governmental interest, Justice O'Connor turns legal analysis largely aside. She spends only a few paragraphs to repeat standard Equal Protection analysis. The heart of the opinion is not a construction or deconstruction of the Equal Protection Clause.

Instead, the analysis really begins when Justice O'Connor offers a non-Equal Protection principle: "[t]he Law School's educational judgment that such diversity is essential to its education mission is one to which we defer."[65] That declaration—the first sentence after the majority states its conclusion that diversity can be a compelling governmental interest—is a driving force in the majority's analysis. This deference means the majority accepts the defendant's story more than questions it, and effectively ensures its constitutionality.

The majority pays little attention to the situation faced by Grutter—that as an individual she would have been treated differently if she were of a different race or ethnicity. The opinion states that "the diffusion of knowledge and opportunity through public institutions of higher education must be *accessible to all individuals regardless of race or ethnicity*."[66] The implication of this statement is not, however, race neutral admissions; the emphasis is on being "accessible" not "regardless of race or ethnicity." The opinion turns immediately to announce the importance of integration: "Effective participation by members of all racial and ethnic groups in the civic life of our Nation is essential if the dream of one Nation, indivisible, is to be realized."[67] How Grutter is treated to achieve this integration is given little appreciation. The majority deemed her position generally acceptable because all persons have the opportunity to take advantage of parts of the law school's multi-faceted diversity policy.

The conclusions in the majority opinion are inconceivable without deference to Michigan Law School, but also without the widespread amici support. The majority references extensively the briefs of other educators, big businesses, and particularly that of the military.

All this allows the majority to deem the benefits of diversity as "substantial."[68] Diversity, according to the majority, promotes classroom learning, but also serves businesses, the military, and society as a whole. In this sense, the majority goes beyond Justice Powell's support of diversity, which was largely internal to the classroom setting.

Nor will the law school's practices lead to the stereotypes O'Connor has faulted other race conscious activity for creating.[69] Its quest for a "critical mass" instead "diminish[es] the force of such stereotypes."[70]

A sixth Justice agreed that diversity could be a compelling governmental interest: Justice Kennedy. He accepts the validity of Justice Powell's *Bakke* opinion with little discussion, and dissented for other reasons.

Justices Scalia and Thomas strongly disagreed. Justice Scalia's opinion argued that the definition of diversity is too broad.[71] He posits that the educational benefits of diversity are "the same lesson taught to ... people three feet shorter and twenty years younger ... in institutions ranging from Boy Scout troops to public-school kindergartens."[72] Justice Thomas belittles the goal of educational diversity. He characterizes it as merely " 'aesthetic.' That is, the Law School wants to have a certain appearance, from the shape of the desks and tables in its classrooms to the color of the students sitting at them."[73] Justice Thomas argues, from both a constitutional and a public policy stance, that African–Americans would be better off without the quest of historically white institutions to become more racially diverse. He also notes the limited nature of diversity in improving the status of African Americans. He reasons that diversity does little for the many African–Americans who are "too poor or too uneducated to participate in elite higher education and [diversity] therefore presents only an illusory solution to the challenges facing our Nation."[74] He allows that diversity means that "the aestheticists will never address the real problems facing 'underrepresented minorities,' instead continuing their social experiments on other people's children."[75]

Diversity in Practice: Narrow Tailoring

Five Justices held that the law school's practices were narrowly tailored to diversity. By validating the law school's approach, the majority revealed a new line-up card for constitutional race conscious decision making for the purpose of diversity. The approach can be expensive, but is largely replicable in any merit-based admissions program, and perhaps elsewhere as well. Given the weight the law school placed on race, *Grutter* leaves ample room for other educators to consider race within constitutional boundaries.

First, a school should never state a fixed number for its use of diversity; this would likely be an unconstitutional quota. While schools can seek a "critical mass" of students, that goal should result in a range of enrollment percentages. The law school, for example, enrolled minorities in a range from 13.5% to 20.1% during the years in question, and no one confessed to having a precise numerical goal. The fact that narrower ranges existed in different time periods, as Justice Kennedy noted in his opinion, does not create an impermissible quota.

Second, each application should receive individual review to ascertain "all the ways an applicant might contribute to a diverse educational environment."[76] In making that individual review, officials can make race a "plus" factor, but must also "meaningfully consider" non-racial/ethnic diversity factors.[77] It is acceptable if this results in admitting non-minorities with lower scores than minority admittees, as was true for Michigan Law School.

Third, the individual review cannot include a point system, as the undergraduate school used. While Justices Ginsburg and Souter argued in their *Gratz* dissent that the point system made explicit what was implicit in the law school program, the majority of the Court found the point system to be an unconstitutional difference.

Fourth, race conscious admissions practices must be terminated "as soon as practicable,"[78] a rather ambiguous standard. Twenty-five years after *Bakke*, Justice O'Connor writes that "[w]e expect that 25 years from now, the use of racial preferences will no longer be necessary to further the interest approved now."[79] Justice O'Connor does not explain why diversity has an expiration date, or how racial preferences will become unnecessary in 2027, but the statement gains the approval of Justices Scalia and Thomas.

Once these four factors are present, the race conscious decision-making for the purpose of diversity is likely to be validated—so long as the school is entitled to the deference afforded to Michigan Law School. The rest of the majority's opinion on narrowly tailoring discusses what is *not* required. Race neutral alternatives that would negatively affect the quality of students, such as a lottery or lowering of admission standards, need not be considered, as Justices Scalia and Thomas strongly advocated. Using "daily reports" to track the racial and ethnic enrollment in an incoming class is acceptable so long as admissions personnel state, as they did in *Grutter*, that these reports do not influence their use of race and ethnicity but are used only to fulfill the goal of a critical mass. Further, it is perfectly acceptable to have different definitions of "critical mass" for different groups. Chief Justice Rehnquist noted, for example, that Native Americans are enrolled at much lower numbers than African–Americans. The range of Native American admittees was from 13 to 19, compared to a range of 91 to 108 for African–Americans.

Admission percentages can also closely track application percentages without indicating an unconstitutional quota. Chief Justice Rehnquist apparently composed his own charts of the statistical evidence to demonstrate that admission rates of racial ethnic groups closely mirror their application rates over time. For example, the percentage of Hispanic applicants in 1995 was 5.1%, with their admission rate at 5.0%. He demonstrated similarly tight correlations for African–Americans, Latinos, and Native Americans from 1995 to 2000. Justice Kennedy argues forcefully that this evidence indicates a quota, a characterization that the other dissenting Justices avoid all together. The majority responded that admission rates differ from enrollment rates. The *enrollment* rates are what matter for the majority, not the admission rates that Chief Justice Rehnquist presents, and the enrollment rates differ more from year to year. The majority takes this approach even though schools have more control over their admission rates than their enrollment rates.

Strict Scrutiny Weakens Diversity

The dissenting Justices fault the rigor of the majority's strict scrutiny analysis. Justice Scalia, for example, scorns the majority's approach, calling it "challeng[ing] even for the most gullible mind."[80] The majority admits that its application of strict scrutiny is different, but maintains it is following *Adarand*'s admonishment that strict scrutiny considers context. Given that "universities occupy a special niche in our constitutional tradition," the majority concludes that deference to the law school is warranted.[81]

In doing so, the Court has clearly signaled a deferential version of strict scrutiny for universities when they engage in racial decision making for the purpose of creating diversity.[82] This has meant a "cost benefit" balancing test that considers the benefits and harms of affirmative action.[83] That analysis focuses not on how applicants benefit, or don't benefit, from affirmative action, but on society as a whole. Neither are Equal Protection principles prominent in defining the societal benefits of affirmative action. Instead the majority turns to the defendants and amici briefs by governments, educators, companies, and the military in articulating the social benefits of affirmative action. The Court defines diversity not as one of its own constitutional principles, but as a worthwhile principle belonging to others that wins the Court's compliant endorsement.

In doing so, the Court divorces diversity from any connection to individual or group legal rights.[84] This may have been necessary to get Supreme Court validation, but it necessarily weakens the prescriptive force of diversity. A choice is allowed, but so long as the choice is akin to that of Michigan Law School's, no one's rights are implicated in making that choice. In short, the deferential strict scrutiny allows other schools to make similar choices to Michigan Law School's, but affords no one any positive rights.

In addition, the choice of voluntary integration may not last. Diversity is validated based on pedagogy and expected social outcomes, but pedagogy can change and expected social outcomes can be proven false.[85] Further, the Court expects that a need for voluntary affirmative action will last no more than twenty-five years.[86] Constitutional principles typically do not expire with time; their shelf life is timeless.[87] Yet, the Court tells schools from the outset to expect diversity's demise.

Diversity Weakens Integration

As compared to school desegregation, diversity seeks a weak version of integration. The *Grutter* majority clearly supports the idea of integration, and links diversity to the benefits of integration. For example, the majority states the value of integrated schools: "Access to legal education (and thus the legal profession) must be inclusive of talented and qualified individuals of every race and ethnicity, so that all members of our heterogeneous society may participate in the educational institutions that provide the training and education necessary to succeed in America."[88]

Yet, the meaning of integration through diversity, unlike school desegregation jurisprudence, is not transformative. No mandate is issued for racial balancing, or even for a great increase in minority enrollment in historically white schools. Instead, historically white institutions are allowed to use diversity so that they are not all-white or almost all-white. Some minorities are thus admitted, but typically not as many to reflect the minority population. Because of this, diversity will likely not be a backdoor attempt to fulfill school desegregation's unfulfilled promise of not having a " 'white' school or 'Negro' school, but just schools."[89] In other words, schools will likely keep a racial identity with diversity.

Indeed, the Court largely validates the status quo and accepts the majority of views expressed to it. By contrast, *Brown I* was clearly intended to change society. The most difficult issue underlying affirmative action—how to redress the uneven playing field—is omitted from discussion all together. The majority posits that "race unfortunately still matters," but without examining the difficult issue of why this might be so and what it might tell us about the need for affirmative action.[90]

In short, the use of diversity is entirely moderate—it is not to remedy societal discrimination, nor does it offer a different standard for benign discrimination. It strives not necessarily to offer further improvement of race relations or to integrate further historically white schools, but to sustain the current approach and allow choice. While *Brown II* was greeted with Massive Resistance and signaled a radical transformation in education, *Grutter* puts race in higher education in a holding pattern, one that is to last presumably until 2027.

*A Post–*Grutter *Report*

In many ways, *Gratz* and *Grutter* brought clarity to what schools can and cannot do in the name of diversity. Schools that used point systems for admissions before the Michigan cases—such as the University of Massachusetts at Amherst, University of Michigan, and Ohio State—have changed their systems to ones that include individual review and other more flexible practices. The University of Texas, the defendant in *Hopwood*, has returned to race-conscious admissions, but the state legislature has kept the Top Ten Percent Plan for undergraduate admissions. Texas A & M, on the other hand, has remained race neutral, but has eliminated its legacy preferences.[91]

In California and Washington, the changes have been more subtle. In 2001, the Regents of the University of California voted unanimously to repeal its prohibition on race-based admissions. Proposition 209 remains in effect, however, so explicit race conscious admissions are still unlawful. California universities have engaged, however, in other ways to increase their minority enrollment, ways that are more implicit in their race consciousness. For example, the University of California, Los Angeles ("UCLA") provides extra points in the admissions process for students who have participated in outreach programs for low-performing high schools or have personal challenges, low income, or attended a low-performing high school, or are first-generation college.[92] The law school at UCLA has started a Critical Race Studies program, and its minority enrollment has increased.[93] The University of California counts scores on SAT II's in Spanish, including the scores of Spanish-speaking students.[94] The State of Washington faces a similar situation, as its Civil Rights Initiative continues to restrict the use of race. The University of Washington no longer prefers applicants who are African American or Latino, but does "favor[] applicants from 'diverse backgrounds' who are 'persevering against substantial obstacles such as prejudice or discrimination.' "[95]

Intervenor Erika Dowdell, who testified in *Grutter* at the district court hearing as an African American junior at the University of

Michigan, was admitted to UCLA School of Law (but not Michigan Law School), with the expectation of studying in the Critical Race Studies program.[96] There she won second place in the 2004 Black Law School Students Association—Western Region Moot Court Competition[97] and received the San Francisco School Desegregation Summer Fellowship.[98] She is presently working at the Los Angeles Public Defender's Office.

Intervenor Agnes Aleogua was a high school junior when Massie visited her downtown Detroit magnet school for potential intervenors. She eventually received an on-the-spot offer of admission to the University of Michigan after an interview with a university admissions officer at her high school. She graduated with a Bachelor of Arts in Education, and is a social studies teacher in Miami as part of the Teach for America program.[99]

Barbara Grutter never attended law school. She has deemed *Grutter* as "neither wise nor just"[100] and has continued to promote public discussion of affirmative action preferences as president of Toward A Fair Michigan ("TAFM"). Grutter describes TAFM as a "non-profit, non-partisan education organization, which, amongst other things, sponsors debates (providing both pro and con speakers) to promote an informed citizenry in support of the best public decision" on affirmative action preferences.[101]

In newspaper interviews, she has emphasized the lessons she has taught her children from her role as named plaintiff: "I had always taught [my kids] discrimination was wrong and the law protects them from that. I could have been angry and bitter—or whine about it—or I could do something positive. I viewed filing a lawsuit as a positive thing."[102]

CIR has no pending cases challenging affirmative action in education, but has continued to challenge racial preferences in other areas, namely government contracting and federal employment. Another group, Center for Equal Opportunity, has filed complaints with the Department of Education challenging how schools have considered race after *Grutter*.[103] The Michigan Civil Rights Initiative, modeled on the California counterpart, was passed by Michigan voters on the November 2006 ballot, and the University of Michigan must one again review how, and if, it will consider race and ethnicity. And the Supreme Court—with two new members since it decided *Grutter*—has accepted review of two cases on *Grutter*'s applicability to K–12 schools.[104] How Chief Justice John Roberts and Justice Samuel Alito will react to diversity and its uses is unknown. BAMN organized another March on Washington on the day of the oral argument.

In short, the story of affirmative action seems to be one that will never end.

Endnotes

1. Thanks to Marvin Krislov, Miranda Massie, Michael Olivas, Wilson Parker, Mike Selmi, and Ted Shaw for their many very helpful comments. I would especially like to thank Barbara Grutter for all her time and effort in commenting on this book chapter. All errors, of course, are my own.

2. Email message from Barbara Grutter to author (June 14, 2006).

3. Id.; Mark Clayton, *The Woman Behind the Law School Admissions Suit*, Christian Science Monitor, April 3, 2001, at 14.

4. 438 U.S. 265 (1978).

5. 539 U.S. 306 (2003).

6. *See generally* Jerome Karabel, *The Chosen: The Hidden History of Admission and Exclusion at Harvard, Yale, and Princeton* 77–136 (2005); Malcolm Gladwell, *Getting In: The Social Logic of Ivy League Admissions*, The New Yorker, Oct. 10, 2005.

7. *See* Gladwell, *supra* note 6.

8. *See* Karabel, *supra* note 6, at 408; Samuel Issacharoff, *Law and Misdirection in the Debate Over Affirmative Action*, 2002 U. Chi. Legal F. 11, 24.

9. Richard H. Sander, *A Systemic Analysis of Affirmative Action in American Law Schools*, 57 Stan. L. Rev. 367, 379 (2004).

10. Griffin v. School Bd. of Prince Edward Co., 377 U.S. 218 (1964).

11. *See* Taylor Branch, *Parting the Waters: America in the King Years 1954–63*, at 634–72 (1988).

12. *See* Michael A. Olivas, *Constitutional Criteria: The Social Science and Common Law of Admissions Decisions in Higher Education*, 68 U. Colo. L. Rev. 1065, 1100–02 (1997) (noting that after Meredith applied, Ole Miss began requiring an ACT score for the first time and that after Meredith was ordered admitted, the school began requiring a minimum ACT score set to exclude almost all minority applicants).

13. Regents of Univ. of Ca. v. Bakke, 438 U.S. 265, 314, 319–20 (1978) (opinion of Powell, J.).

14. Sanford Levinson, *Diversity*, U. Pa. J. Con. L. 573, 578 (2000) (referenced in Justice Kennedy's dissenting opinion in *Grutter*, 539 U.S. at 393); *see also* Anthony T. Kronman, *Is Diversity a Value in American Higher Education?*, 52 Fla. L. Rev. 861, 861 (2002) ("It is striking that a word which a generation ago carried no particular moral weight and had, at most, a modestly benign connotation, should in this generation have become the most fiercely contested word in American higher education."). Yet, schools themselves brought the idea to Justice Powell's attention. *See Bakke*, 438 U.S. at 311–18 (opinion of Powell, J.) (noting that Davis defended its program, in part, on the grounds of diversity and that the Harvard Plan valued diversity as well).

15. *See* Michael Selmi, *The Life of* Bakke*: An Affirmative Action Retrospective*, 87 Geo. L.J. 981, 1002 (1999).

16. *Grutter*, 539 U.S. at 306.

17. Grutter v. Bollinger, 288 F.3d 732, 737 (6th Cir.) (en banc) (quoting law school's policy), *aff'd*, 539 U.S. 306 (2003).

18. Grutter v. Bollinger, 137 F.Supp.2d 821, 828 (E.D. Mich. 2001), *rev'd*, 288 F.3d 732 (6th Cir.) (en banc), *aff'd* 539 U.S. 306 (2003).

19. *See, e.g.*, Adarand Constructors, Inc. v. Pena, 515 U.S. 200 (1995); Shaw v. Reno, 509 U.S. 630 (1993); Richmond v. Croson, 488 U.S. 469 (1989); Wygant v. Jackson Bd. of Educ., 476 U.S. 267 (1986).

20. *Adarand*, 515 U.S. at 220 (quoting Fullilove v. Klutznick, 448 U.S. 448, 537 (1980) (Stevens, J., dissenting)).

21. This telling of the story behind *Grutter v. Bollinger* relies heavily on Greg Stohr, *A Black and White Case: How Affirmative Action Survived Its Greatest Legal Challenge* (2004).

22. Paul Burka, *Law's New Icon: Cheryl Hopwood: She fought affirmative action at the University of Texas—and won*, Tex. Monthly, Nov. 30, 1999, at 113.

23. Hopwood v. Texas, 78 F.3d 932, 945 (5th Cir. 1996).

24. Michael S. Greve, Hopwood *and Its Consequences*, 17 Pace L. Rev. 1, 3 (1996).

25. Cal. Const. Art. I, § 31(a) (2003).

26. *See* Stohr, *supra* note 21, at 49 (quoting McDonald).

27. As she explained later to Michigan undergraduates, "I had struggled with sexist behavior far too long to simply turn around and meekly accept discrimination on yet another basis. That is not progress!" Barbara Grutter, Speech at Race & Admissions Class, University of Michigan Residential College (Oct. 27, 2005) (copy on file with author). Her role as a parent was also critical in her decision to lend her name and time to the lawsuit—she "was most concerned by what I would teach them [her children] if I did nothing in the face of a formal policy of discrimination by a public institution." *Id.*

28. June Kronholz, *Does a White Mom Add Diversity?*, Wall St. J., June 25, 2003, at B3. The plaintiff in the Texas Law School affirmative action case, *Hopwood v. Texas*, also had diversity factors that were not highlighted in her application. *See* Olivas, *supra* note 12, at 1111 n. 218.

29. Email message from Barbara Grutter to author (June 14, 2006).

30. Kronholz, *supra* note 28, at B3.

31. Email message from Barbara Grutter to author (Aug. 21, 2006).

32. BAMN's full name is currently Coalition to Defend Affirmative Action, Integration and Immigrant Rights and Fight for Equality by Any Means Necessary.

33. Email message from Miranda Massie to author (Sept. 7, 2006).

34. Miranda Massie, *Representing the Student Intervenors in* Grutter, *Jurist Online Symposium* (Sept. 5, 2002) (available at <<http://jurist.law.pitt.edu/forum/symposium-aa/massie-printer.php>>).

35. Miranda Massie, *Litigators and Communities Working Together:* Grutter v. Bollinger *and the New Civil Rights Movement*, 15 Berkeley La Raza L.J. 109, 110 (2004).

36. Grutter v. Bollinger, 188 F.3d 394 (6th Cir. 1999) (consolidated appeal with *Gratz*).

37. Judge Friedman alleged procedural irregularities in how other members of the district court handled the defendants' motion to consolidate the cases before Judge Duggan. *See* Stohr, *supra* note 21, at 95–100.

38. Gratz v. Bollinger, 122 F.Supp.2d 811 (E.D. Mich. 2000), *rev'd in part*, 539 U.S. 244 (2003).

39. *See* Stohr, *supra* note 21, at 153.

40. Email message from Barbara Grutter to author (Aug. 21, 2006).

41. For example, on cross-examination, Franklin agreed that he does "not support the admission of less qualified minority applicants over more qualified Asian or white applicants." Stohr, *supra* note 21, at 163.

42. *Grutter*, 137 F.Supp.2d at 840.

43. *Grutter*, 539 U.S. at 348 (Scalia, J., concurring in part and dissenting in part).

44. Wash. Rev. Code § 49.60.400 (2001); Smith v. University of Wash. Law Sch., 233 F.3d 1188 (9th Cir. 2000).

45. Johnson v. Board of Regents, 263 F.3d 1234 (11th Cir. 2001); *see also* Podberesky v. Kirwan, 38 F.3d 147 (4th Cir. 1994) (holding race-based scholarship program unconstitutional).

46. *See* Eisenberg v. Montgomery County Public Schs., 197 F.3d 123 (4th Cir. 1999); Tuttle v. Arlington County Sch. Bd., 195 F.3d 698 (4th Cir. 1999) (per curiam); Wessmann v. Gittens, 160 F.3d 790 (1st Cir. 1998); *see also* Brewer v. West Irondequoit Central Sch. Dist., 212 F.3d 738 (2d Cir. 2000) (upholding voluntary transfer program designed to reduce the racial isolation of Rochester and the surrounding suburban school districts); Hunter v. Regents of the Univ. of Ca., UCLA's Graduate School of Education, 190 F.3d 1061, 1063 (9th Cir. 1999) (upholding the constitutionality of a race conscious admissions program for a "laboratory" elementary school operated with a stated justification of researching to learn how to improve "the quality of education in urban public schools").

47. Two Sixth Circuit judges strongly objected to the timing of the circulation of the petition for initial *en banc* hearings (which effectively excluded the participation of two judges who took senior status) and the assignment of judges in the foregone panel. *See Grutter*, 288 F.3d at 810–814 (Boggs, J., dissenting) (the "Procedural Appendix" to Judge Boggs' dissent, which was joined by Judge Batchelder). This in turn drew the objections of four judges to the accuracy and public nature of the complaints. *See id.* at 752–58 (Moore, J., concurring) (joined by Daughtrey, Cole, and Clay, J.J.) (opining that "Judge Boggs and those joining his opinion have done a grave harm not only to themselves, but to this court and even to the Nation as a whole"); *id.* at 772–73 (Clay, J., concurring) (joined by Daughtrey, Moore, and Cole, J.J.) (deeming "the dissent's procedural attack [as] an embarrassing and incomprehensible attack on the integrity of the Chief Judge and this Court as a whole").

48. *Grutter*, 288 F.3d at 748.

49. *Id.* at 773 (Boggs, J., dissenting).

50. *Id.* at 792 (Boggs, J., dissenting).

51. *Id.* at 794 (Boggs, J., dissenting).

52. *See* Stohr, *supra* note 21, at 214.

53. For a thorough look at the amicus filings, see Neal Devins, *Explaining* Grutter v. Bollinger, 152 U. Pa. L. Rev. 347, 366–372 (2003).

54. Gerald Ford, *Inclusive America, Under Attack*, N.Y. Times, Aug. 8, 1999, § 4, at 15.

55. *See* Devins, *supra* note 53, at 370.

56. Consolidated Brief of Lt. Gen. Julius W. Becton, et al., *Grutter v. Bollinger*, 2003 WL 1787554, at *17 (Feb. 21, 2003).

57. *Id.* at *9–10.

58. *See* Devins, *supra* note 53, at 372 & n.117.

59. *See id.* at 372.

60. Brief of United States, *Grutter v. Bollinger*, 2003 WL 176635, at *8 (Jan. 17, 2003) (starting its summary of argument with "[e]nsuring that public institutions, especially educational institutions, are open and accessible to a broad and diverse array of individuals, including individuals of all races and ethnicities, is an important and entirely legitimate government objective").

61. *Id.* at *12 n.4.

62. Thanks to former UM General Counsel Marvin Krislov for bringing this to my attention.

63. *Grutter*, 539 U.S. at 313.

64. *Id.* at 316.

65. *Id.* at 328.

66. *Id.* at 331 (emphasis added).

67. *Id.* at 332.

68. *Id.* at 330.

69. *See, e.g.*, Shaw v. Reno, 509 U.S. 630, 647 (1993) (O'Connor, J., writing the majority opinion) ("It [racial redistricting] reinforces the perception that members of the same racial group—regardless of their age, education, economic status, or the community in which they live—think alike, share the same political interests, and will prefer the same candidates at the polls. We have rejected such perceptions elsewhere as impermissible racial stererotypes."); Metro Broadcasting, Inc. v. FCC, 497 U.S. 547, 604 (1990) (O'Connor, J., dissenting) ("Racial classifications, whether providing benefits to or burdening particular racial or ethnic groups, may stigmatize those groups singled out for different treatment and may create considerable tension with the Nation's widely shared commitment to evaluating individuals upon their individual merit.").

70. *Grutter*, 539 U.S. at 333.

71. *Id.* at 347 (Scalia, J., concurring in part and dissenting in part) ("If properly considered an 'educational benefit' at all, it is surely not one that is either uniquely relevant to law school or uniquely 'teachable' in a formal educational setting.").

72. *Id.*

73. *Id.* at 354 n.3 (Thomas, J., concurring in part and dissenting in part).

74. *Id.*

75. *Id.* at 372 (Thomas, J., concurring in part and dissenting in part).

76. *Id.* at 337.

77. *Id.* at 338; *see also id.* ("What is more, the Law School actually gives substantial weight to diversity factors besides race.").

78. *Id.* at 343.

79. *Id.*

80. *Id.* at 347 (Scalia, J., concurring in part and dissenting in part); *see also id.* at 350 (Thomas, J., concurring in part and dissenting in part) (deeming "unprecedented [the] deference that Court gives to the Law School, an approach inconsistent with the very concept of 'strict scrutiny' "); *id.* at 380 (Rehnquist, C.J., dissenting) (faulting the majority's " 'unprecedented' deference"); *id.* at 388 (Kennedy, J., dissenting) (declaring the majority's approach not strict scrutiny and "nothing short of perfunctory").

81. *Id.* at 329.

82. *See, e.g.*, Jack Balkin, Plessy, Brown, *and* Grutter*: A Play In Three Acts*, 26 Cardozo L. Rev. 1689, 1724 (2005) ("The fact that the Court engages in this sort of deference is a tell-tale sign that it is not applying a scrutiny as strict as it claims.").

83. *See* Michelle Adams, *Searching for Strict Scrutiny in* Grutter v. Bollinger, 78 Tul. L. Rev. 1941 (2004); Jed Rubenfeld, *Affirmative Action*, 107 Yale L.J. 427 (1997).

84. *See* Rachel Moran, *Of Doubt and Diversity*, 67 Ohio L.J. 201, 226 (2006).

85. *Id.*

86. *See generally* Dorothy A. Brown, *Taking* Grutter *Seriously: Getting Beyond the Numbers*, 43 Houston L. Rev. 1 (2006); Joel K. Goldstein, *Justice O'Connor's Twenty–Five Year Expectation: The Legitimacy of Durational Limits in* Grutter, 67 Ohio L.J. 83 (2006).

87. Similarly, constitutional principles are typically afforded an immediate remedy when violated, but an exception was made in *Brown II*. There the Court held that the remedy need not come at once, but "with all deliberate speed." Brown v. Board of Educ., 349 U.S. 294, 301 (1955).

88. *Grutter*, 539 U.S. at 332–33.

89. Green v. County Sch. Bd., 391 U.S. 430, 442 (1968).

90. *Grutter*, 539 U.S. at 333; *see also id.* at 338 ("By virtue of our Nation's struggle with racial inequality, such students are both likely to have experiences of particular importance to the Law School's mission, and less likely to be admitted in meaningful members on criteria that ignore those experiences.").

91. Daniel Golden, *No More Boost for "Legacies" at Texas A & M*, Wall St. J., Jan. 13, 2004, at B1. The school's original plan was race neutral on its face, but included a preference for legacy. After public criticism from Texas legislators, Texas A & M faculty, and others, the school dropped the legacy preference. *See* Todd Ackerman, *Legislators Slam A & M Over Legacy Admissions*, Hous. Chron., Jan. 4, 2004, at A1. The University of Texas never had legacy preferences in admissions.

92. Daniel Golden, *Extra Credit To Get into UCLA, It Helps to Face "Life Challenges,"* Wall St. J., July 12, 2002, at A1.

93. Daniel Golden, *Case Study: School Find Ways to Achieve Diversity Without Key Tool*, Wall St. J., June 20, 2003, at A1.

94. Daniel Golden, *Admission: Possible: Language Test Gives Hispanic Students a Leg Up in California*, Wall St. J., June 26, 2001, at A1.

95. Golden, *supra* note 93.

96. *Id.*

97. *See* Brett Cook, *UCLA Docket Article* (Spring 2004) (available at <<http://www.law.ucla.edu/moot/awards/awards_BLSA.htm>>).

98. *UCLA Alumni Magazine* (Winter 2004) (available at <<www.law.ucla.edu/docs/alummagwint2004.students.pdf>>).

99. Seth Lewis, *Recruited to Teach for America*, The Miami Herald, March 26, 2006.

100. Barbara Grutter, *Making Progress: A Response to Michigan GOP Chair Betsy DeVos*, National Review, Aug. 19, 2003 (available at <<http://www.nationalreview.com/comment/comment-grutter081903.asp>>).

101. Email message from Barbara Grutter to author (May 23, 2006).

102. Clayton, *supra* note 3.

103. *See* Moran, *supra* note 84, at 231–32.

104. *See* Parents Involved in Community Schools v. Seattle Sch. Dist. No. 1, 426 F.3d 1162 (9th Cir. 2005) (en banc) (holding diversity to be a compelling governmental interest in K–12 setting and that having race be a tie-breaker for high school admissions is narrowly tailored), *cert. granted*, 126 S.Ct. 2351 (2006); McFarland v. Jefferson County Pub. Schs., 330 F.Supp.2d 834 (W.D. Ky. 2004) (holding "maintaining racially integrated schools" as a compelling governmental interest, deeming the use of a goal of each schools having between a 15% and 50% African–American enrollment not a quota in practice with race in a few instances tipping the balance, but not affirming the use of separate admission lists by race and gender at some schools), *aff'd*, 416 F.3d 513 (6th Cir. 2005) (per curiam), *cert. granted*, 126 S.Ct. 2351 (2006); *see also* Comfort v. Lynn Sch. Comm., 418 F.3d 1 (1st Cir. 2005) (en banc) (upholding race-based transfer as a part of voluntary desegregation planing and diversity as a compelling governmental interest in K–12 schools). *But see* Cavalier v. Caddo Parish Sch. Bd., 403 F.3d 246 (5th Cir. 2005) (deeming a goal of 50/50

+/–15% a quota, and different racial admissions scores not narrowly tailored; leaving open the question of whether diversity a compelling governmental interest at K–12 level). *See generally* Maurice R. Dyson, *Towards an Establishment Clause Theory of Race–Based Allocation: Administering Race–Conscious Financial Aid After* Grutter *and* Zelman, 14 S. Cal. Interdisc. L.J. 237 (2005) (examining the constitutionality of race-based financial aid); James E. Ryan, *Voluntary Integration: Asking the Right Questions*, 67 Ohio L.J. 304 (2006) (articulating what questions to ask about the constitutionality of voluntary K–12 integration plans and contending that such plans can be constitutional); Wendy Parker, *Connecting the Dots:* Grutter, *School Desegregation, and Federalism*, 45 Wm. & Mary L. Rev. 1691, 1705–39 (2004) (analyzing the role of local control in school desegregation and its connection with *Grutter*'s deference).

5

The Story of *Lau v. Nichols*: Breaking the Silence in Chinatown

Rachel F. Moran

The story of *Lau v. Nichols*[1] is not an easy one to tell. Although the United States Supreme Court's decision protecting English language learners from discrimination in education has endured for over thirty years, there is a hole at the heart of this case, the place where Kinney Kinmon Lau and his mother should be. The Laus today are silent about the lawsuit. Although Kinney and his mother helped to rectify an injustice and so made civil rights history, they have not laid claim to their legacy and are in fact deeply ambivalent about—indeed, even estranged from—their role in the case.

The reasons for the Laus' distance and detachment are complex, but then so is the case itself. This was a lawsuit with many agendas, only some of which were realized. The Laus just wanted a better education for Kinney, but litigation delays limited how much he could benefit. The Laus' lawyer, Edward Steinman, was eager for a dramatic constitutional victory but instead prevailed on narrow statutory grounds. The Chinese community in San Francisco was in turmoil, buffeted by an influx of immigrants and by newly mobilized Chinese–American college students seeking social justice for Chinatown. *Lau* offered an opportunity to join together in demanding respect for linguistic and cultural autonomy. Faced with escalating conflict, city officials simply wanted the case to go away. In the turbulent 1960s and 1970s, the school system faced desegregation challenges, labor unrest, and protests over the neglect of Chinese and Latino students' special needs.[2] Eventually, a fragile peace would come but at a price.

A Time of Transition

At the time *Lau* was filed in 1970, the nation, the state of California, and the San Francisco Unified School District were grappling with demographic, social, and legal change. The United States Supreme Court had declared official segregation in the public schools unconstitutional in

Brown v. Board of Education[3] in 1954, but this stirring declaration prompted few changes until Congress and administrative agencies backed up the Court's pronouncement with the power of the purse and a threat of vigorous enforcement. The Civil Rights Act of 1964[4] was especially critical in making equal educational opportunity more than mere rhetoric. With the implementation of reform came new battles over the meaning of *Brown*'s desegregation mandate and the scope of federal authority over state and local school districts.

At the time that *Lau* was litigated, there were several important unanswered questions about *Brown*'s legacy. When Chief Justice Earl Warren spoke for a unanimous Court in striking down "separate but equal" schools, he cited not only the damage that segregation inflicted on the "hearts and minds" of black children but also the role of education as the cornerstone of good citizenship and personal success.[5] As a result, some advocates contended that *Brown* was designed not only to combat racial inequality but to enshrine a right to education.[6] There was no express right to education in the Constitution, but the Court had recognized some unenumerated rights, such as the right to travel and the right to privacy, because they were essential to preserve other constitutional guarantees. Activists argued that education easily stood on a par with these implied rights.[7] If education were deemed fundamental, then a denial of access to any child, regardless of race or ethnicity, would trigger strict judicial scrutiny. Almost impossible to meet in practice, this standard of review required school officials to show that their practices were necessary to achieve a compelling state interest.

Declaring education a fundamental right would help to deal with another area of uncertainty about *Brown*'s significance. When *Lau* was filed, it was unclear whether the Justices wanted to eradicate all segregation in the public schools or whether they were concerned only with segregation that resulted from purposeful, official state action. In desegregation cases in the South, federal courts had confronted school assignment laws that explicitly separated children on the basis of race. This *de jure* segregation was part of a Jim Crow caste system that openly relegated blacks to a position of inferiority. As advocates of school desegregation turned to the North and West, they found that racially identifiable schools often resulted from residential housing patterns rather than race-based student assignments. Nearly two decades after *Brown*, the Court had not yet decided whether this *de facto* segregation could be held unconstitutional in the absence of proof of discriminatory intent by the school board.[8]

The plaintiffs in *Lau* faced special challenges in proving that they were victims of wrongful discrimination. There had certainly been a history of anti-Chinese legislation in California.[9] In fact, the hardships were so severe that it became common to say that a person facing long odds "didn't have a Chinaman's chance."[10] However, many Chinese-speaking students in San Francisco were recent immigrants who had not been subject to this history of abuse.[11] Moreover, in the post-World War II era, San Francisco officials prided themselves on their liberal tolerance, and school administrators considered themselves on the cutting edge of experiments with bilingual instruction. Faced with challenges by black, Latino, and Chinese activists, the city's public educators felt surprised and beleaguered.[12]

Not only did city and school officials disclaim any animus, but the Chinese community itself rejected the premise that all school segregation is inherently pernicious. When the local branch of the National Association for the Advancement of Colored People began to press for a busing plan in San Francisco in the late 1960s and early 1970s, Chinatown's residents fought to keep neighborhood schools intact as a way to preserve students' language and culture.[13] Angry Chinese parents staged demonstrations and even chased the school superintendent out of a meeting.[14] Freedom schools were created to serve Chinese students, who boycotted their public school assignments in droves.[15] The message seemed clear: The ethnic enclave of Chinatown did not necessarily fit a model of discrimination forged in the Jim Crow South.

As *Lau* proceeded through the courts, equal protection law was in a state of flux. Education had not been declared a fundamental right, nor had *de facto* segregation been deemed a constitutional violation. Despite these uncertainties, the plaintiffs in *Lau* had reason to be hopeful. The *Brown* decision had prompted congressional action and the rise of federal agencies devoted to civil rights enforcement. Title VI of the Civil Rights Act of 1964 adopted a broad principle of non-discrimination: "No person in the United States shall, on the ground of race, color, or national origin, be excluded from participation, be denied the benefits of, or be subjected to discrimination under any program or activity receiving Federal financial assistance."[16] The provision was not narrowly limited to state-mandated segregation but potentially covered a wide array of exclusionary practices. These practices might include the educational neglect of non-English-speakers, many of whom were non-white.

In 1968, Congress gave unprecedented visibility to the needs of English language learners by passing the Bilingual Education Act.[17] The Act did not establish a right to special assistance but instead promoted research and experimentation to develop appropriate programs.[18] During the *Lau* litigation, the Office for Civil Rights ("OCR") prepared a 1970 memorandum that extended Title VI's protections to students excluded from meaningful access to the curriculum on the basis of language—at least where language was a proxy for race, ethnicity, or national origin.[19] This memorandum later played a pivotal role in *Lau*'s resolution.

California was at the forefront of these efforts to resolve unanswered questions about *Brown*'s legacy. Efforts were underway to attack disparities in per-pupil expenditures that resulted from reliance on a local property tax system to fund public schools. In *Serrano v. Priest*, advocates argued that the disparities offended the state constitution's promise of equal protection because wealth, like race, was a suspect classification and education was a fundamental right.[20] *Lau* was filed the year before the California Supreme Court spoke to these issues. Even so, when the state's high court found that students were constitutionally entitled to an equitable system of school finance, the victory buoyed hopes that a right to language assistance might be similarly protected.[21] These hopes would be dashed just two years later when the United States Supreme Court in a 5–4 decision rejected similar arguments about inequities in school finance under federal equal protection law in *San Antonio Independent School District v. Rodriguez*.[22] Despite this setback, the plaintiffs in *Lau* would pursue a writ of *certiorari* and win a surprising, unanimous victory before the Court.

When *Lau* was filed, the plaintiffs also had reason to believe that proof of animus was not necessary to prevail on their claim of language discrimination. California courts had indicated that *de facto* as well as *de jure* segregation might trigger an equal protection violation under the state constitution.[23] In a San Francisco desegregation suit filed shortly after *Lau*, the federal district court seemed to accept this view under the United States Constitution as well.[24] Only several years after the Court's favorable decision in *Lau* would intent be clearly recognized as a prerequisite to an equal protection violation under both California and federal law.[25]

Meanwhile, San Francisco's Chinatown was undergoing changes and challenges of its own. The city had been a principal destination for Chinese immigrants since the mid- to late 1800s when they arrived to work in gold mines, labor on farms, build the transcontinental railroad, and start small businesses in the ethnic enclave called Chinatown.[26] Initially, associations from distinct regions of China were created to help newcomers. In the face of pervasive discrimination, however, regional differences became less significant than shared hardship. The associations merged to form the Chinese Six Companies, which would represent the entire community's interests.[27] In the 1950s and 1960s, after the Communists took control of mainland China, the number of immigrants coming to San Francisco increased. Chinatown's traditional leadership profited by opposing Communism and developing trade relationships with Taiwan. At the same time, the influx of immigrants offered a ready pool of cheap labor for local entrepreneurs.[28] Because the newcomers were consigned to long hours and low wages, the Great Society programs of the 1960s seemed to offer possibilities to improve conditions in

Chinatown. Yet, the community's established leaders fully expected to control the flow of federal money to fight poverty, even as they exploited the immigrant workforce.[29]

These leaders had not reckoned on a newly mobilized cadre of Asian–American youth. The Bay Area during the 1960s and 1970s was a hotbed of civil rights and anti-war activism. Asian Americans on college campuses joined protests against social injustice. Eventually, these activists began to focus on issues related to their own communities. The students successfully advocated for Asian–American studies and began to question the condition of immigrants in places like San Francisco's Chinatown. Young and idealistic, these college-educated reformers took on both the white and Chinese establishments.[30] Influenced by new voices in Chinatown, teenagers responded by protesting conditions in their high schools.[31] As the college contingent did community outreach, immigrants themselves began to organize to demand improved working conditions, expanded social services, and better schools.[32]

The struggle for leadership in Chinatown was accompanied by a surge in violence. There were rumors that the Chinese Six Companies had issued "hit contracts" to have activists assassinated.[33] At the same time, gangs were recruiting the same teenagers whom idealistic young reformers wanted to save. Guns and drugs were rife in Chinatown, and staff at non-profit community organizations faced real danger. In 1972, the Chinese community in San Francisco was rocked by the murder of Barry Fong–Torres, a former probation officer and the newly appointed director of the Youth Services Center. Reportedly left at the scene was a misspelled note that said "PIG INFOMERS DIE YONG."[34] Chinatown's thin veneer of romantic exoticism, of sightseeing and dim sum, seemed to be falling away.

Amid these difficulties, Chinatown was thrown into even greater upheaval by efforts to desegregate the public schools. The Chinese community had begun to demand programs that addressed students' linguistic and cultural needs. As a result of these efforts, the school district sought federal grant money for a Chinese bilingual program, an initiative that would later figure in the *Lau* litigation.[35] These reforms were expected to take place within Chinatown and to supplement private after-school programs that already taught students to read and write in Chinese. When faced with the prospect of busing, residents resorted to angry protests and boycotts, and the Chinese Six Companies sought to intervene in the desegregation litigation with the help of a young attorney named Quentin Kopp. Kopp would launch a long and successful political career in the city as a result of his high-profile role in the lawsuit.[36] The United States Supreme Court rebuffed efforts to exempt the Chinese from busing. In doing so, Justice William O. Douglas pointedly cited *Yick Wo v. Hopkins*, a case from the late 1800s that struck down a California law that discriminated against Chinese laundries.[37] Noting that *Brown* "was not written for blacks alone," the Court seemed to be saying that Jim Crow had come to Chinatown and so would desegregation.[38]

Although *Lau* was filed a few months before the San Francisco desegregation case, the juxtaposition of the two lawsuits posed interesting questions about equal educational opportunity. *Lau* sought assimilation through the acquisition of English as well as sensitivity to Chinese-speaking students' linguistic needs. The case said nothing about taking children out of Chinatown. At the heart of *Lau* was a deep ambiguity. Did full assimilation require both integration and special language instruction? Or could the Chinese preserve their identities in racially identifiable schools, yet be fairly included in the American dream through programs that taught them English? The uncertain relationship between racial integration and linguistic and cultural autonomy later would lead to confusion and misunderstanding. The price was the Laus' alienation from the very lawsuit that bears their name.

Finding a Voice: The Lau *Litigation*

When Mrs. Kam Wai Lau came to the Chinatown Neighborhood Legal Services office in 1970, she was not concerned with these complex questions of equity and inclusion. Like many Chinese-speaking immigrants, Mrs. Lau and her husband worked in low-wage occupations in Chinatown, struggling to pay the rent and put food on the table. Too poor to afford a lawyer, Mrs. Lau sought free legal advice after a disagreement with her landlord. Housing disputes like hers were among the bread-and-butter issues that poverty lawyers typically handled.[39] While describing her complaint through an interpreter, she mentioned that her son Kinney was having difficulty in school because his classes were conducted entirely in English. Kinney, who had come to the United States from Hong Kong at the age of five, spoke Chinese as his first language and could not follow the bulk of what his teachers were saying.[40]

Mrs. Lau's comments about her son's schooling caught the ear of Edward H. Steinman. He had some personal familiarity with language differences because his family included Russian immigrants who had spoken only Yiddish when they immigrated to North America. Even so, his parents were not particularly supportive of special assistance, given that their relatives had learned English on their own.[41] His family's doubts did not deter Steinman. With his long hair and beard, he thought of himself as an unreconstructed radical, who represented a new breed of neighborhood services lawyer. A recent graduate of Stanford Law School, Steinman had been selected as a Reginald Heber Smith Fellow, or "Reggie." The fellowship program had been created in 1967 to attract high-quality attorneys to the Office of Economic Opportunity's newly created Legal Services Program. Reggies were "to undertake activities calculated to have a broad effect on the problems of poverty instead of taking a regular caseload of routine legal problems affecting only the individual client."[42] For a Reggie like Steinman, Mrs. Lau's complaint about her son's educational neglect was a perfect opportunity to take aim at practices that entrenched poverty.

In fact, Steinman had been monitoring similar complaints from other clients in anticipation of test-case litigation.[43] Steinman thought Kinney would make an excellent lead plaintiff because of his age, his failure to receive any special assistance, and his birthright citizenship. As it turned out, Steinman had been misled by a translation error into thinking Kinney was born in the United States. This was not the only mistake that would hamper Steinman's full understanding of his clients' situation. For instance, he erroneously believed that Mrs. Lau was a widow, which he thought would make her an appealing victim.[44] Convinced that Kinney was the right child to be the public face of the lawsuit, Steinman persuaded Mrs. Lau to sue on her son's behalf.

Having enlisted a lead plaintiff, Steinman thought it imperative to generate support in the Chinese community. Fortuitously for him, a young activist named Ling-chi Wang was working informally out of the legal services office. Born in China, he had come from Hong Kong to study Semitic languages, but as a graduate student at Berkeley in the late 1960s, he got caught up in activism on campus. Once he became committed to social change, Wang devoted the rest of his life to bettering the lives of Asian Americans. Already instrumental in creating the Asian American Studies Department at Berkeley, Wang had been organizing immigrants in Chinatown to protest unfair working conditions. Fluent in Chinese and English, Wang's bilingual skills conferred some unique advantages. His Chinese gave him access to and credibility with Chinatown residents, while his English allowed him to communicate effectively with white officials. With Wang's help, Steinman recruited other parents to allow their children to join the lawsuit.[45] Like the Laus, the other named plaintiffs came from the ranks of Chinatown's working poor. The parents were garment workers, gas station attendants, maintenance workers, kitchen helpers, and dishwashers. Some were retired or unemployed. Like Mrs. Lau, most were mothers concerned about their children's future.[46]

Although many of San Francisco's students were Spanish speakers in need of special services, Steinman was certain that the lawsuit had to be "*Lau*, not *Lopez*."[47] Before *Lau* was filed, he convinced a legal services lawyer in San Francisco's heavily Latino Mission District that the case should be brought solely on behalf of Chinese-speaking students. Steinman believed that the situation facing the Chinese children was starker than that confronting Latino students based on the relative numbers who received little or no assistance. Moreover, Chinatown was perceived as a self-sufficient community, and Asian Americans had achieved notable academic success without the benefit of affirmative action. As a result, they had become the "model minority," and so a request for special assistance by Chinese-speaking students might get a more sympathetic hearing in the courts than one by Spanish-speaking clients.[48]

The District Court Proceedings: An Uphill Battle

On March 23, 1970, Steinman filed a class action on behalf of fourteen named plaintiffs in federal district court. The president and members of the San Francisco school board, the superintendent of schools, and the president and members of the San Francisco board of supervisors were named as defendants.[49] Steinman alleged that "plaintiffs and at least 2,850 other Chinese-speaking students languish in San Francisco Unified School District classrooms, unable to either understand or communicate in the English language."[50] Citing the inadequacies of the district's December 1969 language survey, Steinman estimated that the number of affected students was actually closer to 4,000.[51]

Steinman's complaint divided the students into two sub-classes: at least 1,800 who, like Kinney Kinmon Lau, received no special instruction whatsoever; and 1,050 who received some help. Of those who got special assistance, approximately half received part-time instruction in English for less than one hour per day; the other half were taught in full-time classes designed for Chinese-speaking students.[52] Even those receiving some special instruction had teachers who generally did not speak Chinese. In fact, in the Chinese Bilingual Education Program, about two-thirds of the teachers spoke only English.[53] According to the plaintiffs, the assignment of students to part-time, full-time, or no compensatory instruction in English was wholly arbitrary because the district never conducted tests to determine which students needed help.[54] As Steinman put it, "The school board showed me everything they were doing, which was nothing."[55]

Steinman saw these facts as a way to make constitutional history. Although the complaint alleged that the San Francisco school district had violated federal and state law, both constitutional and statutory, the legal analysis emphasized that education was a fundamental right under the Constitution.[56] Citing *Brown v. Board of Education* as authority, Steinman's memorandum of points and authorities asserted that: "The right to an education in this society is most fundamental and vital. Without an education, an individual is confronted with almost insurmountable barriers in seeking not only an adequate livelihood, but also self-respect."[57] Fundamental fairness required that the Chinese-speaking students' liberty interest in education be safeguarded under due process.

For the plaintiffs, education clearly stood on a par with implied rights to privacy and to travel, neither of which was expressly mentioned in the Constitution but both of which enjoyed protection under the Ninth Amendment.[58]

Steinman concluded that the constitutional mandate was unambiguous:

> There is no longer any question or doubt that the opportunity to attend a public school is of such critical importance as to warrant protection by the Constitution of the United States. Education is essential to the enjoyment of both political and economic rights in American society. Without it, individuals are not able to earn an adequate livelihood nor fulfill their public duties and responsibilities.[59]

If education qualified as a fundamental right, the school system's programs were subject to strict scrutiny. That is, they had to be necessary to promote a compelling state interest. According to Steinman, there was no plausible pedagogical reason for the neglect of Chinese-speaking children, and expense alone could not justify imposing such a grossly disproportionate burden on them.[60] Steinman went even further, asserting that the lack of assistance was so arbitrary and capricious that it could not withstand even an extremely lenient test that asked only whether the district's practices were rationally related to a legitimate state interest.[61]

Steinman insisted that under either strict scrutiny or a rational relation test, the right to education "is not satisfied by merely permitting a child to physically pass through school doors and attend classes" and "must include the right to learn English."[62] He demanded special instruction with bilingual teachers and appropriate testing to assess students' language needs.[63] In his view, these programs were cost-effective alternatives to wholly ineffectual warehousing of Chinese-speaking students.[64] To preempt any claim that the Chinese sought linguistic segregation, Steinman made clear that "English is the dominant and central language" and "[w]ithout knowledge of English, plaintiffs have no opportunity to learn."[65] An English-only program isolated the plaintiffs from their peers, and even those who received limited help were at most marginally better off because without bilingual instructors, the students simply parroted lessons in English without understanding them.[66]

Although Steinman clearly hoped for a constitutional victory, he hedged his bets by including a discrimination claim that relied on Title VI of the Civil Rights Act of 1964. As a recipient of federal funds, the school district had an affirmative duty to rectify past discrimination based on race, ethnicity, or national origin and to ensure equal opportunity in all aspects of the instructional process.[67] Because English-only classes excluded the Chinese-speaking students from full participation, Steinman argued that the school district had engaged in impermissible discrimination. These two claims—the right to an education and the right to be free of discrimination—formed the key arguments in the litigation.

Thomas M. O'Connor and Raymond D. Williamson, who were the city attorney and deputy city attorney respectively, represented the defendants. Irving G. Breyer, who served as legal adviser to the Board of Education, was of counsel on the case.[68] O'Connor and Breyer would hold their positions throughout their careers, while Williamson left to become a municipal court judge as *Lau* was pending on appeal before the Ninth Circuit. O'Connor and Williamson had worked for banks before joining the City Attorney's Office; neither had any special expertise in education law.[69] Because Breyer served as a liaison throughout the lawsuit, Williamson "never met with school board officials nor appeared before them."[70] Apart from consultations with Breyer, the deputy city attorney was largely on his own in crafting a strategy in the case. No one was "looking over his shoulder" or "proofread[ing] his briefs."[71]

In contrast to the plaintiffs' thirty-three page memorandum, the defendants offered only a fourteen-page response. When Williamson wrote the brief, he was juggling a heavy caseload. As he recalls, the City Attorney's Office had only thirty-six lawyers at the time; today, there are over 200.[72] The bulk of Williamson's work was in federal court, and even Steinman admits that the deputy city attorney was "swamped with cases brought by lawyers like me."[73] Overburdened and perhaps confident that this was an easy win for the defense, Williamson conceded a great deal of legal ground, a strategy similar to that adopted in the desegregation lawsuit filed shortly afterwards in San Francisco. There, too, "[a]lthough the board of education lodged a defense, it generally accepted the plaintiffs' arguments."[74]

The defense in *Lau* did little to dispel the stark picture of thousands of pupils being relegated to classes taught in a wholly unintelligible language. In fact, Williamson stipulated to the lack of special assistance for Chinese-speaking students.[75] Williamson recalls that he "rarely got to do any offensive tactics" like "scheduling depositions for the other side," although he would have done so if necessary.[76] Instead, once he verified the plaintiffs' factual allegations with Breyer, they were accepted as correct and the focus shifted to legal arguments. Steinman's complaint had relied on statements, surveys, and reports prepared by the school district itself, and Williamson says that he would have confirmed Kinney Kinmon Lau's placement in a class where he was "asked to learn English by the seat of his pants."[77]

On questions of law, the city conceded that the Chinese-speaking students had a right to education but denied that it was being violated.[78] School officials were "employing all means available limited only by the availability of funds, buildings and qualified personnel to provide as fine an education as possible for all pupils of this School District."[79] According to the defendants, there was no denial of a public education because:

> The same courses of instruction, books, teaching aids and facilities are offered at all of these schools and are available to plaintiffs just as they are available to other students in their same classes and schools. Furthermore, no contention has been made that the schools which plaintiffs attend are inferior to other schools in this School district.[80]

According to the defense, the Chinese-speaking students were seeking not an equal educational opportunity but "special instruction designed for a unique and uncommon . . . problem."[81]

City officials conceded that bilingual education "would provide a fine opportunity for a broad-based education for those who would take advantage of such a program," but rejected any claim that this type of program was constitutionally or statutorily mandated.[82] The school district saw itself in the vanguard of efforts to develop special programs, despite ongoing controversy about the effectiveness of different instructional methods.[83] The defendants worried that a judicial mandate would chill this experimentation by requiring the district to treat all Chinese-speaking students the same. For example, the district could be forced to close "the Chinese Bilingual Education Center which admittedly serves only a few students due to the fact that it is a recent innovation and is also a pilot project. . . ."[84] The defense concluded that the plaintiffs' demands were "properly . . . directed to the state legislature or Congress, which had already taken steps to provide funding for demonstration projects in this area."[85]

Despite these concessions, the plaintiffs were taking no chances and filed a thirty-two page reply brief. Steinman was quick to point out that the defense agreed that education was a fundamental right and that bilingual education was desirable.[86] He used language from the school district's own federal grant application to establish a Chinese Bilingual Program as evidence that current programs were inadequate:

> For [Chinese-speaking] children, the lack of English means poor performance in school. The secondary student is almost inevitably doomed to be a dropout and become another unemployable in the ghetto. The only hope of removing this cause of poverty lies in adequate education, vastly different in extent of services and in kind from what is available at present. The existing sources are woefully inadequate.[87]

According to Steinman, the district's obligations were not discharged by providing the same instruction to students with widely disparate needs and proficiencies.[88] *Brown* plainly rejected the "surface equality" of treating different students as though they were alike by striking down "separate but equal" schools.[89] After *Brown*, special programs were mandated for those with "physical, mental, and other educational handicaps. [Defendants] should not discriminate against students of Chinese ethnicity with language handicaps."[90] Despite the district's professions of good faith, Steinman accused administrators of dragging their feet by pursuing only token amounts of federal money for bilingual programs.[91] In light of school officials' resistance, Steinman sought a preliminary injunction to protect his clients from further irreparable harm.[92]

Although some of Steinman's arguments were novel, he was confident that he could win *Lau* in the generally liberal Northern District of California. His optimism faded when Judge Lloyd H. Burke was assigned to the case. Both Steinman and Wang recall that Burke made his career as a United States Attorney who prosecuted Chinese immigrants facing deportation as part of the war on Communism waged in the 1950s. Wang believes that the federal judgeship was a reward for these efforts.[93] Steinman considered Judge Burke "a monstrosity," explaining that at that time in the Northern District, "there were six certified liberals, one moderate, one conservative, and one far right-winger. I got the far right-winger."[94]

Judge Burke is not alive to defend himself against these charges, but his partisanship does come through in the hearings. At the outset, he made plain his skepticism that Chinese-speaking students had any right to special language assistance, even if they had a right to education. The judge did admit that "by this time, as a broad proposition, it can be accepted that an education of some kind must be made available probably as a constitutional right; although just exactly how you torture yourself into that conclusion, I don't know."[95] Yet, he wondered aloud "whether or not, conceding a right to an education, you have an additional right to a specific kind of education which must be designed to meet the special needs of a particular individual or a particular group of individuals."[96] The court cautioned the plaintiffs against "equating need with right."[97] In Judge Burke's view, any such right could not be limited to the Chinese-speaking but would have to be extended to all children who needed linguistic assistance. Despite Steinman's assurance that the large number of affected Chinese students made their situation distinguishable, Judge Burke believed that the right would accrue to individuals, not groups.[98]

The judge suggested that a sweeping judicial mandate was inappropriate because there was no evidence that the school district was responsible for the Chinese-speaking students' dilemma. As he explained, "their need is something which is unrelated to their participation in School Board-controlled activities"[99] because, there was "no willful attempt to discriminate.... We have what amounts to the product, almost, of a birth defect, if you use the term in its broad sense, that their birth was under such circumstances so as to deprive them of the opportunity to become susceptible of instruction in the English language."[100] For Judge Burke, the plaintiffs' lack of proficiency in English meant that "they aren't students at all; they are just people, they are just bodies in the classroom...."[101] As unfortunate as their situation might be, it "certainly was no fault of the members of the School Board or the Board of Supervisors."[102] In short, under this fault-based approach, Chinese-speaking students could be warehoused without the benefit of an education, but no legal violation arose unless the district had somehow caused their lack of English proficiency.

Without evidence of past discrimination, Judge Burke believed that the plaintiffs' claims should be directed to legislators and school officials, not the courts. Steinman might have sound reasons for wanting reform because "remedial instruction in English is both wise and perhaps essential, and ... the long-range benefits are far out of proportion to the expense which might be entailed in providing such instructions."[103] Even so, good policy was not the same as a judicially enforceable entitlement: "I just seriously question the right of this Court to select—by reason of pleadings brought before it, of course—a group of students, find a need and then follow that with a finding of a right which will be met by the Court in the form of preliminary injunction. I just find the whole theory of such litigation to be a Pandora's box."[104]

Of course, it was precisely this theory of litigation that lay at the heart of Steinman's mission as a Reggie. Steinman believed that judicial activism was necessary because the students and their parents were a discrete and insular minority for whom the political process was ineffective.[105] Judge Burke was "inclined to take issue with [the] conclusion that the Chinese-speaking people are wholly apolitical."[106] In response, Steinman touched on the changing composition of Chinatown and the influx of politically disenfranchised immigrants:

> That was not my point. My point was that those who have not been able to learn to speak English have not been able to make the inroads. Obviously the Chinese are influential in San Francisco. But they are not represented on either the Board of Supervisors or the Board of Education. Many of them have reached positions of prominence; but the fact remains that for ... those who cannot fathom the language on which this system operates, be it political, judicial or otherwise, they are the ones who are not getting attention.[107]

In contrast to Steinman, Williamson remembers Judge Burke as an experienced jurist who was "courteous" and "reasonable," especially given that the overburdened attorney was so busy that "he barely had time to button his shirt" before coming to court.[108] For the defense, Judge Burke was a "very nice man, not one that peppered you with questions."[109] The hearing on the motion for a preliminary injunction bears out this aspect of Williamson's account. Having grilled Steinman extensively, Judge Burke turned to the deputy city attorney to see if "there [is] any argument that you think you can make that I haven't already made for you."[110] After complimenting the court for having "done admirably for the position that we were taking,"[111] Williamson noted that bilingual education was not necessarily the only effective method of instruction.[112] Cutting off this line of argument, Judge Burke interjected that "I don't think that Mr. Steinman has directed his comments to the bilingual aspect of the case to any substantial degree."[113] Sensing victory in the offing, Williamson readily agreed.[114] Steinman then asked to submit documents on the benefits of bilingual programs, but he acknowledged that "[m]y concern is initially with those students that get nothing at all."[115]

Although Steinman wanted further fact-finding, Judge Burke declined to hold a trial on the merits. Instead, his ruling was solely on the pleadings, the hearing on the motion for a preliminary injunction, and some additional documents filed afterwards.[116] Steinman and Williamson disagree about whether the judge's approach was unusual. Williamson recalls that the district court regularly disposed of civil rights cases this way because "none of them really involved a dispute about the facts. It was basically a legal issue so there was no need for a jury trial."[117] Steinman, however, believes that the summary disposition was further evidence of Judge Burke's bias against the plaintiffs.[118] In either case, the judge was obviously eager to kick the case upstairs to the Ninth Circuit. As he remarked to the parties, "it doesn't really matter what happens here, because ... you have got a three-Judge court on appeal."[119]

With the district court litigation coming to an abrupt conclusion, Steinman asked for an additional day to submit exhibits. As he later recalled, Judge Burke was suspicious of the request and agreed to the extension so that Steinman would have just enough rope to hang himself.[120] In fact, Steinman knew that federal officials were about to release a memorandum that for the first time "defined [the OCR's] policies with regard to possible discrimination against national origin minorities."[121] Under the memorandum, the Civil Rights Act of 1964 mandated "that where inability to speak and understand the English language excludes national origin minority group children from effectively participating in a school district's educational program, the district must take positive steps to correct the language deficiency in order to open the program to these students."[122]

The OCR's support for the *Lau* plaintiffs at first might seem puzzling. After all, President Richard Nixon was a Republican, and his administration would seem to have little sympathy for a case that sought to expand *Brown*'s legacy. Ling-chi Wang believes that the stark picture in *Lau* embarrassed federal officials, forcing them to issue the 1970 memorandum.[123] Steinman has a different theory. He thinks that the Nixon administration was receptive because it saw the growing number of Latinos in the United States as likely to become a Republican constituency. As a result, the federal government supported bilingual ballots as well as bilingual education, including the push to teach Chinese-speaking students English in *Lau*.[124] Whatever the reason, the United States proved an invaluable ally in the case.

Even so, Steinman's last-minute machinations did not sway the district court. A brief order dismissing the plaintiffs' case was published shortly after the OCR memorandum was submitted. Although the prevailing party usually assumed the task of drafting the order, Steinman says that he volunteered to do it because of Williamson's heavy caseload. Steinman saw crafting the order as a way to limit the impact of the adverse ruling on appeal and to include the Title VI claim.[125] Williamson, on the other hand, does not recall ever having allowed the other side, and certainly not an attorney from Neighborhood Legal Services, to prepare an order in a case in which the city prevailed. Had Williamson been busy, he says he would have asked for help from another attorney in his office, not from an adversary.[126]

The order must speak for itself. It held that "the plaintiffs have rights to an education and to equal educational opportunities, under the Constitution of the United States, the Constitution of the State of California, and laws enacted by the California State Legislature."[127] Even so, "[the Chinese-speaking students'] special needs, however acute, do not accord them special rights above those granted other students."[128] For that reason, "[a]lthough this Court and both parties recognize that a bilingual approach to educating Chinese-speaking students is both a desirable and effective method, though not the only one, plaintiffs have no right to a bilingual education."[129] Once the order was issued, Steinman promptly filed a motion for leave to proceed in forma pauperis because his clients could not afford the cost of an appeal.[130] That same day, the judge granted the request, and the case was on its way to the Ninth Circuit.[131]

The Ninth Circuit: More Bad News

If Steinman thought that Judge Burke had been an unfortunate draw at the district court level, the lawyer felt he had another round of bad luck before the Ninth Circuit. Chief Judge Richard Chambers assigned the case to himself and Judge Ozell Trask as well as Judge Irving Hill, a federal district court judge sitting by designation. Steinman remembers that Chief Judge Chambers and Judge Trask were the only two members of the court from Arizona, a state that had done almost nothing about bilingual issues. As a result, Steinman worried that the judges would be indifferent or resistant to his clients' claims. He could not believe that it was mere coincidence that out of seventeen judges, he got two likely to be so unreceptive to his case. After facing Burke's hostility, Steinman recalls thinking to himself "here we go again."[132]

Though disappointed with the panel, Steinman persevered with his appeal. The arguments on each side remained largely the same. The defense did add a brief reference to federalism concerns,[133] while Steinman included a section that drew on the OCR memorandum. Citing the agency's language, the plaintiffs contended that: "For non-English-speaking Chinese youngsters in San Francisco, no affirmative steps have been taken to 'rectify [their] language deficiency' or to provide them 'effective participation in the educational program offered by the school district.' "[134] The United States, acting as an amicus curiae or friend of the court, filed a brief asserting that the memorandum was "entitled to be given great weight by the courts"[135] and clearly required the district to take affirmative steps to address the Chinese-speaking students' language needs.[136] The United States was careful, however, to remain agnostic as to remedies, which "will no doubt depend on a variety of considerations, including financial and other resources available to the school district, the efficacy of various alternative compensatory language training programs, and the feasibility of implementing them."[137] The United States suggested a remand so that the Office of Education could work cooperatively with the school district to formulate an appropriate plan.[138]

The Center for Law and Education submitted an amicus brief as well. Located at Harvard University, the Center was funded by the Office of Economic Opportunity to provide research that would bolster test-case litigation brought by legal services lawyers like Steinman.[139] The Center had developed expertise on linguistic barriers to education because "[o]ur recent sampling of neighborhood legal service offices indicates that over 20 such offices are presently actively involved in litigation concerning the educational rights of non-English speaking poor children."[140] The Center's brief cited extensive research to show that despite disagreements about optimal teaching methods, "it is significant that no support could be found in the literature for simply allowing non-English speaking youngsters to sit, uncomprehending in the classroom without making intensive efforts to communicate with them."[141] Indeed, the Center concluded that "[t]his Court needs no experts to recognize that plaintiffs do not receive the same education as other students."[142]

Interestingly, neither the plaintiffs, the United States, nor the Center spent much time analyzing the history of anti-Chinese sentiment in California. In asserting that the San Francisco school district was guilty of national origin discrimination, the amicus brief for the United States cited previous official segregation of Chinese children under a state law that was not repealed until 1947.[143] The Center for Law and Education addressed this history of discrimination at greater length. Yet, even there, the discussion accounted for only a few pages in a forty-page brief with multiple appendices.[144] At the district court level, the failure to offer proof of animus might have been an artifact of Judge Burke's decision to dispense with a trial. At the Ninth Circuit, though, it became clear that Steinman and his allies were making a strategic choice. Steinman did not believe that he could show intentional discrimination because English-language instruction had been a longstanding and universal requirement that was not targeted at a particular group.[145] Instead, he wanted the court to declare education a fundamental right for all children, while the United States wanted exclusionary effects alone to trigger a violation under Title VI. Both theories sought to expand *Brown*'s mandate by going beyond a focus on discriminatory intent.

In elaborating on *Brown*, Steinman and the Center painted a picture of the law in dramatic transition, while the United States treated the OCR memorandum as a natural outgrowth of existing federal enforcement responsibilities under Title VI.[146] The portrait of law in flux rested heavily on the California Supreme Court's school finance decision in *Serrano v. Priest* in 1971. Handed down after Judge Burke's decision in *Lau, Serrano* recognized education as a fundamental right under the state constitution and ordered the equalization of per-pupil school expenditures.[147] To show that this approach was steadily gaining momentum, the Center pointed out that several other state and federal courts already had followed the precedent.[148] In addition, the Center noted that courts were moving to protect linguistic minority students by expanding the reach of anti-discrimination doctrine and at times had incorporated bilingual programs into desegregation orders.[149] With a busing case pending in San Francisco, the Center wanted to assure the Ninth Circuit that "the proceedings in *United States v. Texas* [a desegregation case that included bilingual education as part of the remedy] help make it abundantly clear that compensatory language training for non-English speaking children is the very antithesis of segregation."[150]

Despite the plaintiffs' reformist fervor, the court of appeals took over two years to hold oral argument in *Lau* due to a backlogged docket. In a 2–1 decision affirming the district court, Judge Trask and Chief Judge Chambers held that *Brown*'s mandate was narrowly limited to undoing officially imposed segregation, the very type of discrimination that Steinman and the amici had spent little time addressing.[151] As the majority noted, the plaintiffs had "alleged no such past de jure segregation" nor was there any "showing that [their] lingual deficiencies are at all related to any such past discrimination."[152] Without evidence of animus, the Ninth Circuit insisted that there was no basis for interpreting *Brown* as imposing "an affirmative duty to provide [a student] special assistance to overcome his disabilities, whatever the origin of those disabilities may be."[153] Indeed, the majority found such a "reading of *Brown* ... extreme, and one which we cannot accept."[154]

The school system's decision to focus on English as the language of instruction was "intimately and properly related to the educational and socializing purposes for which public schools were established. This is an English-speaking nation. Knowledge of English is required to become a naturalized United States citizen" and to participate in civic activities.[155] The court could not intervene simply because special assistance for Chinese-speaking students was "commendable and socially desirable."[156] Instead, the court of appeals concluded that:

> Every student brings to the starting line of his educational career different advantages and disadvantages caused in part by social, economic and cultural background, created and continued completely apart from any contribution by the school system. That some of these may be impediments which can be overcome does not amount to a "denial" by the Board of educational opportunities within the meaning of the Fourteenth Amendment should the Board fail to give them special attention, this even though they are characteristic of a particular ethnic group.[157]

In short, the majority found that "[t]he classification claimed invidious is not the result of laws enacted by the State presently or historically, but the result of deficiencies created by the appellants themselves in failing to learn the English language."[158] As for Title VI and the OCR memorandum, the Ninth Circuit disposed of them in a brief sentence: "Our determination of the merits of the [equal protection] claims ... likewise dispose of the claims made under the Civil Rights Act."[159]

Steinman and his clients could take some comfort from the dissent. According to Judge Hill, the majority's wooden interpretation of equal protection was "too narrow"[160] and ignored the realities facing the students:

> The plaintiffs in this case are small, Chinese-speaking children who sue on their own behalf and on behalf of others similarly situated. The majority describe the plight of these children as being "the result of deficiencies created by the appellants themselves in failing to learn the English language." To ascribe some fault to a grade

> school child because of his 'failing to learn the English language' seems both callous and inaccurate. If anyone can be blamed for the language deficiencies of those children, it is their parents and not the children themselves. Even if the parents can be faulted (and in many cases they cannot, since they themselves are newly arrived in a strange land and in their struggle for survival may have had neither the time nor opportunity to study any English), it is one of the keystones of our culture and our law that the sins of the fathers are not to be visited upon the children.[161]

After the ruling, the Ninth Circuit considered granting en banc review, that is, an opportunity for all the judges to hear the case. The petition was rejected over a vigorous dissent by Judges Shirley Hufstedtler and Walter Ely. They argued that the school district could not be characterized as a passive bystander because officials compelled students to attend school and then placed them in classes that "insulate[] the children from their classmates as effectively as any physical bulwarks. Indeed, these children are more isolated from equal educational opportunity than were those physically segregated blacks in *Brown*; these children cannot communicate at all with their classmates or teachers."[162]

When the petition for en banc review was denied, Judge Trask wrote a separate concurrence to defend the disposition of the case. In doing so, he relied heavily on the United States Supreme Court's recent decision in *San Antonio Independent School District v. Rodriguez*.[163] In *Rodriguez*, the Court refused to adopt *Serrano*'s approach to equal protection under the federal Constitution. The Justices rejected a fundamental right to equal educational opportunity but left open the possibility of a right to be free of an absolute deprivation of education.[164] Judge Trask observed that the Chinese-speaking students' need for special help did not mean that they were receiving no educational benefit in English-speaking classrooms. As a result, the plaintiffs did not suffer an absolute deprivation.[165] As Judge Trask explained, equal protection did not require "absolute equality or precisely equal advantages," in part because of the "infinite variables affecting the educational process."[166] A student's native language was simply one of those variables.

The Supreme Court Decides: A Surprising Victory

The Court's decision in *Rodriguez* was very much on Steinman's mind as he petitioned the United States Supreme Court for *certiorari* in *Lau*.[167] Aware that the Court's recent ruling did not bode well for his clients, Steinman nevertheless pursued Supreme Court review because he was confident that an adverse ruling could be limited to the situation of Chinese-speaking students in San Francisco. Attorneys representing Spanish speakers could readily distinguish the case away.[168] Steinman expected the outcome to be close and framed his arguments to appeal to two swing votes, Justices Potter Stewart and Lewis Powell. The majority opinion in *Rodriguez* left little room for hope, but Steinman believed that if the Justices agreed to hear *Lau*, they would use the facts to clarify what amounted to an absolute deprivation of education.[169] For that reason, the *certiorari* petition focused on children like Kinney Kinmon Lau who received no assistance of any kind.[170] To link the deprivation to protected First Amendment liberty interests, Steinman contended that a lack of English proficiency would later interfere with the students' ability to vote and participate in civic affairs.[171]

Rodriguez did not present similar obstacles to Steinman's discrimination claim. The plaintiffs in the Texas school finance case had challenged differential treatment on the basis of wealth. In *Lau*, the Chinese-speaking students were claiming mistreatment on the basis of national origin as well as race and ethnicity.[172] These traits were clearly suspect and triggered vigorous constitutional protection. Unfortunately, in the lower courts, the plaintiffs had not offered evidence of intentional discrimination, and it was not clear that differential treatment based on language was tantamount to racial, ethnic, or national origin discrimination. A caste system rooted in immutable traits was pernicious because individuals could not escape a status ascribed at birth. By contrast, a person who did not speak English could learn the language and so was not consigned to a perpetually inferior position. As a result, the Court might conclude that language was not a suspect classification and so would apply a lenient rational relation test. In that event, Steinman had two lines of response. First, the school district's decision to provide no special assistance was arbitrary and capricious.[173] Alternatively, the school board's inaction had the effect of excluding students based on race, ethnicity, or national origin and therefore violated Title VI, as interpreted in OCR's memorandum.[174]

As Steinman struggled with the implications of *Rodriguez*, the defendants made the most of it. According to San Francisco officials, Steinman previously had demanded perfect equality for his Chinese-speaking clients.[175] Now, the defendants complained, he was changing his theory at the eleventh hour by suddenly focusing exclusively on students who received no special assistance.[176] The defense took Steinman to task for introducing novel legal arguments to evade *Rodriguez*'s fatal effect:

> Petitioners now state that this case involves the First Amendment and certain HEW [i.e., OCR] guidelines. To the best of Respondents' knowledge, such authority has not been cited before, either to the District Court or to the Court of Appeals. This has not before been a First Amendment case [about the right to vote and participate in the political process].[177]

After criticizing Steinman for offering new theories on appeal, the defendants themselves elaborated significantly on federalism issues previously mentioned only in passing. San Francisco officials had good reason to worry that the United States government was undermining local control of the schools. After all, as a Reggie, Steinman was paid by the federal government to bring the case. Throughout the appeal, the Center for Law and Education received federal support to generate expert evidence to bolster Steinman's claims. Finally, the United States was directly involved in producing the OCR memorandum and using it to strengthen the plaintiffs' Title VI argument. As Steinman put it, "the case should been *United States v. Nichols*."[178]

Citing the importance of state autonomy and local discretion, the defense insisted that "the Fourteenth Amendment was not enacted with the intention of destroying the federal system. Nor do the courts view the Fourteenth Amendment as a tool which enables the courts under the auspices of the federal constitution to control the administration of government by the states."[179] To respect the limits of a federalist system, the Court had to base an equal protection violation on intentional discrimination. The plaintiffs here had not shown any animus.[180] For the same reason, Title VI required proof of intent, and any interpretive memorandum that went further was invalid because "the director of the Office for Civil Rights exceeded the authority vested in him by Congress. . . ."[181] The defendants cautioned that the Fourteenth Amendment was not a license for Congress or the courts "to impose on the states their view of what constitutes wise economic or social policy."[182]

Given the high stakes, Steinman enlisted the support of influential allies before the Court.[183] He felt that *Rodriguez* constrained him to focus on the question of whether his clients were suffering a total deprivation of education. He hoped that the amicus briefs would amplify the Justices' perspective on the case by providing historical background, a picture of the abysmal state of instruction for English language learners, and an overview of possible remedies.[184] Steinman recruited ten amici, three of whom wrote in support of the petition for *certiorari* and all of whom filed briefs on the merits. By contrast, no amici wrote in support of the school board's position.[185] The two amici who had participated before the Ninth Circuit once again filed briefs. The United States had a significant stake in the case because the court of appeals, in a brief aside, had summarily dismissed the OCR's interpretation of Title VI.[186] As Assistant Attorney General J. Stanley Pottinger observed, the district court "did not in fact ... give reasonable consideration to Title VI."[187] Directly countering the defendants' federalism arguments, the United States argued that Congress and the OCR could go beyond the scope of equal protection law because their actions were based on the Spending Clause. When the federal government provided grants to state and local agencies, such as the San Francisco school district, Title VI and the OCR memorandum could "place reasonable restrictions upon the use of federal funds by the recipients."[188]

The Center for Law and Education joined with two other amici to contend that minimum access to education was a fundamental right. The Center for Law and Education again offered expert evidence that "if a child cannot understand the language of instruction he is doomed to educational failure."[189] This time, though, the amicus brief included a footnote provided by Ling-chi Wang that was written entirely in Chinese characters.[190] Steinman recalls that he worried about whether the footnote would be deemed improper, and for similar reasons, chose not to begin his oral argument in Chinese.[191] Despite Steinman's apprehensions, the footnote generated lively discussion among the Justices about just what the characters meant.[192] The Court did not get a translation, but according to Roger L. Rice, formerly an attorney for the Center, the sentence was aptly chosen for the *Lau* case: "When playing the lute, one must consider the listener, when shooting an arrow, one must aim at the target."[193]

Another academic think tank, the Childhood and Government Project at the University of California at Berkeley's law school, took up the cause that minimum educational access was a fundamental right. Stephen D. Sugarman, the Project's lead counsel, had been a principal architect of the *Serrano v. Priest* litigation and was interested in limiting the damaging effects of *Rodriguez*.[194] The setback in *Rodriguez* had been by the slimmest of margins, and like Steinman, the Project's lawyers expected the *Lau* decision to be close. As in *Rodriguez*, they directed their arguments to Justice Stewart, whom they expected to be the crucial swing vote.[195] The Project's brief contended that San Francisco's treatment of Chinese-speaking children amounted to a total deprivation of education that stigmatized them and eventually would prevent them from exercising their political rights.[196] The brief expressly rejected the notion that linguistic assimilation would happen naturally without any special assistance. This attitude reflected "a kind of smugness ... we find frightening. Given a sufficient number of generations most people will be assimilated; the rights of the current generation should not be sacrificed in the name of that eventuality."[197]

Like the academic think tanks, the National Education Association ("NEA") and the California Teachers Association ("CTA") jointly filed amicus briefs supporting plaintiffs' argument that without special assistance, linguistic minority students would be unable to participate in political life and exercise their rights as citizens.[198] In their first brief in support of *certiorari*, the NEA and CTA largely ignored Title VI issues, but the brief on the merits devoted more time to these arguments. This shift likely reflected a growing sense that the Court's decision would turn on statutory grounds.[199]

In contrast to researchers and professional educators, racial and ethnic organizations filed briefs that focused on questions of discrimination, rather than the right to education. The brief by the Chinese Six Companies and other organizations in Chinatown was a rare instance of cooperation with the new breed of activists who threatened the established power structure. Once *certiorari* was granted, traditional leaders undoubtedly realized that they could no longer be bystanders to a lawsuit with potentially momentous consequences for the Chinese community.[200] Already rebuffed by the Supreme Court in the desegregation litigation,[201] the Chinese Six Companies in particular could not lose face yet again. The Chinatown establishment did not want to be upstaged in a legal challenge related to language, culture, and education, particularly one brought by low-income residents who could not even afford a lawyer.

Reflecting the Chinese community's long struggle for citizenship, the Chinese Six Companies' amicus brief emphasized that the school district's neglect left both immigrant and native-born youth at risk of succumbing to poverty and delinquency.[202] These concerns were echoed in a brief filed by the San Francisco Lawyers' Committee for Urban Affairs. Though not a racial or ethnic organization, the Committee used its brief to chronicle a "dismal history of official discrimination" against the Chinese in California.[203] The American Jewish Congress along with two other Jewish organizations filed an amicus brief that reviewed discrimination against a range of racial and ethnic groups to bolster the plaintiffs' equal protection claim.[204] Steinman singled out the Chinese and Jewish organizations' briefs as particularly compelling in conveying to the Court the hardships and discrimination faced by newcomers and dispelling the myth that all Jews and Asians had achieved the American dream.[205]

Although the lawsuit began as *Lau* not *Lopez*, Steinman did not believe that the fiction that Chinese-speaking students were the sole group affected could be sustained once the Supreme Court granted *certiorari*.[206] Latino organizations filed amicus briefs to remind the Court that Spanish-speaking students represented far and away the largest group harmed by this form of educational neglect. The Mexican American Legal Defense and Educational Fund drew parallels between Spanish-speaking and Chinese-speaking children. Mexican Americans had been subject to longstanding discrimination, and the number of Spanish speakers was growing due to immigration.[207] As with the Chinese, English-language immersion was linked to high dropout rates and low achievement among Mexican–American students.[208] The Puerto Rican Legal Defense and Education Fund ("PRLDEF") described litigation on behalf of Spanish-speaking children in New York City public schools that mirrored the claims in *Lau*.[209] A victory in *Lau* would assist PRLDEF in negotiating a consent decree of its own.[210] Finally, attorneys from California Rural Legal Assistance filed an amicus brief that largely dispensed with legal arguments and instead told the stories of Spanish-speaking children who received no special assistance in California public schools.[211] Efrain Tostado's story sounded very much like Kinney Kinmon Lau's. Without bilingual teachers, aides, or materials, "Efrain is unable to follow what goes on in the classes. He cannot understand what the teachers or the other students say during the class. The teachers do not give him assignments or homework. They do not call on him. They do not help him."[212] As a result, "Efrain's schooling amounts to no more than his physical presence in the classroom."[213]

During oral argument, the Court gave some clues to how it would decide *Lau*. On the plaintiffs' side, Steinman had split his time with the United States. He believed that an attorney from the Nixon administration would enjoy special credibility with the four Justices who were Nixon appointees.[214] Steinman was to address equal protection issues, while Assistant Attorney General Pottinger would deal with questions related to Title VI and the OCR memorandum. Yet, the Justices used their questions to focus on the statutory claims. The Court wanted Steinman's assurance that the district court had an opportunity to consider the OCR memorandum.[215] With this assurance, the Justices then grilled Pottinger about the memorandum's scope.[216] When City Attorney O'Connor spoke for the defendants, the Court pressed him about the OCR's authority to issue the memorandum and the school district's compliance with it.[217] Justice Harry Blackmun posed a question to the defense that should have sent a chill through any good litigator: "Mr. O'Connor, if you lose this case, what will happen ...?"[218] The Court wanted to know whether the city was likely to give up federal grants to avoid providing special language instruction under Title VI.[219]

Although some attorneys and scholars had expected the decision in *Lau* to be a close and difficult one, the Court handed down a unanimous opinion just six weeks after oral argument. Steinman had hoped for a constitutional victory, but the short opinion by Justice William O. Douglas held only that the school district had violated Title VI by effectively denying Chinese-speaking students access to the curriculum. In overturning the lower courts, the Court made clear that it was relying on the OCR memorandum and that no specific remedy was mandated.[220] In retrospect, Steinman believes that the Justices spoke with one voice because they were still reeling from intense criticism of the *Rodriguez* decision and wanted to show that they had not abandoned *Brown*'s legacy of equal educational opportunity.[221]

As a result, Justices expressed their reservations about *Lau* in separate concurrences rather than in dissent. Justice Potter Stewart,

Chief Justice Warren Burger, and Justice Harry Blackmun wrote separately to note that the OCR guidelines deserved deference and that without them, Title VI would not necessarily be violated by a school district's "laissez-faire attitude."[222] In another concurrence, Justice Blackmun and Chief Justice Burger insisted that "numbers are at the heart of this case" and that "when, in another case, we are concerned with a very few youngsters, or with just a single child who speaks only German or Polish or Spanish or any language other than English, I would not regard today's decision ... as conclusive...."[223] Even with these caveats, the Chinese-speaking students had scored a decisive victory, though not on a grand constitutional scale.

On Remand: Silent No More

Despite Judge Burke's lack of sympathy for the students' position, he had to oversee the contentious process of crafting a remedy on remand. Neither the Justices nor the OCR had provided concrete guidance on designing special programs, an omission that Ling-chi Wang likens to the Court's use of "all deliberate speed" to implement desegregation after *Brown*.[224] Steinman was convinced that Judge Burke would fashion the narrowest possible relief, while Wang worried that the superintendent and school board members would be unreceptive to real reform. Because both Steinman and Wang preferred comprehensive programs that relied on some native-language instruction, the two pursued a negotiated settlement process that would place substantial power in the hands of community representatives. The process would require the district to come up with a proposal in consultation with educational experts, civil rights authorities, and the affected constituencies.[225]

In early February 1974, about two weeks after the Court's decision, the President of the Board of Education, Eugene Hopp, welcomed community input and asked school district staff to conduct "a study of the problem along with an inventory of the present program and then develop a program to present to court."[226] Hopp promised to hold a public hearing on the master plan's preparation. Shortly afterwards, Chinese for Affirmative Action ("CAA"), a local civil rights organization in which Wang was actively involved, wrote a letter proposing a Citizens Task Force on Bilingual Education that would help to craft the master plan. One month later, with no response from the school district, CAA again sent a letter and enlisted support from other local organizations as well as state and federal officials.[227]

With pressure mounting, the district's Director of Bilingual Education, Raymond Del Portillo, called a meeting with invited community participants on April 15, 1974. At the meeting, school personnel presented a preliminary draft of the master plan that would be finalized and filed with the court in mid-May.[228] The plan proposed to build on existing programs and would rely to a substantial degree on intensive English instruction.[229] Del Portillo asked community members to join a special advisory committee that would endorse the plan. Dissatisfied by the inadequate weight given to native-language instruction, they declined the invitation and protested their role as nothing but a rubber stamp.[230]

The next day, a coalition of community organizations held a press conference to call once again for a Citizens Task Force. Because the leadership threatened to sue for contempt of court, local media covered the event extensively.[231] Less than a week later, Judge Burke notified the defendants that he would hold a hearing in mid-June on the master plan. Steinman believes that the judge wanted an expeditious resolution, so that the increasingly politicized planning process would not lead to far-ranging remedies.[232] Whatever the district court's reasons, the United States successfully intervened to avoid an impending crisis in *Lau* in mid-May. Federal officials offered to provide guidance on how to comply with Title VI, thus relieving Judge Burke of responsibility for setting minimum standards.[233] Three days before the United States' intervention, the school board agreed to establish a Citizens Task Force to assist in drafting the master plan. The board also authorized funds for technical assistance from the Center for Applied Linguistics.[234] Judge Burke then cancelled the June hearing to permit the parties to collaborate on an appropriate remedy.[235]

Comprised of a cross-section of the multiracial, multicultural, and multilingual San Francisco population, the Citizens Task Force struggled to find a workable structure.[236] Members eventually prepared a plan that was submitted to school officials in December 1974. This plan called for bilingual-bicultural education whenever feasible and proposed bilingual schools to serve each major language group in San Francisco. For smaller groups, the plan recommended bilingual support.[237] The Task Force then turned to school personnel and the Center for Applied Linguistics to flesh out details related to implementation.

Although school administrators were initially cooperative, they eventually distanced themselves from the recommendations. The relationship between community representatives and the administration grew increasingly strained.[238] In a February 15, 1975 letter to the superintendent, the Task Force wrote: "Our goodwill and strict compliance with Board resolutions apparently was naivete on our part; our good faith effort was rewarded with insult and rejection. The Superintendent clearly abused our trust. . . . "[239] Under pressure from the United States, the school board moved one month later to adopt a resolution that made some modifications to the Task Force recommendations but left the fundamental commitment to bilingual-bicultural education intact.[240] The consent decree was finally filed in late October 1975.[241] By the time programs were in place, Kinney Kinmon Lau was getting too old to participate in them. Eventually, his family moved out of Chinatown.[242]

Lau's *Legacy: Echoes of An Earlier Time*

As the struggle over the master plan dragged on in San Francisco, *Lau* was influencing federal policy. Participants in the case played an important role in ensuring that the Court's mandate was enforced by Congress and federal agencies. For example, Pottinger and Wang testified at committee hearings, and Wang consulted with civil rights officials in developing guidelines for enforcement.[243] These efforts succeeded in ensuring that *Lau* would have an immediate impact. Shortly after the Supreme Court's decision, Congress codified the holding in the Equal Educational Opportunities Act (EEOA) of 1974. Promoted by the Nixon Administration as a package of alternatives to busing, the EEOA declared that districts could not adopt practices and policies that had the effect of excluding children from the curriculum on the basis of language, where language served as a proxy for race, ethnicity, or national origin. Like *Lau* itself, the EEOA mandated "appropriate action" without specifying particular remedies.[244]

To facilitate compliance, Congress allocated increased funding for school districts to develop programs under the Bilingual Education Act.[245] Cognizant of the difficulties that districts like San Francisco were facing, OCR issued the *Lau* Guidelines in 1975.[246] The Guidelines established a clear preference for use of a child's native language, and intensive English instruction was to be employed only for secondary students with limited time to master a second language.[247] OCR began to enforce the standards through compliance investigations.[248] That same year, the United States Office of Education established nine *Lau* Centers, mainly at universities, to provide technical assistance to school districts seeking to comply with the Supreme Court's mandate.[249]

Meanwhile, states followed the federal example and adopted their own bilingual education acts.[250] Wang helped to draft California's Chacon–Moscone Bilingual–Bicultural Act in 1976.[251] This Act mandated native-language instruction whenever feasible for linguistic minority students.[252] The state's Department of Education developed guidelines, and the legislature allocated funds to support new programs. Of particular importance were efforts to increase the number of bilingual teachers and the availability of bilingual materials. The California bilingual education bureaucracy expanded under the new regime.[253]

In the mid- to late 1970s, official support for bilingual programs reached its apex. *Lau* had seemingly transformed the policy landscape. This newfound commitment to bilingual education soon came under attack, however, on both pedagogical and ideological grounds. Some researchers reported that there was no empirical evidence to demonstrate the superiority of native-language instruction.[254] Other critics worried that bilingual programs derogated the role of English as America's common language.[255] These objections eventually led to retrenchment in bilingual education policy at both the federal and state levels. In 1979, a school district challenged the *Lau* Guidelines because they were enforced as rigidly as rules but had not been subject to notice and comment rulemaking.[256] When the newly formed Department of Education held hearings on the Guidelines in 1980, the ensuing political free-for-all forced officials to dispense with formalizing new rules. Instead, the Department reverted to the 1970 OCR memorandum.[257] The hearings that spelled disaster for the Guidelines happened during Secretary Shirley Hufstedtler's tenure, and her successor Terrel Bell officially revoked the provisions.[258] As a Ninth Circuit judge, Hufstedtler had dissented vigorously from the denial of en banc review in *Lau*, sharply criticizing the view that Chinese-speaking students were seeking special, rather than equal, treatment. Despite her commitment to language assistance, she could not withstand the intense political controversy that engulfed bilingual programs only five years after the Guidelines were put in place.

With the Guidelines' demise, federal enforcement efforts waned, and bilingual education advocates had to look primarily to the courts to protect the entitlement recognized in *Lau*.[259] Just as this shift was taking place, the Justices began to confine the decision to its facts. In 1978, the Court concluded that under both Title VI and the Equal Protection Clause, plaintiffs had to show invidious intent to establish a violation.[260] *Lau* technically remained good law only because the Justices left open the possibility that rules and regulations like the OCR memorandum could prevent discrimination by prohibiting practices with exclusionary effects.[261] Then, in 2001, the Court held that there was no private right of action under these rules and regulations. As a result, only federal agencies could enforce the OCR memorandum. To bring a claim under Title VI, concerned parents and students had to establish discriminatory intent just as they would under equal protection law.[262] The EEOA, already a cornerstone of language rights litigation, took on even greater importance after this retrenchment under Title VI. In codifying *Lau*, Congress had expressly adopted an effects test and included a private right of action.[263]

Even so, the EEOA has some limitations of its own. School districts can avoid liability if their instructional programs are based on a sound educational theory, are implemented in a reasonable way, and are monitored appropriately to assess their effectiveness. This standard allows teachers and administrators considerable latitude in developing programs.[264] In 2006, state defendants in *United States v. Texas* asserted immunity under the Eleventh Amendment to insulate themselves from lawsuits brought by parents and students under the EEOA. Echoing the defendants' arguments before the Supreme Court in *Lau*, Texas officials cited the importance of federalism and insisted that Congress must clearly abrogate their immunity under the statute.[265] Other critics of the EEOA have argued that because it was anti-busing legislation, Congress did not develop evidence of a clear pattern of discrimination against linguistic minority students to justify the statutory protections.[266] Steinman points out that the *Lau* case itself could be part of such a record,[267] but ironically the litigation's authoritative force is weakened precisely because the plaintiffs did not choose to emphasize a history of animus. To date, attacks on the EEOA have not succeeded,[268] but the verdict is still out on whether the Court will invoke federalism concerns to limit the statute's reach.[269]

In California, policymakers similarly retreated from their earlier commitment to native-language instruction. The 1980 Bilingual Education Improvement and Reform Act emphasized the central goal of learning English and increased state support for intensive English instruction.[270] In 1986, voters passed an initiative declaring English the official language of California.[271] Then, in June 1987, the state's bilingual education act lapsed under a sunset law. The governor vetoed a bill that would have renewed the act, and the legislature could not muster the votes to override his decision. As a result, California was left without any state statutory provisions for bilingual programs.[272] To fill the gap, the California Department of Education adopted guidelines that preserved some preference for native-language instruction.[273] The guidelines put the Department at loggerheads with its more conservative counterpart, the California Board of Education. The Board began to grant waivers to districts that did not wish to comply with the Department's bilingual education requirements. Eventually, some parents and students went to court to challenge the waivers' validity.[274]

All of this in-fighting was rendered moot, however, when a wealthy entrepreneur, Ron Unz, put an "English for the Children" initiative on the state ballot. The measure required public schools to use intensive English instruction with some limited exceptions.[275] Voters approved the proposal by a margin of 61% to 39%.[276] In spite of litigation challenging the initiative's legality, it remains good law.[277] The impact on achievement in California schools is disputed, but the policy sends a clear signal that native-language instruction has fallen from grace.[278]

Amid this turmoil on the federal and state levels, the *Lau* consent decree has brought relative stability to bilingual programs in San Francisco. Controversy and conflict have given way to routine procedures. As a consequence of the litigation, the district hired bilingual teachers and administrators with core operating funds rather than temporary grant money.[279] After the lawyers went on to other cases, these professionals oversaw implementation and monitored compliance. Each year, school personnel are expected to provide the district court with statistics on program evaluation, reclassification of children in bilingual programs, personnel, management, staff development, and community participation.[280] The consent decree has sheltered the district from changes under federal and state law, most notably the Unz initiative.[281] In 2006, Judge William Alsup, who had taken over the case from Judge Burke, suggested terminating the decree because it had been reduced to largely perfunctory reporting. Judge Alsup already had ruled that San Francisco's desegregation consent decree would draw to a close at the end of 2005.[282] Concerned advocates lobbied to keep the bilingual education order in place, and Steinman joined forces with the school district and the OCR to file an affidavit opposing termination. Ron Unz already had expressed an interest in challenging the San Francisco decree, and supporters of the master plan did not want to lose *Lau*'s protection from the statewide mandate to use intensive English instruction.[283]

Conclusion

Lau leaves a mixed legacy for those who began the case with high hopes. The Laus themselves became bitter and estranged from the lawsuit and their lawyer, Edward Steinman. Mrs. Lau wanted a better education for her son, but the delays in litigation meant that Kinney received relatively little direct benefit from the Supreme Court victory. After the family moved out of Chinatown, he struggled with English all through high school and mastered the language only when he attended San Francisco City College. Nor could he read Chinese, a skill that might have been useful to him as a software engineer when new markets opened up in Asia.[284]

After years of silence, Kinney finally reflected openly on the case in 2002. Looking back, he could not say whether he was an unwitting hero or a pawn: "My mother told me that having equal opportunity was important, but I think this movement was brought on by other groups and they just needed a face, and that's where we came in."[285] Interestingly, Steinman agrees with this assessment, saying that he did strategically pick Kinney to be the lead plaintiff. Even so, Steinman does not believe that this fact accounts for the Laus' subsequent anger and alienation. Instead, he attributes their change of heart to a mistaken belief that the bilingual education lawsuit was part of the desegregation effort in San Francisco. Steinman is convinced that the Laus did not want to be associated with busing.[286] Whatever the reason, neither Mrs. Lau nor her son has laid claim to the case. As Kinney sums it up, "I don't know how many people the whole thing helped. If I knew, I would think it was great, and that we stood for something, that we did something to help people."[287] Yet, he adds: "I don't know if bilingual education is better—I'm still trying to work it out."[288]

As for Steinman, he is proud of his role in the lawsuit and continues to lecture about it widely. He is now a law professor at Santa Clara University, a position he has held since he represented the Laus before the Ninth Circuit. Although Steinman did not achieve a grand constitutional victory, he has come to appreciate the virtues of prevailing under Title VI.[289] The lawsuit ensured special attention to the needs of English language learners. Even if debates over instructional methods persist, doing nothing is not an option. Had he prevailed on constitutional grounds, Steinman is not sure that bilingual education would look different today because "courts can't overcome th[e] essentially political reality" of school systems.[290]

In fact, the experience in California suggests that declaring a fundamental right to education would not have accomplished dramatically more than Title VI, the OCR memorandum, and the EEOA have. The California Supreme Court did recognize a right to education.[291] In the years after *Lau*, as state policy shifted away from native-language instruction, advocates primarily turned to federal law, rather than the right to education under state law, to challenge the retrenchment.[292] It is not clear that invoking a fundamental right could have succeeded in attacking changes in California's bilingual education law. Courts still would have deferred to school officials in fashioning a remedy. Disagreements about the optimal method of instruction remain unresolved, and even today, the only consensus seems to be that a complete denial of assistance is inappropriate. Because no one has proposed total neglect, every reformer can at least plausibly claim to be promoting students' interests and thus advancing their right to education. Without a way to mandate a particular remedy, the realization of a fundamental right to education seems as bedeviled by underlying pedagogical uncertainty as federal anti-discrimination law.

The Chinatown community wanted respect for its linguistic and cultural autonomy. Although *Lau* was a victory of sorts, residents like Mrs. Lau remained preoccupied with the desegregation mandate. In the ensuing years, the Chinese continued to challenge race-based school assignments, which limited their children's ability to attend neighborhood schools. The desegregation plan also forced Chinese applicants to meet tougher standards than any other racial or ethnic group to gain admission to San Francisco's premier high school.[293] Eventually, the Chinese community's efforts culminated in success: The district ceased to consider race in making pupil assignments in 1999.[294] Despite efforts to use socioeconomic status to preserve some degree of integration, public schools in San Francisco have grown increasingly identifiable by race. As a result, officials once again have begun to discuss ways to factor race into assignments, even though California has banned racial preferences in state decisionmaking.[295]

Meanwhile, at a national level, *Lau*'s legacy has to a substantial degree been claimed by advocates for Spanish-speaking students. Most of the subsequent litigation under Title VI and the EEOA has involved the very Latino children whom Steinman chose not to include as plaintiffs.[296] In a few cases, Asian-language groups have been used to thwart Spanish speakers' demands for native-language instruction. Just across the bay from San Francisco, the Berkeley Unified School District gathered statistics on small numbers of students who spoke Vietnamese, Cantonese, Laotian, Mandarin, and Tagalog, among others, and who enjoyed academic success in English as a Second Language classes. The statistics were used to refute Spanish-speaking plaintiffs' arguments that their poor school performance was due to a lack of bilingual teachers and materials.[297] The lawsuit once again cast Asian students in the role of model minority, and Latinos received a bitter reminder that the Supreme Court decided *Lau*, not *Lopez*.

The San Francisco school district appears to have achieved the peace, at least with respect to special language instruction, that it wanted. The case has not gone away, but the controversy largely has. The bilingual bureaucracy quietly generates its reports, and the consent decree in *Lau* has enabled the district to escape much of the turbulent politics surrounding language rights in the rest of the state. In this regard, *Lau* stands in marked contrast to San Francisco's desegregation case, which still sparks intense debate over the meaning of educational equity and how best to achieve it. Though most have accepted the regime instituted under *Lau*, Ling-chi Wang, who retired in 2006 after a long and distinguished career in Berkeley's Asian American Studies Department, still hopes for more. He would like to see a program of bilingual-bicultural education for every child in the city's public schools.[298]

All in all, the compromise in *Lau*—a federal right with state and local discretion to craft a remedy—has proven remarkably durable. If the case has not fulfilled everyone's hopes, it also has not wholly succumbed to civil rights reversals. Much like Kinney Kinmon Lau himself, the lawsuit beat the odds—getting to the Supreme Court, generating unanimity, and enduring for over thirty years as a benchmark of basic decency for students who simply want the chance to learn.

Endnotes

1. 414 U.S. 563 (1974).

2. For an account of some of these controversies, see David L. Kirp, *Just Schools: The Idea of Racial Equality in American Education* 82–116 (paperback ed. 1982).

3. 347 U.S. 483 (1954).

4. 42 U.S.C. § 2000d.

5. 347 U.S. at 493–94.

6. *See* Jack M. Balkin, *Rewriting* Brown*: A Guide to the Opinions*, in *What* Brown v. Board of Education *Should Have Said* 56–59 (Jack M. Balkin ed. 2001).

7. Tristan W. Fleming, *Education on Equal Terms: Bilingual Education Must Be Mandated in the Public Schools for Hispanic LEP Students*, 17 Geo. Immigr. L. J. 325, 338–42 (2003); Susan H. Bitensky, *Legal Theory: Foundations for a Right to Education Under the U.S. Constitution: A Beginning to the End of the National Education Crisis*, 86 Nw. U. L. Rev. 550, 574–642 (1992); Stephen E. Gottlieb, *Compelling Governmental Interests: An Essential But Unanalyzed Term in Constitutional Adjudication*, 68 B.U. L. Rev. 917, 926–32 (1988).

8. *See* David A. Strauss, *Discriminatory Intent and the Taming of* Brown, 56 U. Chi. L. Rev. 935, 946–50 (1989).

9. *See, e.g.*, Act of Apr. 6, 1850, ch. 99, § 14, 1850 Cal. Stat. 229, 230 (prohibiting Chinese from testifying against whites as interpreted in *People v. Hall*, 4 Cal. 399 (1854)); Foreign Miners' License Tax, Act of Apr. 13, 1850, ch. 97, §§ 1, 5, 1850 Cal. Stat. 221, 221–22; Act of May 4, 1852, ch. 37, 1852 Cal. Stat. 84, *repealed and superseded by* Act of Mar. 30, 1853, ch. 44, 1853 Cal. Stat. 62 (officially repealed by Act of Apr. 26, 1939, ch. 93, 1939 Cal. Stat. 1067, 1215); Chinese Police Tax, Act of Apr. 26, 1852, ch. 339, 1862 Cal. Stat. 462 (officially repealed by Act of May 16, 1939, ch. 154, 1939 Cal. Stat. 1274, 1376) (levying capitation tax on Chinese and held to be an unconstitutional invasion of federal control over immigration in *Lin Sing v. Washburn*, 20 Cal. 534 (1862)); Act of Apr. 28, 186, ch. 329, § 8, 1860 Cal. Stat. 321, *amended by* Act of Mar. 24, 1866, ch. 342, 1866 Cal. Stat. 398; Act of Apr. 14, 1870, ch. 556, 1869–70 Cal. Stat. 839; Act of Apr. 7, 1880, ch. 80, 1880 Cal. Stat. 142–43, 152; Act of Mar. 12, 1885, ch. 97, 1885 Cal. Stat. 99–100. The legislature subsequently amended the law to include Japanese children, Charles Wollenberg, *All Deliberate Speed: Segregation and Exclusion in California Schools, 1855–1975* at 72 (1976). Local ordinances in San Francisco also were directed against the Chinese. *See, e.g.*, Ho Ah Kow v. Nunan, 12 F. Cas. 252 (C.C.D. Cal. 1879) (pigtail ordinance); Yick Wo v. Hopkins, 118 U.S. 356 (1886) (laundry ordinance). For an excellent overview of these efforts, see Charles McClain, *In Search of Equality: The Chinese Struggle Against Discrimination in Nineteenth Century America* 9–76, 79–144 (1994).

10. William Poy Lee, *The Eighth Promise: An American Son's Tribute to His Toisanese Mother* 73 (2007).

11. Complaint for Injunction and Declaratory Relief (Civil Rights), Lau v. Nichols, Civ. No. C–70 627 LHB 11–12 (Mar. 25, 1970).

12. Kirp, *supra* note 2, at 83–84, 97–99; Response to Order to Show Cause; Memorandum in Opposition to Motion for Preliminary Injunction; Motion to Dismiss, Lau v. Nichols, Civ. No. C–70 627 LHB 6 (Apr. 27, 1970).

13. Daryl Lembke, *S.F. Integration Plan Evokes Chinese Wrath*, L.A. Times, June 27, 1971, at A5; Narda Z. Trout, *Worry in Chinatown: "No One Understands,"* L.A. Times, Sept. 14, 1971, at A3.

14. *Chinese Parents Protest Busing*, S.F. Chron., May 27, 1971, at 10; Donovan Bess, *S.F. School Busing Plans Are Assailed*, S.F. Chron., June 3, 1971, at 2; Harry Johanesen,

Chinese Protest School Bus Plans, S.F. Chron., June 6, 1971, at 3; *S. F. Anti-Busing Group Forms*, S.F. Chron., Aug. 18, 1971; Daryl Lembke, *School Bussing Plan Starts Monday in S.F.*, L.A. Times, Sept. 12, 1971; *S.F. School Chief Run Out of Chinatown by Angry Parents*, L.A. Times, Feb. 8, 1972, at A3.

15. Philip A. Lum, *The Creation and Demise of San Francisco Chinatown Freedom Schools: One Response to Desegregation*, 5 Amerasia J. 57, 60–67 (1978); *Boycott in S.F. Heavy; Some Buses Roll Empty*, L.A. Times, Sept. 13, 1971, at 3; Daryl Lembke, *School Attendance in S.F. Slashed by Boycott of Bussing*, L.A. Times, Sept. 14, 1971, at A1; Julie Smith, *Chinese Schools Set to Open*, S.F. Chron., Sept. 14, 1971, at 4; *Boycott in S.F.*, L.A. Times, Sept. 19, 1971, at O4; Mitchell Thomas, *Chinatown "Freedom School,"* S.F. Chron., Sept. 21, 1971, at 2; Daryl Lembke, *"Freedom School" Problems Multiply, Chinatown Divided*, L.A. Times, Oct. 17, 1971; Rose Pak, *A Day of Fury in Chinatown*, S.F. Chron., Feb. 8, 1972, at 1; Rose Pak, *Chinese "Freedom Schools" to Go On*, S.F. Chron., Aug. 31, 1972, at 1.

16. 42 U.S.C. § 2000d.

17. Bilingual Education Act of 1968, Pub. L. No. 90–247, 81 Stat. 783, 816–19 (codified as amended at 20 U.S.C. §§ 3420, 3423d, 3473, 6002, 6825, 6842, 6931, 6951 (2006)).

18. Guadalupe San Miguel, *Contested Policy: The Rise and Fall of Federal Bilingual Education in the United States 1960–2001* at 14–17 (2004); Rachel F. Moran, *The Politics of Discretion: Federal Intervention in Bilingual Education*, 76 Cal. L. Rev. 1249, 1259–65 (1988).

19. Identification of Discrimination and Denial of Services on the Basis of National Origin, 35 Fed. Reg. 11,595 (1970).

20. Serrano v. Priest, 5 Cal.3d 584 (1971).

21. *See* Brief Amicus Curiae Center for Law and Education in Support of the Appellants at 24–26, Lau v. Nichols, 483 F.2d 791 (9th Cir. 1973) (No. 26155) (1972); Letter to Mr. William B. Luck, Clerk, United States Court of Appeals for the Ninth Circuit, from Edward H. Steinman, Attorney for Appellants, dated June 26, 1972 (filed June 27, 1972).

22. 411 U.S. 1 (1973).

23. Jackson v. Pasadena City Sch. Dist., 59 Cal.2d 876 (1963).

24. Kirp, *supra* note 2, at 96–97 (noting that the district court judge cut off fact finding so that "[t]he merits of the charge that San Francisco had deliberately segregated its schools consequently were not thoroughly examined").

25. The California Supreme Court's decision that the state constitution prohibited both de facto and de jure segregation, Crawford v. Board of Educ., 17 Cal.3d 280 (1976), was overturned by a popular initiative that mandated that the state would go no further than federal law in combating racially identifiable schools. The United States Supreme Court upheld the initiative in Crawford v. Board of Educ., 458 U.S. 527 (1982).

26. Ronald Takaki, *Strangers From a Different Shore* 79–94 (paperback ed. 1990); Iris Chang, *The Chinese in America: A Narrative History* 29–77 (2003).

27. Chang, *supra* note 26, at 78–80; Takaki, *supra* note 26, at 119: L. Ling-chi Wang, Chinatown in Transition 3 (Mar. 7, 1969) (manuscript on file with author).

28. Chang, *supra* note 26, at 262–68; Takaki, supra note 26, at 415; Wang, *supra* note 27, at 6.

29. Chang, *supra* note 26, at 269–70; Wang, *supra* note 27, at 5–8.

30. Peter Kwong and Dusanka Miscevic, *Chinese America: The Untold Story of America's Oldest New Community* 267–93 (2005); Chang, *supra* note 26, at 270–74; Wang, *supra* note 27, at 10–11.

31. *See, e.g.*, Lee, *supra* note 10, at 174–82 (describing efforts by a Chinese-American student body president to protest conditions at Galileo High School in the late 1960s); *see also* L. Ling-chi Wang, *Major Education Problems Facing the Chinese Community* (1972), *reprinted in Chinese American Voices: From the Gold Rush to the Present* 312, 317–18 (Judy Yung et al. eds. 2006) (describing problems at Galileo during this time).

32. *See, e.g.*, Alex Hing, *The Need for a United Asian-American Front, 1970*, *reprinted in The Columbia Documentary History of the Asian American Experience* 371–73 (Franklin Odo ed. 2002).

33. Chang, *supra* note 26, at 272; Lee, *supra* note 10, at 172–73; Interview with Ling-chi Wang, Professor Emeritus of Asian American Studies, University of California at Berkeley, in Berkeley, California (Nov. 15, 2006).

34. Ben Fong-Torres, *The Rice Room: Growing Up Chinese-American—From Number Two Son to Rock 'n' Roll* 209 (paperback ed. 1995).

35. Interview with Ling-chi Wang, *supra* note 33.

36. *Chinese Lose Fight to Stay School Bussing*, L.A. Times, Aug. 30, 1971, at 3; *High Court Bars Stay in S.F. Busing*, S.F. Chron., Aug. 31, 1971, at 1; Interview with Ling-chi Wang, *supra* note 33.

37. Guey Heung Lee v. Johnson, 404 U.S. 1215, 1216 (1971) (Douglas, J.) (citing Yick Wo v. Hopkins, 118 U.S. 356 (1886)).

38. *Id.*

39. Earl Johnson, *Justice and Reform: The Formative Years of the OEO Legal Services Program* 9–10 (1974).

40. Garance Burke, *Ambivalent in Any Language Subject of Landmark Bilingual Case Uncertain of Role*, Boston Globe, July 22, 2002, at A1.

41. *Id.*; Interview with Edward H. Steinman, Professor, University of Santa Clara School of Law, in San Francisco, California (Oct. 10, 2006).

42. Johnson, *supra* note 39, at 179–80; *see also* Lawrence J. Fox, *Legal Services and the Organized Bar: A Reminiscence and a Renewed Call for Cooperation*, 17 Yale L. & Pol'y Rev. 305, 305–07 (1998). At one point, Reggies made up nearly 25% of professional legal services staff. Alan W. Houseman, *Political Lessons: Legal Services for the Poor—A Commentary*, 83 Geo. L.J. 1669, 1683 (1995). The program ended in 1983. Reginald Heber Smith Fellows Alumni News, Equal Justice Update, *available at* http://www.equaljustice update.org/reggiealumninews.htm (last visited Nov. 27, 2006).

43. Cynthia Gorney, *The Suit That Started It All; The Lau Case: When Learning in a Native Tongue Becomes a Right*, Wash. Post, July 7, 1985, at A12.

44. Burke, *supra* note 40, at Al; Interview with Edward H. Steinman, *supra* note 41.

45. Interview with Ling-chi Wang, *supra* note 33; Interview with Edward H. Steinman, *supra* note 41.

46. Motion for Leave to Proceed on Appeal In Forma Pauperis, Lau v. Nichols, Civ. No. C–70 627 LHB 2 (June 22, 1970); Affidavit in Support of Motion to Proceed on Appeal In Forma Pauperis, Lau v. Nichols, Civ. No. C–70 627 LHB 2 (June 19, 1970) (Mrs. Fung Yee Lee); Affidavit in Support of Motion to Proceed on Appeal In Forma Pauperis, Lau v. Nichols, Civ. No. C–70 627 LHB 2 (June 19, 1970) (Mrs. Kam Wai Lau); Affidavit in Support of Motion to Proceed on Appeal In Forma Pauperis, Lau v. Nichols, Civ. No. C–70 627 LHB 2 (June 19, 1970) (Yue Bew Leong); Affidavit in Support of Motion to Proceed on Appeal In Forma Pauperis, Lau v. Nichols, Civ. No. C–70 627 LHB 2 (June 19, 1970) (Mrs. Choi Kam Tom); Affidavit in Support of Motion to Proceed on Appeal In Forma Pauperis, Lau v. Nichols, Civ. No. C–70 627 LHB 2 (June 19, 1970) (Mrs. Julia Sun); Affidavit in Support of Motion to Proceed on Appeal In Forma Pauperis, Lau v. Nichols, Civ. No. C–70

627 LHB 2 (June 19, 1970) (Kun Cheung); Affidavit in Support of Motion to Proceed on Appeal In Forma Pauperis, Lau v. Nichols, Civ. No. C–70 627 LHB 2 (June 19, 1970) (Mrs. Moy Hor Chiu); Affidavit in Support of Motion to Proceed on Appeal In Forma Pauperis, Lau v. Nichols, Civ. No. C–70 627 LHB 2 (June 19, 1970) (Henry Lee).

47. Burke, *supra* note 40, at Al; Interview with Edward H. Steinman, *supra* note 41.

48. Interview with Edward H. Steinman, *supra* note 41.

49. Complaint for Injunction and Declaratory Relief (Civil Rights), *supra* note 11, at 7.

50. *Id.* at 2 (emphasis in original).

51. *Id.* at 11; Memorandum of Points and Authorities in Support of Motion for Preliminary Injunction, Lau v. Nichols, Civ. No.C–70 627 LHB 4 (Apr. 8, 1970).

52. Complaint for Injunction and Declaratory Relief (Civil Rights), *supra* note 11, at 10–11.

53. *Id.* at 11; Memorandum of Points and Authorities in Support of Motion for Preliminary Injunction, *supra* note 51, at 3; Affidavit of Edward H. Steinman, Lau v. Nichols, Civ. No. C–70 627 LHB 1–2 (May 12, 1970).

54. Memorandum of Points and Authorities in Support of Motion for Preliminary Injunction, *supra* note 51, at 3.

55. Interview with Edward H. Steinman, *supra* note 41.

56. Complaint for Injunction and Declaratory Relief, *supra* note 11, at 3–4.

57. Memorandum of Points and Authorities in Support of Motion for Preliminary Injunction, *supra* note 51, at 2.

58. *Id.* at 7–8.

59. *Id.* at 6.

60. *Id.* at 21–23.

61. *Id.* at 20–21.

62. *Id.* at 12.

63. Complaint for Injunction and Declaratory Relief (Civil Rights), *supra* note 11, at 23–24; Order to Show Cause, Lau v. Nichols, Civ. No. C–70 627 LHB 2–3 (Apr. 8, 1970).

64. Memorandum of Points and Authorities in Support of Motion for Preliminary Injunction, *supra* note 51, at 23–24.

65. *Id.*

66. *Id.* at 15–18.

67. *Id.* at 25–26.

68. Breyer's older son, Stephen, would go on to become a United States Supreme Court Justice, while his younger son, Charles, would serve on the federal district court for the Northern District of California. David Lauter, *Breyer's Public Life Offers Few Clues to Private Beliefs; Though Ambitious, Nominee Has Tried to Have Practical Impact. But Leanings Are Unclear*, L.A. Times, May 31, 1994, at A1, col. 5; Mark Simon, *Judge's Handling of Pot Ruling Seen as "Classic Chuck Breyer," S.F. Federal Jurist Known for Exercising His Own Discretion*, S.F. Chron., June 5, 2003, at A14. When Raymond Williamson's father served as a state legislator, he created the position that Breyer occupied. Interview with Raymond Williamson, Member, National Roster of Arbitrators and Mediators, American Arbitration Association, in San Francisco, California (Oct. 10, 2006).

69. J.L. Pimsleur, *Former City Attorney Thomas M. O'Connor*, S.F. Chron., July 29, 1998, at A20; Hon. Raymond D. Williamson, Jr., Action Dispute Resolution Services, *available at* http://www.adrservices.org/neutrals/neutrals_williamson.htm (last visited Nov.

27, 2006). Williamson subsequently became a superior court judge and later retired from the bench to do arbitration and mediation. Interview with Raymond Williamson, *supra* note 68.

70. Interview with Raymond Williamson, *supra* note 68; Telephone Interview with Raymond Williamson, Member, National Roster of Arbitrators and Mediators, American Arbitration Association (Dec. 15, 2006).

71. Interview with Raymond Williamson, *supra* note 68; Telephone Interview with Raymond Williamson, *supra* note 70.

72. Interview with Raymond Williamson, *supra* note 68.

73. Interview with Edward H. Steinman, *supra* note 41.

74. Kirp, *supra* note 2, at 95.

75. Stipulation, Lau v. Nichols, Civ. No. C–70 627 LHB 1–2 (May 12, 1970).

76. Interview with Raymond Williamson, *supra* note 68; Telephone Interview with Raymond Williamson, *supra* note 70.

77. Interview with Raymond Williamson, *supra* note 68; Plaintiffs' Reply Brief to Memorandum of Defendants Opposing Motion for Preliminary Injunction, Lau v. Nichols, Civ. No. C–70 627 LHB 1 (May 8,1970) (citing San Francisco Unified School District, Pilot Program: Chinese Bilingual (May 5, 1969)).

78. Response to Order to Show Cause; Memorandum in Opposition to Motion for Preliminary Injunction; Motion to Dismiss, Lau v. Nichols, Civ. No. C–70 627 LHB 3 (Apr. 27, 1970).

79. *Id.* at 4.

80. *Id.* at 5.

81. *Id.*

82. *Id.* at 6.

83. *Id.* at 7–8. The school district did submit an affidavit from its Acting Director of Research and Program Evaluation, Yvon Johnson, stating that there was disagreement about the most effective method of teaching children with limited English proficiency. Like the defendants' legal memorandum, the affidavit did not cite to any educational experts. Affidavit in Opposition to Motion for Preliminary Injunction and in Support of Motion to Dismiss, Civ. No. C–70 627 LHB 1–2 (May 4, 1970).

84. Response to Order to Show Cause; Memorandum in Opposition to Motion for Preliminary Injunction; Motion to Dismiss, *supra* note 78, at 9.

85. *Id.* at 13–14. In a supplemental filing, the defense argued that the members of the board of supervisors were not proper parties to the case because they had no authority to alter the school district's budget to support bilingual programs. Supplemental Memorandum in Opposition to Motion for Preliminary Injunction and in Support of Motion to Dismiss, Lau v. Nichols, Civ. No. C–70 627 LHB 1–3 (May 5, 1970).

86. Plaintiffs' Reply Brief to Memorandum of Defendants Opposing Motion for Preliminary Injunction, *supra* note 77, at 7–8.

87. *Id.* at 1 (emphasis added in reply brief) (citing San Francisco Unified School District, *supra* note 77, at 6A).

88. *Id.* at 2–4.

89. *Id.* at 3–5.

90. *Id.* at 6.

91. *Id.* at 18–20.

92. *Id.* at 21–32.

93. Interview with Ling-chi Wang, *supra* note 33; Interview with Edward H. Steinman, *supra* note 41. There are some reported cases related to deportation proceedings against Chinese in which Lloyd H. Burke represented the federal government as the United States Attorney. Cheng Lee King v. Carnahan, 253 F.2d 893 (9th Cir. 1958); Leng May Ma v. Barber, 241 F.2d 85 (9th Cir. 1957); Chiu But Hao v. Barber, 222 F.2d 821 (9th Cir. 1955); Ly Shew v. Dulles, 219 F.2d 413 (9th Cir. 1954); Jew Sing v. Barber, 215 F.2d 906 (9th Cir. 1954); Cheng Fu Sheng v. Barber, 144 F. Supp. 913 (N.D. Cal. 1956); United States v. Chow Bing Kew, 141 F.Supp. 253 (N.D. Cal. 1956). For a description of the deportation of Chinese Americans during the 1950s, see Kwong and Miscevic, *supra* note 30, at 220–26; Xiaojian Zhao, *The Immigration and Naturalization Service's Campaign Against Chinese Americans During the Cold War*, in *Major Problems in Asian American History* 350–56 (Lon Kurashige and Alice Yang Murray eds. 2003).

94. Interview with Edward H. Steinman, *supra* note 41.

95. Reporter's Transcript, Lau v. Nichols, Civ. No. C–70 627 LHB 5 (May 12, 1970).

96. *Id.* at 6.

97. *Id.* at 7.

98. *Id.* at 15–17.

99. *Id.*

100. *Id.* at 31.

101. *Id.* at 18.

102. *Id.*

103. *Id.* at 28.

104. *Id.* at 28–29.

105. *Id.* at 57–58.

106. *Id.* at 58.

107. *Id.* at 58–59.

108. Interview with Raymond Williamson, *supra* note 68; Telephone Interview with Raymond Williamson, *supra* note 70.

109. Interview with Raymond Williamson, *supra* note 68.

110. Reporter's Transcript, *supra* note 95, at 37.

111. *Id.*

112. *Id.* at 37–38.

113. *Id.* at 38.

114. *Id.*; Telephone Interview with Raymond Williamson, *supra* note 70.

115. Reporter's Transcript, *supra* note 95, at 40.

116. Answer to Complaint for Injunction and Declaratory Relief, Lau v. Nichols, Civ. No C–70 627 LHB (May 26, 1970); Answers to Interrogatories, Lau v. Nichols, Civ. No. C–70 627 LHB (May 26, 1970); Non–Jury Hearing on Defendants' Motion to Dismiss and Plaintiffs' Motion for Preliminary Injunction, Etc., Lau v. Nichols, Civ. No. C–70 627 LHB (May 26, 1970) (noting exhibits introduced at the May 12, 1970 hearing and those added on May 26, 1970).

117. Interview with Raymond Williamson, *supra* note 68.

118. Interview with Edward H. Steinman, *supra* note 41.

119. Reporter's Transcript, *supra* note 95, at 34.

120. School District's Memorandum of Points and Authorities Regarding Reasonable Attorney's Fee Award, Lau v. Nichols, Civ. No. C–70–627 LHB 6–7 n.4 (Dec. 13, 1978).

121. HEW News, HEW–Z7 at 1 (May 25, 1970); School District's Memorandum of Points and Authorities Regarding Reasonable Attorney's Fee Award, *supra* note 120, at 6–7 n.4.

122. HEW News, *supra* note 121, at 2.

123. Interview with Ling-chi Wang, *supra* note 33.

124. Interview with Edward H. Steinman, *supra* note 41. Steinman's theory is borne out by materials unearthed during the Watergate hearings. Presidential Campaign Activities of 1972, Senate Resolution 60, Hearings Before the Senate Select Comm. on Presidential Campaign Activities, 93d Cong., 1st Sess. 5532–5698 (1973); 8617–72 (1974). In some cases, Assistant Attorney General Stanley Pottinger is mentioned in the documents, *id.* at 5538, 5554, 5558, 5691, and on one occasion, a memorandum dated March 3, 1972 refers to arranging a meeting with Pottinger "regarding a black-brown problem we're having in San Francisco," *Id.* at 5538. In addition, "The Plan to Capture the Spanish Speaking Vote" prepared by The Campaign to Re–Elect the President describes the 1970 OCR memorandum and increased federal funding for bilingual education as highlights of Nixon's record. *Id.* at 8634–35.

125. Interview with Edward H. Steinman, *supra* note 41.

126. Telephone Interview with Raymond Williamson, *supra* note 70.

127. Order, Lau v. Nichols, Civ. No. C–70 627 LHB at 2–3 (May 26, 1970).

128. *Id.* at 3.

129. *Id.*

130. Motion for Leave to Proceed on Appeal in Forma Pauperis, Lau v. Nichols, Civ. No. C–70 627 LHB 2 (June 22, 1970).

131. Order Granting Leave to Appeal in Forma Pauperis, Lau v. Nichols, Civ. No. C–70 627 LHB 2 (June 22, 1970).

132. Interview with Edward H. Steinman, *supra* note 41.

133. Brief of Appellees at 17–18, Lau v. Nichols, 483 F.2d 791 (9th Cir. 1973) (No. 26155) (1970).

134. Appellants' Opening Brief at 43, Lau v. Nichols, 483 F.2d 791 (9th Cir. 1973) (No. 26155) (1970).

135. Memorandum for the United States as Amicus Curiae at 22, Lau v. Nichols, 483 F.2d 791 (9th Cir. 1973) (No. 26155) (1971).

136. *Id.* at 13–17.

137. *Id.* at 24.

138. *Id.* at 24–25.

139. Johnson, *supra* note 39, at 180–82.

140. Brief Amicus Curiae Center for Law and Education in Support of the Appellants at 3, Lau v. Nichols, 483 F.2d 791 (9th Cir. 1973) (No. 26155) (1972).

141. *Id.* at 15.

142. *Id.* at 9.

143. Memorandum for the United States as Amicus Curiae, *supra* note 135, at 16 n. 7.

144. Brief Amicus Curiae Center for Law and Education in Support of the Appellants, *supra* note 140, at 29–31.

145. Interview with Edward H. Steinman, *supra* note 41.

146. *Compare* Appellant's Opening Brief, *supra* note 134, at 21–22, 25–26; Brief Amicus Curiae Center for Law and Education in Support of the Appellants, *supra* note 140, at 23–25, *with* Memorandum for the United States as Amicus Curiae, *supra* note 135, at 20–25. Steinman reinforced a picture of legal transformation by filing periodic letters with the court of appeals that were tantamount to litigation updates. Letter to William B. Luck, Clerk, United States Court of Appeals for the Ninth Circuit, from Edward H. Steinman, Attorney for Appellants, in Lau v. Nichols, No. 26,155 (filed June 27, 1972); Letter to William B. Luck, Clerk, United States Court of Appeals for the Ninth Circuit, from Edward H. Steinman, Attorney for Appellants, in Lau v. Nichols, No. 26,155 (filed December 4, 1972).

147. See *supra* notes 20–21 and accompanying text.

148. Brief Amicus Curiae Center for Law and Education in Support of the Appellants, *supra* note 140, at 24–26.

149. *Id.* at 20, 36–37.

150. *Id.* at 37 (footnote omitted) (citing United States v. Texas, 330 F. Supp. 235 (E.D. Tex. 1971), *modified in part and affirmed*, 447 F.2d 441 (5th Cir. 1971)). For an account of the tensions between desegregation and bilingual education that were emerging at the federal level, see Gary Orfield, *Must We Bus?: Segregated Schools and National Policy* 302–04 (1978).

151. Lau v. Nichols, 483 F.2d 791, 794–95 (9th Cir. 1973).

152. *Id.* at 797.

153. *Id.* at 794. The Ninth Circuit noted that the Supreme Court would be deciding *Keyes v. School District No. 1*, a lawsuit involving desegregation in the Denver Public Schools, the following term. Denver had never adopted an official policy of segregation, but the school board had allegedly manipulated the drawing of attendance boundary lines, the use of mobile classrooms, and the construction of new facilities to perpetuate racially identifiable schools. One question was whether these practices were sufficient to establish discriminatory intent in the absence of explicitly racial student assignments. *Id.* at 795 n.8.

154. *Id.* at 794. For that reason, the majority distinguished the desegregation litigation in *United States v. Texas*, which was remedying past intentional wrongdoing by school officials. *Id.* at 797.

155. *Id.* at 798.

156. *Id.*

157. *Id.* at 797.

158. *Id.* at 799.

159. *Id.* at 795.

160. *Id.* at 800.

161. *Id.* at 805.

162. *Id.* at 806.

163. 411 U.S. 1 (1973).

164. *Id.* at 36–37.

165. 483 F.2d at 808.

166. *Id.*

167. Interview with Edward H. Steinman, *supra* note 41. *See also* Linda Mathews, *School Funds Ruling to Have Broad Impact*, L.A. Times, June 29, 1973, at K1 (suggesting that *Lau* might "provide some insight into the significance of Rodriguez").

168. Interview with Edward H. Steinman, *supra* note 41; E-mail correspondence with Edward H. Steinman (Dec. 10, 2006).

169. Interview with Edward H. Steinman, *supra* note 41.

170. Brief for the Petitioners at 10–13, Lau v. Nichols, 414 U.S. 563 (1974) (No. 72–6520) (1973); Reply Brief of Petitioners at 2–3, Lau v. Nichols, 414 U.S. 563 (1974) (No. 72–6520) (1973).

171. Brief for the Petitioners, *supra* note 170, at 13; Reply Brief of Petitioners, *supra* note 170, at 13–14 n.32.

172. Petition for Writ of Certiorari and Affidavit in Forma Pauperis at 12–14, Lau v. Nichols, 414 U.S. 563 (1974) (No. 72–6520) (1973); Petitioners' Reply Memorandum at 3, Lau v. Nichols, 414 U.S. 563 (1974) (No. 72–6520) (1973).

173. Petition for Writ of Certiorari and Affidavit in Forma Pauperis, *supra* note 172, at 14–15; Petitioners' Reply Memorandum, *supra* note 172, at 3.

174. Petition for Writ of Certiorari and Affidavit in Forma Pauperis, *supra* note 172, at 16; Brief for the Petitioners, *supra* note 170, at 44–48; Reply Brief of Petitioners, *supra* note 170, at 14.

175. Brief for Respondents in Opposition to Petition for Writ of Certiorari at 11–12, Lau v. Nichols, 414 U.S. 563 (1974) (No. 72–6520) (1973); Brief of Respondents at 13–20, Lau v. Nichols, 414 U.S. 563 (1974) (No. 72–6520) (1973).

176. Brief for Respondents in Opposition to Petition for Writ of Certiorari, *supra* note 175, at 4.

177. *Id.* at 2–3.

178. Interview with Edward H. Steinman, *supra* note 41.

179. Brief of Respondents, *supra* note 175, at 31.

180. *Id.* at 66–67.

181. *Id.* at 61.

182. *Id.* at 67.

183. School District's Memorandum of Points and Authorities Regarding Reasonable Attorney's Fee Award, *supra* note 120, at 28–29.

184. Interview with Edward H. Steinman, *supra* note 41.

185. Docket Sheet for Lau v. Nichols, 414 U.S. 563 (1974) (No. 72–6520) (docketed Apr. 9, 1973).

186. Memorandum of the United States as Amicus Curiae at 5, Lau v. Nichols, 414 U.S. 563 (1974) (No. 72–6520) (1973); Memorandum of the United States as Amicus Curiae at 5, Lau v. Nichols, 414 U.S. 563 (1974) (No. 72–6520) (1973).

187. Transcript of Oral Argument at 23, Lau v. Nichols, 414 U.S. 563 (1974) (No. 72–6520) (1973). Although the memorandum in support of granting the petition for *certiorari* was filed with Erwin N. Griswold as lead counsel, by the time the brief was submitted, Robert H. Bork had taken over as Solicitor General. Only two months before the amicus brief was filed, Bork had fired Special Prosecutor Archibald Cox after Attorney General Elliot Richardson and Deputy Attorney General William Ruckelshaus refused to do so. President Nixon had ordered that Cox be fired when he sought tape recordings of White House conversations in conjunction with the Watergate investigation. The departure of Cox, Richardson, and Ruckelshaus was dubbed the Saturday Night Massacre, and Bork's role mired him in controversy. Fred Emery, *Watergate: The Corruption of American Politics and the Fall of Richard Nixon* 397–401 (paperback ed. 1995).

188. Memorandum of the United States as Amicus Curiae, *supra* note 186, at 14–15 (May 18, 1973).

189. Brief Amicus Curiae of the Center for Law and Education, Harvard University in Support of the Petitioners at 4, Lau v. Nichols, 414 U.S. 563 (1974) (No. 72–6520) (1973).

190. Brief Amicus Curiae of the Center for Law and Education, Harvard University, in Support of the Petition at 16 n.14, Lau v. Nichols, 414 U.S. 563 (1974) (No. 72–6520) (1973).

191. Interview with Edward H. Steinman, *supra* note 41.

192. E-mail correspondence with Roger L. Rice, Attorney, Multicultural Education, Training and Advocacy, Inc. (July 17, 2006).

193. *Id.*

194. E-mail correspondence with Stephen D. Sugarman, Roger J. Traynor Professor of Law, University of California at Berkeley School of Law (Boalt Hall) (July 19, 2006). The Project's five-person legal team included notable education and family law scholars. Mark Yudof and David Kirp went on to write a leading textbook on educational law and policy. Mark Yudof, David Kirp, Betsy Levin, and Rachel F. Moran, *Educational Policy and the Law* (4th ed. 2002). Robert Mnookin eventually left Berkeley to join the Harvard Law School faculty. Harvard On–Line Faculty Directory, *available at* http://www.law.harvard.edu/faculty/directory/facdir.php?id=46 (last visited Nov. 27, 2006).

195. E-mail correspondence with Stephen D. Sugarman, Roger J. Traynor Professor of Law, University of California at Berkeley School of Law (Boalt Hall) (July 20, 2006).

196. Brief Amicus Curiae of the Childhood and Government Project in Support of Petitioner Children at 1–2, 5–6, 10–12, Lau v. Nichols, 414 U.S. 563 (1974) (No. 72–6520) (1973).

197. *Id.* at 13.

198. Brief for the National Education Association and the California Teachers Association as Amici Curiae in Support of the Petition for a Writ of Certiorari to the United States Court of Appeal for the Ninth Circuit at 2 & n.2, 6–10, Lau v. Nichols, 414 U.S. 563 (1974) (No. 72–6520) (1973); Brief for the National Education Association and the California Teachers Association as Amici Curiae at 7–17, Lau v. Nichols, 414 U.S. 563 (1974) (No. 72–6520) (1973).

199. Brief for the National Education Association and the California Teachers Association as Amici Curiae, *supra* note 198, at 18–23.

200. Interview with Ling-chi Wang, *supra* note 33.

201. Guey Heung Lee v. Johnson, 404 U.S. 1215 (1971) (Douglas, J.) (denying petition for stay of desegregation order). The Chinese Six Companies' efforts to control the Freedom Schools that were established to evade the busing order also failed. Lum, *supra* note 15, at 67–69.

202. Brief of Amici Curiae The Chinese Consolidated Benevolent Association et al. at 9–13, Lau v. Nichols, 414 U.S. 563 (1974) (No. 72–6520) (1973).

203. Brief for San Francisco Lawyers' Committee for Urban Affairs as Amicus Curiae in Support of Petitioners at 10, Lau v. Nichols, 414 U.S. 563 (1974) (No. 72–6520) (1973).

204. Brief of American Jewish Congress, et al. at 7–33, Lau v. Nichols, 414 U.S. 563 (1974) (No. 72–6520) (1973).

205. Interview with Edward Steinman, *supra* note 41.

206. *Id.*

207. Brief of Amici Curiae Mexican American Legal Defense and Educational Fund et al. at 4–12, Lau v. Nichols, 414 U.S. 563 (1974) (No. 72–6520) (1973).

208. *Id.* at 12–19.

209. Brief *Amicus Curiae* of the Puerto Rican Legal Defense & Education Fund, Inc., in Support of Petitioners at 2–9, Lau v. Nichols, 414 U.S. 563 (1974) (No. 72–6520) (1973).

210. *See* Luis O. Reyes, *The* Aspira *Consent Decree: A Thirtieth-Anniversary Retrospective of Bilingual Education in New York City*, 76 Harv. Educ. Rev. 369, 370–73 (2006). Even with the Supreme Court's decision in *Lau*, the plaintiffs in New York faced resistance from school officials in implementing the consent decree. *Id.* at 374–77.

211. Brief of Efrain Tostado, et al. as Amici Curiae at 3–21, Lau v. Nichols, 414 U.S. 563 (1974) (No. 72–6520) (1973).

212. *Id.* at 4–5.

213. *Id.* at 6.

214. Interview with Edward H. Steinman, *supra* note 41.

215. Transcript of Oral Argument, *supra* note 187, at 16.

216. *Id.* at 21–22, 25–27, 30–32. Later, during the time that Steinman had reserved for rebuttal, the Court asked him whether it needed to reach the constitutional questions if there was a Title VI violation. Although Steinman insisted that it might be appropriate to address equal protection concerns, the Court seemed unpersuaded. *Id.* at 63–64.

217. *Id.* at 47–50, 57–58.

218. *Id.* at 52.

219. *Id.* at 52–54.

220. Lau v. Nichols, 414 U.S. 563, 564–69 (1974).

221. Interview with Edward Steinman, *supra* note 41.

222. 414 U.S. at 569–70 (concurring opinion of Stewart, J.).

223. *Id.* at 572 (concurring opinion of Blackmun, J.).

224. Interview with Ling-chi Wang, *supra* note 33.

225. *Id.*; Interview with Edward H. Steinman, *supra* note 41.

226. L. Ling-chi Wang, Lau v. Nichols: *History of a Struggle for Equal and Quality Education*, in *The Asian American Educational Experience* 58, 67 (Don T. Nakanishi and Tina Yamano Nishida eds. 1995) (quoting press release).

227. *Id.* at 67–68.

228. Preliminary Report to Dr. Lane E. DeLara on Bilingual/ESL/Newcomer Staff Response to Implications of *Lau v. Nichols* (Apr. 3, 1974).

229. *Id.*; Dexter Waugh, *The Legal Struggle for Bilingual Education*, S.F. Examiner, May 27, 1974, at 1; Dexter Waugh, *"One-a-Day" English Is Bitter Pill to Swallow*, S.F. Examiner, May 29, 1974; Dexter Waugh, *Money Is Key Word in Bilingual Programs*, S.F. Examiner, May 31, 1974.

230. Wang, *supra* note 226, at 68–69.

231. *Id.* at 69; *Angry Push for Bilingual Study*, S.F. Chron., Apr. 17, 1974, at 5.

232. Interview with Edward H. Steinman, *supra* note 41.

233. Complaint in Intervention, Lau v. Nichols, Civ. No. C–70 627 LHB 3–4 (May 17, 1974); United States' Notice of Motion and Motion for Leave to Intervene as Party Plaintiff, Lau v. Nichols, Civ. No. C–70 627 LHB 2–3 (May 17, 1974); United States' Memorandum of Points and Authorities in Support of Motion for Leave to Intervene, Lau v. Nichols, Civ. No. C–70 627 LHB 3–9 (May 17, 1974). The request for leave to intervene was granted the same day. Order, Lau v. Nichols, Civ. No. C–70 627 LHB (May 17, 1974).

234. Wang, *supra* note 226, at 70; Dexter Waugh, *The Legal Struggle for Bilingual Education*, *supra* note 229, at 1.

235. Affidavit of Counsel for Defendants Dr. Eugene Hopp, et al., Lau v. Nichols, Civ. No. C–70 627 LHB 1–2 (May 30, 1975); Wang, *supra* note 226, at 70.

236. Wang, *supra* note 226, at 71.

237. *Id.* at 71–73.

238. *Speaking Up for Bilingual Plan*, S.F. Chron., Jan. 29, 1975, at 5; Dexter Waugh, *Bilingual Education: 2 Years Later*, S.F. Chron., Feb. 1, 1976, at 23.

239. Wang, *supra* note 226, at 77.

240. *Id.* at 78–80.

241. Consent Decree, Lau v. Nichols, No. C–70 627 LHB (Oct. 22, 1975); Dexter Waugh, *supra* note 238, at 23.

242. Burke, *supra* note 40, at A1.

243. Interview with Ling-chi Wang, *supra* note 33.

244. 20 U.S.C. § 1703; Moran, *supra* note 18, at 1271–72.

245. *Id.* at 1279.

246. Office for Civil Rights, Task–Force Findings Specifying Remedies Available for Eliminating Past Educational Practices Ruled Unlawful Under *Lau v. Nichols* (1975), *reprinted in Bilingual Education* 213 (Keith Baker and Adriana de Kanter eds. 1983).

247. *Id.* at III, *reprinted in Bilingual Education*, *supra* note 246, at 215–18.

248. Moran, *supra* note 18, at 1282–83.

249. *Id.* at 1280 n.138.

250. *Id.* at 1283–84.

251. Interview with Ling-chi Wang, *supra* note 33.

252. Cal. Educ. Code §§ 52100–52179 (1976).

253. For example, the California Association for Bilingual Education was incorporated in 1976. It now has over sixty chapters and affiliates and 5,000 members. About CABE, *available at* http://www.bilingualeducation.org/about_n.html (last visited Nov. 27, 2006). See generally San Miguel, *supra* note 18, at 39 (describing the rise of professionally oriented organizations in bilingual education in the 1970s).

254. *See, e.g.*, American Institutes for Research (AIR), *Evaluation of the Impact of ESEA Title VII Spanish/English Bilingual Education Program* (1977–78); Beatrice Birman and Alan Ginsburg, *Addressing the Needs of Language–Minority Children: Issues for Federal Policy* (1981); Keith Baker and Adriana de Kanter, *Effectiveness of Bilingual Education: A Review of the Literature* (1981).

255. Rachel F. Moran, *Bilingual Education as a Status Conflict*, 75 Cal. L. Rev. 321, 331–33 (1987).

256. Northwest Arctic School District v. Califano, No. A–77–216 (D. Alaska Sept. 29, 1978).

257. Moran, *supra* note 18, at 1294–96.

258. *Id.* at 1295, 1296 n.212.

259. San Miguel, *supra* note 18, at 66–68.

260. Regents of the Univ. of Cal. v. Bakke, 438 U.S. 265, 284–87 (1978) (opinion of Powell, J.); *id.* at 325, 328–40 (opinion of Brennan, White, Marshall, and Blackmun, JJ.).

261. *Id.* at 303–05 (opinion of Powell, J); Peter Margulies, *Bilingual Education, Remedial Language Instruction, Title VI, and Proof of Discriminatory Purpose: A Suggested Approach*, 17 Colum. J.L. & Soc. Probs. 99, 130 (1981).

262. Alexander v. Sandoval, 532 U.S. 275, 289–93 (2001).

263. 20 U.S.C. §§ 1703, 1706; Castaneda v. Pickard, 648 F.2d 989, 1007–08 (5th Cir. 1981); Flores v. Arizona, 48 F.Supp.2d 937, 940 (D. Ariz.1999); Rachel F. Moran, *Undone by Law: The Uncertain Legacy of* Lau v. Nichols, 16 Berkeley La Raza L.J. 1, 6 (2005).

264. Castaneda v. Pickard, 648 F.2d at 1009–10; Eden Davis, *Unhappy Parents of Limited English Proficiency Students: What Can They Really Do?*, 35 J.L. & Educ. 277, 280–81, 282–83 (2006).

265. Response to Motion for Further Relief, United States v. Texas, Civ. No. 6:71–CV–5281 WWJ 7–8 (Feb. 23, 2006); Defendants' Consolidated Motion for Reconsideration of Memorandum Opinion and Order Rejecting Defendants' Eleventh Amendment Immunity Defense and Retaining Jurisdiction and Conditional Motion to Stay Proceedings, United States v. Texas, Civ. No. 6:71–CV–5281 WWJ 11–14 (June 16, 2006). For the countervailing view, see Response of Plaintiff–Intervenors to Defendants' Consolidated Motion for Reconsideration of Memorandum Opinion and Order Rejecting Defendants' Eleventh Amendment Immunity Defense and Retaining Jurisdiction and Conditional Motion to Stay Proceedings, United States v. Texas, Civ. No. 6:71–CV–5281 WWJ 11–21 (July 10, 2006); United States' Response to the Defendants' Motion for Reconsideration and Conditional Motion to Stay, United States v. Texas, Civ. No. 6:71–CV–5281 WWJ 5–17 (July 10, 2006).

266. Geoffrey Landward, Board of Trustees of the University of Alabama v. Garrett *and the Equal Education Opportunity Act: Another Act Bites the Dust*, 2002 BYU Educ. & L.J. 313, 327–29.

267. Interview with Edward H. Steinman, *supra* note 41.

268. *See, e.g.*, Memorandum Opinion and Order, United States v. Texas, Civ. No. 6:71–CV–5281 WWJ 9–11 (May 30, 2006); Memorandum Opinion in Support of Order Denying Motio for Reconsideration and Staying District Court Proceedings Against State Defendants, United States v. Texas, Civ. No. 6:71–CV–5281 WWJ 12–34 (Aug. 11, 2006).

269. Moran, *supra* note 263, at 7–8.

270. Cal. Educ. Code §§ 52161–52179; Rachel F. Moran, *Bilingual Education, Immigration, and the Culture of Disinvestment*, 2 J. Gender, Race, and Justice 163, 169 (1999).

271. Cal. Const. art. III, § 6 (1986).

272. Sunset Review Advisory Committee II, Reports to the Legislature on Categorical Programs Scheduled to Sunset on June 30, 1987 (Sept. 1985); Lou Cannon, *Bilingual Education Under Attack; California Ballot Initiative Backers Hope Effort Will Resonate Elsewhere*, Wash. Post, July 21, 1997, at A15; Richard C. Paddock, *Deukmejian Vetoes Bill on Bilingual Education; Cites Legal Spending Limit, Calls for Review of Programs Set to Expire at End of School Year*, L.A. Times, Oct. 1, 1986, at pt. 1, p. 1, col. 2.

273. Program Advisory to County and District Superintendents from Bill Honig, Superintendent of Public Instruction re Education Programs for Which Sunset Provisions Took Effect on June 30, 1987 Pursuant to Education Code Sections 62000 and 62000.2 (Aug. 26, 1987).

274. Comite de Padres de Familia v. State Sup't of Pub. Instr., No. 281824 (Cal. Sup. Ct. Feb. 5, 1995); Quiroz v. State Bd. of Educ., No. CIV.S–1600 WBS/GGH, 1997 WL 661163 at *1 (E.D. Cal. 1997).

275. Proposition 227, 1998 Cal. Legis. Serv. (West) (codified at Cal. Educ. Code §§ 300–340 (West Supp. 1999)).

276. Ramon McLeod, *Prop. 227 Got Few Latino Votes*, S.F. Chron., June 5, 1998, at A19.

277. Valeria G. v. Wilson, 12 F.Supp.2d 1007 (N.D. Cal. 1998), *aff'd*, 307 F.3d 1036 (9th Cir. 2002); California Teachers Ass'n v. Davis, 64 F.Supp.2d 945 (C.D. Cal. 1999), *aff'd sub nom.* Cal. Teachers Ass'n v. Board of Educ., 271 F.2d 1141 (9th Cir. 2001).

278. Rene Sanchez and William Booth, *Calif. Rejection A Big Blow to Bilingualism; Decisive Vote Could Set Pace for Rest of Nation*, Wash. Post, June 4, 1998, at A16. For a comprehensive evaluation of the effects of Proposition 227, see Thomas B. Parrish, et al., Effects of the Implementation of Proposition 227 on the Education of English Learners, K–12: Findings from a Five–Year Evaluation vii–x (Jan. 24, 2006) (describing barriers to implementation and lack of clear evidence of superiority of a particular teaching methodology; a key factor in the success of any program was qualified staff).

279. Interview with Ling-chi Wang, *supra* note 33.

280. *See, e.g.*, Board of Education, The Lau Report, 1994–95, Part I at 1 (filed Nov. 23, 1995) (indicating that "Although the timetable for the Master Plan has expired since the Fall of 1980, the SFUSD continues to operate all Master Plan activities. The SFUSD continues to submit the Lau Consent Decree Report annually as an expression of its good faith and continued effort to serve non-English-proficient (NEP) and limited-English-proficient (LEP) students of various language backgrounds.").

281. San Francisco Unified School District, Bilingual Education & Learning Academy, 1999–2000 Lau Report (filed Nov. 11, 1999); Interview with Ling-chi Wang, *supra* note 33.

282. San Francisco NAACP v. San Francisco Unified Sch. Dist., 413 F.Supp.2d 1051, 1061–72 (N.D. Cal. 2005); Heather Knight, *San Francisco: New Changes Await School Assignment Plan*, S.F. Chron., Nov. 10, 2005, at B3.

283. Interview with Ling-chi Wang, *supra* note 33; Interview with Edward H. Steinman, *supra* note 41.

284. Burke, *supra* note 40, at A1.

285. *Id.*

286. Interview with Edward Steinman, *supra* note 41.

287. Burke, *supra* note 40, at A1.

288. *Id.*

289. Interview with Edward Steinman, *supra* note 41.

290. *Id.*

291. See Hanif S.P. Hirji, *Inequalities in California's Public School System: The Undermining of Serrano v. Priest and the Need for a Minimum Standards System of Education*, 32 Loyola L.A. L. Rev. 583, 589–99 (1999) (describing the California Supreme Court's strict scrutiny of disparities in school finance and the leveling down that resulted). Concerns that the requirement of strict equality had led to a race to the bottom prompted advocates to seek guarantees of an opportunity to learn in California's troubled public schools. Jeannie Oakes and Martin Lipton, *"Schools that Shock the Conscience":* Williams v. California *and the Struggle for Education on Equal Terms Fifty Years After* Brown, 11 Asian L.J. 234, 234–45 (2004).

292. The one reported state court challenge to Proposition 227 involved a question of statutory interpretation rather than an allegation that the measure violated the fundamental right to education. McLaughlin v. Board of Educ., 75 Cal. App. 4th 196 (1999).

293. Ho v. San Francisco Unified Sch. Dist., 965 F. Supp. 1316 (N.D. Cal. 1997), *appeal dismissed*, 147 F.3d 854 (9th Cir. 1998); San Francisco NAACP v. San Francisco Unified Sch. Dist., 413 F.Supp.2d 1051, 1055–57 (N.D. Cal. 2005) (describing the *Ho* litigation);

Caitlin M. Liu, *Beyond Black and White: Chinese Americans Challenge San Francisco's Desegregation Plan*, 5 Asian L.J. 341, 342–45 (1998).

294. San Francisco NAACP, 413 F.Supp.2d at 1057.

295. Jill Tucker, *Berkeley; School District Sued Over Racial Policy*, S.F. Chron., Oct. 5, 2005, at B1.

296. *See, e.g.*, Cortez v. Calumet Pub. Sch. Dist., 2002 WL 31177378 (N.D. Ill. 2002); Quiroz v. State Bd. of Educ., 1997 WL 661163 (E.D. Cal. 1997); Gomez v. Illinois State Bd. of Educ., 811 F.2d 1030 (7th Cir. 1987); Castaneda v. Pickard, 781 F.2d 456 (5th Cir. 1986); Guadalupe Org. v. Tempe Elem. Sch. Dist., 587 F.2d 1022 (9th Cir. 1978); Otero v. Mesa County Valley Sch. Dist., 568 F.2d 1312 (10th Cir. 1977).

297. Teresa P. v. Berkeley Unified Sch. Dist., 724 F.Supp. 698, 700, 710–11, 714 (N.D. Cal. 1989).

298. Interview with Ling-chi Wang, *supra* note 33.

*

6

The Story of the *Virginia Military Institute*: Negotiating Sameness and Difference

Rosemary C. Salomone

> There is no reason to believe that the admission of women capable of all the activities required of VMI cadets would destroy the Institute rather than enhance its capacity to serve "the more perfect union."[1]

More than ten years have passed since the Supreme Court drew that conclusion, giving the Virginia Military Institute, an all-male state college founded in 1839, little practical choice but to admit women into the Corps of Cadets. By the time the case reached the Court, it was freighted with more than two decades of litigation on behalf of women, the still unresolved debate over sameness and difference, unhealed wounds and suspicion dating from the Civil War, and southern pride in a culture of "manliness" that seemed out of step with the times. As the drama of the lawsuit unfolded, these external factors formed a veiled but intricately woven subtext as both sides remained locked in a life or death struggle, one resolutely trying to preserve the past, the other pushing mightily to forge a new future, each fearing the immediate and broader consequences for the present. Buried within that subtext lies a compelling account of this high profile lawsuit that plumbed the depths of gender and threw open the Institute's doors to women.

The Backdrop

Over the past two centuries, the education of women has been subject to intermittent waves of resistance, ambivalence, and qualified support, each reflecting enduring disagreements over women's place in society. Much of the dispute has focused on whether women and men are inherently the same or different. Remarks made several years ago by the now former President of Harvard University, suggesting by his "best guess" that "intrinsic aptitude" primarily accounts for the paucity of women holding senior academic positions in math and science,[2] conjured up memories of yet another Harvard figure whose opposition to women's education is legendary. Going back to the 1870s, Dr. Edward Clarke, a member of Harvard's Board of Overseers and a former member of Harvard's medical faculty, warned with great certitude that secondary and higher education would harm women's reproductive abilities. Clarke was especially averse to educating women in the masculine and academically challenging atmosphere of the coeducational school. His book, *Sex in Education*,[3] was widely read for decades and stalled early efforts to extend education to women beyond the primary grades. Clark's thesis obviously sounds outrageous by today's understandings. Nonetheless, as the more recent firestorm over women and science demonstrates, the stereotypical attitudes that historically denied women access still linger in remote, and not so remote, corners of academe even three decades after most institutions, including Harvard, removed admissions barriers.

The historical exclusion of women from higher education initially gave rise to women's colleges, beginning with Mount Holyoke in 1837, the same year that Oberlin College opened its Collegiate Department to women. It also was the year that the abolitionist and feminist Sarah Grimke stridently proclaimed that men should grant no special favors to women, but merely "take their feet off [women's] necks and permit [them] to stand up straight."[4] Education was no exception. Many nineteenth century women's advocates, heartened by Oberlin's success, championed coeducation as a right crucial to liberating women from a "separate spheres" ideology that placed men dominant over the public sphere of work, politics, and intellectual life while consigning women to the private sphere of home and family. At the same time, however, many early feminists touted women's moral superiority over men, a justification they used to promote women's suffrage.

This somewhat equivocal view of equality as sameness among women's advocates found more definitive support in the beginnings of the modern-day women's movement. While ideological disagreements over sameness and difference would soon divide their ranks, early second-wave (post 1950s) feminists built their arguments on an assimilationist model that called for fairness as equal treatment based on male norms. Taking their cue from the struggle against racial segregation, they believed that as the law was color-blind, so it should be sex blind.[5] Proponents defined their goals by what white, middle-class men valued: public respect and recognition, gratifying careers with the attendant monetary rewards and status, and freedom from the rigid social expectation of bearing and raising children. By focusing on equal rights, they could avoid the complex and politically sensitive issue of whether differences between the sexes were biological or cultural.[6] One of their primary goals was education, where they struggled to make schools gender-neutral in their inputs—admissions, resources, expectations, climate, and curriculum—and thus in their outputs.[7]

A key player in the development of what is generally known as "liberal feminism" was Ruth Bader Ginsburg, who would ultimately speak for the Court in *United States v. Virginia.* As a young lawyer, Justice Ginsburg experienced first hand the downside of "separate spheres" ideology. Years later, as a Supreme Court justice, she recounted that Justice Felix Frankfurter had refused to offer her a Court clerkship despite her stellar academic credentials, including editorial positions on the law review boards of both Harvard and Columbia. "The Justice was told of my family situation," she recalled. "I was married and had a five-year-old daughter. For whatever reason, he said no." That initial rejection made her keenly aware that educational opportunity alone was not enough. Social and economic barriers had to be officially removed before women could claim their rightful place in society.[8]

In the early 1970s, while teaching on the Columbia University law faculty, Justice Ginsburg served as founding director of the American Civil Liberties Union ("ACLU") Women's Rights Project ("WRP"), the same organization that later influenced the VMI litigation. Throughout the decade, she participated in writing the main brief in nine cases decided by the Court. In six of them, she presented oral argument. She and her colleagues at the WRP incrementally whittled away at separate spheres doctrine.[9] Through their efforts, the Court in 1971, for the first time, ruled in favor of a woman who claimed that she had been denied equal protection of the laws under the Fourteenth Amendment.[10] With "equal treatment" as their overarching philosophy, their goal was to achieve the same exacting judicial scrutiny as for racial discrimination, requiring that government policy must be narrowly tailored to achieve a compelling state justification. When that effort proved fruitless, they shifted strategy and in 1976 successfully moved the Court toward a somewhat less demanding level of intermediate scrutiny. Here the state must demonstrate that sex classifications are substantially related to an important governmental interest.[11] Two decades later, the case against VMI would present a long-awaited opportunity to convince the Court to ratchet up that standard.

Throughout the 1970s, a combination of social, legal, and market pressures moved most all-male educational institutions to admit women. By 1994, men's colleges had all but disappeared, while women's colleges were less than one-third the number they had been in the early 1960s.[12] A confluence of forces likewise moved Congress in 1975 to open the federal military academies to women. The end of the draft, declining respect for the military in the aftermath of the Vietnam War, and the sheer force of the movement to achieve equality for women all came to bear on that decision. With the military's ranks noticeably dwindling, women could help meet the demands for career officers who, in turn, would attract more female recruits to fill the gap. After much debate and resistance, Congress reached a compromise that distinguished between the academies' responsibility to prepare officers for combat and to prepare them for careers in the armed forces. By legislative fiat, West Point and the Naval and Air Force Academies began admitting women into the 1976 entering class.[13]

Public Law 94–106, § 803(a) called for the academies to make only "minimal essential adjustments" to accommodate "physiological differences" between men and women. Otherwise, all "academic and other relevant standards" would remain the same.[14] Initially denying any change in physical standards, the academies eventually adopted the doctrine of "equivalent training" designed to evoke "equal effort rather than equal accomplishment." Classes in karate and self-defense replaced boxing and wrestling. Females had neat and stylish haircuts in contrast to the "buzz cut" imposed on males. Traditional forms of hazing and harassment lost their official and unofficial sanction.[15] The focus was to integrate women, allowing them to remain distinct in limited ways, rather than totally assimilate them into the male-normed life of the academies. The change in training styles, however, was also driven by the advent of the all-volunteer military just as women were entering the academies. As one Annapolis official noted, "We can't have people quitting because they weren't treated with dignity." And so the academies developed more positive, teaching-oriented leadership practices across the board.[16]

Meanwhile, VMI and its South Carolina counterpart The Citadel, the two remaining state military colleges in the country, tenaciously held on to their all-male status. That tactic seemed to work until the late 1980s. At that point, both came under increased pressure from women's rights advocates and young women themselves who viewed them as symbols of gender exclusion and perpetuators of harmful stereotypes. Yet for their students, alumni, state officials, and many of the women in their lives, the institutions represented manliness and tradition of an order that particularly resonated in the South. VMI and The Citadel soon found themselves in the vortex of a contentious dispute over these two opposing views. They also found their fates joined in the Supreme Court's final resolution.

The Seeds of Litigation

The most compelling law stories begin with a named plaintiff, one who presents a portrait of heart-wrenching harm and unstoppable resilience in the face of institutional wrongdoing and resistance to change. The VMI case took a different route into court and so the story takes on a different, though nonetheless interesting, cast. Here the Justice Department in Washington set the legal machinery in motion based on a complaint filed in early1989 by a northern Virginia high school student.

She had applied to VMI and been rejected on the basis of her sex. The student, now presumably in her mid-thirties, has remained nameless and faceless without any details of her aspirations, the sincerity of her interest, or her qualifications.

The seeds for the case, however, were sown three years earlier when Judith Keith, a lawyer for the Justice Department's Civil Rights Division, noticed a headline in the *Washington Post* reading: "VMI Runs Rear–Guard Action Against Admitting Women."[17] The article reported that nothing short of a court order would move the college to change its all-male admissions policy. That unequivocal decision had come from the recommendation of a Mission Study Committee appointed by the VMI Board of Visitors in 1983 as part of a regional re-accreditation self-study. A key component of the study was to re-examine the legality and merits of the college's male-only policy in the wake of the Court's 1982 decision in *Mississippi University for Women v. Hogan*. There the Court had struck down the university's all-female nursing program.[18] The report noted that VMI was highly unlikely to attract a critical mass of at least 10% female cadets, while the necessary accommodations would have a negative impact on the college's "spirit" and "ethos." It also raised the question of combat service toward which, it claimed, VMI graduates were especially inclined.[19] To any informed observer, it was clear that the institution was bracing itself for a court challenge. A full decade had passed since Congress had ordered the federal military academies to admit women.

The news article particularly piqued Judith Keith who was eager to challenge what she saw as a "flagrant example of illegal discrimination" on the part of the VMI Board.[20] But she had to sit back and wait for a live claimant to come forward, either directly or through the women's advocacy network. Three years later, when the complaint from the northern Virginia student arrived on her desk, she ran with it. She began by informing VMI's Acting Superintendent, Major General John William Knapp, that he had twenty days to justify the all-male policy in writing. The pointed demand provoked immediate but mixed responses in Virginia. Then Governor Gerald L. Baliles, a former state Attorney General, urged VMI officials to concede.[21] Aside from the potential state and federal constitutional violations, he could find no "moral ... or educational rationale" to justify the policy.[22] The implicit warning, however, held no punch in Lexington where the VMI Board of Visitors and the VMI Foundation both "dug in" their heels. With marching orders in hand, Knapp sent a letter to Washington simply confirming that VMI had always been all-male and that there had been little interest among women in attending.[23] In reply, Justice threatened to bring suit if the school failed to "develop and implement a full and timely remedial plan" to admit women.[24]

The VMI Board of Visitors passed a unanimous resolution stating that the policy was not in violation of the law, but rather provided "diversity and balance" in the Virginia system of higher education.[25] That same day, in a preemptive strike and to the dismay of Justice attorneys, both the state Attorney General Mary Sue Terry and the VMI Foundation filed separate suits in the federal district court in Roanoke, where they were more certain to get a sympathetic hearing. They challenged what they considered federal encroachment on the state's system of higher education and asked the court to declare the Institute's admissions policy constitutional. The following month, the Civil Rights Division brought its own suit in the same court. The government argued that excluding women violated the equal protection clause of the Fourteenth Amendment.

This was not the first time that claimants had hauled the Commonwealth of Virginia before the federal judiciary to defend education policies that discriminated against women. Two decades earlier, a federal court had forced the state to admit women to the University of Virginia at Charlottesville, the state's flagship institution. At that time, the court declined to address the state's four other single-sex colleges, specifically noting that one of them (VMI) was "military in character." The year was 1970 and the court, unaware that it was sitting on the cusp of a feminist revival that would transform society, mused, "Are women to be admitted on an equal basis, and if so, are they to wear uniforms and be taught to bear arms?"[26] Fast forward to 1990 and that same military college found itself fiercely justifying its right to exclude women based on what the opposition considered archaic and overbroad generalizations of female capabilities and tendencies.[27]

VMI officials had long anticipated legal action. When it finally came, their visceral reaction and resolute defense were reminiscent of a remark made by General Thomas "Stonewall" Jackson, a revered past professor, as he led Confederate forces in the Battle of Charlottesville: "The Institute will be heard from today."[28] To many VMI alums and supporters, this was an issue of "states' rights vs. federal intrusion, Southern tradition vs. Northern self-righteousness." For some it evoked images of the Civil War, when VMI had trained officers for the Confederacy.[29] Close to 1800 cadets and former cadets had served in the Confederate Army, earning the Institute the name "West Point of the South."[30] Buried deep within the institution's collective memory was the devastation that Union troops had wreaked on VMI's buildings, including its library, hospital, and scientific collection, in retaliation for cadets fighting in the Battle of New Market in May 1864. All that remained were the thick walls of the Barracks and the Superintendent's Quarters, where there was an ill daughter. Ten thousand books had been destroyed or stolen.[31]

The valiant charge of the VMI cadets at New Market has inspired the work of artists and historians. A huge painting replicating the event hangs above the altar in the chapel. A moving bronze statue of a female representing *Virginia Mourning Her Dead*, the creation of Moses Ezekiel, a noted sculptor and sergeant of the Corps in that battle, stands in front of Nichols Engineering Hall as a tribute to the cadets who lost their lives. Every spring the school honors their memory in an elaborate ceremony. A journey through the VMI Museum and Archives gives clear testament to the institution's overwhelming and almost romantic identity with the lost Confederate struggle and the school's symbolism of Old Dominion tradition and valor. Much of the Civil War movie *Gods and Generals* was filmed at VMI. As the Civil War had created the very essence of VMI, there was a pervasive feeling, especially among alumni, that this new battle over gender could potentially destroy it.

Educating Citizen Soldiers

VMI's history and culture, largely a function of geography, played a key role in shaping the arguments throughout the lawsuit. The college is located about 200 miles southwest of Washington, D.C. in the Shenandoah Valley town of Lexington, nestled between the Blue Ridge and Allegheny Mountains. It sits on 134 acres directly adjacent to Washington and Lee University, a once all-male private institution, whose physical layout, tone, and typical college ambiance stand in stark contrast with VMI. Crossing over the dividing line, one immediately senses VMI's unmistakable insularity and separation from the outside world. The change is almost jolting. From the Washington and Lee "campus" and its maze of old and new buildings, where young women and men in jeans and tee shirts rush to class or chat casually with friends or faculty, one suddenly encounters the VMI "post" and its austere beige stucco Gothic Revival buildings, forming a fortress-like circle around a grassy twelve acre parade ground, a National Historic Trust District. The cadet Barracks dominates the complex. Athletic facilities and fields circle the outer rim. Uniformed cadets walk erect and with purpose, men tip their hats to women visitors, and all cadets salute faculty, who hold officer titles and wear military uniforms, as they make their way along the perimeter. Any interactions with adults are brief and to the point, greeted with a direct look in the eye, and followed by "ma'm" or "sir." When classes are not in session, one may encounter cadets, in athletic clothes, jogging along the paths or socializing in groups, but even here there is a palpable sense of order and uniformity.

Established in 1839 as the country's first state-supported military college, VMI initially assigned cadets to guard the state militia arsenal in the town. Many of the early cadets were young men, as young as sixteen, poorly educated and from the lower classes of rural Virginia. Unbeknownst to many, in its early years the college functioned by a 1842 legislative act as the state's first normal school, training teachers to improve the state's appalling educational system. After the War, when school teaching became women's work carrying low prestige and low pay, VMI redefined its mission and offered a baccalaureate degree that emphasized science and engineering. By 1900, it had expanded its engineering curriculum, raised academic standards, opened its doors to out-of-state students, and improved the credentials of its faculty.[32] Over the next century, VMI gradually improved its reputation, both in Virginia and nationally. It now offers the baccalaureate degree in engineering, the sciences, and the liberal arts. In the 2005–06 academic year, its 1300 cadets came from 37states and 9 foreign nations.[33]

One critical point that surfaced in the course of the lawsuit was the apparent disconnect between VMI's consciously-guarded military appearance and ethos on the one hand, and its broader core mission on the other. Threaded throughout the VMI narrative, as reflected in its museum exhibits, archival files, official publications, and promotional materials, is the institution's vaunted role in producing soldiers and military leaders who have served valiantly in wartime. That piece of the VMI story seems to eclipse all others. Chief among VMI's most venerated sons is General George C. Marshall, Class of 1901, Army Chief of Staff during World War II and architect of the Marshall Plan to rebuild war-torn Europe, for which he was awarded the Nobel Prize for Peace. On the grounds stands the Marshall Library, a research center for scholars of twentieth century military and diplomatic history.

All cadets take four years of ROTC. Yet unlike the federal military academies which aim to produce professional officers and require graduates to "commission" in one of the armed forces, VMI primarily trains students for corporate and government leadership. Its founding mission was to "prepare young men for the varied work of civil life."[34] In fact, at the time the Justice Department began its investigation in 1989, only 15% of VMI graduates pursued military careers, an even smaller number than the 30% at The Citadel. Among the remaining 85% were prominent alumni including two Virginia congressmen, two state senators, a former speaker of the state House of Delegates, the managing partners of the state's two largest law firms, and a flock of Richmond industrialists and investors. Even by today's numbers, only about 20 to 25% of VMI graduates choose the military as a career while between 40 and 50% accept military commissions upon graduation.[35]

When taken to court, VMI was the sole remnant of an educational system in Virginia where most of the state colleges historically had been single-sex. Its offerings in the liberal arts, sciences, and engineering were available at other public institutions in the state. What made VMI special was its unique mission "to produce educated and honorable men, prepared for the varied work of civil life . . . ready as citizen soldiers to defend their country in time of national peril."[36] The idea of the "citizen soldier" goes back to the very beginnings of the institution and is based on the model of Cincinnatus, the Roman farmer, who temporarily gave up civilian life in 458 B.C. when called to help defend his country in time of need. A seven-foot tall multi-sided granite monument, honoring this legendary figure, stands prominently near the New Barracks. On the side of the monument facing the parade ground is a bronze bas relief depicting Cincinnatus accepting the call of duty.

Like The Citadel, the way that VMI carries out this charge is through an "adversative" or doubting model of education. The purpose is to strip cadets of their individuality in a way that builds camaraderie and bonding. The key features are physical rigor, mental stress, absolute equality of treatment, total lack of privacy, minute regulation of behavior, and indoctrination in desirable values.[37] Bathrooms are communal and, until 1997 when women entered, had no partitions or stalls. Students are assigned as many as five to a room whose doors have shadeless windows and whose sight line to the back must remain unobstructed. Rooms are spartan, lacking the televisions, telephones, carpets, wall decorations, and air conditioning now the norm in college dormitories. The Barracks is a four-story structure made up of two adjoining quadrangles; first year cadets live on the top floor. All rooms open onto porch-like structures or "stoops." Outdoor staircases link each of the levels. While the college is in session, three cadet guards patrol the Barracks area round the clock in two-hour shifts to "keep and teach order."[38]

Incoming freshmen are called "rats." The designation officially dates back to 1850. According to legend, it comes from the name that then neighboring Washington College students called cadets who, in turn, called them "minks" because of their mean and sly tactics in joint military drills.[39] Rats immediately receive the regulation haircut and uniforms along with a copy of "The Bullet," or "rat bible," which they must keep in their possession at all times. This small booklet covers disciplinary rules, the honor code, institutional history, campus layout, and songs and yells. It includes a list of "cardinal sins," such as showing "disrespect to an upper classman," and a catalogue of "customs and courtesies" advising cadets on when to tip their hats and on the essentials of table etiquette.

Rats endure a life of high stress, both physically and mentally. Intense exercise, marching in a contortion called a strain, sitting at attention through meals, and the constant harassment of upper-class students—push-ups demanded at whim, pre-dawn exercises called "sweat parties," in-the-face interrogations on arcane institutional trivia—yield a high attrition rate among first year students. About 10% of the entering class leaves within the first month. The "ratline" ends in February with what is called "breakout." Classes for all cadets run from Monday through Saturday. The day begins before 7 a.m. with reveille and ends at 11 p.m. with taps. Travel off post is regulated even on weekends. Any violation of the Honor Code, which prohibits lying, cheating, stealing, or tolerating those who do, is punishable with expulsion. Unlike the federal service academies, there are no second chances.

From the very beginning of the government's investigation, VMI's attorneys argued with certitude that women were unfit to withstand the rigors of the adversative method. They made it clear that this was a "highly specialized program for the distinctive physiological and developmental characteristics of males."[40] They insisted that if forced to admit women, VMI would have to modify the program, which inevitably would destroy its success. From that position, one would never suspect that almost 50% of the new male cadets regularly failed the physical fitness test and received remedial training, while 2% graduated without ever having passed it.[41] In fact, the school's arguments masked the truth behind the most physically demanding and unremittingly brutal aspects of the VMI experience. Many of these practices were neither related to the school's physical education program, nor were they official policy. They were merely part of a hazing scheme of arbitrary tests that upperclass cadets imposed on the rats and which the institution tacitly sanctioned. A group of high-ranking military women described it as "an abusive method of imposing stress on cadets, but it [was] an artificial stress, not a real-life or combat-type stress."[42] Yet those who make it through and ultimately graduate speak of the ordeal as the worst and best of their lives and hail the "rat line" as the ultimate bonding experience. That feeling undoubtedly has helped create the unstinting alumni loyalty and unmatched level of "giving" that makes the VMI per student endowment the largest of any state college in the country.

Throughout the litigation, school officials and alumni deeply resented change of any kind, particularly when forced on them by outsiders. They especially feared that women would shatter the esteemed "VMI experience." Yet neither a majority of Virginians nor the faculty shared this sentiment. In a February 1990 poll, four out of five Virginians believed that VMI should admit women. In a faculty poll released the following month by VMI's chapter of the American Association of University Professors, 63% showed like support.[43] For some faculty, coeducation was a way to raise academic standards and to improve the quality of an applicant pool with less than stellar SAT scores. For others, it was simply a matter of equality.[44] The immediate reaction to the lawsuit from beyond VMI and Virginia was similarly polarized and even strident. In an article in the *Washington Post*, feminist author Judy Mann described VMI as "a medieval time warp, in which a brotherhood is forged through sadomasochistic rituals in a forgotten monastery supported by the state for its own Byzantine purposes."[45] Phyllis Schlafly, President of the conservative Eagle Forum, shot back, claiming that the lawsuit was mere "mischief-making" whose "real purpose [was] to force VMI to feminize its educational system and force it to conform to the androgynous society demanded by the radical feminists."[46] Another battle in the modern-day culture wars was about to begin.

The Lower Courts

The case was assigned to Judge Jackson Kiser, a Reagan Administration appointee and alum of Washington and Lee Law School. Before going to trial, Judge Kiser dismissed VMI's lawsuit against the Justice Department. At the same time, he permitted the VMI Foundation and the VMI Alumni Association to intervene as defendants in the Department's case against Virginia despite objections from the federal government. He subsequently released Governor Douglas Wilder, also named as a defendant, and granted the state Attorney General Mary Sue Terry permission to withdraw from representing the Commonwealth. Although Wilder at first had seemed neutral on the complaint, he later sought to be removed, stating that "the failure to admit females to [VMI was] against [his] personal philosophy." As Virginia's first African-American Governor, he undoubtedly was sensitive to exclusion. "No person," he said, "should be denied admittance to a state supported school because of her race or gender." Terry, who planned to make a bid for Governor in 1993 and whose campaign treasurer was a VMI alum, initially indicated that she would defend the school but later backed down, ostensibly in response to the Governor's withdrawal. More pragmatically, she had come under heavy criticism from women and progressive elements in the Democratic Party. Meanwhile, both she and Wilder realized that the all-male policy was unpopular with Northern Virginia voters and other recent migrants who were shaping "the New Dominion."[47] Virginia obtained a stay of proceedings while the court considered the state's liability.[48]

The litigation went through two phases, the first addressing the constitutionality of the all-male admissions policy and the second the constitutionality of the remedy that VMI proposed. With the state's lawyer removed at least during the liability phase, the remaining public defendants, along with VMI and its Superintendent, all shared the same attorneys. And so the initial legal theories, factual analysis, and institutional vision were shaped not by the state but primarily by the private interests of the alumni, the VMI Foundation, and the VMI Board of Visitors. Since 12 of the 17 members of the Board were alumni by law, they effectively carried the defense. The VMI forces realized that to maintain VMI's credibility, the battle had to be won not only in the courtroom but also in the court of public opinion. In that regard, they looked to the North, hiring a Manhattan public relations firm which held daily briefings with the school's legal team. By the same token, school officials welcomed the media to present the personal side among the cadets, most of them bitterly opposed to admitting women. Barely two months into the lawsuit, news reporters from New York to Australia were descending upon the post.

The VMI Foundation easily assembled a high-powered and politically positioned legal team. They engaged Griffin Bell, a partner in the Atlanta firm of King and Spalding and former U.S. Attorney General in the Carter Administration. They also enlisted the services of Robert H. Patterson Jr., VMI class of 1949 and senior partner at McGuire, Woods, Battle & Boothe, one of the most powerful law firms in Virginia, and Anne Marie Whittemore, a partner in the same firm and one whose hiring Patterson had questioned on gender grounds twenty years earlier. Patterson, described in the *Washington Post* as a "barrel-chested, vodka-drinking, chain-smoking big-game hunter, with an expletive-spiked vocabulary" and "pillar of the arch-conservative Old Dominion establishment," had replaced Mary Sue Terry in carrying the state's argument before the court.[49] On the other side were Justice Department attorney Judith Keith and her more junior colleague Michael Maurer who had entered the case as the trial date drew close.[50]

Virginia played on the broad theme to preserve single-sex education. Justice attorneys drew from a different text, focusing on the history of sex discrimination and the need to preserve, as a matter of fairness, equal opportunity for women. At trial, Patterson pounded away on VMI's uniqueness and how VMI "did not want to be like West Point . . . a half-baked version of what we are now." He insisted that the demand for a VMI-type education was minuscule among women. Keith retorted with written inquiries from female students interested in applying for admission. Using the fictitious name "Jackie Jones" to place a human face on the blackened-out signatures, one of them, later identified as Dana Hudson, a 15–year–old high school freshman, wrote: "I would like to demonstrate that women, and in particular me, can make a distinct contribution to your current dedication to develop young people." As she later told the press, the women writing these letters "are real women who want to change things. They don't want to ruin the school . . . They just respect it enough to want to be part of it." Keith argued that these women deserved to be admitted on their merits and not denied access on the basis of their sex.[51] But for Patterson, the issue was even bigger. Virginia, he argued, "should not have to bow to what the federal government does in any case." His very tone evoked memories of segregation battles from the 1960s.[52] Joining in on VMI's closing argument, Griffin Bell likewise accused Justice attorneys of wanting to "make the world over in their images."[53]

To courtroom observers, VMI's arguments seemed "more detailed and more cogently presented." Compared to Patterson's "soaring rhetorical flights," the Justice Department's case was flat and unemotional.[54] Whether it was substance or style or cultural affinity, Judge Kiser ruled in favor of VMI.[55] Among his findings of fact, he noted that "[m]ales tend to need an atmosphere of adversativeness or ritual combat" while "females tend to thrive in a cooperative atmosphere in which the teacher is emotionally connected with the students."[56] Best capturing the sentiments among VMI supporters, the *Washington Times* called the ruling "a timely reminder that [the Justice Department's] brand of social engineering, however lauded in elite circles, is not the law of the land."[57]

While the defense may have convinced the court that few women were not only suited for, but also interested in, VMI's unique program, it seemed like males also were losing their enthusiasm for the grueling 17–hour days of VMI's rat line. The following fall, the school's entering class of 351 cadets was the smallest since 1976. And with a 76% acceptance rate, the academic quality of the class was slipping. More academically prepared high school graduates interested in a military career could head to West Point where the tuition was free, hazing had been eliminated, the academic reputation was stronger, and cadets received a monthly stipend of $544.[58] Those not interested in a long-term military commitment could attend any number of ROTC programs, including the Corps of Cadets at Virginia Polytechnic Institute.

The Justice Department appealed the decision to the Fourth Circuit Court of Appeals, a court known for its conservative leanings and tendency to support states' rights.[59] It was the same court that would hear appeals in The Citadel litigation. This time VMI attorneys faced Jessica Dunsay Silver, a seasoned attorney in charge of the appellate section of the Department's Civil Rights Division which, in the months ahead, would fall under the new Clinton Administration. They also faced a joint amicus brief prepared by the National Women's Law Center in Washington and the ACLU Women's Rights Project. Signing on to the brief were major women's rights groups and some of the most prominent female litigators on women's issues. The exclusion of women from VMI, they maintained, relied on "archaic and overbroad generalizations about the differences between men and women, reminiscent of arguments previously advanced in support of race segregation."[60] The concerted effort proved fruitful. The appeals court reversed and remanded the case to Judge Kiser, offering the state three options to remedy the constitutional violation: admit women, establish a separate parallel institution for women, or forgo state support and pursue its policies as a private institution.[61]

Both the three-judge panel and the full Fourth Circuit denied VMI's request for a rehearing.[62] Undaunted, the attorneys moved for a stay of the appeals court's decision, which was granted, and petitioned the Supreme Court to hear the case. Seven women's colleges filed amicus briefs supporting VMI's request, arguing that the case put their legality at risk. There was some speculation that wealthy VMI alums had pressured the colleges into taking that questionable position.[63] The Justice Department asked the Court not to hear the case, arguing that the possibility of a parallel women's program had yet to be argued in the trial court. VMI, in reply, drew the state autonomy card, noting how it was "disheartening that the government would seek to impose coeducational conformity on American public education."[64] The Court denied the petition, opting to wait for the lower courts to rule on VMI's chosen remedy.[65] The VMI Board of Visitors directed the attorneys to prepare a plan for their consideration. The privatization option was especially appealing to many alumni, although it could mean financial suicide. VMI was receiving $8.4 million a year from the state, a sizable sum that gave serious pause even to the school's most ardent supporters.

The state proposed a separate all-female program, the Virginia Women's Institute for Leadership ("VWIL"). The site would be at Mary Baldwin, a private women's liberal arts college located in Staunton, about thirty-five miles northeast of Lexington. The promise of a $5.5 million permanent endowment from the VMI Foundation, plus an annual state allocation of $5,900 for each Virginia student enrolled, made this an offer college officials could not refuse. Mary Baldwin established a task force to develop the VWIL plan, which the college's faculty approved by a vote of 52 to 8. Neither the state nor Mary Baldwin intended this to be a "women's VMI" but rather a "leadership" program designed to meet the "distinctive developmental characteristics and educational needs of women."[66] The Corps of Cadets would be little more than ceremonial, while the ROTC program would provide the main military experience. VWIL students would not live in barracks, would only wear uniforms two or three hours a week for ROTC training, and would not eat all meals together. Training in self-defense and self-assertiveness would replace the VMI adversative approach.[67] The proposal did not sit well in some circles. The *St. Louis Post–Dispatch* called it a "marriage of convenience."[68]A *New York Times* editorial was more caustic, rebuking Governor Wilder for endorsing a "separate and clearly unequal military program for women," calling it "a scrawny imitation of the VMI program," and "a new form of resistance to equality."[69]

Through the course of two trials, both sides bolstered their legal arguments with testimony from experts in the social sciences, higher education, and gender studies. As the attorneys hammered away at the witnesses and turned their testimony upside down on cross-examination, it became an evidentiary war between the forces of sameness and difference. When the parties returned to the trial court, the programmatic aspects of VMI and VWIL took center stage. A squadron of eleven lawyers was led this time by newly elected state Attorney General James S. Gilmore III, a Republican, representing the new Republican Governor George Allen. The VMI expert line-up, including David Riesman, Harvard's preeminent professor (emeritus) of sociology, and Elizabeth Fox–Genovese, the noted feminist historian from Emory University, offered numerous generalizations about the distinct abilities and proclivities of males and females.

The eighty-two-year-old Riesman's testimony in the first trial appeared before the court on videotape. In a deposition read to the court in the second trial, he clearly stated that the "undisciplined nature of many men" and the "overdisciplined, oversubdued, self-mistrustful nature of many women from most coed high schools" were "relevant" to the design of the VWIL program. Yet he also noted that he had known "many women who do not fit this picture at all."[70] His remarks seemed less a testament to all-male schools than a critique of young males and their need for VMI's uniquely punishing educational approach. Perhaps he simply believed that VMI was not denying women anything worth their wanting. Fox–Genovese more decidedly affirmed that belief, lending particular credibility to the state's parallel program for women. She testified that adolescent girls lag in self-confidence; unlike boys, they do not need the adversative method to beat the "uppityness and aggression" out of them. In her view, the leadership experiences offered in the VWIL program would produce young women who can "imagine themselves as leaders."[71]

The government countered with testimony from, among others, Carol Nagy Jacklin, dean of social sciences and communication at the University of Southern California and coauthor of the 1974 classic, *The Psychology of Sex Differences*.[72] Based on more than two decades of research, Jacklin maintained that there are greater learning differences within than between genders. Asked on cross-examination whether she was aware of any educational authorities supporting the adversative method for educating women, Jacklin pointedly responded, "No, nor for men."[73]

The government also presented testimony from Alexander Astin, Director of the Higher Education Research Institute at the University of California at Los Angeles. Both VMI and the district court had placed considerable weight in the first trial on Astin's 1977 book *Four Critical Years*,[74] in which he had touted the academic benefits of all-male colleges. Concerned that the state had misappropriated his research, Astin swiftly published a clarification in *The Chronicle of Higher Education*. He suggested that his earlier findings did not justify an all-male VMI because the original colleges were elite and selective institutions. The students and faculty at all-male colleges arguably might have changed in the intervening years.[75] In the second trial Astin testified that the VWIL and VMI programs were not in fact comparable. VWIL could not measure up, especially on such important intangible benefits as the power of VMI's peer group network and its effect on student outcomes. The VMI model, with all its military rigor and trappings, would attract a different type of student than the program at Mary Baldwin, he told the court, and the experience would produce a different type of graduate. Like Jacklin, Astin could not offer any authority supporting the adversative method, whether for women or for men.[76]

There were, in fact, concrete disparities in the quality of the two educational programs that the court could not easily dismiss. The VWIL curriculum did not offer the advanced math, engineering, and physics courses available at VMI. A VWIL student interested in pursuing an engineering degree would have to attend Washington University in St. Louis for two years and pay the tuition at the private school rate. Only 68% of Mary Baldwin's faculty held Ph.D. degrees compared with 86% at VMI. Meanwhile, the facilities at the two campuses, especially for athletics, were arguably incomparable. As one commentator put it, this was "VMI-lite," the place where girls went because "they just [were] not cut out to take the real tough, manly citizen-soldier leadership training."[77]

The unavoidable question was how to define "comparable." The United States looked for equal inputs. And so a newly minted parallel program for women could never offer VMI's intangible features, including its powerful alumni network, its stellar reputation, its prestige, and its traditions, all resting on more than a century and a half of history. Virginia, on the other hand, looked for comparable outputs, that is, a state-supported female college that would attain an outcome comparable to (but not exactly the same as) the one achieved for the male cadets at VMI. Applying the concept of "substantive comparability," a divided appeals court found the parallel program constitutionally permissible. It warned that the state had to "mitigate the effects" of gender classification by offering both men and women benefits that were "comparable in substance, but not [identical] in form or detail."[78] The programs, therefore, could reflect differences in needs between women and men as long as they did not tend to lessen the dignity or societal regard of either sex. Senior Circuit Judge J. Dickson Phillips, a Carter appointee from North Carolina, disagreed in a sharply worded dissent that harkened back to *Sweatt v. Painter*,[79] the case that had desegregated the University of Texas School of Law in 1950. His characterization of the VWIL program as "but a pale shadow of VMI" would later guide Justice Ginsburg's opinion for the Court, as would much of his rationale. For him, the two programs were not "substantially equal" in all the "tangible" and especially the "intangible" criteria conventionally used to evaluate educational institutions.[80]

In August 1995, as the first class of forty-two women entered the VWIL program, the Justice Department, then under the Clinton Administration, was even more committed to seeing the case to the finish. The appeals court denied the Department's request for a rehearing before the full membership,[81] leading Justice to petition the Supreme Court for consideration. The differences between the two programs, the government argued, were "substantial" and "deliberate," and premised on "explicit and archaic sex-based stereotypes" that merely served to "reinforce patterns of historical discrimination." But Justice also saw the opportunity to move beyond the facts of the case and chart new terrain in the law of sex equality. The Department entreated the Court to apply to sex classifications the same level of strict scrutiny review traditionally applied to race.[82] In other words, VMI's all-male admissions policy should stand only if it were "narrowly tailored" to serve a "compelling" state interest.

As the government's attempt to intrude on Virginia's educational system evoked images of the Civil War among VMI's southern supporters, for its detractors the parallel program at Mary Baldwin dredged up more recent memories of Virginia's willful resistance to racial integration. Those memories surfaced in a notably blunt *New York Times* editorial urging the Court to hear the case. Decrying the "constitutional evasions" of a state "unmoved by social progress," the editors proposed that the case "might do for gender discrimination what *Brown v. Board of Education* [had done] for state-sponsored racial apartheid."[83]

Outside Voices

The Court's decision to grant review elicited an onslaught of amicus briefs, including some surprising alliances, from across the political spectrum. Among VMI supporters were a number of conservative organizations, including the Family Research Council and the Eagle Forum[84] as well as the Independent Women's Forum, whose president Anita Blair was a member of the VMI Board of Visitors.[85] The states of Pennsylvania and Wyoming argued that VMI had a valid interest in protecting diversity and experimentation.[86] Others, including Hawaii, Maryland, Massachusetts, Nevada, and Oregon, expressed more concern for individual rights than state autonomy.[87] A brief signed by Dr. Kenneth Clark, whose research had proven critical in the Supreme Court's 1954 decision in *Brown*, weighed in on the side of Virginia to preserve public single-sex education.[88]

Three amicus briefs particularly resonated with the Court. The first came from the American Association of University Professors. Leading scholars in gender studies, among them Carol Gilligan, Harvard professor and noted author of the groundbreaking book, *In a Different Voice*,[89] challenged the "time-worn" generalizations threaded throughout the trial record. "While it is undoubtedly true that there are average differences between the sexes," they argued, many individual women and men "do not conform to the 'average' for their sex."[90] The second brief, from the International Coalition of Boys' Schools, expressed reservations among some of the signatories with the VMI philosophy, yet they all shared a concern with the potential consequences for single-sex education. Included in the group were representatives of urban school districts and private single-sex schools. The first were interested in exploring the approach, especially for disadvantaged boys, while the latter feared the loss of state or federal aid.[91] The third influential brief spoke for a group of private women's colleges noting similar concerns.[92]

The numerous amicus briefs, however, were not the only outside influence weighing on the Court. As the justices pored over the copious record and listened to oral arguments, one cannot help but assume that a compelling videotape playing in the back of their minds unofficially yet unavoidably shaped their thoughts. The setting of that tape, The Citadel in South Carolina, and the vivid events surrounding strikingly similar legal claims, provided the Court with a dramatically personal element that the VMI litigation sorely lacked. It also offered a more compelling narrative. The case against VMI, with only the mythical and abstract female Jackie Jones seeking admission, did not directly confront the justices with any palpable harm suffered by real women challenging the gender stereotypes implicit in policies that excluded them. The district court, in fact, had characterized the enemy as the United States, dating back to the Civil War, but this time intruding on Virginia's right to educational autonomy. The Citadel, on the other hand, presented a real but tragic heroine (or villain, depending on where you stood) in the person of Shannon Faulkner, a young woman who took the college to court when denied admission. The Justice Department only intervened later as a party.

Here was a more personalized struggle between an actual female applicant and school officials. And here the appeals court had framed the remedy as an individual right to immediate relief from a constitutional violation. The hair-raising ordeal that Shannon Faulkner suffered at the hands of angry and mean-spirited cadets, tacitly encouraged by a defiant administration, was well-documented and brought to life in the local and national media. When put on the defensive, The Citadel engaged in a "campaign of massive resistance" reminiscent of those once waged against racial segregation.[93] Meanwhile, the lurid history of The Citadel's punishing form of hazing had inspired a rich literature, including Citadel alum Pat Conroy's *The Lords of* Discipline,[94] a novel set in an all-male southern military school. Susan Faludi's 1994 *New Yorker* exposé of Citadel culture was equally gripping and even more timely.[95]

This is the story of a high school honors student from rural Powdersville, South Carolina who, having learned about The Citadel in a *Sports Illustrated* article, decided to apply for admission to the 1993 entering class. She convinced her high school guidance counselor to "white out" from her school transcripts all references to her gender while using completely gender-neutral terms in the attached school appraisal. She soon received an acceptance letter with the opening: "Dear Mr. Faulkner." But as news of the error worked its way through the grapevine, The Citadel unapologetically rescinded the offer. Coming from a generation of women unaccustomed to such blatant inequality, she found herself willingly in court, surrounded by a flock of New York City lawyers from the ACLU Women's Rights Project and the prestigious firm of Shearman and Sterling, along with the president of the South Carolina chapter of the National Organization for Women ("NOW").

For the next two and half years, as her lawsuit ground through the courts, she was taunted, vilified, and humiliated. She received telephone death threats and hate mail. Her car was pelted with eggs. The Citadel newspaper dubbed her "the Divine Bovine" and "Mrs. Doubtgender." "Die Faulkner" was scrawled across a billboard in Charleston, and a local radio station made her the subject of parodies in song. Her parents' home was sprayed with obscene epithets. Women stopped her on the street and berated her for trying to destroy a tradition. The Citadel's lawyer argued in court that she was setting about to impose a "unisex worldview" on the Constitution.[96] Meanwhile, Citadel officials dragged their feet on devising a remedy even after the Fourth Circuit had concluded that VMI's identical policy violated the Constitution. They simply argued that there was no demand for a Citadel-type institution or program for women. They made it unmistakably clear that Shannon Faulkner would never be accepted into the powerful network that she was fighting to join. In fact, as they saw it, she was more likely to destroy it.

In July 1994, following a bench trial, the district court ordered the school to admit her into the Corps of Cadets and to develop a plan to admit additional women.[97] Days before classes were to commence, officials won a stay, pending appeal. The following April, a divided appeals court affirmed the district court ruling, ordering The Citadel to admit Faulkner or develop an acceptable alternative plan.[98]After much wrangling and resistance on the part of Citadel officials, on August 12, 1995, Shannon Faulkner reported to The Citadel as the first female cadet in the school's 152–year history. She lasted less than a week, mostly in the infirmary, ostensibly suffering from heat exhaustion. As she later recalled, "hell week" was nothing compared to what she had endured on her way there. She had gained fifty pounds and felt battle worn. By late afternoon of day six, despite her lawyers' desperate urging that she hang on in, she announced that she was withdrawing from the school.

She exited the gates in a jeep to the strains of "Hey, hey, the witch is dead," sung by three dancing cadets in soaking uniforms. Flashed across newspapers nationwide were images of young men whooping and howling, running in circles and chanting with arms raised in victory. Their euphoria underscored the institutional culture—that only "real men" could survive the rigors of The Citadel's program. The fact that thirty male cadets also had withdrawn within the first week could not dispel this pervasive belief.[99] When an unusually high number of upper-class students did not return after Christmas break, Citadel officials realized the high toll the litigation had taken on the institution. Not surprisingly, the public nature of Shannon Faulkner's experience evoked sympathy from many observers who could not "wrap their minds" around the impersonal and abstract arguments emerging from the VMI litigation.[100]

Before the High Court

The Supreme Court heard arguments in *United States v. Virginia* in January 1996, barely six months following the spectacle of Shannon Faulkner's departure from The Citadel. Representing the Justice Department was Paul Bender, Deputy Solicitor General and former high school classmate of Ruth Bader Ginsburg. On Virginia's side was Theodore Olson, a Washington insider and former Assistant Attorney General in the Reagan Administration. As the justices put the lawyers through their paces, perhaps the most telling comment came from Justice Stephen Breyer. When confronted with Olson's argument that the VMI way of life might disappear with the admission of women, he coolly replied, "So what."[101] Late the following June, the Court in a seven-to-one decision ruled that Virginia's categorical exclusion of women from the citizen-soldier training program at VMI violated the Constitution, and that the VWIL parallel program proved an inadequate remedy.[102] Justice Clarence Thomas, whose son was enrolled in VMI at the time, had not participated in the deliberations.

Reading her opinion slowly from the bench to a rapt audience, Justice Ginsburg stressed the narrowness of the decision, the unique facts presented, and the historical background of women's educational exclusion. She began by noting that government must defend its gender-based actions with an "exceedingly persuasive justification," a phrase she invoked nine times and which she described as the "core instruction" of prior decisions, including *Hogan*.[103] Government actors must show "at least that the [challenged] classification serves 'important governmental objectives and that the discriminatory means employed' are 'substantially related to the achievement of those objectives.' " Calling it "skeptical scrutiny," she noted that this "demanding" burden of justification rested "entirely on the state." Courts must take a "hard look" at "generalizations or tendencies" based on gender.[104] Borrowing language from race desegregation cases, she warned that the remedy must "closely fit the constitutional violation," placing the claimants in "the position they would have occupied in the absence of [discrimination]."[105]

She made clear that even benign justifications will not necessarily support categorical exclusions. Although she recognized the "Commonwealth's prerogative evenhandedly to support diverse educational opportunities," the state's actions, she concluded, were anything but "evenhanded." Virginia effectively denied women a unique educational opportunity available solely at the state's "premier military institute." Looking back over VMI's history, it was apparent to the Court that diversity had not driven the decision of its founders, nor had it played a part in continuing to exclude women. "However 'liberally' this plan served the Commonwealth's sons," she noted, "it makes no provision whatever for its daughters."[106]

Justice Ginsburg also dismissed Virginia's arguments preserving the adversative method which, the state claimed, was critical. The state had argued that the modifications needed to accommodate women would be so "radical" and "drastic" that they would "transform" and even "destroy" the VMI program.[107] She noted the success of the federal service academies in admitting women and how the minor necessary alterations were "manageable."[108] That notation belied reality. The academies, in fact, had made a number of accommodations for women and had softened their training program to meet other needs. Nonetheless, expert testimony had established, and the parties had agreed, that "some women [were] capable of all the individual activities required of VMI cadets." Moreover, the district court had recognized that "some women . . . would want to attend [VMI] if they had the opportunity." It was "on behalf of these women," Justice Ginsburg stated, that the litigation had been brought and a "remedy must be crafted."[109] She recalled how similar arguments had been used in the past to exclude women from the practices of law and medicine. Citing *Hogan* she warned that "state actors controlling gates to opportunity . . . may not exclude qualified individuals based on 'fixed notions concerning the roles and abilities of males and females.' "[110] The implication was that women could enter VMI through a process of assimilation, that is, they could blend into the existing program without significant modifications. It was on this assumption that VMI officials consequently sold coeducation to the alumni and students, some of them merely reluctant, others openly hostile.

Throughout the opinion, we see Justice Ginsburg navigating a winding course between competing visions of equality, one based on sameness, the other on difference. Despite her grounding in absolute equality, she recognized that women should be compensated for socially imposed disabilities, or accommodated for different educational needs. Although she used what men have as the norm and looked for equal treatment in this case, she acknowledged the inherent physical differences between the sexes, thereby leaving open the possibility for different treatment under other circumstances. At the same time, she showed sensitivity to women's history of exclusion and subordination, particularly in education. She chose her words more carefully than one might initially comprehend.[111] While recognizing the reality of "physical" (but not all) differences between the sexes, she also cautioned against the potential danger of misapplying that understanding. She acknowledged, and not grudgingly, that unlike race for which the law admits of no differences, the physical or " 'inherent differences' between men and women" are "cause for celebration ... [and] enduring ... The two sexes are not fungible." That language is indeed noteworthy from someone so strongly wedded in the past to the sameness ideal and who, in her early career as a litigator, so forcefully argued for the Court to consider race and sex classifications with equal skepticism. Yet while she conceded that sex classifications "are permissible" as long as they "advance the full development of the talent and capacities of our Nation's people," she also warned that they could not be used to "denigrat[e]" either men or women or to place "artificial constraints on an individual's opportunity."[112] Decisions must be made on a case-by-case basis.

In a critical footnote, Justice Ginsburg affirmed the position that a group of women's college's had taken in their amicus brief. Using language that would lend support to single-sex education and at the same time define its contours, she recognized "the mission of some single-sex schools to 'dissipate, rather than perpetuate, traditional gender classifications.' "[113] And while she made clear that the Court was not addressing the question of whether states could provide "separate but equal" undergraduate institutions, she nevertheless offered specific guidelines on what courts might consider in judging whether the education offered both sexes is "substantially equal." Like Judge Phillips in the court of appeals, she drew on *Sweatt v. Painter*,[114] counseling that equality must be measured by tangible and intangible qualities, including curricular and extracurricular choices, the stature of the faculty, funding, prestige, library resources, and alumni support and influence. On that count, the program at Mary Baldwin, as Judge Phillips had noted, was merely a "pale shadow of VMI."[115]

For Justice Ginsburg, the VMI case vindicated her entire legal career. As one commentator captured it, the decision was the one "she had hoped the [C]ourt would one day arrive at when she first started arguing cases of discrimination in the 1960s.''[116] The language, reasoning, and spirit of her opinion drew heavily from a brief she had prepared in an early unsuccessful round of litigation challenging Philadelphia's all-male Central High School.[117] She herself later recalled that, ''[I]t was [like] winning [that] case twenty years later.''[118] In a speech at the University of Virginia, she went so far as to claim that there was ''no practical difference'' between what had ''evolved'' and the proposed federal Equal Rights Amendment that had failed to win ratification in the early 1980s. Yet in that same Virginia speech, she also revealed a narrower view, that the VMI decision merely represented ''the codification of a social revolution in the role of military academies that had occurred a decade earlier.''[119] In any event, the constitutional implications of her unusually forceful language, her repeated emphasis on the ''exceedingly persuasive justification,'' and her reliance on standards borrowed from race discrimination cases continue to invite speculation within the legal community. Was she merely restating what has been called ''intermediate scrutiny''? Or was ''skeptical scrutiny'' something closer to, but not quite as rigorous as, the ''strict scrutiny'' used for racial classifications? If so, then was it a mere aberration or would it withstand the test of time given recent changes in the Court's membership?[120]

In a concurring opinion, Chief Justice Rehnquist expressed concern on that precise point. He feared that Justice Ginsburg's forceful reliance on the phrase ''exceedingly persuasive justification'' had ratcheted up the standard for reviewing sex-based classifications, misapplied prior case law, and introduced an ''element of uncertainty'' into sex discrimination analysis. To his mind, the phrase was merely ''an observation on the difficulty of meeting the applicable test, not . . . a formulation of the test itself.''[121] Nevertheless, he concluded that the state violated the equal protection clause not because it excluded women but because the VWIL program was not ''comparable,'' and in fact ''distinctly inferior'' to the program offered to men.[122] For Justice Antonin Scalia, the lone dissenting voice, the majority's opinion was ''politics smuggled into law.''[123] In a forty page opinion, just one page short of the majority's, he took the Court to task for distorting judicial precedent, denying the real differences between women and men, and in the end even threatening the vitality of private single-sex schools whose tax-exempt status and government funding would be placed in jeopardy. Striking an ominous note, he predicted that the decision would render ''single-sex public education . . . functionally dead.''[124]

The Court remanded the case to the Fourth Circuit which, in turn, sent it back to Judge Kiser to require Virginia to either develop and implement a plan that met the constitutional standards set by the Court or forego state funding.[125]

The Immediate Response

While the Court's ruling technically applied only to VMI, by implication it also affected The Citadel. The two institutions responded quite differently and with dramatically different results. Within two days, The Citadel announced that it would "enthusiastically accept qualified female applicants into the Corps of Cadets."[126] Officials, in hindsight perhaps too hastily, submitted to the district court a twenty-one-page plan to admit women. The following September, four women entered the Corps without any overt signs of opposition. But even an edict from the highest court in the land could not precipitously change such a deeply embedded culture. By January, two of the women had filed harassment complaints and withdrawn from school. Their claims may have proven shocking and even unthinkable in another setting. Their fellow cadets had sprayed them with nail polish remover and set them on fire, washed their mouths out with cleanser, and kicked them and subjected them to unwelcome sexual advances.[127]

Fourteen male cadets were punished in the wake of the allegations. Two of them were dismissed and three resigned. Both women subsequently sued The Citadel. One of them ultimately settled for $100,000 and the other for $33,750, although the school admitted no wrongdoing. The incidents had once again placed the institution's hidden culture of violence and cruelty under intense public scrutiny. A *Washington Post* editorial urged the school's leaders to "make a judgment about how this worse-than-fraternity nonsense prepares their students for military service in the real world."[128]

The response from VMI was more deliberate and initially resistant. It took an additional three months to decide on a course of action. During that time, VMI alumni explored privatization, while school officials considered the possibility of coeducation. Meanwhile, passions ran high within and without the institution which again became a lightening rod in the gender wars. For some, privatization was a national cause with stakes much larger than VMI itself. Phyllis Schlafly once again stepped in, capturing the depths of those feelings. In an open letter sent to VMI alumni and posted on their unofficial website, she called the "massive government lawsuit" a "no-holds-barred fight to feminize VMI waged by the radical feminists and their cohorts in the Federal Government." Schlafly knew her audience well. She challenged their masculinity and warned them, "If you allow Ginsburg et al. to do what Pat Schroeder et al. have done to the United States Navy, you are not the exemplars of manhood we thought you were. And that goes for the Citadel alumni too."[129]

The task of walking this field of landmines was left not to a son of the Old South but to a Philadelphia Main Line Yankee, Major General Josiah ("Sy") Bunting III, VMI Class of 1963. (The title is by Governor's designation in the Virginia militia.) In 1995, in the thick of the lawsuit, Bunting had returned to his alma mater to take on the possible challenges that loomed ahead. As a student, Bunting had distinguished himself academically and served as First Captain of the Corps. On graduation he went off to Oxford University on a Rhodes scholarship before a stint in Vietnam as Commander of the 505th Infantry. A noted author, his novel *The Lionheads*, based on his Vietnam experiences, won critical acclaim but angered army brass for its "angry indictment of careerism's effect on the military."[130] Before returning to VMI, he had a peripatetic career as a professor, college president, and private school headmaster. At six feet four inches, Bunting is a physically imposing man, and as his friends describe, "a creature out of the nineteenth century." At VMI he taught a seminar on Victorian prose.[131] In person, now in civilian attire as President of a private foundation, he comes across much closer to Mr. Chips (with just a tinge of General Patton) than the hard-nosed military brass one would intuitively expect. Well regarded in higher education circles, he has a keen understanding of institutional culture, which clearly guided his approach to overseeing the transition to coeducation. He also has a profound sense of military duty to carry out orders from higher authorities. Words like honorable, noble, and earnest pepper his discussion of VMI's response to the Court's decision.[132]

As a witness for The Citadel, Bunting had "likened the admission of women to the introduction of a 'toxic kind of virus' whose presence even in small numbers would destroy the entire institution."[133] Immediately following the decision, he lamented how it was a "savage disappointment" for VMI alumni who had helped pay the $14 million in legal fees brought on by the litigation.[134] He insisted that schools such as VMI and The Citadel would be "radically transformed" if they admitted women, and in ways that he did not believe would prove "useful." The changes would be "seismic, profound."[135] Nonetheless, Bunting respected the authority of the Court. He immediately moved his staff toward planning to admit females in the event that the Board of Visitors gave the go-ahead. Within a month of the Court's decision, VMI had up and running an executive committee and eight subcommittees, including over 160 members from across the VMI community, to draw up an "Assimilation Plan." In the meantime, the Board continued deliberating until it finally surrendered in an 8 to 9 vote following three days of meetings. Surprisingly, most of the "yes" votes came from Board members who had graduated before 1970. The cost of going private, estimated at between $100 and $400 million, had proven prohibitively high. But even more was at stake, not the least being the possibility that the Department of Defense might suspend the college's ROTC program for discriminating against women.[136] There were also political risks to consider. Privatization would have dredged up memories of Virginia's resistance to court desegregation orders, making VMI a pariah in the eyes of the media.

From the very beginning, Bunting asserted the college's autonomy. He made clear that the Institute was "anxious to protect the principles and elements of what we are" and refused Justice Department demands to submit an assimilation plan up front. He also made clear that VMI would closely follow the Court's opinion, for better or worse. Unlike the federal academies, it would hold women to the exact same dress and physical requirements, including the buzz haircut, as men.[137] As for the plan, Judge Kiser ultimately brokered a consensus whereby VMI would file quarterly progress reports over which the Justice Department would have no veto power. By that point, the VMI Admissions Office had shown good faith, having initiated a massive direct-mail campaign to female high school seniors, guidance counselors, and athletic directors.

The outrageous acts against Shannon Faulkner and the women who followed her at The Citadel had given VMI officials much to reflect upon as they more cautiously and thoughtfully prepared for admitting women. Over the following year, VMI staff and faculty visited other colleges and universities that had made the transition to coeducation. With the Justice Department prohibiting them from any contact with the Army, Navy, and Air Force academies, Bunting went so far as to visit the Ecole Polytechnique, the prestigious French engineering institution. The administration invited consultants and groups to visit the post and review the committee's plans. It held sexual harassment seminars for staff and cadets.[138] It hired women to fill administrative posts, established complaint procedures outside the chain of command to afford women a level of comfort in reporting incidents, and worked hard to bring the cadets on board. In the end, the committee decided to issue uniforms, including skirts appropriate to females, and to modify the buzz cut by barely a half inch. Meanwhile, VMI had recruited two male and nine female cadets as exchange students from Norwich University in Vermont and Texas A & M, schools with a large cadet corps, the one to engage the male cadets on the acceptability of coeducation, the other to mentor the female cadets. Looking back, Bunting now muses that perhaps they should have recruited additional female faculty, especially lacking in the sciences, and offered more athletic scholarships to attract more women cadets.[139] Yet throughout the process, the term consistently and consciously used was "assimilation" whereby women would conform to the existing male standards, with only essential modifications, as compared to the more accommodating "integration" that had occurred at the federal academies.

In August 1997, 30 women and 430 men entered VMI's first coed "rat line." As cadets and parents sat packed in Jackson Memorial Hall, Bunting told the crowd, "VMI does not care if you are poor or rich, if you are white or black, female or male, Taiwanese or Finn or Virginian. We care only about your heart, your integrity and your determination." Colonel Alan Farrell, acting Dean of Faculty, sounded a more somber note. "This is a world that may be unfamiliar to you," he warned. "It is ritual. It is language. It is symbols. It is customs. It's pomp. It's ferocious nostalgia. It is occasionally, well brutality ... a certain intolerance to human frailty that can appear brutal."[140] By the following March, six women and 69 men from the entering class had dropped out. Yet for the women who remained, the pay off was significant. Graduation that May saw five female cadets, including one from Taiwan, earning rank within the Corps of Cadets. At that point General Bunting noted, with more than a twinge of vindication, that "VMI was instinctively right to say this is what we are, we're not going to change, come take us for what we are."[141] In January, 1999 Judge Kiser dismissed the lawsuit, ruling that VMI had succeeded in guaranteeing women equal treatment. The Justice Department filed no objections.[142]

The Long View

Looking back over a decade of coeducation at VMI, Justice Ginsburg was right. The assimilation of "capable" women did not destroy the Institute or the "VMI Spirit." VMI officials themselves have since conceded that the admission of women did not create the cataclysmic changes they had feared. By 2000, when the first class of women reached their final year, Bunting admitted to feeling "elegiac and enthusiastic." "In the end," he allowed, "VMI had changed very little."[143] At that point, VMI had named its first female battalion commander, one of only two students chosen out of a class of 298, while two women joined the ranks of the "cadre," the elite group of cadets who train and brow-beat the incoming class. In fact, the move to coeducation was far less painful than The Citadel experience. That ease, no doubt, came with the advantage of not being first, along with a $5.1 million state grant to renovate the barracks, and a year to thoughtfully plan the transition. Bunting suggests, however, that regional and institutional culture also played an important role. In Lexington, which is heavily Scots–Irish Presbyterian, he notes, everyone is "orally earnest" and committed to resolving problems by way of committee. Besides, he says, there was "a pervasive sense of dutifulness" that they had to make the school "look good," to "do this honorably," in the model of their most venerated alum, General George Marshall.[144]

VMI made an institutional commitment to assimilate women into the Corps uneventfully. And to some extent it has been reasonably successful. Not surprisingly, there have been bumps along the way. There also remains work to be done. During the first year, a male cadet was found having a sexual encounter on campus with a female exchange student. Both were expelled. The following year, VMI dismissed its top-ranking cadet for allegedly using his position to pressure freshmen women for sex. By the fourth year, when the college permitted its first pregnant cadet to remain in the barracks and continue attending classes, some of her classmates as well as alums seized the opportunity to vent their hostility toward women at VMI. The Commandant himself admitted that a group of cadets was waging a "guerilla campaign," ranging from "verbal insults" to "petty cruelties" against women.[145] (In 2005, VMI adopted a policy requiring any cadet who marries or becomes a parent to resign from the Corps.[146]) As one female alum now recalls, "About five of the guys in our class gave us a hard time. The rest didn't care. There were occasions when these guys were verbally abusive, calling us 'bitches" and other offensive names. We just learned to take it and handle it on a one-on-one basis or just avoid these guys. Once we got through the rat line, we knew we could take more charge of our lives. I had tons of male friends."[147] Yet some of the men who "befriended women" were ostracized from their own groups.[148] Today, such incidents are isolated while any residual hostility is largely kept beneath the surface.[149] None of this, however, is startling. The federal military academies, thirty years into coeducation, continue to battle hostile attitudes and the inappropriate treatment of women.[150]

Some of the problems women cadets faced, especially in the early years of coeducation, were mostly the result of being in such a minute minority with essentially no role models. For some, trying to maintain their femininity while being a good cadet proved unsettling. As one alum recollects, "I had a hard time trying to figure out who I was. College is a time when you're trying to find yourself. Having my hair cut short and not wearing make-up was difficult."[151] Even the uniform skirt generated tension. For some, it was a means of asserting gender identity. For others, it was a symbol of resistance to the pressure of "blending in."[152] One of the biggest challenges was the intense scrutiny. "Everyone knew everything about you—your grades, how fast you ran, whether you were dating someone in the Corps," recalls another alum. In fact, dating between cadets still raises some eyebrows. Their personal successes and failures were common topics of discussion among the male cadets. "They would show up on the back page of the *The Cadet*, the school newspaper, where the editors had free reign to make fun of people."[153] For Jackie Tugman, a member of the second class of women and now Assistant Director of Admissions at VMI, the picture carries into the present. As she pointedly describes it, "Everyone is thrown into this testosterone driven system and women are trying to fit in. And they have to do it the men's way. They have to figure out how to do it."[154] There seems to be a general consensus that female cadets who are not attractive and not physically fit still have the hardest time gaining acceptance by males or females.[155] Yet there is a pervasively stoic attitude among these women. As one female alum sums it up, "VMI is not for the faint of heart, and I would never want it to be."[156]

As for the college itself, little has changed programmatically. The "adversative method," the grueling "rat line," and the traditional rituals continue. Renovations and the addition of a new Barracks building over the next few years will reduce overcrowding but living conditions otherwise will remain essentially the same.[157] The school still sponsors sexual harassment seminars for staff and cadets, while *The Cadet*'s "Humor Page" still considers females as fair game. As a seminar leader explained, VMI must carefully navigate the fine line between harassment and First Amendment free speech protections.[158] And while the college has barely attracted the desired "critical mass" of female cadets, up to 11% (43 women) in the Fall 2006 incoming class, their presence has not deterred males from applying. In fact, it may have proven an incentive. Applications have soared in recent years, helped no doubt by the baby "boomlet," making the school more selective in admissions.[159] Many of the alums once vehemently opposed to admitting women have come around, some even facilitating the careers of former female cadets through the powerful alumni network. A female graduate from the first coed class now sits on the Alumni Advisory Board.

Whatever accommodations VMI has made for women have been minor. Some changes have evolved over the years. Female rats now sport hair about two inches in length. Beyond "breakout," there are no restrictions so long as they tuck their hair under their cap when in uniform. The "Bullet," or "rat bible," has undergone some changes, most of them linguistic but some substantive. Gone is "The Code of a Gentleman," warning the cadet not to "speak more than casually about his girlfriend", or "hail a lady from a club window," or "display his wealth, money, or possessions."[160] Yet references unexpectedly remain to the "brotherhood" created in the corps[161] and to the bonding among "Brother Rats," a term that females have left unchallenged.[162] The aura of male normativity remains alive and well. Perhaps Sy Bunting was right. It could be that a critical mass of women is essential to creating an organic coeducational program. A 2005 Pentagon task force investigating sexual harassment at West Point and Annapolis, where women comprise 15% to 17% of the student body, drew a similar conclusion.[163] Only time will tell just how large that figure must be for the culture to change, if ever.

Although some male cadets continue to lament the loss of the "Old VMI," many if not most have adjusted and even come to appreciate the assimilation of women into the "New VMI." As for Bunting, he still feels "saddened" that VMI did not remain all-male. Nonetheless, he unequivocally would recommend VMI over the VWIL program to any woman who is looking for the "real thing" in military training.[164] It all depends on how you define the "real thing." General Michael Bissell, who oversaw the assimilation process at VMI and now serves as Commandant at Mary Baldwin, sees it differently. "Coeducation," he says, "takes away the good qualities that women can take into the military, their patience, their compassion." From his observations, the VWIL cadets, now numbering around 120, are more self-confident and "don't worry about being the token or rocking the boat" as the female cadets at VMI.[165] "They have a chance to develop their style," he says. But, as Justice Ginsburg noted, some women apparently prefer the VMI experience, for whatever benefits it brings.

Fears that women would wreak havoc on VMI were not the only ones that proved unfounded. Throughout the litigation, VMI attorneys argued that single-sex education itself was at stake, while Justice Scalia, in dissent, forecast its total demise. The past decade has proven them wrong. Private all-women's colleges like Smith, Mount Holyoke, Barnard, and Wellesley continue without legal challenge or administrative threat to their tax-exempt status. Meanwhile, single-sex schooling at the elementary and secondary levels, especially for girls but increasingly for boys, has continued on an upward trajectory begun in the early 1990s. Even more surprisingly, single-sex schools and classes have gained renewed appeal among public school parents and school officials particularly in poor urban communities. The most recent spurt of concentrated interest in the South seemingly reflects the same cultural attitudes that supported all-male admissions policies at VMI and The Citadel. At the time of the Court's decision in 1996, there were only two originally single-sex public schools remaining in the country—the Philadelphia High School for Girls and Western High School in Baltimore, both dating from the 1840s. As of March 2007 there were 52 single-sex schools and 210 coed schools offering single-sex classes in certain subjects.[166]

Ironically, some of the arguments supporting this revival draw on emerging developments in brain research, far advanced since 1996, and the arguable differences in learning styles between girls and boys. The jury is still out on whether these are real differences or merely overbroad generalizations, or even whether they have significant relevance to education.[167] In the meantime, in 2002 as part of the No Child Left Behind Act, Congress authorized the use of federal funds for innovative programs, including single-sex schools and classes.[168] In October 2006, the federal Department of Education issued revised Title IX regulations giving school districts greater flexibility in establishing programs that separate students on the basis of sex.[169] The new rules track the language of the Court's decision, particularly requiring that programs for both sexes meet the Court's test of "substantial equality" based on both "tangible" and "intangible" factors. While these programs have proven controversial, inviting sharp criticism from civil liberties and women's groups, the courts have yet to measure them against Justice Ginsburg's "skeptical scrutiny" standard under the federal Constitution.[170]

Conclusion

The Supreme Court's decision in *United States v. Virginia* is important for its immediate effect in allowing women access to a unique and valued education and for its sweeping rejection of gender stereotypes. Nonetheless, it is equally compelling for its underlying story, with its many twists and turns, of how history, politics, and cultural attitudes can affect the course of constitutional litigation and consequently public policy. It also underscores the role played by outside interests and the national and local media in shaping public opinion on conflicting narratives that at times mask deeper issues of broad social importance. In the end, this deceptively simple case of sex, schooling, and the military merits serious reflection as it continues to evolve against the enduring yet ever-changing debate over sameness and difference.

Endnotes

1. United States v. Virginia, 518 U.S. 515, 558 (1996).

2. Lawrence A. Summers, Remarks at NBER Conference on Diversifying the Science & Engineering Workforce, Cambridge Massachusetts, Jan. 14, 2005, available at http://www.president.harvard.edu/speeches/2005/nber.html.

3. Edward Clarke, Sex in Education; Or, A Fair Chance for the Girls 133 (1873).

4. Sarah Grimke, Letters on the Equality of the Sexes and the Condition of Women 10 (1838), quoted in Barbara Deckard, The Women's Movement 253 (1975), and in Ruth Bader Ginsburg, Sex Equality and the Constitution: The State of the Art, 14 Women's Rts. L. Rep. 361 (1992).

5. U.S Government Printing Office, A Matter of Simple Justice: The Report of the President's Task Force on Women' Rights and Responsibilities iii (1970).

6. Rosemary C. Salomone, Same, Different, Equal: Rethinking Single–Sex Schooling 47 (2003).

7. Rosemary C. Salomone, Feminist Voices in the Debate Over Single–Sex Schooling: Finding Common Ground, 11 Mich. J. Gender & L. 63, 79 (2004).

8. Justice Ruth Bader Ginsburg, The Washington College of Law Founders Day Tribute, 5 Am. U. J. Gender Soc. Pol'y & L. 1, 3 (1996); Salomone, *supra* note 6, at 50.

9. *See* Ruth Bader Ginsburg, Gender and the Constitution, 44 U. Cin. L. Rev. 1 (1975).

10. Reed v. Reed, 404 U.S. 71 (1971); U.S. Const. amend. XIV, § 1 states: "No state shall ... deny to any person within its jurisdiction the equal protection of the laws."

11. Craig v. Boren, 429 U.S. 190 (1976); Deborah L. Markowitz, In Pursuit of Equality: One Woman's Work to Change the Law, 14 Women's Rts. L. Rep. 336, 346 (1992).

12. Leslie Miller–Bernal, Co-education: An Uneven Progression, in Going Coed: Women's Experiences in Formerly Men's Colleges and Universities, 1950–2000, 10 (Leslie Miller–Bernal and Susan L. Paulson eds., 2004).

13. Brian Mitchell, Weak Link: The Feminization of the American Military 37–42 (1989).

14. *Id.* at 42; 10 U.S.C. § 4342 (2005).

15. Mitchell, *supra* note 13, at 70–71.

16. Matt Chittum, VMI Out of Step with Academies, Roanoke Times, Aug. 30, 1998, at A1 (statement of Capt. Glenn Gottschalk, Director of Institutional Research).

17. Philippa Strum, Women in the Barracks 84 (2002); VMI Runs Rear–Guard Action Against Admitting Women, Wash. Post, June 1, 1986, at A22.

18. Mississippi Univ. for Women v. Hogan, 458 U.S. 718 (1982).

19. Mission Study Comm. of the Bd. of Trustees, Virginia Military Institute, Final Report, May 16, 1986, at 2 (copy on file with author).

20. Strum, *supra* note 17, at 86 (citing author's interview with Judith Keith).

21. Va. Const., art. 1, § 2 (stating that the "right to be free from any governmental discrimination upon the basis of religious conviction, race, color, sex or national origin shall not be abridged").

22. Letter from Gerald L. Baliles, Governor, St. of Va., to VMI Bd. of Visitors (Apr. 18, 1989) (copy on file with author).

23. Letter from John W. Knapp, Acting Superintendent, VMI, to James P. Turner, Acting Assistant Att'y Gen., Civil Rts. Div., U.S. Dept. of Justice (Apr. 23, 1989) (copy on file with author).

24. Letter from James P. Turner, Acting Ass't Att'y Gen., Civil Rts. Div., U.S. Dept. of Justice, to Honorable Lawrence Douglas Wilder, Governor, St. of Va. and Joseph M. Spivey, III, President, Bd. of Visitors, Virginia Military Institute (Jan. 30, 1990) (copy on file with author).

25. Resolution, Virginia Military Institute Board of Visitors (Feb. 5, 1990) (copy on file with author).

26. Kirstein v. Rectors and Visitors of Univ. of Va., 309 F.Supp. 184, 187 (E.D. Va. 1970).

27. Salomone, *supra* note 6, at 152.

28. Kent Jenkins, Jr., Candidates Lend an Ear to VMI Issue, Wash. Post, Oct. 2, 1989, at D1.

29. Laura Fairchild Brodie, Breaking Out: VMI and the Coming of Women 11 (2002).

30. John G. Barrett and Richard M. McMurry, VMI in the Civil War, in A Crowd of Honorable Youths: Historical Essays on the First 150 Years of the Virginia Military Institute 331, 32 (Thomas W. Davis ed., 1988); Jennings C. Wise, The Military History of the Virginia Military Institute from 1839 to 1865, 49 (1915).

31. Brodie, *supra* note 29, at 11; Henry A. Wise, Drawing Out the Man: The VMI Story 43 (1978).

32. Diane Avery, Institutional Myths, Historical Narratives, and Social Science Evidence: Reading the "Record" in the Virginia Military Institute Case, 5 S. Cal. Rev. of L. & Women's Stud. 189, 240–67 (1996).

33. VMI: A Profile, Virginia Military Institute Office of Admissions (2005–06) (copy on file with author).

34. Wise, supra note 31, at 12 (quoting speech of John Thomas Lewis Preston, Member of the Organizing Board and Professor of Languages (Nov. 11, 1889)), reprinted in William Couper, One Hundred Years at VMI, I, 33 (1939).

35. VMI New Cadet Handbook 2005–06, 8 (2005) (copy on file with author).

36. Mission Study Comm. Of the Bd. of Trustees, *supra* note 19, at 1.

37. United States v. Virginia, 766 F.Supp. 1407, 1421–24 (W.D. Va. 1991).

38. Wise, *supra* note 31, at 1.

39. *Id.* at 17.

40. Brief for Appellees at 20, United States v. Virginia, 976 F.2d 890 (4th Cir. 1992).

41. Brief for Petitioner at 29, United States v. Virginia, 518 U.S. 515 (1996).

42. Brief of Amicus Curiae Lieutenant Colonel Rhonda Cornum et al. in Support of the Petition of the United States at 11–12, United States v. Virginia, 518 U.S. 515 (1996); Salomone, *supra* note 6, at 153–54.

43. A Challenge to VMI's Admissions Policy: Chronological Events, VMI Alumni Rev. 2 (Spring 1990).

44. Brodie, *supra* note 29, at 19.

45. Judy Mann, Neanderthal Bonding, Wash. Post, Feb. 7, 1990, at B3.

46. Phyllis Schlafly, Leave the Military Colleges Alone, USA Today, Feb. 22, 1990, at 10A.

47. John F. Harris, Terry Excused from Defending VMI, Wash. Post, Dec. 11, 1990, at B8.

48. Virginia, 976 F.2d at 894.

49. John F. Harris, For VMI, An Unlikely Defender of Discrimination, Wash. Post, Apr. 11, 1991, at A1.

50. Strum, *supra* note 17, at 106.

51. Stephen Foster, The Real "Jackie Jones" Changed Mind, Not Beliefs, Roanoke Times, Feb. 12, 1994, at C1.

52. John F. Harris, Ghosts of Old Virginia Haunt VMI Bias Trial, Wash. Post, Apr. 5, 1991, at C1.

53. John F. Harris, VMI Trial is a Study in Contrasts, Wash. Post, Apr. 12, 1991, at D3.

54. *Id.*

55. Virginia, 766 F.Supp. 1407 (W.D. Va. 1991).

56. *Id.* at 1435.

57. Editorial, One for the Cadets, Wash. Times, June 19, 1991, at G2.

58. Male Bastion Finding Fewer Good Men, N. Y. Times, Oct. 20, 1993, at B7.

59. Neil A. Lewis, A Court Becomes a Model of Conservative Pursuits, N.Y. Times, May 24, 1999, at 23.

60. Brief Amici Curiae for the American Civil Liberties Union et al. at 17, United States v. Virginia, 976 F.2d 890 (4th Cir. 1992).

61. Virginia, 976 F.2d 890 (4th Cir. 1992).

62. *Id.*

63. The seven colleges were Mary Baldwin, St. Mary's of North Carolina, Southern Virginia College for Women, Hollins, Randolph–Macon Women's College, Sweet Briar, and Wells; Scott Jaschik, 7 Women's Colleges Back VMI's Appeal to Retain All–Male Student Body, Chron. Higher Educ., April 7, 1993, at 39.

64. Petitioners' Reply Brief on Petition for Writ of Certiorari to the U.S. Court of Appeals for the Fourth Circuit at 1, United States v. Virginia, 518 U.S. 515 (1996).

65. United States v. Virginia, 976 F.2d 890 (4th Cir. 1992), cert. denied, 508 U.S. 946 (1993).

66. VMI Defendants' Proposed Remedial Plan, Sept. 3, 1993 (copy on file with author).

67. *Id.*

68. Editorial, A Marriage of Convenience, St. Louis Post–Dispatch, May 5, 1994, at 6B.

69. Editorial, V.M.I.'s Unacceptable Remedy, N. Y. Times, Oct. 1, 1993, at A30.

70. United States v. Virginia, 852 F.Supp. 471 (E.D. Va. 1994) (transcript of proceedings on remand at 489–90) (testimony of David Riesman).

71. *Id.* at 251, 253 (testimony of Elizabeth Fox–Genovese); *see also*, Elizabeth Fox Genovese, Save the Males?, Nat'l Rev. Aug. 1, 1994, at 49.

72. Eleanor E. Maccoby and Carol Nagy Jacklin, The Psychology of Sex Differences (1974).

73. Transcript of proceedings, *supra* note 70, at 857–58, 894 (testimony of Carol Nagy Jacklin).

74. Alexander W. Astin, Four Critical Years: The Effects of College on Beliefs, Attitudes, and Knowledge (1977).

75. Alexander Astin, VMI Case Dramatizes Issues in the Use of Educational Research, Chron. Higher Educ., July 24, 1991, at A36.

76. Transcript of proceedings, *supra* note 70, at 1247–48 (testimony of Alexander William Astin).

77. Lucinda Finley, Sex–Blind, Separate But Equal, or Anti–Subordination? The Uneasy Legacy of Plessy v. Ferguson for Sex and Gender Discrimination, 12 Ga. S. U. L. Rev. 1089, 1107 (1996).

78. Virginia, 44 F.3d 1229 (4th Cir. 1995).

79. 339 U.S. 629, 633–34 (1950).

80. 44 F.3d at 1250 (Phillips, J., dissenting).

81. Virginia, 52 F.3d 90 (4th Cir. 1995).

82. Brief of Petitioner for Writ of Certiorari to the United States Court of Appeals for the Fourth Circuit at 21, United States v. Virginia, 518 U.S. 515 (1996).

83. Editorial, V.M.I., A Constitutional Throwback, N.Y. Times, June 1, 1995, at A24.

84. Brief Amici Curiae of the Center for Military Readiness et al. in Support of Respondent, United States v. Virginia, 518 U.S. 515 (1996).

85. Brief of Amici Curiae Independent Women's Forum et al. in Support of Respondents, United States v. Virginia, 518 U.S. 515 (1996).

86. Brief of Amici Curiae States in Support of the Commonwealth of Virginia, United States v. Virginia, 518 U.S. 515 (1996).

87. Brief of the States of Maryland, Hawaii. Massachusetts, Nevada, and Oregon, and the Commonwealth of the Northern Mariana Islands as Amici Curiae in Support of Petitioner, United States v. Virginia, 518 U.S. 515 (1996).

88. Brief Amici Curiae in Support of Respondents by Dr. Kenneth E. Clark, et al., United States v. Virginia, 518 U.S. 515 (1996).

89. Carol Gilligan, In a Different Voice: Psychological Theory and Women's Development (1982).

90. Brief Amici Curiae in Support of Petitioner by the American Association of University Professors et al. at 10, United States v. Virginia, 518 U.S. 515 (1996).

91. Brief Amici Curiae of Women's Schools Together, Inc. et al. in Support of Respondents, United States v. Virginia, 518 U.S. 515 (1996).

92. Brief of Twenty–Six Private Women's Colleges as Amici Curiae in Support of Petitioner, United States v. Virginia, 518 U.S. 515 (1996).

93. Valorie K. Vojdik, At War: Narrative Tactics in the Citadel and VMI Litigation, 19 Harv. Women's L. J. 1, 12–13 (1996).

94. Pat Conroy, The Lords of Discipline (1986).

95. Susan Faludi, The Naked Citadel, New Yorker, Sept. 5, 1994, at 62; *see*, John Sedgwick, Guess Who's Coming to VMI? Gentlemen's Quarterly, July 1997, at 124, 128.

96. Claudia Smith Brinson, Shannon Faulkner, Ms. Magazine, Jan. 1996, at 48.

97. Faulkner v. Jones, 858 F.Supp. 552 (D.S.C. 1994).

98. Faulkner v. Jones, 51 F.3d 440 (4th Cir.), cert. denied, 516 U.S. 938 (1995).

99. Debbi Wilogren, The Citadel Reasserts Its All–Male Tradition, Wash. Post, Aug. 20, 1995, at A3; Catherine S. Manegold, In Glory's Shadow 271–76 (2001); Catherine S. Manegold, Female Cadet Quits the Citadel, Citing Stress of Her Legal Battle, N.Y. Times, Aug. 13, 1995, at A1.

100. Manegold, In Glory's Shadow, *supra* note 99, at 293; Salomone, *supra* note 6, at 144–47.

101. Transcript of Oral Argument, United States v. Virginia, 518 U.S. 515 (1996), at 23.

102. Virginia, 518 U.S. at 534.

103. Virginia, 518 U.S. at 531 (citing Hogan, *supra* note 18, at 724).

104. Id. at 533 (quoting Hogan, *supra* note 18, at 724).

105. United States v. Virginia, 518 U.S. at 547 (quoting Milliken v. Bradley, 433 U.S. 267, 280 (1977)).

106. Virginia, 518 U.S. at 540.

107. *Id.*

108. *Id.* at 551 n. 19.

109. *Id.* at 550 (quoting United States v. Virginia, 766 F.Supp. at 1412, 1414).

110. *Id.* at 541 (quoting Miss. Univ. for Women v. Hogan, 458 U.S. at 725).

111. For a discussion of Justice Ginsburg's reliance on competing strands of feminist thought, see Salomone, supra note 7, at 88–92.

112. Virginia, 518 U.S. at 533.

113. *Id.* at 534 n. 7 (quoting Brief of Twenty-six Private Women's Colleges as Amici Curiae, at 5).

114. 339 U.S. 629 (1950).

115. Virginia, 518 U.S. at 551–54, quoting 44 F.3d 1229, 1250 (Phillips, J., dissenting).

116. Robert Marquand, Court Bolsters Protections for Women in Virginia Case, Christian Sci. Monitor, June 27, 1996, at 1 (quoting Mark Tushnet, Former Dean, Georgetown University Law Center).

117. See Petition for Writ of Certiorari to the United States Court of Appeals for the Third Circuit, Vorchheimer v. School Dist. of Phila., 532 F.2d 880 (3d Cir. 1976).

118. Strum, *supra* note 17, at 285.

119. Jeffrey Rosen, The New Look of Liberalism, N.Y. Times Magazine, Oct. 5, 1997, at 60.

120. See Heather L. Stobaugh, The Aftermath of United States v. Virginia: Why Five Justices Are Pulling in the Reins on the "Exceedingly Persuasive Justification," 55 SMU L. Rev. 1755 (2002).

121. Virginia, 518 U.S. at 572, 559.

122. *Id.* at 555–56 (Rehnquist, C.J., concurring).

123. *Id.* at 569.

124. *Id.* at 595–98 (Scalia, J., dissenting).

125. Virginia, 96 F.3d 114 (4th Cir. 1996).

126. Michael Janofsky, Citadel, Bowing to Court, Says It Will Admit Women, N.Y. Times, June 29, 1996, § 1, at 6.

127. Judith Havemann, Two Women Quit Citadel Over Alleged Harassment, Wash. Post, Jan. 13, 1997, at A01.

128. Editorial, Not Raining, Bullying, Wash. Post, Jan. 16, 1997, at A20; Salomone, *supra* note 6, at 148.

129. Brodie, *supra* note 29, at 59.

130. Peter Finn, Leading the March into Coeducation—The Man Himself, Wash. Post, Aug. 17, 1997, at A01.

131. Sedgwick, *supra* note 95, at 124, 131.

132. Interview with Josiah Bunting III, President, Harry Frank Guggenheim Foundation, New York City (July 18, 2006).

133. Vojdik, *supra* note 92, at 13–14, citing deposition of Josiah Bunting at 30, Johnson v. Jones (No. 2:92–1674–2), aff'd, 42 F.3d 1385 (4th Cir. 1994).

134. Joan Biskupic, Supreme Court Invalidates Exclusion of Women by VMI, Wash. Post, June 27, 1996, at A01.

135. The Pros and Cons of Single–Sex Education, U.S. News & World Rep., July 8, 1996, available at http://www.usnews.com/usnews/culture/articles/960708/archive_034186.htm.

136. Donald P. Baker, Admit Women, Keep "Rat Line," Wash. Post, July 2, 1996, at B01.

137. Eric Lipton, VMI Cuts No Slack for Female Applicants, Wash. Post, Sept. 24, 1996, at B01.

138. VMI Assimilation Plan (Executive Version), Virginia Military Institute, Aug. 13, 1997 (copy on file with author).

139. Interview with Josiah Bunting III, in New York City (July 18, 2006).

140. Peter Finn, 30 Women Enroll at VMI, All–Male Since 1839, Wash. Post, Aug. 19, 1997, at D01.

141. Wes Allison, The Rat Line is Alive and Well, Richmond Times Dispatch, May 17, 1997, at A–1.

142. VMI Suit That Opened Admissions Is Dropped, N.Y. Times, Jan. 17, 1999, at 22.

143. Lynn Rosellini, A Leader Among Men, U.S. News & World Rep., Apr. 10, 2000, at 46.

144. Interview with Josiah Bunting III, in New York City (July 18, 2006).

145. Laura Brodie, Pregnant on the Parade Ground, Wash. Post., Apr. 1, 2001, at B08.

146. Virginia Military Institute, General Order No. 12, revised, Dec. 12, 2005 (copy on file with author).

147. Telephone interview with female graduate, VMI Class of 2001 (May 2, 2006).

148. E-mail from female graduate, VMI Class of 2004, to author (Sept.21, 2006) (copy on file with author).

149. Interview with female cadet, VMI Class of 2007, in Lexington, Va. (April 20, 2006).

150. United States Department of Defense, Report of the Defense Task Force on Sexual Harassment & Violence at the Military Service Academies (June 2005), available at http://www.dtic.mil/dtfs_recd/High_GPO_RRC_tx.pdf.

151. E-mail message from female graduate, VMI Class of 2004, *supra* note 148.

152. Diane Diamond and Michael Kimmel, "Toxic Virus" or Lady Virtue: Gender Integration and Assimilation at West Point and VMI, in Miller–Bernal and Poulson, *supra* note 12, at 263, 277–78.

153. Telephone interview with female graduate, VMI Class of 2002 (May 9, 2006).

154. Interview with Jackie Tugman, VMI Class of 2002 and VMI Assistant Director of Admissions, in Rye, N.Y. (May 10, 2006).

155. Telephone interview with Carol Green, VMI Director of Alumni Activities (May 1, 2006).

156. E-mail message from female graduate, Class of 2004, supra note 148.

157. VMI and the Corps of Cadets Undergo Renovations, Collegiate Times, Nov. 2, 2006, 1.

158. Tim Green, Leadership Receives Diversity Training, The Cadet, Apr. 14, 2006, at 1.

159. E-mail message from Jackie Tugman, VMI Assistant Director of Admissions, to author (Sept. 9, 2006) (copy on file with author).

160. The Bullet, Virginia Military Institute, 1990–91, at 13–14 (copy on file with author).

161. The Bullet, Virginia Military Institute, 2004–05, 33 (copy on file with author).

162. *Id.* at 53.

163. United States Department of Defense, Report of the Defense Task Force, *supra* note 150, at 9.

164. Interview with Josiah Bunting III, in New York City (July 18, 2006).

165. Interview with Brig. Gen. N. Michael Bissell, Commandant, Virginia Women's Institute for Leadership, Mary Baldwin College, in Staunton, Va. (April 21, 2006); *see*, Mary Anne Case, Two Cheers for Cheerleading: The Noisy Integration of VMI and the Quiet Success of Virginia Women in Leadership, U. Chi. Legal F. 347 (1999).

166. National Association for Single Sex Public Education, www.singlesexschools.org/schools-schools.htm (last visited June 4, 2007).

167. *See, e.g.*, Leonard Sax, Why Gender Matters: What Parents and Teachers Need to Know About the Emerging Science of Sex Differences (2005); Michael Gurian, Boys and Girls Learn Differently! (2001); *but see*, Rosalind Barnett and Caryl Rivers, Same Difference: How Gender Myths Are Hurting Our Relationships, Our Children, and Our Jobs (2004); Rosemary C. Salomone, Myths and Realities in the Sameness/Difference Debate, 11 Cardozo Women's L.J. 583 (2005).

168. No Child Left Behind, Pub. L. No. 107–118, 115 Stat. 1425, § 5131(a)(23) (pending legislation amended at 20 U.S.C.A. § 7215(a)(23) (2003)).

169. Nondiscrimination on the Basis of Sex in Education Programs or Activities Receiving Federal Financial Assistance, 71 Fed. Reg. 62,530 (2006).

170. *See generally*, Salomone, *supra* note 6.

7

The Story of *Southeastern Community College v. Davis*: The Prequel to the Television Series "ER"

Laura Rothstein

The popular television series "ER" has featured many characters with disabilities.[1] These include Drs. John Carter and Abby Lockhart (who are both alcoholics), Dr. Kerry Weaver (who uses a crutch),[2] Dr. Robert Romano (a surgeon who lost an arm in a helicopter accident), Dr. Nathan, played by Don Cheadle (a surgical resident with Parkinson's disease), third year medical student Lucy Knight (who had a learning disability), Dr. Mark Greene (who died of brain cancer), Dr. Gabriel Lawrence (played by Alan Alda) a highly regarded physician with Alzheimer's, and Jeanie Boulet (a physician's assistant who had gotten HIV from her promiscuous husband).

Before the 1970s, the popular doctor shows were "Dr. Kildare,"[3] "Ben Casey,"[4] and "Marcus Welby MD".[5] None of these shows featured lead roles or major characters with disabilities. It is unimaginable that a whole cast of characters with disabilities would be part of a hospital staff in that era.

Four Stories

This is the story of how Frances Davis played a role in changing the culture of how people with disabilities are treated in society. It is the story of how people with disabilities in higher education were increasingly included as a result of her case. It is the story of how higher education disability discrimination standards play an important part in developing disability discrimination law generally. And finally, it is the story of how disability discrimination law changed the way society views individuals with disabilities.

Supreme Court Justice Sandra Day O'Connor recognized the importance of higher education in America when she held in the landmark *Grutter* decision that "universities, and in particular, law schools, represent the training ground for a large number of our Nation's leaders."[6] The importance of higher education as an avenue into full participation in American society makes it particularly significant that the first case in which the Supreme Court addressed any aspect of federal disability discrimination was one involving higher education, specifically nursing school.[7] In 1979, the Court for the first time, in *Southeastern Community College v. Davis,*[8] considered the Rehabilitation Act of 1973 and its application. The 1973 Rehabilitation Act[9] was the first of several major federal discrimination laws. The *Davis* decision was the first of a number of major Supreme Court decisions[10] to address a variety of issues under federal disability discrimination policy.

The story here is about how individuals who today seek to enter into American society through colleges and universities are affected by these laws and Ms. Davis's attempt to use them. While she lost the case, the decision set the stage for implementation of a nondiscrimination policy not only to higher education, but to other aspects of society. The decision affects individuals with conditions ranging from depression and drug addiction, to sensory impairments (such as hearing and vision), mobility impairments, and learning disabilities. And it affects areas of employment, K–12 education, public accommodations, public services, transportation, justice systems, housing, and health care.

Without this story, other stories would not be part of our everyday lives—such as the television series "ER"—in which many of the health care professionals have disabling conditions. Many of the characters on the television series "ER" and even President Jed Bartlett (who had multiple sclerosis) on "West Wing" would have different stories to be told without Frances Davis. In fact, the very idea of their presence in these shows and in the mainstream of America would be less likely, and their stories might not be told at all.

The story starts with the passage of the Rehabilitation Act in 1973. It was a law passed with very little detailed planning (unlike most civil rights laws) and without an advocacy movement behind it. Rather, it was the result primarily of some Senate staffers who were working on the reauthorization of the Vocational Rehabilitation Act Amendments of 1954.[11] The Vocational Rehabilitation Act's initial purpose had been to expand funding for rehabilitation services for returning war veterans for the purpose of returning them to work.

Because other federal funding statutes had required that the recipient of federal support not discriminate on the basis or race or gender, it seemed logical that a similar requirement should be applied with respect to nondiscrimination on the basis of disability.[12] The 1973 amendments to the Rehabilitation Act thus prohibited federal employers (Section 501),[13] federal contractors (Section 503),[14] and federal recipients of federal financial assistance (Section 504)[15] from discriminating against otherwise qualified individuals with disabilities. Most colleges and universities received federal financial assistance in some form, and thus they were subject to Section 504 of the Rehabilitation Act. The statutory provisions were deceptively short, without language to define many of the key terms. Private higher education programs, along with private health care providers were the only major private sectors of society affected to a great extent by Section 504 of the Rehabilitation Act.

Then, nothing much happened. Because the Rehabilitation Act had been amended with little fanfare or press coverage, there was little awareness about it. Initially and for some time, few advocacy groups existed and those that did were not connected by websites, Listservs, and cell phones. As a result, the 1973 Rehabilitation Act was not used initially in any major comprehensive way to bring about broad social change.

Perhaps the exception was the activism occurring with respect to groups seeking change in public education and trying to deinstitutionalize individuals who were mentally ill and/or mentally retarded. But the Rehabilitation Act was certainly not the basis for any broad activism by individuals seeking greater access to colleges and universities. Perhaps the most apparent reason for this lack of activism was that in 1973, there were few students with disabilities of college age with the skills and preparation to attend college. The reason was that it was not until 1975, when Congress enacted the Education for All Handicapped Children Act (now Individuals with Disabilities Education Act)[16] that comprehensive education of students with disabilities began. And it would not be until several years later that a student would have been identified at an early age so as to benefit throughout his or her years in school from the special education mandates, and thus be ready for college.

In the meantime, except for the lawyers and advocates for special education and deinstitutionalization, there were few attorneys with the expertise, interest, or willingness to handle a disability discrimination case even if there were clients out there seeking their services. Most lawyers had never taken a course in law school on disability discrimination. Taking a case in a brand new area of law would certainly be a daunting proposition, particularly where the statute had very little legislative history and no regulatory guidance. While Congress had contemplated that the Department of Health, Education and Welfare[17] would promulgate regulations, it took a lawsuit[18] and a sit-in (or "roll-in") by a large number of wheelchair users at HEW to convince Secretary Joseph Califano in 1976[19] to develop the model regulations. And it was not until 1978 that the regulations became final.[20] Frances Davis initially sought entry into the registered nurse training program at

Southeastern Community College in Whiteville, North Carolina, in 1973, well before the regulations were in place.

So, between the newness and vagueness of the law, the lack of legal expertise, and the lack of potential clients in a position to seek relief from discrimination, it is not surprising that it was not until 1979, six years after the enactment of Section 504 of the Rehabilitation Act, that the Supreme Court issued its first opinion on any law involving disability discrimination.

Why Did Frances Davis Bring This Case and How Did It Evolve?

Frances Burchette was born on August 31, 1932, later married Ray Davis, and worked in a dry cleaning plant for three years before applying to Southeastern Community College. Before her application to the registered nurse (RN) program, she was licensed as a Licensed Practical Nurse (LPN) in 1967, by the North Carolina authorities.[21] This license required working under constant supervision. An LPN is not permitted to perform medical tasks requiring a great degree of technical sophistication.[22] Ms. Davis had only done a small amount of private duty work as an LPN at the time she applied to Southeastern Community College. She had had a hearing loss in both ears for many years, at the time she applied.

In pursuit of a license as a Registered Nurse, Frances Davis applied to Southeastern Community College and was accepted on August 17, 1973, for admission to the College Parallel program. Her letter of acceptance noted her understanding that she wanted to enter the Associate Degree Nursing Program in September of 1974, and advised her that her progress would be evaluated at the end of the 1973–74 academic year, after which two additional years would be required to receive the degree.[23]

Significant to the ultimate decision by the Supreme Court in this case, and significant in subsequent litigation involving health care professional training programs is the fact that this academic program is intended to prepare an individual to be certified to practice a specific profession. The program content is designed for that purpose, including clinical and practice training and is not solely academic in nature. The first year at Southeastern Community College was preliminary to the nurses training program. Her coursework included English, biology, and psychology courses in which she received B's and C's.[24] The criteria for admission to the program included both scholastic criteria and a required physical examination, and these criteria were made known to all prospective applicants.[25]

During an interview for entry into the Associate Degree program, Ms. Davis's difficulty in understanding speech was noticed, and she was referred to the Center for Speech and Hearing Disorders at Duke University Medical Center because of her identified hearing loss. Her April 18, 1974, hearing evaluation by an independent audiologist, resulted in a finding that she had a significant hearing loss in both ears with "marked speech discrimination loss." A hearing aid evaluation recommended a replacement of her current hearing aid, but noted that even with the new hearing aid, she would need to use her lipreading skills to supplement hearing to understand speech. The hearing aid improved her hearing level to the outer limits of normal hearing levels. Based on that evaluation, a May 6, 1974, letter advised Ms. Davis that she did not qualify for admission to the Associate Degree in Nursing Program.[26]

On May 13, the Director the Nursing Programs requested by phone (and on May 14 by letter) that the North Carolina Board of Nursing Executive Director provide an opinion as to the effect of Mrs. Davis's hearing disability on her ability to practice nursing. The May 17, letter noted concurrence that the level of hearing disability could preclude her from being safe for practice in any setting allowed by a license as an RN or by a license as an LPN. It further noted that:

> Moreover, we would question the advisability of you and the faculty's assuming responsibility for Mrs. Davis's involvement in patient care as a student in nursing. To adjust patient learning experiences in keeping with Mrs. Davis's hearing limitations could, in fact, be the same as denying her full learning to meet the objectives of your nursing programs....

The letter further noted that the basis of the opinion was the audiologist's response about the expectations of nurses in patient care, that she needs to have the speaker get her attention and to look directly at her to understand speech. It further noted the innumerable patient care situations in which her abilities would be inadequate to respond to patient needs that might be critical in life and death situations.[27]

After she was denied admission, Ms. Davis visited Dr. McCarter, the college president's office in June, and asked for a review and reconsideration of her application. Although she visited without an appointment, the president immediately called together several faculty and administrative staff to meet with her.[28] Following the visit, President McCarter asked for a committee of staff members to review the application and to report to the Dean of Students. The committee's review confirmed the original decision. A college grievance procedure existed, but it was not pursued, apparently because it seemed futile, perhaps because the president had already considered the matter.[29]

Represented by counsel from a small firm in North Carolina, Ms. Davis challenged the denial in federal district court claiming a violation of Section 504 of the Rehabilitation Act and denial of equal protection and due process.[30] Ms. Davis claimed that she had been discriminated against under Section 504 of the Rehabilitation Act. That section provides:

> No otherwise qualified handicapped individual ... shall, solely by reason of his handicap, be excluded from the participation in, be denied the benefits or, or be subjected to discrimination under any program or activity receiving Federal financial assistance....[31]
>
> The term "handicapped individual" means any individual who ... (A) has a physical or mental impairment which substantially limits one or more of such person's major life activities, (B) has a record of such an impairment, or (C) is regarded as having such an impairment.[32]

The focus of the case at all judicial levels of consideration was the meaning of "otherwise qualified." The question was whether the determination is to be made that the individual meets the requirements in spite of the impairment, or whether the individual meets the requirements if the impairment is disregarded.

The evidence presented by Ms. Davis's counsel at the October 18, 1976, bench trial before Judge Robert W. Hemphill was solely the letters, tests, and exhibits, which were basically the college records and correspondence involving her application.[33] The college offered defense through testimony by several members of the nursing admissions staff and the college president, all testifying that she was not qualified because of the hearing disability.[34] One witness for the defense admitted that she could adequately perform in some fields of nursing with special training and individualized supervision.[35] The college claimed that such supervision would not be practical and would be unduly expensive.[36]

The District Court of the Eastern District of North Carolina upheld the denial of admission, concluding that her inability to be licensed as a Registered Nurse was a legitimate basis for denial of admission to the Associate Degree Program.[37] The district court held that her hearing impairment prevented her from safely performing in either the training program or in the nursing profession. The court held that "otherwise qualified" means "otherwise able to function sufficiently in the position sought in spite of the handicap, if proper training and facilities are suitable and available."[38] The court held that it was not discriminatory to exclude Ms. Davis based on the facts and evidence before it.

Subsequent to the District Court opinion, the Department of Health, Education, and Welfare interim model regulations under the Rehabilitation Act became effective.[39] Ms. Davis appealed the trial court decision on

January 5, 1977 and the Fourth Circuit issued its opinion on March 28, 1977.[40] The new regulations were a major factor in the Fourth Circuit's remand of the case.[41] Although it did not dispute the findings of fact, the court thought the case should be reconsidered in light of the regulations that had been promulgated after the district court's decision.[42] The Fourth Circuit found that the new regulations clarified that the impairment should not be taken into account in deciding whether Ms. Davis was "otherwise qualified." Of significance is its determination that Section 504 requires "affirmative conduct" to a degree that accommodations are required even where they "become expensive."[43]

The Supreme Court Decision

Southeastern Community College's petition to the Supreme Court for certiorari[44] was granted because the issue was of such importance to institutions covered by Section 504.[45] The case was argued on April 23, 1979, and decided on June 11, 1979, the first Supreme Court decision to interpret the Rehabilitation Act of 1973.

Eugene Gressman prepared the petition for certiorari, the brief on behalf of the college, and argued the case before the Court. Although he did not have experience on disability discrimination issues, he was and is a noted Supreme Court practice expert. He had no assistance in any of these matters.[46] Marc Charmatz, an experienced and well known advocate on behalf of rights of individuals who are deaf,[47] wrote the brief and argued the case for Ms. Davis. More than 50 amicus briefs were filed in the case.[48] Among other issues, the briefs for higher education institutions noted the burden on states to support certain types of accommodations and concerns about liability. The briefs for Ms. Davis emphasized the history of treatment of individuals with disabilities, the importance of individualized determinations, the improvements in technology of hearing aids.

On June 11, 1979, the Supreme Court, with Justice Powell writing the unanimous opinion, tracked to a substantial degree the arguments made by Professor Gressman in Southeastern's brief.[49] The Court detailed the events leading up to the case, noting that it would be necessary for Ms. Davis to rely on lipreading for effective communication.[50]

The Court reversed the Fourth Circuit's decision, holding that it had misconstrued the regulations, and that the district court's interpretation was closer to the statutory meaning. "An otherwise qualified person is one who is able to meet all of a program's requirements in spite of his handicap."[51] The Supreme Court thought it appropriate to determine qualification based on both academic and technical standards. Furthermore, technical standards include *all* nonacademic admissions criteria essential to participation.[52] The Court referenced the HEW Regulatory Guidance and noted that without such an interpretation, a blind person with all the qualifications to drive a bus, other than sight, would be otherwise qualified,[53] an argument found in Southeastern's brief.[54]

The Court applied this standard to the specific facts before it, noting that the record indicated that close, individual attention would be required to ensure patient safety.[55] This would mean she could not participate in the clinical aspects of the class, and this would be a *fundamental alteration*, not a required modification.[56] In the view of the Court, this would be "affirmative action" requiring substantial expenditures.[57] The Court emphasized, however, that

> Technological advances can be expected to enhance opportunities to rehabilitate the handicapped or otherwise to qualify them for some useful employment. Such advances also may enable attainment of these goals without imposing undue financial and administrative burdens....[58]

The Court dismissed the argument that because Ms. Davis might be licensed in another jurisdiction, the college could admit her. The Court determined that even if that were the case, this does not require the college to lower its standards.[59] The Court reversed and remanded for further proceedings.

The decision has proven to be a landmark decision and a reference point for all disability discrimination claims that focus on whether the individual bringing the claim is "qualified."

The Rest of the Story

The "rest of the story" is really not so much what happened to Frances Davis. It is unknown whether she ever worked as a Licensed Practical Nurse or whether her desire to serve as a nurse was foreclosed because of this decision.[60] The real story is not so much about her, but about the others who followed behind her, and how this case established so many principles for how other disability discrimination cases would be handled by the courts after the *Southeastern Community College v. Davis* interpretation of who is protected under disability discrimination law and how that is to be decided.

Professional education programs leading to licensing, particularly programs for health care professions are given substantial deference by the courts regarding what are the essential requirements of the program, what constitutes a direct threat, and what would be unduly burdensome. The courts are consistent, however, in following the Supreme Court's expectation that assessments about qualifications for admissions must be individualized.

Since *Southeastern Community College*, courts have addressed cases involving admission of a blind applicant to medical school,[61] enrollment by a medical student with serious mental illness,[62] admission of a dental student with HIV,[63] admission and performance of students with learning disabilities to medical school,[64] enrollment of an individual with multiple sclerosis into a psychiatry residency program,[65] enrollment of a nursing student with obesity,[66] and a number of other enrollment and professional licensing cases.[67] In all cases where the substantive issues were addressed, the courts required individualized assessments of whether the individuals were able to carry out the essential functions of the program with or without reasonable accommodations in spite of the disability. Courts have not allowed myths or stereotypes or prejudices to be determinative, but instead have required that appropriate officials made rationally justifiable decisions.[68]

In most cases, the courts determined that the individual was not "otherwise qualified." One significant exception was a case involving a medical student with multiple sclerosis who was applying to the psychiatric residency program.[69] The court found that the medical school's denial was based on short interviews by three members of the admissions committee who had made assumptions about how Dr. Pushkin's multiple sclerosis would affect patient care, assumptions that were not based on the evidence. The denial was found to be discriminatory. The fact that Dr. Pushkin had already received an M.D. may explain this unusual decision. The school's approach to the decision process, however, may be a more significant factor.

The increased awareness and the standard for decision making have surely been the reasons that it is no longer unusual to see doctors and nurses on popular television programs, such as "ER" with a variety of disabling conditions. The "ER" series has also done a good job of showing the hospital's challenge in balancing patient care with the conditions of the health care professionals.

This standard of decision making has carried over from health care professional programs to other higher education and licensing situations and to the employment setting. Courts have now grappled with qualifications of individuals with a wide array of disabling conditions in a wide variety of settings.[70]

How Did Higher Education Disability Policy Evolve After the Case?

Contrary to what many advocates feared, this decision was not the end of opportunities for individuals with disabilities in higher education and professional education. While it defined the key terms of qualification, other parallel legal developments in the 1970s were critical to the inclusion of individuals with disabilities in higher education and ultimately in professions, including medical professions as well as in society generally.

Special Education as a Parallel Policy

The Individuals with Disabilities Education Act (IDEA),[71] enacted in 1975 under the title Education for All Handicapped Children Act, requires public K–12 education to provide a free appropriate education in the least restrictive environment to all age eligible students. The education is to be individualized to each student. It also incorporated a very detailed set of requirements related to finding and identifying students with disabilities and developing individualized educational programs. Essential to its impact, the IDEA provides for an elaborate set of detailed procedural safeguards, ensuring that parents had access to an impartial hearing and right of judicial review for students with disabilities.

While it took some time for special education mandates to be phased in, and while there are still substantial challenges with full implementation, the IDEA has made an enormous difference in the presence of individuals with disabilities in society. The IDEA made it possible for students with a wide array of impairments (ranging from mental retardation to sensory impairments to learning disabilities to psychological conditions) to participate in public education.

The IDEA differs from the Rehabilitation Act and the Americans with Disabilities Act by requiring more than nondiscrimination and reasonable accommodation. It requires schools to provide appropriate education, which in many cases may be much more costly and complex than what is required at the college level. The result, however, was that many individuals who in the past would have been institutionalized as children, or who would simply have dropped out of public schools were graduating from high school and were in a position to consider and apply to college and the work force.

The 1973 Rehabilitation Act, Section 504, and the 1975 Individuals with Disabilities Education Act thus worked in tandem to set the stage for a push by students with disabilities for admission and accommodations at the higher education level. While a few cases relating to disability discrimination were decided before 1979, none provided any guidance for the issue in this case.[72] *Southeastern Community College v. Davis* was the first case to reach the Supreme Court, and it was one of the few cases to focus on and interpret the substantive aspects of the Rehabilitation Act.

Regulatory Guidance

Apparent from the case history is the fact that it took policymakers some time to provide the guidance to the colleges and universities about how to handle the influx of students with disabilities. Although the Rehabilitation Act was enacted in 1973, it was not until 1978 that regulatory guidance was provided. So it is not surprising that it took a few years for there to be extensive litigation at the college level.

Because the Rehabilitation Act only applies to federal agencies, federal contractors, and recipients of federal financial assistance, most of the private sector was not affected. Only programs such as colleges and universities and health care programs such as major hospitals, where most private institutions receive federal grants or other support, were comprehensively affected. The private sector was not substantially affected by disability discrimination laws until the 1990 passage of the Americans with Disabilities Act. Thus, for almost two decades, higher education was the primary laboratory for interpreting disability discrimination policies.

Immediately after the 1973 enactment of the Rehabilitation Act and for several years after, colleges and universities were unprepared for handling issues relating to applicants and students with disabilities. Higher education did not have comprehensive or appropriate practices, policies, and procedures to handle these situations. An individual with a disability whose application was rejected or whose request for accommodation was denied was unsure where to seek redress or even if the adverse action was permissible under the law.

As a result of the regulatory guidance, institutions subject to Section 504 were required to engage in a self evaluation a year after the effective date of the model regulations.[73] This self-examination process began to improve the awareness and understanding for college policymakers and administrators that more attention to this issue was needed. Questions began to be asked about who was responsible for payment, how much was reasonable, just how far were colleges required to go with these new types of students. The combination of the 1978 regulations and case law began to provide guidance. *Southeastern Community College v. Davis* in 1979, combined with the 1978 regulations was a turning point. States began to develop more extensive Rehabilitation Act programs and departments that provided both funding for services and technical assistance on rehabilitation and accommodations for education, higher education, and employment. Colleges and universities started paying attention and improvements resulted.[74]

The Americans with Disabilities Act Enhances Protection Against Disability Discrimination

Higher education institutions were already fairly experienced with these issues by the time the Americans with Disabilities Act (ADA)[75] was enacted in 1990. The ADA was much more comprehensive than the

Rehabilitation Act because of its substantially greater prohibition of discrimination in the private sector. Title I of the ADA applies to all but the smallest employers. Title II applies to state and local governmental agencies. And Title III applies to twelve categories of private providers of public accommodations, one of the categories being educational programs. The ADA incorporates into the statutory language substantial clarifying language that resulted from the evolution of Rehabilitation Act case law. The ADA nondiscrimination language and definition of who is protected is virtually identical to the Rehabilitation Act. As a result, colleges and universities are not only subject to Section 504, but they are subject to Title I (for employment), Title II (if they are a state or local institution), and/or Title III (if they are a private institution).

Unlike other programs, colleges and universities were already somewhat adept at addressing these issues and were much further along in developing policies, practices, and procedures related to disability discrimination. Given the importance of higher education as an avenue into full participation in American society, that was a good thing. Higher education could and has provided leadership in this area.

How the Courts Have Guided the Debate

In the three decades since the *Davis* decision, a number of significant judicial decisions, at the Supreme Court and at lower court levels, have helped to implement full (or at least greater) participation by individuals with disabilities into higher education and society in general. While some of the cases providing this guidance arose in contexts other than higher education, many of the higher education based cases have provided guidance to the debate for other aspects of society.

For Frances Davis there was not really a disagreement that she was "handicapped" within the definition of the Rehabilitation Act. Her impairment clearly substantially limited her major life activity of hearing. Most of the earlier cases, both in higher education and in other settings did not focus on whether the individual was disabled. It was almost always assumed that was the case.

The ADA's coverage of the private sector substantially increased the amount of litigation. With virtually all employers and places of public accommodation now covered, lawsuits abounded. But as the floodgates opening, and more individuals with conditions such as back injuries and depression began seeking accommodations, particularly in the employment setting, the courts began focusing more on that issue and narrowing the definition of who is covered. This trend in lower courts ultimately led to the Supreme Court decisions known as the "*Sutton* trilogy."[76] In the context of nearsighted airline pilot applicants (whose vision was correctable with eyeglasses), a truck driver with monocular vision, and an individual with high blood pressure controlled by medication, the Court determined that whether a condition is "substantially limiting" must take into account the effect of mitigating measures. The individuals in these cases were found not to be covered.

In 2002 the Supreme Court focused even further on coverage in addressing what constitutes a major life activity, again a response to the groundswell of employment discrimination cases involving a wide range of conditions. In the context of a woman working on an automobile assembly line, claiming that her repetitive stress syndrome was a disability, the Court set the standard. [77]Major life activities are those that involve tasks central to the daily lives of most people.[78] The case was remanded for further decision making, but was settled, resulting in no further judicial guidance in the case. Also in 2002, the Court established that the standard for direct threat applies not only to threats to the health and safety of others, but also to oneself.[79]

The fallout of those cases combined was a substantial narrowing of the definition. Cases were much more quickly being dismissed at an early stage through summary judgments determining that the individual was not covered by the ADA. Individuals with conditions such as epilepsy, diabetes, and cancer, whose conditions were routinely almost presumed to be disabilities before the late 1990s were no longer protected. The courts thus did not reach the issue of whether the person was "otherwise qualified" or whether accommodations being requested were "reasonable."

Again, probably related to the increase in litigation resulting from the ADA, defendants began raising procedural issues, such as immunity from damages (for state agencies). The result was that the courts did not focus on the substantive aspects of qualifications and reasonable accommodations and thus there is little guidance on these issues. Lower courts have only recently begun refocusing on the substantive issues.

This trend in litigation had an interesting evolution in higher education. Very early after the passage of the Rehabilitation Act, the courts addressed some procedural issues, such as program specificity and immunity. Congress responded to some of these cases with amendments to the Rehabilitation Act. By 1979, and the decision in *Southeastern Community College v. Davis*, the courts were focusing on whether the individual was otherwise qualified and whether the program could accommodate the condition. The evolution of these issues was often in the higher education context because most colleges and universities received federal financial assistance, and most employers and public accommodation programs did not. As a result, when looking for precedent on the issue of whether one is otherwise qualified or on reasonable accommodation issues, more precedent is found in the pre–1999 cases, particularly in higher education contexts.

While colleges and universities seemed rarely to raise defenses of immunity or whether the individual was disabled before the late 1990s, today they are much more likely to do so. In fact, in 1999, the same day the Court decided the *Sutton* trilogy, it remanded the *Bartlett v. New York State Board of Law Examiners* case,[80] which involved an individual with a learning disability seeking accommodations on the bar exam. The Court instructed the lower court to determine whether Marilyn Bartlett's learning disability had been mitigated so that it was not substantially limiting to any major life activity. Ultimately on remand, it was determined that she was substantially limited in the major life activity of reading, and that her self accommodations in getting herself through law school had not changed that. Therefore, she did have a substantial impairment justifying reasonable accommodations.

It is important to note, however, that colleges and universities seem still to be less likely to raise these defenses, perhaps because they had become much more adept in the decade between *Southeastern Community College v. Davis* (1979) and the passage of the Americans with Disabilities Act (1990). Higher education had evolved practices, policies, and procedures before other sectors affected by the ADA (with the exception of K–12 education). Because they were more experienced at finding ways to accommodate the student with chemical sensitivities who requested not to be in a classroom with chalk dust, they were unlikely to argue that they did not have to provide the accommodation because that condition is not a covered disability. Colleges and universities have also followed the admonition in *Southeastern Community College v. Davis* that

> Technological advances can be expected to enhance opportunities to rehabilitate the handicapped or otherwise to qualify them for some useful employment. Such advances also may enable attainment of these goals without imposing undue financial and administrative burdens upon a State.[81]

Colleges and universities have been the leaders in finding ways to use technology to accommodate students with a wide range of disabilities.

Although higher education was ahead of employers and places of public accommodation on these issues, the road was not entirely smooth. Beginning in the mid–1980s, the number of students with disabilities who had received the benefits of special education because of the 1975 Individuals with Disabilities Education Act, began reaching college age. Their special education had better prepared them for college. They expected a certain level of services in college as a result. What became apparent was that these students and their parents did not realize that not everything that the IDEA required in high school was required in college. In high school, the burden was on the school to proactively identify and evaluate (including payment for testing and evaluating) the student. In high school, the student was to be provided education designed to provide appropriate education, not just to be provided reasonable accommodations. In contrast, the college student has the responsibility to make known the disability and to request the accommodations. That includes paying for the cost of an evaluation. The burden shifts in college.

For students with learning disabilities, there have been a number of challenges.[82] With the increased number of such students, and reinforced by the *Bartlett* and other decisions, higher education has become insistent that students with learning disabilities provide appropriate documentation to justify the requested accommodations. That means evaluations must be done by professionals with appropriate expertise and that these evaluations must be recent. It also means that the student pays for these evaluations. These new expectations came as a shock to some parents. With increased awareness, however, today there is less surprise.

Disability rights advocates fought early on for expansion of the 1973 Rehabilitation Act rights, so that more than those receiving federal support would be covered. Because the expansion took 17 years, the interpretation of the Rehabilitation Act (after which the substantive rights under the ADA are modeled) developed to a large extent within higher education. A broader application of disability discrimination law at an earlier stage might have resulted in an earlier groundswell of litigation and in a much earlier narrowing of these laws, as occurred in *Sutton* and the recent immunity decisions. We would not have the body of case law that provides guidance on a variety of issues to draw on.

For example, *Wynne v. Tufts University Medical School*,[83] established the standard for determining the burden related to reasonable accommodation. The case involved a medical student with a learning disability. He had been accommodated during the early part of his medical education, by receiving accommodations such as additional time on exams. After the school denied his request to take exams in a format other than multiple choice, he brought a Section 504 claim. The First Circuit in remanding the case, established a standard for making decisions about reasonable accommodations. The court required that the institution submit

> undisputed facts demonstrating that the *relevant officials* within the institution considered alternative means, their feasibility, cost and effect on the academic program, and came to a *rationally justifiable* conclusion that the available alternatives would result either in

lowering academic standards or requiring *substantial program alteration*. (emphasis added).[84]

In establishing this standard, the court referenced *Southeastern Community College v. Davis* and the Supreme Court's expectation that programs consider technological advances in making these assessments.[85]

Further proceedings applying this standard resulted in a decision that Wynne could not be reasonably accommodated by alternative format exams. The decision, however, set out an extremely useful and often-cited standard for making determinations about reasonable accommodations, and indeed about making other decisions in disability discrimination cases. Because of the *Sutton* decision in 1999, narrowing the definition of who is covered, if *Wynne* were brought today, it would be much more likely to be dismissed because a court might well find that Wynne did not have a disability protected under the Rehabilitation Act or the ADA.[86]

The same could be said for a number of the pre–1999 higher education cases. The courts would have been less likely to reach the substantive issues of qualification and reasonable accommodation if the institutions had raised the issue of whether the individual was covered through a motion to dismiss. It is because higher education cases did not focus on that issue that there is a well developed and useful body of case law, which is a valuable reference not only in the higher education context, but in other areas as well.

The Four Stories of Frances Davis

So, there are really four stories here. There is the story of Frances Davis—what happened to her, how she came to bring the case, and that she did not reach her dream of becoming a registered nurse.

There is the story of how this case began setting the standard in higher education cases for what it means to be otherwise qualified for academic programs, particularly those that lead to professional certification, and even more particularly those involving health care professions.

There is the story of how this case and other early higher education cases reached substantive issues and provided a valuable framework through those decisions for a much broader range of cases—employment, public accommodations, housing, and so on.

And finally, there is the story of how, because of the earlier cases that focused on issues of qualification and accommodation, that society became much more open to the mainstream participation of individuals with disabilities. While many claimants lost their cases in court, many did not. And because these claims were not summarily dismissed, based on noncoverage (at least in the years from 1973 to the mid 1990s), colleges and universities (including professional education programs) developed policies, practices, and procedures that opened the doors to a much greater presence for individuals with disabilities.

Flash Forward—The "ER" Cast of Characters

The open door and more positive attitudes about individuals with disabilities in higher education and society generally is exemplified by the television series *ER*, and the characters on that program. The beginning of this chapter listed several characters with disabilities with roles in a teaching hospital in Chicago. These include doctors, nurses, physician assistants, and medical students. Their stories really highlight the evolution of the law.

Lucy Knight, a third year medical student in the ER, had a learning disability. How did she get into medical school? Was she given reasonable accommodations? Was her learning disability a direct threat to patients because she could not read the charts quickly?

Dr. John Carter and Dr. Abby Lockhart both had problems with alcohol. Dr. Mark Greene died of brain cancer, with symptoms affecting his performance. The story lines often highlighted the tension in ensuring that these problems did not interfere with patient care.

Dr. Robert Romano was a surgeon who lost an arm when he caught it on the life flight helicopter. He struggled to resume some ability to practice medicine with only one arm, although it became apparent quickly that the essential functions of being a surgeon required the use of two arms.

Jeanie Boulet was a physician's assistant who had become HIV positive. The ER staff was aware of her condition, and worked to accommodate her work in the ER by not requiring her to perform invasive procedures with sharp instruments. Ultimately she decided herself that this accommodation could not anticipate all circumstances and she resigned from the staff.

When Dr. Nathan's Parkinson's disease made it difficult for him to work long hours and at certain times of the day, there was at least an attempt to explore whether that could be accommodated. The story line demonstrated a recognition that he had valuable qualities related to patient interaction, and that qualities would be lost if he could not be a doctor.

Alan Alda played a highly regarded and experienced physician. When symptoms of Alzheimer's began to be apparent to other members of the staff, they addressed this issue with sensitivity rather than being dismissive.

It is safe to assume, that without the Rehabilitation Act and its early interpretations, including the *Southeastern Community College v. Davis* decision, and the resulting proactive approach taken by programs subject to disability discrimination law, that the presence of individuals with disabilities in the mainstream of society would be significantly less. These individuals would be unlikely to even be admitted to nursing school or medical school without the Rehabilitation Act and the judicial interpretations that opened those programs.[87] A television show with the frequent and ongoing presence of health care professionals with a variety of disabling conditions would simply be a fantasy, rather than reflecting reality.

The portrayal of these characters is not so far from reality. While it is true that there are still only a handful of physicians, nurses, and other health care professionals with major disabilities (such as blindness, deafness, and paraplegia or quadriplegia), the attitudes have changed significantly. In 1997, a medical student with paraplegia received his M.D. from Georgetown University.[88] In that same year, a medical student with quadriplegia received his M.D. from Albert Einstein College of Medicine.[89] The University of Michigan enrolled a medical student with quadriplegia in 2003.[90] In 2005, a blind medical student received his M.D. at the University of Wisconsin–Madison, graduating in the top sixth of his class.[91] The presence of nurses with disabilities has increased also, [92] although, as with physicians, the numbers still remain small.

In 2004, Jordan Cohen, then President of the Association of American Medical Colleges, discussed this issue in his column in the association's monthly magazine.[93] He noted the importance of the ADA in opening consideration to applicants with disabilities. He also noted that it remains the case today that medical students must be able to perform the essential functions of the program, and that each school determines the standards for its own program. Schools need not make accommodations that are an undue hardship for the institution. He also points out that medical schools "vary in their ability, financially and otherwise, to implement reasonable accommodations even if their technical requirements could permit the admission of a given student." It is noteworthy that the medical students with significant disabilities mentioned in the preceding paragraph were apparently all admitted and enrolled without litigation.

The medical schools that provided the opportunity were in the position to take on the burden. The burden can be substantial,[94] and the fact that medical students with significant impairments have graduated does not mean that in every case litigation against a medical school would be successful. The academic and other abilities of each individual above were different. The types and severity of the impairments varied, and the resources of the medical school varied. So the institutions did what the Court in *Southeastern Community College v. Davis* and its progeny and what the Rehabilitation Act and the ADA tell them to do—they made individualized assessments.

The Rest of the Story—How Davis Affected Other Areas Beyond Higher Education

Because of the Rehabilitation Act, the *Davis* case, and the early case law development in the higher education context, today (even with the narrowed definition of who is disabled), courts require that individualized assessments be made about who is covered and who is qualified. Courts continue to constructively apply principles of least restrictive environment. Courts apply appropriate tests of reasonableness, considering issues of undue burden and fundamental alteration thoughtfully. This is true in cases involving employment, K–12 education, public accommodations, state and local governmental services, transportation, housing, access to justice, access to health care, and other areas.

With advances in technology, one can imagine in the future a television series in a teaching hospital setting, a nurse who is deaf or a doctor who is blind and how those individuals would be portrayed. Although she lost her case, without the Frances Davis story, and what made it possible for her to bring the case in the first place, these stories might never have been possible.

Endnotes

1. The series began airing in 1994.

2. On the April 27, 2006, show, Dr. Weaver was able to walk without the crutch as a result of surgery for degenerative hip dysplasia. Before the change in the character, however, Laura Innes, who plays Dr. Weaver, noted that she wanted to explore the choice to have surgery and what that would do to the character's identity. "Their crutch can be a big part of the identity of the disabled. After playing one of the highest-profile disabled people on television for so many years, I felt some guilt at abandoning this group." Interview with Laura Innes, from the St. Louis Post–Dispatch, May 7, 2006. See also Mary Murphy, ER's Weaver Stands on Her Own, TV Guide p. 33, March 6, 2006. *See also*, Linda Villarosa, Barriers Fall for Disabled Medical Students, New York Times (November 25, 2003) (including reference to Dr. Julie Madorsky, a physician who uses a crutch as a result of childhood polio, who was the prototype for Dr. Kerry Weaver).

3. The series ran from 1961 to 1966.

4. The series ran from 1961 to 1966.

5. The series ran from 1969 to 1976.

6. Grutter v. Bollinger, 539 U.S. 306, 332 (2003).

7. Similarly, the *Brown v. Board of Education*, 347 U.S. 483, 74 S.Ct. 686 (1954) decision in which separate but equal was struck down by the Supreme Court, was preceded by a number of lower court cases involving desegregating higher education, often law schools. The advocates knew then that higher education in general, and professional education in particular, were important avenues to participation in society. For a discussion of that point, see Richard Kluger, Simple Justice (2004).

8. 442 U.S. 397, 99 S.Ct. 2361, 60 L.Ed.2d 980, 1 A.D.D. 60 (1979).

9. 29 U.S.C. §§ 791, 793, 794.

10. A number of lower court cases under the Rehabilitation Act and the special education statute were decided before 1979, but this was the first to reach the Supreme Court.

11. For a detailed discussion of the development of disability discrimination policy, see R. Scotch, From Good Will to Civil Rights: Transforming Federal Disability Policy (1984). For a brief summary overview of all disability discrimination laws, see Laura Rothstein and Julia Rothstein, Disabilities and the Law, Ch. 1, 3rd ed. (Thomson/West 2006).

12. In 1973, the term used was "handicap" but by 1990, that term was disfavored, and the term "disability" replaced it in virtually all federal legislation.

13. 29 U.S.C. § 791.

14. 29 U.S.C. § 793.

15. 29 U.S.C. § 794.

16. 20 U.S.C. §§ 1400 *et seq.*

17. HEW later became the Department of Health and Human Services, and the Department of Education was created.

18. See Cherry v. Mathews, 419 F.Supp. 922 (D.D.C. 1976).

19. Executive Order No. 11,914, 41 Fed. Reg. 17871 (Apr. 28, 1976).

20. 47 Fed. Reg. 2132 (Jan. 13, 1978). The regulations relevant to colleges and universities included a number of provisions related to admissions and recruitment, treatment of students, academic adjustments, housing, financial and employment assistance for students, and nonacademic services (physical education and athletics, counseling and placement services, and social organizations). 34 C.F.R. Part 104, Subpart E.

21. *Southeastern Community College v. Davis*, No. 78–711, Petition for Certiorari, Appendix at 17a (Stipulation of Facts, #3) and 116a (application for admission).

22. 442 U.S. at 401–02.

23. Petition for Certiorari, Appendix at 123a.

24. Petition for Certiorari, Appendix at 135a–136a.

25. Petition for Certiorari, Appendix at 110a–115a.

26. Petition for Certiorari, Appendix at 129a–130a.

27. Petition for Certiorari, Appendix at 132a–135a.

28. 442 U.S. at 402.

29. Petition for Certiorari, Appendix at 62a–69a.

30. The constitutional claims were dismissed at the District Court level, and no review of that dismissal was pursued. The complaint was filed on September 8, 1975. Petition for Certiorari, Appendix at 1a. The firm that represented her, Diehl and Gibson was bought out in 2003 by another firm. Philip Diehl, who was her counsel of record, died a few years ago.

31. 29 U.S.C. section 794 (1976 ed., Supp. II). Subsequent to the time this case was decided, the statute was amended to use the term "disabled" instead of "handicapped" and a number of other amendments have further defined who is covered.

32. 29 U.S.C. section 706(6) (1976 ed.). A number of amendments and Supreme Court decisions have refined and clarified the definition of who is covered.

33. Petition for Certiorari, Appendix at 23a–162a. The only defense witnesses to testify were representatives of Southeastern Community College.

34. *Id.*

35. Davis v. Southeastern Community College, 424 F.Supp. 1341, 1346 (E.D.N.C. 1976).

36. 424 F.Supp. at 1345.

37. 424 F.Supp. 1341 (E.D.N.C. 1976).

38. 424 F.Supp. at 1345.

39. 42 Fed. Reg. 22676 (May 4, 1977); 45 C.F.R. part 85 (1978).

40. Petition for Certiorari, Appendix at 1a.

41. 574 F.2d 1158 (4th Cir. 1978).

42. Subsequent to the Fourth Circuit remand, the Rehabilitation Act was amended to potentially affect the interpretation related to the Davis case, but the amendments did not affect the case in any way. Section 119 of the Rehabilitation, Comprehensive Services, and Developmental Disabilities Amendments of 1978, 92 Stat. 2982. See 442 U.S. at 403.

43. 574 F.2d at 1161–62.

44. Petition was filed on October 27, 1978 and granted on January 8, 1979. Petition for Certiorari, Appendix at 1a.

45. Southeastern Community College v. Davis, 442 U.S. 397, 404 (1979).

46. Phone interview with Professor Gressman, Professor Emeritus, University of North Carolina School of Law, April 18, 2006 (Professor Gressman's 89th birthday). Although he has emeritus status, he still works at his law school office every day and continues to write on Supreme Court practice. He has the distinction of serving as a Supreme Court clerk longer than any other individual (from 1943 to 1949). He was not sure how he had come to be asked to represent Southeastern Community College, but he distinctly remembers Ms. Davis's presence when he argued the case before the Court.

47. Marc Charmatz is currently an attorney with the National Association of the Deaf Law Center. He teaches disability law at the University of Maryland School of Law. Unlike Professor Gressman, whose expertise is in Supreme Court practice, rather than disability law, Marc Charmatz has a long record of involvement in disability rights issues, particularly relating to individuals who are deaf.

48. Briefs supporting Southeastern Community College were filed by the Department of Justice Office of the Attorney General, the American Council on Education, the American Medical Colleges, the National Institute for Independent Colleges and Universities, the Board of Governors, and a number of state governments. Briefs supporting Ms. Davis were filed by the American Civil Liberties Union, the American Coalition of Citizens with Disabilities, the State of California, the New York City Council of Organizations Serving the Deaf, several California advocacy organizations, and a number of other advocacy organizations. Briefs on both sides addressed procedural issues, including whether there is a private right of action, burdens of proof, and exhaustion of administrative remedies. The procedural issues were not the focus of the Supreme Court's decision, and are not addressed in this story.

49. 442 U.S. 397 (1979).

50. 442 U.S. at 407.

51. 442 U.S. at 406.

52. 442 U.S. at 406, referring to 45 C.F.R. section 84.3(k)(3), and pt. 84 App. A, p. 405 (1978).

53. 442 U.S. at 407.

54. Petitioner's Brief, pp. 17–18, citing HEW Regulatory Guidelines, 45 C.F.R. Part 84, Appendix A, p. 376. The petitioner noted that this analysis was available to, but was not utilized by the Fourth Circuit.

55. 442 U.S. at 409.

56. 442 U.S. at 410.

57. 442 U.S. at 411. This use of the term "affirmative action" is not the traditional use of the term, and was not used by other courts in disability discrimination cases after this decision.

58. 442 U.S. at 412. *See also* Burton Bollag, *The Debate Over Deaf Education*, The Chronicle of Higher Education A18 (May 12, 2006) (referencing progress in cochlear implants).

59. 442 U.S. at 413.

60. Ms. Davis's current address and activities are unknown.

61. Ohio Civil Rights Commission v. Case Western Reserve University, 76 Ohio St.3d 168, 666 N.E.2d 1376 (1996).

62. Doe v. New York University, 666 F.2d 761 (2d Cir. 1981).

63. Doe v. Washington University, 780 F.Supp. 628 (E.D. Mo. 1991).

64. Wong v. Regents of University of California, 192 F.3d 807 (9th Cir. 1999); Zukle v. Regents of University of California, 166 F.3d 1041 (9th Cir. 1999); Betts v. Rector and Visitors of the University of Virginia, 191 F.3d 447 (4th Cir. 1999); Wynne v. Tufts University School of Medicine, 932 F.2d 19 (1st Cir. 1991); Gonzalez v. National Board of Medical Examiners, 60 F.Supp.2d 703 (E.D. Mich. 1999); Price v. National Board of Medical Examiners, 966 F.Supp. 419 (W.D.W. Va. 1997).

65. Pushkin v. Regents of the University of Colorado, 658 F.2d 1372 (10th Cir. 1981).

66. Russell v. Salve Regina College, 890 F.2d 484 (1st Cir. 1989).

67. See Laura Rothstein and Julia Rothstein, Disabilities and the Law Section 10.03 (Thomson/West 2006).

68. Wynne v. Tufts University School of Medicine, 932 F.2d 19 (1st Cir. 1991). This case set the standard by requiring that these decisions be made by "relevant officials within the institution" who came to "rationally justifiable conclusions" about whether an action would lower academic standards or require substantial program alteration. While not a Supreme Court decision, the case has the precedential value of such a decision and has been widely and consistently cited for this standard of decision making within higher education.

69. Pushkin v. Regents of the University of Colorado, 658 F.2d 1372 (10th Cir. 1981).

70. Laura Rothstein and Julia Rothstein, Disabilities and the Law (Thomson/West 2006).

71. 42 U.S.C. § 1400. For an overview and history of special education law, see Laura Rothstein and Julia Rothstein, Disabilities and the Law Chapter 2 (Thomson/West 2006).

72. Laura Rothstein and Julia Rothstein, Disabilities and the Law (Thomson/West 2006). *See, e.g.*, Trageser v. Libbie Rehabilitation Center, Inc., 590 F.2d 87 (4th Cir. 1978) (employment discrimination claim could not be brought under Section 504 in nursing home receiving limited government benefits); Hairston v. Drosick, 423 F.Supp. 180 (S.D. W. Va. 1976) (case involving whether Section 504 requires catheteriziation as a health service in public schools).

73. 34 C.F.R.§ 104.6(c).

74. I was in the unique position in my own professional life to observe this first hand. In 1979, I had been appointed as a visiting professor at the University of Pittsburgh School of Law. I had requested only one course because I was pregnant. Before the appointment began, I decided that I could take on more and when I inquired whether there were additional things I might do at the law school, it was suggested that because I was a member of the Pennsylvania bar, that I could handle some of the cases in the Developmental Disabilities Law Project, a clinic in which law students under the guidance of the clinic director took on disability discrimination cases. When I indicated that I didn't know anything about that area of law, the response was "that's OK, neither does anyone else." I accepted the assignment, and this began my work in this area of law. The following year (1980), when I began teaching at West Virginia University College of Law, I was assigned to serve as faculty editor of the Journal of College and University Law. I began developing teaching materials on disability law at that time, which eventually evolved into textbooks and a treatise. I was in the unique position to study and teach about the intersection of higher education and disability discrimination issues at a critical time in the evolution of these legal issues.

75. 42 U.S.C. §§ 12101 *et seq. See also* Sara Hebel, *How a Landmark Anti-Bias Law Changed Life for Disabled Students*, The Chronicle of Higher Education, p. A23 (January 26, 2001).

76. Sutton v. United Air Lines, Inc., 527 U.S. 471 (1999); Albertsons, Inc. v. Kirkingburg, 527 U.S. 555 (1999); and Murphy v. United Parcel Service, Inc., 527 U.S. 516 (1999). A 1998 Supreme Court decision involving a dental patient with HIV had addressed whether she was disabled. Bragdon v. Abbott, 524 U.S. 624 (1998). Previously, courts had determined with very little analysis that individuals with HIV or similar conditions were covered. See School Board of Nassau County v. Arline, 480 U.S. 273 (1987).

77. Toyota Motor Mfg. Kentucky, Inc. v. Williams, 534 U.S. 184 (2002). The case was settled after remand.

78. 534 U.S. at 197.

79. Chevron U.S.A. Inc. v. Echazabal, 536 U.S. 73 (2002).

80. Bartlett v. New York State Board of Law Examiners, 226 F.3d 69 (2d Cir. 2000).

81. 442 U.S. at 412.

82. The courts have recently addressed issues of learning disabled students in a number of cases involving medical school. While the focus has been on whether the condition was a covered disability, courts have also reverted to earlier determinations, and addressed whether the medical student was otherwise qualified.

83. 932 F.2d 19 (1st Cir. 1991).

84. 932 F.2d at 26

85. 932 F.2d at 26, citing *Southeastern Community College v. Davis.*

86. See cases cited in Laura Rothstein and Julia Rothstein, Disabilities and the Law § 3.22 (Thomson/West 2006).

87. While in most cases, these individuals developed the disabilities after admission, it is likely that they would have faced discrimination in continued employment as health care professionals in the era before *Southeastern Community College* and subsequent developments.

88. Alexandria Berger, *Student Copes With Paraplegia, Becomes M.D.*, Houston Chronicle at p. 4D (December 12, 1997).

89. Irwin M. Dannis, M.D., *Profile in Courage: Jim Post, M.D., Class of '97*, E=MD2, p. 2 (Summer 2004). Jim Post received substantial national media attention during this process.

90. Mary Beth Reilly, *Quadriplegic Medical Student Flexes His Muscles with "Murderball,"* AP (December 14, 2005); http://www.med.umich.edu/opmnewspage/2005/mudergball.htm.

91. Andy Mandis, *Blind Medical Student Earns M.D.*, http://www.msnbc.msn.com/id/7318398, Associated Press, April 5, 2005; Gina Shaw, Blind Medical Student Beats the Odds, 9 AAMC NewsRoom Reporter (July 2000).

92. Donna Carol Maheady, Nursing Students with Disabilities: Change the Course (Exceptional Parent Press 2003) (includes eight stories of nursing students with disabilities); *Students with Disabilities Can Succeed in Nursing*, Kansas City Nursing News, KS (October 14, 2002) (http:://www.deaftoday.com/news/archives/pppp77.html).

93. *A Word From the President—Reconsidering "Disabled" Applicants*, AAMC Reporter (June 2004).

94. Gina Shaw, *Blind Medical Student Beats the Odds*, AAMC Reporter (Volume 9) (July 2000) (noting that it took substantial faculty time to make materials accessible); Irwin M. Dannis, *Profile in Courage: Jim Post, M.D., Class of '97*, E=MD2, p. 3 (Summer 2004) (Jim Post paid a physician's assistant to provide motor skills).

8

The Story of *Hazelwood School District v. Kuhlmeier*: Student Press and the School Censor

Anne Proffitt Dupre[1]

A Narrower Spectrum

"I want to work on the school newspaper." These are not words that usually would cause parents to place the family lawyer on retainer. Maybe they should.

Three teenagers signed up for the Journalism II class at Hazelwood East High School in St. Louis County, Missouri, in the spring of 1983. Little did they know that this decision would lead to a battle with school officials that would end in the United States Supreme Court and an opinion that was "probably the most significant free speech case involving public school students since the Court decided *Tinker v. Des Moines Independent Community School District*" almost twenty years before.[2]

The three teenagers—Cathy Kuhlmeier, Leslie Smart, and Leanne Tippett—took the journalism class after first completing Journalism I the previous fall. As part of this class, the young women worked as editors of the school newspaper, the *Spectrum*, which was published about six times a semester by the journalism class. The *Spectrum* covered issues of interest to the1800 students in grades nine through twelve, including stories on sports, interviews with faculty members, prom news, general news items, movie reviews, editorials, and other items of current interest.

During the spring of 1983, Ms. Kuhlmeier served as the *Spectrum's* layout editor, Ms. Smart was a newswriter and movie reviewer, and Ms. Tippett was a news feature writer, cartoonist, and photographer. Although students who were not enrolled in the journalism class could submit items to the paper, it was mostly written and entirely edited by members of Journalism II. In the Curriculum Guide, the course description for Journalism II stated, "Journalism II provides a laboratory situation in which the students publish the school newspaper applying the skills they have learned in Journalism I."[3] For the most part, students worked on the paper during class time, although it also took some after-school time. Overall, the newspaper was run as part of an academic class and not as an extra-curricular activity.

Mr. Robert Stergos taught Journalism I and Journalism II from 1981 until April 1983. Mr. Stergos exercised a great deal of editorial control over the newspaper. He selected the students who were to be editors, scheduled publication dates, approved stories and other content, and had control over the editing process. During the school year, there had been discussion between Mr. Stergos and the administration over how much control the school should have over what was published in the *Spectrum*. At a meeting in January 1983, several of Mr. Stergos's superiors informed him that the Board of Education's policies should not be questioned in the paper. Moreover, they told him that all issues of the newspaper should be submitted to and approved by the school principal, Mr. Robert Reynolds, before publication and distribution to the student body.[4] In April 1983, after Stergos resigned to enter the private sector, Mr. Howard Emerson took over as journalism teacher and supervisor of the *Spectrum*, and his duties were identical to those of Mr. Stergos.[5]

The *Spectrum* was published every three weeks, and it had a distribution of 4500 copies. Before the events that precipitated this famous case, previous issues of the *Spectrum* included stories on topics such as teenage dating, drug and alcohol use among students, race relations, teenage marriage, the death penalty, school desegregation, runaways, teenage pregnancy, religious cults, and the draft.[6]

The May 13, 1983 issue of the *Spectrum* was the genesis of the lawsuit that ultimately defined the scope of freedom of the press in a public high school setting (and perhaps, as we shall see later in the chapter, even the scope of freedom in the college setting). The usual publication practice was for the teacher—Stergos, and later Emerson—to submit page proofs to the principal Reynolds for review before publication. When the teacher delivered the proofs on May 10 for the May 13 issue, Reynolds' reaction to two articles started events in motion that would end almost five years later with a divided opinion from the United States Supreme Court.

The May 13 issue of *Spectrum* was printed and sold to the student body, but it was not the issue that the student editors expected to see, at least not in its entirety. The issue was two pages and five articles short of the issue they had laid out and edited. When Principal Reynolds read over the newspaper, he discovered two articles that appeared on two different pages of the paper that he believed should not be published. He did not think that there was enough time to edit these articles before the paper had to be sent off for publication, and so he told Mr. Emerson to remove the entire two pages on which these articles were printed. Because of the publication setup, this resulted in several other articles being pulled from publication, despite the fact that the principal did not have a problem with those particular articles.[7]

The first of the two articles was entitled *Student Pregnancy: Three Personal Accounts* (hereinafter "the pregnancy article").[8] It was written by a student named Christine De Hass and consisted of three personal accounts of Hazelwood East students who were pregnant.

The second article was entitled *Divorce's Impact on Kids May Have Life Long Affect* [sic] (hereinafter "the divorce article"). Written by student Shari Gordon, it contained interviews with students who discussed their parents' divorce. The article included quotes from a named freshman student who said, "My dad wasn't spending enough time with my mom, my sister and I. [sic] He was always out of town on business or out late playing cards with the guys. My parents always argued about everything," and "In the beginning I thought I caused the problem, but now I realized it wasn't me."[9] Similar quotes were provided by two other students, who were identified by name. Both De Hass and Gordon had circulated questionnaires to fellow students that required the students to sign the questionnaire as acknowledgement that they were aware that the information they provided was to be used in *Spectrum* articles.

After the newspaper went to print without the articles, the students found a notice posted in the journalism room: "The content of some of the articles were *personal* and highly sensitive—people and names were used. [sic] The information was sensitive and totally unnecessary to be included in the school newspaper. They have many other opportunities to achieve goals in journalism class or publishing of the school newspaper that do not require that kind of reporting. [sic] Learning can take place in research and reporting that is less sensitive, less controversial, and certainly something that is just as beneficial to students."[10]

The students were upset that the articles were cut from the published newspaper, and so they decided to take action. At a loss for how to handle the situation, they first contacted their former teacher, Mr. Robert Stergos. According to an article that appeared in *The Nation* while the case was before the Supreme Court, Stergos had resigned from his post as *Spectrum* advisor because of a disagreement with the school board.[11] Stergos, who was 26 years old at the time, believed fervently that teaching journalism to students meant allowing them to explore important school issues and expose the problems they discovered. He had been taken to task by the school administration the semester before he resigned when his students published one article exposing grading inconsistencies and another comparing the salaries of male and female coaches.

The school district's associate superintendent Francis Huss wanted tighter control over what was published in the school newspaper, and Huss was critical of Principal Reynolds over his alleged lack of control over the student journalists and Mr. Stergos. When Huss demanded that the newspaper no longer run stories questioning board policy and insisted on the review of all editions of the paper before it went to print, Stergos decided that he had had enough. He found a job as a consultant and decided to end his teaching career at Hazelwood East. He was released from his contract and left the school just two weeks before the controversial articles were to be published. Stergos wanted high school journalism to mean "more than profiles of prom queens. He taught the values of the free press."[12] Although Stergos knew about the articles, he decided not to say anything to the administration about them before his departure.

When the students sought out Stergos to ask him how they should handle the administration's decision, he advised the Ms. Kuhlmeier and her co-editors to talk to the American Civil Liberties Union. The ACLU did not represent the students, but told them they likely had a good case, and the students brought suit against the school district, administrators, the principal and members of the faculty. The students claimed that the school violated their First Amendment (right to) freedom of speech, freedom of expression and freedom of press and their Fourteenth Amendment right of due process.

The Trial Court: Editing or Censorship?

Chief Judge Nangle of the United States District Court of the Eastern District of Missouri divided the case into two parts. He first ruled that he would not grant injunctive relief to the students. Since the students had already graduated by the time of the trial, injunctive relief was no longer possible.[13] He then conducted a bench trial on the first amendment issue.

Sitting without a jury, Judge Nangle had the job of deciding which view of the facts he found more credible. His opinion starts with a lengthy section of factual findings, many of which have been set forth above. Since the factual findings of a trial court are granted deference by courts of appeals, these factual findings would prove to be important as the case worked its way up through the Eight Circuit Court of Appeals and beyond.

First, Judge Nangle found that student testimony that they believed they had free rein to publish practically anything was "not credible."[14] They were well aware of the control that Stergos (and later Emerson) exercised over the newspaper. In addition, their textbook in the journalism class reprinted the ethical rules adopted by the American Society of Newspaper Editors, as well as the Chicago Sun–Times code of professional standards. Both of these documents contained sections discussing "Fair Play." The former stated that the reporter must stand accountable to the public for the accuracy of their reports and should give persons accused the earliest opportunity to respond. The latter stated that a person whose reputation is attacked is entitled to simultaneous rebuttal, that every attempt should be made to present all sides of controversial issues, and that the anonymous quote should be avoided except in cases where the reasons for anonymity are made clear to the reader.[15] Thus, the ethical rules of journalism were a part of the class and the laboratory experience.

Although the pregnancy article stated that "all names have been changed to keep the identity of these girls a secret,"[16] Principal Reynolds testified that he was concerned that "the girls had been described to the point where they could be identified by their peers."[17] At the time, there were eight to ten girls in the high school who were pregnant. Because of the limited number of pregnant students at the high school and details given by the girls in the article, their identities were not as secret as the author and *Spectrum* editorial staff had hoped.[18] One could be identified because of her due date and because she dropped out of school. One teacher testified that at the time the articles were deleted she thought she could identify two of the three girls, testimony that Judge Nangle found credible. Although the pregnant girls were told that their names would not be revealed in the newspaper, they were not given instructions on parental consent. The fathers of the pregnant students were not interviewed or given a chance to respond.

The student reporters did not solicit the consent of the parents of the students who were quoted in Ms. Gordon's article on divorce, and the parents were not given a chance to respond to the accusations made against them by their children. Moreover, a student was named in the divorce article that Mr. Reynolds cut. Although the *Spectrum* editorial staff later decided to remove the name from the article, at the time that the principal made his decision, the name was there, and Reynolds believed it was unfair that the parents did not have a chance to respond to their child's disparaging statements.[19] Reynolds thought that fairness required that the parents should be notified and given a chance to respond, testimony that Judge Nangle again found credible.

Both sides presented expert witnesses, and it is clear from Judge Nangle's order that the school district won "the battle of the experts" hands down. The plaintiff's expert was Dr. Robert Knight, a professor of journalism from the University of Missouri–Columbia. During direct examination, he testified that the articles complied with recognized journalism standards. But skillful questioning during the cross-examination brought out facts that caused Knight to lose credibility with Judge Nangle. In Judge Nangle's view, Knight's actions with respect to the case had been "less than objective and independent."[20] At a conference of reporters and investigators, Knight had passed out copies of the stories in question with his own summary, attempted to convince others to come to the aid of the students, and later tried to get the executive committee of the convention to help the student press.[21]

The defendant's expert witness, Mr. Martin Duggan, a recent appointee to the Federal Commission on Compensation and former editorial page editor for the Saint Louis Globe Democrat, fared much better. He testified that "fairness and balance" is a term of art in journalism and requires journalists to present all sides of a story. He testified that the divorce story did not meet this standard and that both the divorce story and the pregnancy story were not suitable for publication because they were invasions of privacy. He also explained the difference between censorship and editing; censorship comes from an outside source, where editing is the prerogative of an authority within the publishing entity.[22]

This trial may very well have been won and lost with these experts. Judge Nangle simply stated that Duggan was more credible than Knight—his opinion was "entitled to more weight."[23] Knight is "deeply and personally involved with high school press issues and his own personal interests are basically aligned with an expansion of student press rights. Mr. Duggan, on the other hand, was an objective and independent witness who was not even compensated by defendants for his testimony."[24]

Judge Nangle noted that the students all received academic credit and a grade for their work in the journalism class. He also pointed out that the judgment of the professional educators with many years of experience dealing with high school students was both reasonable and entitled to great deference.[25]

Judge Nangle's order delved deeply into the rich well of case law involving the First Amendment in a public high school setting. Not surprisingly, he started with *Tinker v. Des Moines Independent Community School District*.[26] In *Tinker*, a group of students were suspended when they disobeyed a school policy and wore black armbands to school to protest the Vietnam War. In an opinion written by Justice Fortas, the Supreme Court made clear that students "do not shed their constitutional rights at the school house gate."[27] School officials could restrain student speech only when it "materially disrupts classwork, or involves substantial disorder or invasion of the rights of others."[28]

Two lines of cases had developed since *Tinker* with respect to student press issues. One line of cases addressed the situation where the student speech arose outside of official school programs. This is where student speech rights are at their strongest. Educators must show that the speech will materially disrupt the educational process (and they are rarely able to do so because it is more difficult for the school to prove that the conduct or speech was materially disruptive to the education process when the speech is not a part of that process).[29] In line with *Tinker*, courts generally decided that students' free speech rights would prevail when students engage in speech that is privately-initiated, not sponsored by the school, and independent of any official school activities or publications.[30]

But there was another line of cases where the analysis had not been so clear. In these cases, the speech in question occurred in the context of a school-sponsored program, and here the results were mixed.[31] When a school-sponsored program was at issue, courts focused on whether the school program was part of a public forum for free expression or whether the program was a part of the school curriculum over which school officials had greater control. If school officials created an open forum, they would be more limited by the First Amendment when attempting to restrain student speech.

With regard to the *Spectrum* newspaper at Hazelwood East High School, Judge Nangle determined that the newspaper was an integral part of the school curriculum, not a public forum for free expression for students.[32] It was part of a class, taught by a faculty member with a textbook, and students received class credit and a grade. Most importantly, the teacher had control over almost every aspect of the newspaper's production.

Even though the newspaper was an integral part of the curriculum, this did not mean that school authorities were completely unconstrained by the First Amendment. They must still show that there was a reasonable basis for the action that they took.[33] According to Judge Nangle, Principal Reynolds' concern that students would lose their anonymity was reasonable and involved an invasion of privacy. Invasion of the rights of others was one of the bases in *Tinker* that would justify a restraint on student speech. Reynolds' concern about the divorce article was also reasonable because there was serious doubt that it complied with rules of fairness that are standard in the field of journalism. Moreover, school authorities wished to avoid the impression that the school endorsed the sexual norms portrayed in the story, and Judge Nangle explicitly "credit[ed] the judgment of [the school] officials that such material, especially in the context of a school newspaper produced by a journalism class, is not appropriate for some of the *Spectrum*'s readers, given their age and maturity."[34]

Thus, the school did not violate the students' First Amendment rights. The defendants "merely exercised their discretion, in a proper manner, with respect to a product of the Hazelwood East curriculum."[35]

Moving Up the Appeals Ladder: Scylla and Charybdis

Given the differing views on this issue, as even Judge Nangle acknowledged, it is hardly surprising that a panel of the Eighth Circuit Court of Appeals could neither agree with Judge Nangle nor among themselves. The court of appeals reversed Judge Nangle in a 2–1 decision.[36]

Unlike the district court, the court of appeals, in an opinion written by Judge Heaney and joined by Judge Arnold, held fast to the *Tinker* analysis. The appeals court flat-out disagreed with Judge Nangle's finding that the *Spectrum* was not a public forum. Although the *Spectrum* was published by the journalism class and was essentially part of the curriculum, the newspaper was "something more" than just a class exercise.[37] Judge Heaney described the newspaper as "a forum in which the school encouraged students to express their views to the entire student body freely."[38] This was a student publication in every sense of the word. The students ran the paper in almost every aspect of its creation and publication: picking staff members, choosing subject matter, writing articles, and editing the final edition. The court focused on the testimony of the former *Spectrum* advisor Stergos who stated at trial, "It's a student paper, so that the students, first of all, decided the stories, and, you know, wrote the stories, so they obviously were deciding the content. They were writing them. I would help if there were any matters that they had questions of, legalwise or ethicalwise, but—."[39] Accordingly, the newspaper was not an integral part of the curriculum over which school officials could exercise a certain degree of control, but a public forum that operated as a conduit for student viewpoints.

It appears that the court of appeals read the evidence in the record and found its own set of facts from that record. Every first-year law student learns that appeals courts must not disturb a trial court's finding of fact unless that finding is "clearly erroneous," a high standard for change.[40] Although the evidence before the two courts could have been read differently, it is hard to see how Judge Nangle was clearly erroneous in his finding, and it is curious that the appeals court never even claimed that its analysis met this standard.

Of course, the extent of First Amendment protection for a public forum is greater than for an integral part of the school curriculum. The *Tinker* disruption analysis comes back into the picture, and school officials must show that the restraint on student speech is "necessary to avoid material and substantial interference with school work or discipline . . . or the rights of others."[41] Whittled to its essence, the crux of the case comes down to how much deference judges are willing to give to the educators making a decision. The two judges in the majority were not willing to defer to the professional judgment of educators to the same degree Judge Nangle was, and this tougher scrutiny spelled defeat for the school district.[42]

The majority saw no evidence in the record that the school principal or board could have reasonably forecast that any of the censored articles would have disrupted class or caused any sort of substantial disorder among the students. The judges saw no evidence either that the publication of these articles in *Spectrum* would lead anyone to believe that the school board endorsed teenaged pregnancies or that the article was inappropriate for the age and maturity level of some of its readers.[43]

Most significantly, the majority disagreed with the educators regarding what it called "the heart of the case"—whether the pregnancy article and the divorce article invaded the privacy rights of others. Even *Tinker* allows for First Amendment restraint if student speech invades the rights of others. But what does this mean? Taking its cue from a Student Note in the *Michigan Law Review*,[44] the court decided that school officials are justified in constraining student speech in this context only when the speech could result in tort liability for the school.[45]

This standard is, of course, a high one. The court found no potential tort emanating from any of the stories. The name was removed from the divorce story before it went to the printer (Judge Heaney does not mention that Principal Reynolds did not know of the removal when he made his decision to omit the article). Thus, the stories were no more than "anecdotal treatment of the subject of divorce."[46] No tort here. With respect to the pregnancy article, the three girls agreed to be the subjects of a newspaper article, but their parents and the fathers of their babies did not. The court focused on the parents and the fathers: The only possible tort they could claim was invasion of privacy—publicity exposing the details of the life of a person, which exposure would be offensive and objectionable to a reasonable person.[47] The parents would have no claim as no details of their lives were exposed. The fathers were not named in the articles (although the court does not address the fact that the fathers could have been identified if the female students were identified). The female students consented to the article. No tort here either.

The court of appeals did not address to what extent the students should be restrained from writing journalism that did not meet journalistic ethical standards. Nor did the court discuss whether educators have an interest in their students that exceeds or differs from the dollar amount that the school district is willing or able to pay during tort litigation. The court of appeals reversed Judge Nangle and remanded the matter back to him for a determination of damages, noting that the facts would not give rise to any damages other than nominal damages.[48]

Given the complexity of the issues, it was not surprising that one of the three judges on the panel dissented. Judge Wollman acknowledged that *Tinker* spelled out First Amendment rights for students, but it did not give students the unfettered right to publish a school-sponsored, faculty-supervised paper with the same lack of restraint enjoyed by the commercial press. "The majority opinion consigns school officials to chart a course between the Scylla of a student-led first amendment suit and the Charybdis of a tort action by those claiming to have been injured by the publication of student-written material."[49] For those unfamiliar with Greek mythology, the Scylla and Charybdis were two sea monsters that inhabited either side of a narrow straight between which Odysseus had to sail in Homer's classic tale. Choosing to sail further from one monster meant that the hero had to sail closer to the other and face certain doom. Judge Wollman pointed out that while the commercial press can afford to retain counsel to advise them on questions that arise daily regarding liability, school districts do not usually have these kinds of resources to spend on legal fees, rather than instruction.[50]

The United States Supreme Court: "Legitimate Pedagogical Concern"

The Supreme Court granted the school district's petition for certiorari and heard oral argument in the case right after the lunch recess on October 13, 1987.[51] First to present was the lawyer for the school district, Mr. Robert Baine, Jr. of St. Louis, Missouri. The Justices asked questions about the use of public forum analysis, pointing out that *Tinke*r never mentioned it. Somewhat helpful to Mr. Baine and his clients was the Court's opinion in *Bethel School District No. 403 v. Fraser*[52]—decided only the year before—which added to the *Tinker* rule by allowing school officials to constrain "vulgar and lewd" speech that undermined the basic educational mission of the school. This helped the school district, because the *Fraser* Court had not required material disruption or substantial interference with the educational process as required by *Tinker*. Baine tried to use this more recent opinion to bolster his argument that courts should defer to the judgment of educators regarding two important issues: (1) the subject matter that is appropriate for the students in their schools and (2) whether it would appear that the school had condoned the activities discussed in the articles.

He received help from one Justice, who pointed out that even if the school district might not appear to condone the activity, it was certainly providing the means to discuss it.[53] Unlike *Tinker*, where the students provided their own armbands, the school district here provided and paid for the ink, the paper and the publication costs. This would seem to tie the school district to the newspaper in a way that did not occur in *Tinker*.

The Justices kept asking Baine what the standard would be for the school district to constrain student speech in the context of the school newspaper, and Baine got himself in a corner by seeming to claim that the school district would have unlimited power. Although it was apparent that at least some of the Justices were not buying this, Baine remained adamant until pressed with a hypothetical asking if the school official could decide to publish all articles favorable to Democrats and none for Republicans. Baine tried to backtrack by suggesting that viewpoint discrimination would be a problem, and one Justice told him, "You can't have it both ways." His argument bogged down, and he reserved the remainder for rebuttal.[54]

The Justices probed the attorney for the students, Leslie Edwards, also of St. Louis, about the significance of any representation made to the students about who had control over the newspaper. Edwards maintained that there was an important distinction between a curricular activity and one that was extracurricular, arguing that the *Spectrum* was more like an extracurricular activity. She, too, got tangled up in the argument when presented with the hypothetical question whether a faculty advisor could reserve the right to say no to any article that is morally undesirable for high school students. Ms. Edwards stated that the school board could delegate this function to an advisor, but that the decision to delete could not be content-based. Now the Justices had her:

> QUESTION: So the advisor cannot say I reject this article which encourages what I think is immorality in [sic] the part of high school students, but I will accept this article which I think encourages morality?
>
> MS. EDWARDS: It does not serve an editorial function and it does not serve an educational interest. I do not think that would be constitutional.
>
> QUESTION: So you either have to have no school paper or you have to have a school paper that carries articles like smoking pot is fun, that is the constitutional choice?
>
> MS. EDWARDS: I do not think so. I think that you can allow the school to set up one that is related to their educational interests, so long as they do not tell the students now go and exercise your *Tinker* First Amendment rights.
>
> QUESTION: I do not understand.
>
> MS. EDWARDS: I do not think that it only has to be one or the other. I mean I think that the school can—

> QUESTION: I could set up a newspaper then and say you are not going to have any articles in it that encourage the smoking of pot, I can do that?
>
> MS. EDWARDS: If it is viewpoint based, I do not think that they can.
>
> QUESTION: They cannot. So I either have to have no newspaper or I have to have a newspaper that has articles encouraging the kids who go to that school to smoke pot.

The Justices seemed unconvinced by this argument, but things soon went from bad to worse.

> QUESTION: So the only way to avoid all of the good stuff that you are doing in the classroom teaching them that smoking pot is no good is not to have a student newspaper, that is the only way that you could avoid the school formally subsidizing that opposing value judgment.
>
> MS. EDWARDS: Not to pay for it, not to have an advisor.
>
> QUESTION: Right.
>
> MS. EDWARDS: And not to allow the other viewpoint to be presented. To only have one viewpoint, you would have to have no school newspaper, yes.
>
> QUESTION: So I take it on your theory that the school could not even require that the students include in the newspaper the idea that smoking pot is bad.
>
> MS. EDWARDS: Oh, sure. That is both viewpoints to be presented.
>
> QUESTION: That is not First Amendment law, that is not First Amendment law.

The questions veered off in another direction, but the argument bogged down once again.

> QUESTION: May I ask you this question about this case. As I understand it, part of the problem arose because the person who normally exercised responsibility, Mr. Stergos left, and there was kind of confusion about it.
>
> Supposing that he had not left and everybody was used to working with him and recognized that he was the teacher who controlled it, and he took plenty of time to reach the same decision that the principal reached here, told the students all about it, and had just as weak reasons as the principal did, but he came to that conclusion that this is not a very good article for the paper and you cannot print it.
>
> Would you still have a case?

MS. EDWARDS: If he—

QUESTION: If he ended up after all of the deliberations had gone into whether these articles ought to go in or not, and he comes to the conclusion that these are not very good articles for this school, I think that I will cut them.

Do you have the same right to say?

[Author: There may be an error in the transcript here, since this makes no sense. The question may have been "Do you have the same case?" or something along that line.]

MS. EDWARDS: Frankly, I think that it is not very strong, no. I would say that the advisor has the ability and the right because of his expertise to do some editorial function. That has been delegated by the school to him, and that is different than the principal.

QUESTION: So you would say that is a different case?

MS. EDWARDS: Yes, sir.

QUESTION: So what you are really complaining about is the fact that this principal did not use very good judgment?

MS. EDWARDS: That they reached up and got someone who was not part of the editorial function who was not skilled in journalism or experienced, and did it for a reason other than journalistic standards or editorial discretion.

QUESTION: Well, say he decided journalistic standards, this article does not show the degree of maturity that we think that it ought to show to have the school name on it and all of the rest, there is some misspelling in it and some bad grammar, a mixture of reasons, that is not enough?

MS. EDWARDS: The advisor, that he could do that?

[Author: Ms. Edwards seems to be agreeing that the advisor could cut the article.]

QUESTION: If the advisor can do it, I do not understand why the principal cannot.

MS. EDWARDS: Because the advisor is part of what has been delegated by the school to be the training and practicing of student expression.

QUESTION: It seems to me what you are saying is if you are going to have censors that they have to be good censors.

MS. EDWARDS: No, I think that they have to be journalistically involved, so the motivation of the school is good journalism and not a viewpoint.

> QUESTION: It is a constitutional line [?] [W]hether you are violating the Constitution depends on whether you have a good journalist involved or not in the censorship?

Of course, Ms. Edwards probably did not mean for the constitutional line to be placed there, but her answer—"The constitutional line comes with whether student expression is protected or not"—begged the question and did not seem to impress the Justices either.

Mr. Baine seemed to have regained his composure when he returned for his brief rebuttal. He focused his argument on the evidence that that newspaper was part of the school curriculum, a good strategy since courts traditionally defer to school officials with regard to curriculum issues. At 1:52 p.m. on October 13, 1987, Chief Justice Rehnquist announced that the case was submitted.

By Supreme Court standards, the wait was not a long one. Just three months later, in an opinion written by Justice White (joined by Chief Justice Rehnquist and Justices Stevens, O'Connor, and Scalia), the Court held that there was no First Amendment violation.[55] Attorney Baine was correct in discerning that the case *Bethel v, Fraser*, decided in the year before *Hazelwood* was argued, had changed the landscape that had been carved out by *Tinker*.[56] Although the opinion began with the "schoolhouse gate" quote from *Tinker*, the Court then immediately quoted *Fraser*, noting that a student's right to free speech "are not automatically coextensive with the rights of adults in other settings," and that a school need not tolerate speech that was inconsistent with its "basic educational mission." [57]Justice White, who had joined the majority in *Tinker*, wrote an opinion that dramatically changed the landscape that *Tinker* had formed.

First addressing the public forum issue, the majority simply agreed with Judge Nangle's view of the evidence, rather than that of the Eighth Circuit. The newspaper was produced as part of the Journalism II class, which was taught by a faculty member, and which students took for class credit and a grade. As such a teaching tool, the newspaper was not a public forum at all. The faculty never opened up the newspaper as a forum to the outside public or even to the student body as a whole; it was limited to members of the journalism class. In fact, the paper was produced in a laboratory setting, as the students applied the skills they learned in class to the newspaper. The day-to-day publication process underscored that the production of the newspaper was part of a classroom activity. The faculty advisor had the final say on all quotes and articles published, and the principal had the power to review each issue before publication. Because it was not a public forum, teachers and school officials may place reasonable restrictions on the types of speech that students can engage in through the newspaper.[58]

The Court took great pains to distinguish *Tinker*. *Tinker* addressed independent student speech that happened to occur on school grounds, and school officials were placed in the position of having to deal with it. When speech generates from an independent source, like an unofficial underground newspaper, most people who hear or read that speech will understand that the opinions expressed therein are those of the student delivering the message. But when student speech comes from a school-sponsored newspaper or in some other forum established and funded by the school, the public is much more likely to believe that the views are endorsed by the school itself. For this reason, a school may exercise greater control over the speech that is presented through a medium that belongs to the school itself and not to its students.

How much greater control may school officials exert under these circumstances than in circumstances where the facts are closer to *Tinker*? Instead of manipulating the *Tinker* standard to fit these facts, the Court simply articulated a new standard entirely: "We hold that educators do not offend the First Amendment by exercising editorial control over the style and content of student speech in school-sponsored expressive activities so long as their actions are *reasonably related to a legitimate pedagogical concern*."[59]

Once the Court articulated its new standard, all that remained was to apply it to the actions of Principal Reynolds. Reynolds had concerns about the anonymity of the pregnant students, the privacy interests of their parents and boyfriends, the journalistic fairness issues in the divorce article and the maturity level of the newspaper readers.[60] Thus, "we cannot reject as unreasonable" Reynolds' conclusion that these articles were not suitable for publication in the *Spectrum*.[61]

Justice Brennan wrote a lengthy and impassioned dissent, in which he was joined by Justices Marshall and Blackmun. He accused his colleagues of allowing "brutal censorship,"[62] giving school officials the right to act as "thought police."[63] By pulling the articles, Principal Reynolds demonstrated "unthinking contempt for human rights."[64] Justice Brennan viewed the distinction between personal and school-sponsored speech as a mistake, and he would have held fast to the *Tinker* standard that protects student speech unless it materially disrupts the education process. Justice Brennan stated that the censorship did not serve the curriculum purposes of the school newspaper, "unless one believes that the purpose of the school newspaper is to teach students that the press ought never report bad news, express unpopular views, or print a thought that might upset its sponsors."[65] He argued that the school could have achieved its purposes by using less restrictive means to dissociate itself from the views expressed in the newspaper, such as printing a disclaimer with each issue of the *Spectrum* stating that the views expressed therein are those of the student editors and not endorsed by the school. The school board also could have issued an official response stating its position on the matter and pointing out the faults in the students' positions. Justice Brennan famously concludes his dissent with the lament, "The young men and women of Hazelwood East expected a civics lesson, but not the one the Court teaches them today."[66]

Justice John Paul Stevens, often an enthusiastic advocate for broad and deep student rights was strangely silent. Although he wrote a spirited dissent in *Bethel School District No. 403 v, Fraser*,[67] which had curtailed student speech rights, he joined the *Hazelwood* majority, and he did not even write a separate concurrence that would shed light on this apparent change of heart. Because only eight Justices heard the case, Justice Stevens vote was a crucial one. If the opinion had been decided on a 4–4 vote, the decision of the Eighth Circuit upholding the rights of the students would stand.

One aspect of the opinion that deserves careful attention is the genesis of the standard that the Court set for school officials who wish to constrain student speech: Their actions must be "reasonably related to a legitimate pedagogical concern."[68] This standard, set forth by a Justice who joined the *Tinker* majority, revives another standard that was suggested by Justice John M. Harlan almost two decades earlier in his *Tinker dissent.* Justice Harlan stated that "school officials should be accorded the widest authority in maintaining discipline and good order in their institutions."[69] To turn this into a constitutional standard, Justice Harlan would require that the school district demonstrate that its actions were motivated by something other than *"legitimate school concerns.*"[70] This construction, similar to that of the *Hazelwood* majority, envisioned a "best interest" analysis, assuming that the educator making the decision—who is trained in the pedagogical needs of students—would act in the best or "legitimate" interests of the students unless the students could show otherwise.[71]

In Hazelwood's *Wake*

The decision "sent immediate shock waves throughout the educational and legal communities."[72] The mainstream media described the outcome as granting expansive powers to schools. The front page of the Washington Post stated, "The Supreme Court gave public school officials sweeping power to censor school-sponsored student publications yesterday, rejecting the complaints of three dissenting justices that it was approving 'brutal censorship.' "[73] Many school officials and their advocates approved of the decision. Within an hour of the Supreme Court's decision being announced on the radio, one high school in California censored its newspaper by removing an article that was to be published discussing AIDS.[74] A Missouri school administrator stated that this decision "made his day."[75] Ivan Gluckman, counsel for the National

Association of Secondary School Principals in Reston, Virginia., claimed that most high school principals do not want to censor school newspapers but they still must have the final word on what is printed.[76] "They are responsible for what comes out in the newspaper," Gluckman said, just like a chief editor is responsible for what appears in a regular newspaper. "No reporter has an unfettered right to publish whatever he wants in the paper," he said.[77]

Not all educators were enthusiastic about the opinion. The school board in Dade County, Florida, had an official policy regarding school newspapers that student newspapers were not censored. In addition, the faculty, administration, students and a professional journalist had created guidelines for the newspaper providing that students made all final editorial decisions. School officials decided that this policy would remain in place despite the *Hazelwood* decision.[78] In the same vein, some teachers, administrators and students in the Washington, D.C. area said censorship had not been much of an issue and that students had been given free rein to report on such subjects as teen-age pregnancy and drug and alcohol use.[79]

Editorial comment on the opinion was also mixed.[80] While some writers hailed the opinion as "a lesson in reality" for students that "with freedom goes responsibility and that goes for the First Amendment,"[81] others were highly critical of its reasoning and result.[82] Richard M. Schmidt Jr., general counsel of the American Society of Newspaper Editors, said the ruling could open the door to increased use of censorship. Schmidt said school officials confronted with a controversial story may decide "it's easier to just pull it out of the paper rather than arouse the natives."[83] Nat Hentoff, journalist and advocate for broad First Amendment rights stated that "students, including those old enough to vote—are now in peril if they write opinion articles on political issues or candidates. Yet, speech about how we govern ourselves is at the core of First Amendment values. The Soviet Union's cultural attaches in the United States must be much bemused by this decision."[84]

The opinion generated spirited discussion in the legal literature as well, with many commentators viewing the opinion with aggravation and/or apprehension. Some commentators decried the diminution of student rights that eroded *Tinker* because of the effect it would have on the students' education as citizens and their perceptions of democratic values:

> *Hazelwood's* lenient reasonableness standard, which permits wide latitude for self-government, subordinates national democratic ideals to local values; it allows schools, in pursuit of their inculcative mission, to dictate what students can hear and say. As a result, students not only are deprived of the education necessary to func-

> tion as democratic citizens, but also are implicitly taught that their government is arbitrary and authoritarian.[85]

Others saw *Hazelwood* as depriving students of creativity and the ability to challenge the status quo: After *Hazelwood*, "a simple statement that deviation from orthodoxy is the reason for the punishment or censorship of juvenile speech may be sufficient."[86]

Not all commentators saw only the negative repercussions of the *Hazelwood* decision, however. Dean Bruce Hafen argued that "rather than weakening the Court's commitment to the constitutional rights of students, *Hazelwood* seeks to strengthen students' fundamental interest in the underlying principles of free expression: the right to develop their own educated capacity for self-expression."[87] According to Hafen, the *Hazelwood* Court recognized that schools, as well as courts, can advance and protect the values of the First Amendment. Far from harming the First Amendment, *Hazelwood* advances *institutional* First Amendment freedoms, giving educators' broad authority to define and supervise the educational mission of public schools both in and out of the classroom.[88]

Most commentators saw *Hazelwood* as a watershed opinion. As Professor Rosemary Salomone pointed out,

> The Court's sweeping language ... moved far beyond the narrow issue of school censorship. It even moved beyond the question of appropriate or acceptable speech in public secondary schools. It was clear that *Hazelwood* could have far-reaching consequences for student rights, school governance, and the scope of official authority to make curricular decisions that reflect the values of the local community.[89]

What of the standard set forth in *Hazelwood*—actions that are "reasonably related to a legitimate pedagogical concern?" If *Tinker* admonished courts to use strict scrutiny in addressing student claims of First Amendment violations by requiring "*material* disruption" and "*substantial* interference," *Hazelwood* racheted the scrutiny down, by requiring only a "*legitimate* pedagogical concern." Thus, for a court to overturn a decision by a school official, it is necessary to find that the professional educator in question did not have a legitimate reason for his or her decision. It does not have to be the best decision under the circumstances, or even a good decision, as long as a court can find that there was a "legitimate" concern with respect to education.

With this in mind, school officials and their attorneys now come to court having briefed how and why the actions of the educators were based on a legitimate a pedagogical concern. Most of the time, courts will defer to the judgment of educators regarding which concerns about pedagogy are legitimate. The Sixth Circuit presents one example of how courts address the issue:

> [I]ndependence of thought and frankness of expression occupy a high place on our scale of values, or ought to, but so too do discipline, courtesy, and respect for authority. Judgments on how best to balance such values may well vary from school to school. Television has not yet so thoroughly homogenized us that conduct deemed unexceptionable in New York City, for example, will necessarily be considered acceptable in rural Tennessee.
>
> Local school officials, better attuned than we to the concerns of the parents/taxpayers who employ them, must obviously be accorded wide latitude in choosing which pedagogical values to emphasize, and in choosing the means through which those values are to be promoted. We may disagree with the choices, but unless they are beyond the constitutional pale we have no warrant to interfere with them.[90]

The court determined that civility was a legitimate pedagogical concern and held that there was no First Amendment violation when a student was declared ineligible for an election after he made rude remarks about the high school assistant principal at a campaign speech at a school assembly.[91]

In a similar vein, a high school principal in Virginia ended the use of a school mascot, a cartoon symbol of "Johnny Reb," because of complaints from minority students and parents that they found the symbol offensive.[92] The court of appeals stated that because "[a] school mascot or symbol bears the stamp of approval of the school itself," it was sufficient that the principal's decision to eliminate the symbol was "based on legitimate concerns."[93] The question whether the concerns were legitimate did not hold the court up for long:

> "[The principal] received complaints that Johnny Reb offended blacks and limited their participation in school activities, so he eliminated the symbol based on legitimate concerns. Except to make the rough threshold judgment that this decision has an educational component, we will not interfere, and it is clear that educational concerns prompted [this] decision."[94]

Students may turn to underground newspapers to avoid the sting of *Hazelwood*. Since underground newspapers are not school-sponsored, many courts focus instead on the *Tinker* disruption test. This does not necessarily mean that students have a carte blanche to write with total abandon, however, as some courts have determined that articles inciting violent or destructive acts could lead school officials reasonably to forecast material disruption or substantial interference with the operation of the school.[95] Particularly in the wake of the massacre at Columbine and other mass shootings at schools, it seems likely that courts would tend to err on the side of preventing violence and defer to school officials regarding this issue.

The effect of the *Hazelwood* decision has not been limited only to newspapers or to students. Other creative activities in school have also been caught in its net, and the *Hazelwood* framework has been used to decide cases when school officials attempt to restrain *teacher* expression. For example a teacher in a Creative Writing class was disciplined when she allowed her students to use profanity in their work in violation of school policy. The students wrote plays with repeated use of the words "fuck," "shit," "ass," "bitch," and "nigger" and described sexual encounters in graphic detail.[96] Using the *Hazelwood* standard, the court stated that "[a] flat prohibition on profanity in the classroom is reasonably related to the legitimate pedagogical concern of promoting generally acceptable social standards."[97]

When another teacher was disciplined for making a remark in class about the lack of moral values of some students,[98] the parents of the students complained, and he was placed on administrative leave. The court used the *Hazelwood* standard for evaluating the teacher's classroom speech, and then analyzed whether the school officials' actions were based on a legitimate pedagogical concern.[99] The school officials set forth three concerns to justify the sanctions for the teacher—(1) the school has an interest in preventing a teacher from using his position of authority to confirm an unsubstantiated rumor; (2) the school has an interest in ensuring that its teacher exhibit professionalism and sound judgment: and (3) the school has an interest in providing an educational atmosphere where teachers do not make statements about students that embarrass those students among their peers.[100] The court had no trouble deciding whether the asserted concerns were legitimate, simply stating: "The interests asserted by the school in this case clearly are legitimate pedagogical interests."[101] Placing the teacher on paid administrative leave and writing a letter of reprimand explaining the school's concerns were both reasonably related to serving those pedagogical interests.[102] Thus, *Hazelwood* has moved a long way from it base, which merely allowed a school principal to remove student-written articles from a school-sponsored newspaper.

Not all courts defer to the judgment of educators regarding what is and what is not a legitimate pedagogical interest, but when a court rules against a school on this matter, it is unusual enough to garner some attention. *Desilets v. Clearview Regional Board of Education*[103] is a case that is often used to show how courts occasionally will buck the tide. In that case, school officials refused to allow middle school students to review R-rated movies in the school newspaper. The asserted pedagogical concern was that the educators did not want the school to be perceived as promoting R-rated movies to middle-school-aged children. The trial court determined that the decision to restrict the articles was reasonably related to a legitimate pedagogical concern, but the court of appeals disagreed. "Substantial deference to educational decisions does not require a wholesale abandonment of First Amendment principles simply because the medium for the student's expression is funded by a school board."[104] The court first read *Hazelwood* as applying only to decisions based on content or journalistic style. Then the court stated that the school's decision was not based on content, which it defined as "what is written," but on subject matter, which it defined as "what is written about."[105] The articles were not lewd, lacking in grammar or likely to cause disruption. The only reason school officials wanted to restrict them was because the movies in the reviews were R-rated. The court ruled that the decision whether to allow a middle-school child to view an R-rated movie is a parental decision, not an educational one, and the pedagogical interests of the school simply did not extend to this matter.[106]

In addition to those infrequent instances where court decisions may knock down a school's rationale, students in some states have broader rights under state law than those allowed under the *Hazelwood* ruling. In addition to the First Amendment to the U.S. Constitution, states can provide additional free speech protection to their own citizens under the state constitution or by enacting state laws or regulations. For example, at least six states—Arkansas, California, Colorado, Iowa, Kansas, and Massachusetts—have passed statutes,—often called "anti-*Hazelwood* laws"—that provide student journalists attending schools with added protection against administrative censorship.[107] For example, Chapter 71, Section 72 of the Annotated General Laws of Massachusetts states:

> § 82. Right of Students to Freedom of Expression.
>
> The right of students to freedom of expression in the public schools of the commonwealth shall not be abridged, provided that such right shall not cause any disruption or disorder within the school. Freedom of expression shall include without limitation, the rights and responsibilities of students, collectively and individually, (a) to express their views through speech and symbols, (b) to write, publish and disseminate their views, (c) to assemble peaceably on school property for the purpose of expressing their opinions. [108]

Other states, including New Jersey, Ohio, Hawaii, Nevada Oregon, Rhode Island, Kentucky, Wyoming, Illinois, Montana, Washington, New Hampshire and Indiana, have defeated initiatives for anti-*Hazelwood* statutes.[109]

Organizations like Student Press Law Center have been significantly shaped by the *Hazelwood* decision and continue to work as staunch advocates for anti-*Hazelwood* legislation. The Center, a non-profit organization based in Arlington, Virginia, was established in 1974 and offers free information, advice, and legal assistance to students and faculty alike who face censorship issues. It is the only agency in the United States that exclusively offers services to high school and college journalists. It offers a comprehensive website that equips students with tools on how to avoid censorship and how to handle such censorship when it is encountered.[110] The Center also provides daily news coverage of events that affect student press issues and provides analysis of major legal decisions that deal with student freedom of speech. To further assist student journalists, the Center operates a formal Attorney Referral Network comprised of about 150 lawyers who are willing to provide free legal representation to students. Each year, approximately 2,500 student journalists and teachers from all across the United States contact the Center for assistance or information.[111]

University of Hazelwood?

One issue that has concerned The Student Press Law Center and legal commentators is the extent to which *Hazelwood* applies to student press in higher education. The Supreme Court has decided one case directly concerning student press rights in higher education, although the newspaper in question was underground. In *Papish v. Board of Curators of University of Missouri*,[112] the University dismissed a graduate student who distributed a newspaper on campus that contained a cartoon depicting a policeman raping the Statue of Liberty and the Goddess of Justice. The caption read, "With Liberty and Justice for All." An article in the paper was entitled, "Mother Fucker Acquitted," and discussed the trial and acquittal of a New York City youth who was a member of a group called "UP Against the Wall, Mother Fuckers."[113] The Court ruled that the student's First Amendment rights had been violated, stating, "mere dissemination of ideas—no matter how offensive to good taste—on a state university campus may not be shut off in the name alone of conventions of decency."[114]

But *Papish* did not answer the question how *Hazelwood* should affect newspapers that were sponsored by a university. Footnote 7 of the *Hazelwood* opinion explicitly left that question for another day.[115] But it did not take long for tentacles from the opinion to reach into the college campus. After *Hazelwood* was decided, several colleges reorganized their student newspapers and one administrator ordered the removal of a play from a campus literary magazine.[116] But courts still had to weigh in on *Hazelwood* at college, and, not surprisingly, the results have been mixed and more than a little confusing.[117]

For example, advocates for student press rights gained some measure of comfort when the First Circuit—only one year after *Hazelwood* was decided—stated unequivocally that "Hazelwood School District v.

Kuhlmeier, in which the Court held that a high school newspaper whose production was part of educational curriculum was not a public forum, is not applicable to college newspapers.''[118] But the statement appeared in a one-sentence footnote. It had no explanation or analysis, and it had little to do with the facts of that particular case, so it was not clear how much weight this statement would bear. Adding to the confusion, two other circuits used the *Hazelwood* framework in the collegiate setting, but neither involved the student press.[119]

The idea that *Hazelwood* could be used in the university setting got some traction in what has been called ''one of the most significant student press legal battles of the 1990s.''[120] The Sixth Circuit needed a full en banc review in *Kincaid v. Gibson* to decide whether administrators could confiscate the *Thorobred*, a yearbook that was fully funded by Kentucky State University.[121] The yearbook had only one student editor who took any interest in the project, and she took it upon herself to present a yearbook unlike any in the past. She created a foil purple cover (the school colors are green and gold) and conceived a theme for the book—Destination Unknown. The vice-president for student affairs claimed the yearbook was of poor quality and objected to the cover, the theme, the lack of captions under the photos and the inclusion of current events not relating to KSU. She and the university president decided to confiscate the yearbook and withhold them from distribution. The district court found that the yearbook was not a public forum since it was not a journal of expression but a ''journal of the 'goings on' in a particular year at KSU.''[122] Relying on the *Hazelwood* framework, the court determined that the refusal to distribute the yearbook because the university officials believed that it was of poor quality and did not represent the school as it should was reasonable.[123]

A divided tree-judge panel of the Sixth Circuit Court of Appeals affirmed the district court, but the Circuit heard the case en banc (all the judges in the circuit) and reversed their colleagues. The majority of the en banc court cited the case from the First Circuit, and determined that *Hazelwood* has ''little application to this case.''[124] Since the majority went on to find that the yearbook was a limited public forum, the court seemed to be saying that *Hazelwood* was not applicable because the *Hazelwood* ''reasonableness'' standard would apply only if the yearbook was a nonpublic forum. Yet the quote and cite from the First Circuit—*Hazelwood* ''is not applicable to college newspapers'' could allow for the broader argument that *Hazelwood* has no place at all in the university setting.

Those who viewed *Kincaid* as one of the most important college press freedom cases ever needed to hold onto their hats when *Hosty v. Carter* hit the Seventh Circuit.[125] Heads are still reeling from the final missive from that en banc court, which upended the notion that the college press might be immune from *Hazelwood*.

In 2003, the United States Court of Appeals for the Seventh Circuit was asked whether the principles of *Hazelwood* applied to public colleges and university students. The plaintiffs were students at Governors State University[126] who served as editors and reporters for the *Innovator*, the school newspaper that was supported by student activity fees. The case arose when the university dean of student affairs called the newspaper's printer and stated that a university official needed to review any paper before it went to print. The printer wrote to the students and told them of his conversations with the dean. A printing company representative later told the students that the printer did not wish to risk printing the paper and then not get paid for their work. The students filed suit.

Because of the procedural posture of the case when it reached the court of appeals, the court needed to decide whether the dean was immune from the lawsuit. The standard for this immunity is whether the law was "clearly established" that the dean's request to review and approve the issues of the *Innovator* would violate the student's First Amendment rights. The main focus therefore is to what extent the law regarding university student speech rights was clear at the time the conduct occurred. The court observed that for several decades courts had consistently held that the student press in colleges and universities was entitled to strong First Amendment protection. Under this view, administrators can constrain student media only if the speech is unprotected or if it would cause significant and imminent physical disruption of the campus. The court cited numerous cases that had been decided before *Hazelwood*. Based on those cases, the dean's actions, if proved, violated clear constitutional rights of the students *unless Hazelwood* "muddled the landscape to such an extent that the law has become unclear."[127]

The Seventh Circuit panel ruled that a decision about the First Amendment in a high school setting had no effect on the rights of university students. Because the landscape in colleges differs so much from the landscape in high school, even *Hazelwood*'s landmark ruling did not affect student rights in higher education. There are obvious differences between the two in the areas of curriculum and extra-curricular activities. Moreover, the missions of the two institutions are distinct and reflect the needs of students of differing ages and maturity levels. Because only one per cent of the students in the nation's colleges is under 18, they should not be treated like 15-year-old high school students. The court was emphatic that there was nothing in the *Hazelwood* opinion that changed the general view favoring broad First Amendment rights for university students.[128]

Two years later, the majority of the judges in the entire Seventh Circuit came to the opposite conclusion on the identical facts. The en banc opinion, written by Judge Frank Easterbrook, dissected the *Hazelwood* opinion and determined that age was a factor only when determining if the school officials had a legitimate pedagogical justification for their actions. If the asserted justification is based on the maturity level of the students, the age difference between high school and college may be important. There may be no crucial difference between high school and college students, however, if the justification is based on the quality of the written work—whether it is ungrammatical, inadequately researched, biased or profane—or if the school wishes to disassociate itself from any position other than neutrality on controversial political matters. Thus, the court stated unequivocally that *Hazelwood*'s framework applies to subsidized student newspapers at elementary schools, high schools, and colleges.[129]

The first question to address under that framework, of course, is whether the newspaper is a public forum. To answer this question, the trial court had focused on the fact that unlike the *Hazelwood* case, the newspaper was not a part of the college curriculum. This was the wrong question to ask, according to the en banc court. Although being part of the university curriculum may be a sufficient reason to find a non-public forum, it is not a necessary condition.[130] An alumni magazine may not be part of the university curriculum, but it would not be a public forum, and the university could choose to publish articles of its choice. Thus, the court needed to delve further into the facts surrounding the creation of the *Innovator* to decide the forum issue. Based on the facts the court had before it (the appeal occurred before a trial, so this could change if there is a trial upon remand), the court determined that the university had established a public forum because its Media Board rules stated that the *Innovator's* content and format would be determined "without censorship or advanced approval."[131]

Even if the *Innovator* operated in a public forum, the dean was immune from suit unless it was "clearly established" that her particular actions violated the students' rights. Unlike the three-judge panel of the Seventh Circuit, the en banc majority concluded that the law was *not* clearly established that these particular actions were unlawful. The court below had determined that the dean should have known both that *Hazelwood* would not apply to colleges and that only curricular speech is subject to supervision. The en banc court decided that both these propositions were wrong. And even if the lower courts were correct that *Hazelwood* did not apply here, the law in this area is not clear. The *Hazelwood* opinion expressly reserved the question, and courts since then have not clearly established that all college newspapers are off limits for administrators. Two circuit courts have applied *Hazelwood* to collegiate speech, and one has refused to do so. Thus, the dean was entitled to qualified immunity from liability for money damages.[132]

From the time of *Tinker*, the school speech analysis has changed depending on the perspective of the analyst. Not surprisingly, four judges on the Seventh Circuit dissented from the opinion, taking an entirely different tack from that of Judge Easterbrook. The dissenters argued that there is a legal distinction between college students and high school students, and they focused on cases where courts have recognized that minors have a unique status under the law. Because high school students are less mature than college students and because the mission of the high school differs from the mission in higher education, there is no reason to apply *Hazelwood* beyond the high school context. As a general matter, college students are more mature, independent thinkers. Where K–12 education is concerned with the inculcation of values (citing *Fraser*), the mission of the university is to expose students to the "marketplace of ideas."[133]

The dean should not have been entitled to qualified immunity, claims the dissent, because courts were clear before *Hazelwood* that university administrators could not require prior restraint and courts after *Hazelwood* did not change this rule. The cases cited by the majority in support of its position were not cases about college newspapers but addressed speech within the classroom.[134]

At the end of the day, the district court and four circuit judges—Evans (who wrote the panel opinion and the en banc dissent), and Rovner, Wood and Williams—would have refused to apply *Hazelwood* in this context. Judge Coffey, who joined the panel opinion, apparently changed his mind during the en banc court, and voted with Judge Easterbrook, along with Judges Flaum, Posner, Ripple, Mannion and Kanne. The next step was a petition for *certiorari* to the United States Supreme Court. The Court denied *certiorari* on February 21, 2006, leaving the issue to percolate more throughout the lower courts before intervening on this important issue.[135] "For now, it remains unclear how much the law lets college administrators regulate student expression."[136]

Hazelwood School District v. Kuhlmeier: *Winners and Losers*

Professor Rosemary Salmone, a noted scholar who has authored another chapter in this book, studied the impact of *Hazelwood* four years after the opinion was handed down.[137] As Professor Salomone points out, the significance of a Supreme Court opinion is not apparent right away, but it develops over time.

> [T]he extent to which the decision influences public policy or practice depends on whether, over time, other interpreting and enforcing populations reaffirm the norms established by the Court. The more

the Court appears in step with the dominant values of those populations, the more likely the decision will be reinforced at the state and local levels and vice versa. [138]

Professor Salomone maintains that *Hazelwood* changed *Tinker*'s "anti-institutional presumption to a presumption of constitutional validity for the school's educational policy decisions."[139] Using this presumption, courts have been willing to move beyond the context of the school principal and the school newspaper. State legislatures—with few exceptions—have not been willing to lessen the effects of the decision, resulting in an "apparent chilling effect" on school journalism.[140] This suggested to Professor Salomone that, despite all the criticism, Hazelwood School District v. Kuhlmeier was "in step with dominant social values."[141]

There is no indication in court opinions or in state legislation that these social values and the institutional response to them have changed dramatically since Salomone's 1992 analysis. Indeed, in the wake of the massacre at Columbine and other well-publicized school shooting cases, courts may be even more willing to defer to the policy decisions of educational institutions, at least when those decisions appear to involve a fear of violence. Thus, nearly two decades since the Supreme Court handed down the opinion, *Hazelwood School District v. Kuhlmeier* has proved to be a dynamic force that continues to shape the public schools. How deeply it will gore into the education process in our nation still remains to be seen. It has been used to address creative activities in school well beyond the school newspaper, as well as speech by professors and teachers. Only recently we have seen a divided Court of Appeals for the Seventh Circuit unequivocally insert *Hazelwood* into the college newspaper setting.

Robert Baine, the school board attorney in *Hazelwood*, said in 2001 that he (not surprisingly) believed the Court got it right. "I think the *Tinker* case had been abused. The original basis for *Tinker* was good but some lower courts had expanded *Tinke*r to the point where school officials would have had to permit the printing of anything the students wrote. There is a saying that 'all education is local,' and I think the *Hazelwood* case stands for that principle."[142]

Cathy Kuhlmeier, now Cathy Cowan, is understandably less satisfied. By the time the case reached the Supreme Court, she was a senior at Southeast Missouri State University, and she did not attend the oral argument because she says her attorney failed to inform her about it. She does not regret her decision to fight, but she says the ordeal left a "bad taste in her mouth" for journalism.[143] Cowan said, "Students don't have enough First Amendment freedoms. There are a lot of very intelligent kids out there, and we should listen to them more. Maybe if we did, the world would be a better place.''[144]

It is hard to tell if the world would be a better place if *Hazelwood* had never been decided, or if it had come out the other way. There is little evidence to show that schools in Kansas, California or Colorado—all states with anti-*Hazelwood* legislation—are necessarily better places than schools in South Dakota or New Hampshire. Even if there were some showing—based on test scores or some other objective measure—it would be difficult to connect any difference to the presence or absence of *Hazelwood*.

Nevertheless, *Hazelwood* has unquestionably left its mark on the way we view our nation's schools and the students inside them. Barring any momentous change in the social climate or another Supreme Court case that drastically changes the landscape, *Hazelwood v. Kulhmeier* will continue to play a vital part in the analysis of First Amendment rights in public schools. The civics lesson that Justice Brennan recounted in his *Hazelwood* dissent is still ongoing.

Endnotes

1. Faith E. Snyder and James Donovan provided excellent research assistance on this project.

2. Bruce Hafen, *Hazelwood School District and the Role of First Amendment Institutions* 1988 Duke L.J. 685, 685.

3. Kuhlmeier v. Hazelwood School Dist., 607 F.Supp. 1450, 1452 (E.D. Mo. 1985). Some of the pedagogical concepts underlying the Journalism II class included publishing a newspaper under the pressures of pre-established deadlines, the legal moral and ethical restrictions placed upon journalists within the community, responsibility and acceptance of criticism for articles of opinion, leadership responsibilities, layouts that present the news within an accurate, fair and balanced format, pride in the school newspaper, and journalism as a potential career choice. *Id.*

4. *Id.* at 1453–54. The student plaintiffs were aware of Stergos' control over the *Spectrum*. In addition, the School Board allocated operating funds to the newspaper in its annual budget. For example, in 1982–83, printing expenses for the newspaper amounted to $4668.50, only $1166.84 of which was deferred by sales. *Id.* at 1452. In fact, the Chair of the English Department and the school principal had such control over the *Spectrum* that they had discussed omitting the last two issues of the paper due to budget overruns. *Id.* at 1454.

5. *Id.* at 1451.

6. *Id.* at 1452.

7. *Id.* at 1458. These additional articles became irrelevant as the lawsuit proceeded.

8. The text of this article is reprinted at *infra* note 18.

9. 607 F.Supp. at 1457–58. *See also* Brief for American Society of Newspaper Editors et al. as Amici Curiae Supporting Respondents, Hazelwood School District v. Kuhlmeier, 484 U.S. 260 (1988). (No. 86–836), which printed both articles in their entirety. The reprint of this article as it appears in the amicus brief follows:

WHEN PARENTS SPLIT

Kids Can Bear the Scars

By Shari Gordon

In the United States one marriage ends for every two that begin. The North County percentage of divorce is three marriages end out of four marriages that start. There are more than two central characters in the painful drama of divorce. Children of divorced parents, literally millions of them, are torn by the end of their parents' marriage. What causes a divorce? According to Mr. Ken Kerkhoff, social studies teacher, some of the causes are:

- Poor dating habits that lead to marriage.
- Not enough things in common.
- Lack of communication.
- Lack of desire or effort to make the relationship work.

Figures aren't the whole story. The fact is that divorce brings a psychological and sociological change to the child.

One junior commented on how the divorce occurred, "My dad didn't make enough money, so my mother divorced him."

"My father was an alcoholic and he always came home drunk and my mom really couldn't stand it any longer," said another junior.

One freshman said, "My dad wasn't spending enough time with my mom, my sister and I. He was always out of town on business or out late playing cards with the guys. My parents always argued about everything."

"In the beginning I thought I caused the problem, but now I realize it wasn't me," she added.

"I was only 5 when my parents got divorced," said Susan Kiefer, junior. "I didn't quite understand what the divorce between my parents really meant until about the age of 7. I understood that divorce meant my mother and father wouldn't be together again."

"It stinks!" exclaimed Jill Viola, junior. "They can, afterwards, remarry and start their lives over again, but their kids will always be caught in between."

Out of the 25 students interviewed, 17 of them have parents that have remarried. The feeling of divorce affects the kids for the rest of their lives, according to Mr. Kerckhoff. The effects of divorce on the kids lead to the following:

- Higher rate of absenteeism in school.
- Higher rate of trouble with school, officials and police.
- Higher rate of depression and insecurity.
- A higher rate of divorce when they themselves get married.

All of these are the latest findings in research on single parent homes.

There is a discrepancy between the text and title of the divorce article as reported by the district court and that quoted above from the Appendix to the Amicus Brief filed by the American Society of Newspaper Editors, et al. The district court stated that the title of the article was *Divorce's Impact On Kids May Have Lifelong Affect* [sic]. 607 F.Supp. 1457–58. The Amicus Brief lists the title as *When Parents Split, Kids Can Bear the Scars*. In addition, the district court stated that a freshman identified as Diana Herbert was quoted in the article as saying that her dad did not spend enough time with the family. The article set forth in the amicus brief does not name the student. It is not clear why or how this discrepancy between the text as reported by the district court and the text as reported by the amici occurred. What is clear is that the title and text changed from the time the district court reviewed the case to the time the amici filed briefs before the U.S. Supreme Court.

10. 596 F.Supp. at 1459 (emphasis in original).

11. Steve Visser, *A Civics Lesson at Hazelwood East*, *The Nation*, Oct. 24, 1987, at 442.

12. *Id.*

13. Kuhlmeier v. Hazelwood School District, 596 F.Supp. 1422, 1424 (E.D. Mo. 1984) (granting in part and denying in part the district's Motion for Summary Judgment).

14. Kuhlmeier v. Hazelwood School District, 607 F.Supp. 1450, 1456 (E.D. Mo. 1985).

15. *Id.* at 1456–57.

16. *Id.* at 1457.

17. *Id.* at 1459.

18. The article as it was meant to be published was later published in the *St. Louis Globe–Democrat* and can also be found in an amicus brief filed on behalf of the student-plaintiffs by the American Society of Newspaper Editors, National Association of Broadcasters, Reporters Committee for Freedom of the Press and Sigma Delta Chi. Brief for American Society of Newspaper Editors et al. as Amici Curiae Supporting Respondents, Hazelwood School District v. Kuhlmeier, 484 U.S. 260 (1988) (No. 86–836). The following is the reprint from the amicus brief:

Student Pregnancy: Three Personal Accounts

By Christine De Hass

These stories are the personal accounts of three Hazelwood East students who became pregnant. All names have been changed to keep the identity of these girls a secret.

Terri:

I am five months pregnant and very excited about having my baby. My husband is excited too. We both can't wait until it's born.

After the baby is born, which is in July, we are planning to move out of his house, when we save enough money. I am not going to be coming back to school right away (September) because the baby will only be 2 months old. I plan on coming back in January when the second semester begins.

When I first found out I was pregnant, I really was kind of shocked because I kept thinking about how I was going to tell my parents. I was also real happy. I just couldn't believe I was going to have a baby. When I told Paul about the situation, he was real happy. At first I didn't think he would be because I wasn't sure if he really would want to take on the responsibility of being a father, but he was very happy. We talked about the baby and what we were going to do and we both wanted to get married. We had talked about marriage before so we were both sure of what we were doing.

I had no pressures (to have sex). It was my own decision. We were going out four or five months before we had sex. I was on no kind of birth control pills. I really didn't want to get them, not just so I could get pregnant. I don't think I'd feel right taking them. At first my parents were upset, especially my father, but now they're both happy for me. I don't have any regrets because I'm happy about the baby and I hope everything works out.

Patti:

I didn't think it could happen to me, but I knew I had to start making plans for me and my little one. I think Steven (my boyfriend) was more scared than me. He was away at college and when he came home we cried together and then accepted it.

At first both families were disappointed, but the third or fourth month, when the baby started to kick and move around, my boyfriend and I felt like expecting parents and we were excited! My parents really like my boyfriend. At first we all felt sort of uncomfortable around each other. Now my boyfriend supports our baby totally (except for housing) and my parents know he really does love us, so they're happy.

After I graduate next year, we're getting married. My boyfriend and I have a beautiful relationship and it's been that way ever since three years ago. Therefore, I really do think that the future looks good for baby Steven. I want to say to others that it isn't easy and it takes a strong, willing person to handle it because it does mean giving up a lot of things. If you're not willing to give your child all the love and affection around, you can't be a good parent.

Lastly, be careful because the pill doesn't always work. I know because it didn't work for me.

This experience has made me a more responsible person. I feel that now I am a woman. If I could go back to last year, I would not get pregnant, but I have no regrets. We love our baby more than anything in the world (my boyfriend and I) because we created him! How could we not love him? ... He's so cute and innocent ...

Julie:

At first I was shocked. You always think, "It won't happen to me." I was also scared because I did not know how everyone was going to handle it. But, then, I started getting excited.

There was never really any pressure (to have sex), it was more of a mutual agreement. I think I was more curious than anything. I had always planned on continuing school. There was never any doubt about that. I found that it wasn't as hard as I thought it would be. I was fairly open about it and people seemed to accept it. Greg and I did not get married. We figured that those were not the best circumstances, so we decided to wait and see how things go. We are still planning on getting married when we are financially ready. I also am planning on going to college at least part-time.

My parents have been great. They could not have been more supportive and helpful. They are doing everything they can for us and enjoy being "grandma and grandpa." They have also made it clear it was my responsibility.

19. *Kuhlmeier*, 607 F.Supp. at 1459.

20. *Id.* at 1460.

21. *Id.* at 1460–61.

22. *Id.* at 1461.

23. *Id.* at 1460.

24. *Id.*

25. *Id.* at 1461.

26. 393 U.S. 503 (1969).

27. *Id.* at 506.

28. *Id.* at 513. For an analysis of the *Tinker* opinion in its jurisprudential and historical context see Anne Proffitt Dupre, *Should Students Have Constitutional Rights? Keeping Order in the Public Schools*, 65 Geo. Wash. L. Rev. 49 (1996) and Anne Proffitt Dupre, *School Speech* (Harvard Press forthcoming).

29. This standard is analogous to the strict scrutiny standard in equal protection law.

30. *See, e.g.*, Tinker v. Des Moines Indep. Community School Dist., 393 U.S. 503 (1969); Nitzberg v. Parks, 525 F.2d 378 (4th Cir. 1975) (school could not establish regulations that prevented distribution of an independent student newspaper); Shanley v. Northeast Indep. School Dist., 462 F.2d 960 (5th Cir. 1972) (school could not place prior restraint on the distribution of underground newspaper); Fujishima v. Board of Education, 460 F.2d 1355 (7th Cir. 1972) (school could not make a rule that prohibited the distribution of underground newspaper); Eisner v. Stamford Bd. of Education, 440 F.2d 803 (2d Cir. 1971) (school could not place prior restraint on distribution of an underground newspaper).

31. *See, e.g.*, Bethel School Dist.No. 403 v. Fraser, CV 83–306T (W.D. Wash. 1983) (school enjoined from disciplining student for sexual content in speech in school assembly). After the district court decided *Hazelwood*, the U.S. Supreme Court overruled the Ninth Circuit (which had affirmed the district court) in Bethel School Dist.No. 403 v. Fraser, 478 U.S. 675 (1986) (school could prevent student from using lewd language in a speech at a school assembly). *See also* Nicholson v. Board of Educ., 682 F.2d 858 (9th Cir. 1982) (upholding review of class-produced school newspaper before publication); Seyfried v. Walton, 668 F.2d 214 (3d Cir. 1981) (school could prevent the performance of school-sponsored theatrical play); Gambino v. Fairfax County School Bd., 564 F.2d 157 (4th Cir. 1977) (school not allowed to prohibit publication of article in school newspaper); Trachtman v. Anker, 563 F.2d 512 (2d Cir. 1977) (school could forbid distribution of a sex questionnaire in school newspaper); Stanton v. Brunswick School Dep't, 577 F.Supp. 1560 (D. Me. 1984) (school officials enjoined from preventing publication of student quote in yearbook); Frasca v. Andrews, 463 F.Supp. 1043 (E.D.N.Y. 1979) (school officials could prevent publication of letter in official school paper since it would cause substantial disruption of education); Zucker v. Panitz, 299 F.Supp. 102 (S.D.N.Y. 1969) (school officials enjoined from preventing publication of Vietnam protest advertisement in school newspaper).

32. 607 F.Supp. at 1464.

33. This standard may be compared to the rational basis standard in equal protection analysis.

34. 607 F.Supp. at 1466.

35. *Id.* at 1467.

36. Kuhlmeier v. Hazelwood School District, 795 F.2d 1368 (8th Cir. 1986).

37. *Id.* at 1373.

38. *Id.*

39. *Id.* at 1372. Although the quote appears to leave off in mid-sentence at a odd place, this is precisely the way the Eighth Circuit opinion quoted it.

40. *See* Anderson v. Bessemer, 470 U.S. 564, 573–74 (1985).

41. *Tinker*, 393 U.S. at 511.

42. For a discussion of judicial deference to the opinions of professional educators, see Anne Proffitt Dupre, *Disability, Deference, and the Integrity of the Academic Enterprise*, 32 Ga. L. Rev. 393 (1998).

43. The court cited to the policy statement that *Spectrum* published at the beginning of each school year, which stated that "it was a student newspaper, that its publication policy would be guided by the first amendment, that the articles and editorials reflected the view of the staff and not the administrators or faculty of the high school, and that it followed the standards set forth in the journalism class textbook." 795 F.2d at 1376.

44. Note, *Administrative Regulation of the High School Press*, 83 Mich. L. Rev. 625, 641 (1984) ("Limiting school action under the invasion-of-rights justification to torts or potential torts means that a school can refer to previously defined legal standards to decide if it may constitutionally restrain student expression.").

45. 795 F.2d at 1376. Judge Heaney wrote, "Any yardstick less exacting than potential tort liability could result in school officials curtailing speech at the slightest fear of disturbance." *Id.*

46. *Id.*

47. The court referred to W. Prosser & W. Keaton, *The Law of Torts* 809 (4th ed. 1971) and *The American Bar Association Juvenile Justice Standards Project Relating to Schools and Education* 84 (1982).

48. 795 F.2d at 1377.

49. *Id.* at 1378–79 (Wollman, J. dissenting).

50. *Id.* at 1379 (Wollman, J., dissenting).

51. By this time, the case had garnered considerable attention, *see e.g.*, Glen Elsasser, *School Paper Case Raises Court Test, Chicago Tribune* October 14, 1987, at 3; Stuart Taylor, Jr., *Court Hears Censorship Case, N.Y. Times*, October 14, 1987, at A18, and the Court had received briefs from the ACLU, the American Society of Newspaper Editors, the People of the American Way, NOW Legal Defense and Education Fund, Planned Parenthood Federation of America, and the Student Law Center urging affirmance. The Pacific Legal Defense Fund filed a brief urging reversal, and the National School Boards Association and the Dade County School Board filed briefs of amicus curiae. The number of briefs filed for and against amounted to six briefs for the students, one for the school district and two that were neutral.

52. Bethel School Dist. No. 403 v. Fraser, 478 U.S. 675, 682 (1986). In *Fraser*, a high school student delivered a speech during a school assembly that contained an obvious sexual metaphor for a man's penis and ejaculation. The Supreme Court held that the mission of the public school was to inculcate the habits and manners of civility, and that school officials could restrain vulgar or lewd speech as a part of that mission.

53. 1987 U.S. TRANS LEXIS 152 at 12. Individual Justices are not identified in the transcript, although they sometimes can be identified in context (*e.g.*, "Your answer to Justice Scalia's question seems vague.").

54. 1987 U.S. TRANS LEXIS 152 at 20.

55. Hazelwood School District v. Kuhlmeier, 484 U.S. 260 (1988). Only eight Justices heard this opinion. Justice Lewis Powell resigned in 1987, and Justice Anthony Kennedy did not take the oath of office until February 1988.

56. *See Fraser*, 478 U.S. 675.

57. *Id.* at 682, 685.

58. The Court quoted Cornelius v. NAACP Legal Defense & Educational Fund, Inc., 473 U.S. 788 (1985):

> The government does not create a public forum by inaction or by permitting limited discourse, but only by intentionally opening a nontraditional forum for public discourse.

Id. at 802.

59. *Hazelwood*, 484 U.S. at 273 (emphasis added). Creating a new standard had the added benefit of allowing the Court to avoid deciding whether the Eighth Circuit was correct when it determined that the part of the *Tinker* rule that included "invasion of the rights of others" precluded school officials from restraining student speech unless the speech could result in tort liability for the school.

60. In their amicus brief, The National School Boards Association and National Association of Secondary School Principals pointed out that teenage pregnancy in the early 1980s was on the rise and was a sensitive issue. Brief for National School Boards Association and National Association of Secondary School Principals as Amicus Curie Supporting Petitioners, Hazelwood School District v. Kuhlmeier, 484 U.S. 260 (1988) (No. 86–836), 1987 WL 864175. The brief argued that "[b]ecause teen pregnancy poses such a serious problem and because students receive inaccurate, unreliable or irresponsible information from a variety of sources outside the schools, it is particularly important that the information they get from school-sponsored sources is accurate." Moreover, the brief maintained that schools have the responsibility of protecting the pregnant teenagers who gave interviews for the articles, pointing out that "[s]tudents in a high school setting may not have the maturity to understand the potential adverse consequences that flow from making public the most intimate details of their lives."

61. *Hazelwood*, 484 U.S. at 276.

62. *Id.* at 289 (Brennan, J., dissenting).

63. *Id.* at 285 (Brennan, J., dissenting).

64. *Id.* (Brennan, J., dissenting).

65. *Id.* at 284 (Brennan, J., dissenting).

66. *Id.* at 291 (Brennan, J., dissenting).

67. *See Fraser*, 478 U.S. at 691 (1986) (Stevens, J. dissenting).

68. *Hazelwood*, 484 U.S. at 273 (emphasis added).

69. *Tinker*, 393 U.S. at 526 (1969) (Harlan, J., dissenting).

70. *Id.* (emphasis added).

71. *See* Anne Proffitt Dupre, *Should Students Have Constitutional Rights? Keeping Order in the Public Schools*, 65 Geo. Wash. L. Rev 49, 102 (1996). Professor Marci Hamilton has written about the attorneyship model of representation, describing the role of the representative in a liberal representative democracy. See Marci A. Hamilton, *Discussion and Decisions: A Proposal to Replace the Myth of Self-Rule with an Attorneyship Model of Representation*, 69 N.Y.U.L. Rev. 477, 483 (1994). Looking at public schools through this lens would mean that school officials are entrusted with the delegated responsibility to act in the best pedagogical interest of both student and parent, while they also fulfilled an obligation of continued communication to both student and parent. Dupre, *supra* at 103. "In short, parents would delegate to school officials—teachers and principals—the power to make independent judgments regarding 'legitimate pedagogical concerns.' "

72. Rosemary C. Salomone, *Free Speech and School Governance in the Wake of Hazelwood*, 26 Ga. L. Rev. 253 (1992).

73. Al Kamen, *Schools' Power to Censor Student Publications Widened; "Basic Educational Mission" Takes Precedence*, Wash. Post, Jan. 14, 1988, at A1. *See also* David A. Savage, *Justices OK Censorship by Schools: Say Educators Can Control Content of Pupil Publications*, L.A. Times, Jan.14, 1988, at 1 ("broad powers to censor school newspapers"); Stuart Taylor, Jr., *Court 5–3 Widens Power of School to Act as Censor*, N.Y. Times, Jan.14, 1988, at A1 ("broad power to censor school newspapers, plays and other 'school-sponsored expressive activities' ").

74. Nat Hentoff, *School Newspapers & the Supreme Court*, School Library Journal, March 1988, at 116.

75. *Id.*

76. Savage, *supra* note 73, at 1.

77. *Id.* Gwendolyn H. Gregory, deputy general counsel for the National School Boards Association, said there would actually be little real change after the ruling since most school officials believed they already had substantial authority over student publications. Kamen, *supra* note 72, at A1.

78. Hentoff, *supra* note 74, at 116.

79. Claudia Levy, *Views Diverse on Censorship Rulings, Some Area Teachers, Editors Fear Restraints on Student Papers*, Wash. Post, Jan 15, 1988, at A4.

80. *See, e.g.*, Editorial, *The Wrong Lesson*, St. Petersburg Times, Jan. 15, 1988, at 16A ("It would have been better for the court not to have accepted the case than to have decided it as it did."); Editorial, *First Amendment Lessons*, N.Y. Times, Jan. 15, 1988, at 30A (decision was "basically correct, but 'it's a pity that the justices, who did not hesitate to sustain school officials beyond the strict needs of the case before them, could not find space to admonish school systems to wield their power with wisdom, care and restraint' "); Editorial, *Education and the School Press*, Christian Sci. Monitor, Jan. 15, 1988, at 13 (A newspaper is a school activity, not an individual expression of opinion, as in *Tinker*, but decision is nonetheless disappointing on several levels); Editorial, *Censorship as a Lesson*, L.A. Times, Jan. 16, 1988, at 8 ("trashing what young writers and editors produce in concert with a faculty adviser, as was the case with *Spectrum*, can scarcely be dignified by the name teaching").

81. *See, e.g.*, Judy Mann, *Principal as Publisher*, Wash Post, Jan. 15, 1988, at C3.

82. *See, e.g.*, Thomas Collins, *First Amendment Haves and Have-nots*, Newsday, Jan 1988, at 8 ("Besides mocking the Constitution and going against a vital American tradition, the ruling also ignores the world the students encounter outside the school.").

83. Kamen, *supra* note 73, at A1.

84. Hentoff, *supra* note 74 at 115.

85. *The Supreme Court, Leading Cases: 1987*, 102 Harv. L. Rev. 143, 278 (1988).

86. William S. Geimer, *Juvenileness: A Single-edged Constitutional Sword*, 22 Ga. L. Rev. 949, 959 (1988).

87. Hafen, *supra* note 2, at 684.

88. *Id.* There has hardly been a dearth of commentary on the opinion. *See, e.g.*, Mark G. Yudof, *Tinker Tailored: Good, Civility, and Student Expression*, 69 St. John's Law Rev. 365 (1995); William G. Buss, *School Newspapers, Public Forum, and the First Amendment*, 74 Iowa L. Rev. 505 (1989); J. Marc Abrans & S. Mark Goodman, *End of an Era? The Decline of Student Press Rights in the Wake of Hazelwood School Dist v. Kuhlmeier*, 1988 Duke L.J. 707, Shari Golub, *Tinker to Fraser to Hazelwood, Supreme Court's Double–Play Combination Defeats High School Students' Rally For First Amendment Rights*, 38 DePaul L. Rev. 487 (1988).

89. Salomone, *supra* note 72, at 253–54.

90. Poling v. Murphy, 872 F.2d 757, 762 (6th Cir. 1989).

91. *Id.* at 758.

92. Crosby v. Holsinger, 852 F.2d 801 (4th Cir. 1988).

93. *Id.* at 802.

94. *Id.* at 802.

95. *See* Pangle v. Bend–Lapine School Dist., 10 P.3d 275 (Ore. Ct. App. 2000) and other cases discussed in Martin R. Gardner and Anne Proffitt Dupre, *Children and the Law: Cases and Materials* 478–79 (2d ed. 2006).

96. Lacks v. Ferguson Reorganized School Dist., 147 F.3d 718 (8th Cir. 1998).

97. *Id.* at 724.

98. Referring to a rumored incident from the previous day, he said, "I don't think in 1967 you would have seen two students making out on the tennis court." Miles v. Denver Public Schools, 944 F.2d 773, 774 (10th Cir. 1991).

99. *Id.* at 776.

100. *Id.* at 778.

101. *Id.*

102. *Id.*

103. Desilets v. Clearview Regional Board of Education, 630 A.2d 333 (N.J. Super. App. Div. 1993).

104. *Id.* at 541.

105. *Id.* at 542.

106. *Id.* at 543.

107. See A.C.A. § 6–18–1201; Cal. Educ. Code § 48907; C.R.C.A. § 22–1–120; I.C.A. § 280.22; K.S.A. § 72–1506; M.G.L.A. 71 § 82.

108. M.G.L.A. 71 § 82 (2006).

109. *See* Salomone, *supra* note 72, at 305–06 for a description of state legislative initiatives.

110. The Student Press Law Center, *available at* http://www.splc.org.

111. Student Press Law Center, *available at* http://www.splc.org. In 1992, the Center issued guidelines for students and their advisors that is available at its website. The

Student Press Law Center, *Fighting Censorship After Hazelwood, available at* http://www.splc.org/legalresearch. The Center instructs students not to withhold well-written and accurate stories out of such fear, but rather to publish them and leave any possible censoring to the administration. It warns students, "If you head down the road of self-censorship, it will not be long until your publication is as superficial and unchallenging as many student publications were a generation ago. It is up to you not to let that happen." *Id.* The website also instructs students to talk to their principals and boards of education about adopting policies that define their newspapers as public forums and spells out the decision-making responsibilities that the students have regarding content of their publications.

112. 410 U.S. 667 (1973). *Papish* was decided before *Hazelwood* and thus did not consider that case's application to higher education.

113. The Supreme Court opinion used dashes instead of completing the words: "M—— F——."

114. *Id.* at 670.

115. "We need not now decide whether the same degree of deference is appropriate with respect to school-sponsored expressive activities at the college and university level." *Hazelwood*, 484 U.S. at n 7.

116. Michael A. Olivas, *The Law and Higher Education: Cases and Materials on Colleges in Court* 826–827 (3d ed. 2006).

117. A detailed analysis of this issue appears in Anne Proffitt Dupre, *School Speech* (Harvard University Press forthcoming).

118. Student Government Association v. Board of Trustees of the University of Massachusetts, 868 F.2d 473, n.6 (1st Cir. 1989).

119. Axson–Flynn v. Johnson, 356 F.3d 1277 (10th Cir. 2004) involved a student, a Mormon, who did not want to utter the word "fuck" or take the Lord's name in vain in acting class at the University of Utah. The court applied *Hazelwood*, but remanded the case for a determination whether the school's justification was truly pedagogical or whether it was a pretext for religious discrimination. In Bishop v. Aronov, 926 F.2d 1066 (11th Cir. 1991), the court addressed the classroom speech of a professor at the University of Alabama. The court held that the classroom was not an open forum, and that the University's restrictions were sufficiently narrow and clear as to put the professor on notice of what he could not do. The university, as an employer, should be entitled to place reasonable restrictions on the learning experiences of its students, and the university could direct the professor to refrain from expressing his religious viewpoints in the classroom.

120. *Freedom Fighter*, Student Press Law Center 10 (Fall 1999).

121. Kincaid v. Gibson, 236 F.3d 342 (6th Cir. 2001) (en banc).

122. *Id.* at 346 (describing district court opinion).

123. *Id.*

124. *Id.* at n.5.

125. 412 F.3d 731 (7th Cir. 2005) (en banc).

126. "Governors" has no apostrophe.

127. *Id.* at 949.

128. 325 F.3d 945 (7th Cir. 2003).

129. 412 F.3d at 735.

130. *Id.* at 736.

131. *Id.* at 737.

132. *Id.* at 738–39 *Cf.* Edwards v. California University of Pennsylvania, 156 F.3d 488 (3d Cir. 1998). Then-judge Alito authored the opinion addressing a professor's claim that he had been deprived of his right to free speech when his dean restricted his choice of classroom materials, criticized his teaching and suspended him without pay. The opinion does not rely (or even cite) *Hazelwood*, but it stresses that a university controls its curriculum.

133. *Id.* at 740 (Evans, J., dissenting).

134. *Id.* at 743 (Evans, J., dissenting).

135. 546 U.S. 1169 (2006). Thirty organizations, including press freedom groups and university journalism departments joined in three amicus briefs on behalf of the students. Sara Lipka, *Stopping the Presses*, Chron. of Higher Educ., March 3, 2006, at A35. The Student Press Law Center has been encouraging student journalists, especially those in the Seventh Circuit jurisdiction (Illinois, Indiana and Wisconsin) to request school administrators to designate student publications as public forums. *Id.* at A36 (pointing out success at Illinois State University, the University of Southern Indiana and the University of Wisconsin at Platteville, but noting that administrators at the University of Louisville at Monroe had imposed a prior review policy on the student newspaper). In response to *Hosty*, California passed a statute that enhances student free speech rights and prescribes how campus administrators should oversee student publications that are financed by the university. *See* 2006 Cal. Legis. Serv. 1536 (West); *see also California Bill Would Curb Official Censorship of Student Newspapers*, Chron. of Higher Educ., May 26, 2006, at A28. A handful of other states are considering similar measures. *Id.* It seems likely that more litigation will be forthcoming: "The inclination to censor is already there. The *Hosty* case may embolden administrators to take steps that they may not have taken, because they'll think that legally they can defend them. And they're going to have to because we and other advocates of the First Amendment will come after them." Lipka, *supra* at A36.

136. Lipka, *supra* note 135, at A36.

137. *See* Salomone, *supra* note 72, at 253. The article explores the impact of the opinion, drawing on the methodology of "impact theory," a body of research developed in the 1960s and 1970s that focuses on the empirical consequences of legal decisions. Although a detailed description of the methodology and results of her research is beyond the scope of this book chapter, I highly recommend Professor Salomone's superb article for those who wish to read more about this fascinating opinion.

138. *Id.* at 254.

139. *Id.* at 318–19.

140. *Id.* at 319.

141. *Id.*

142. David Hudson, *Cathy Cowan reflects on her high school journalism fight in Hazelwood case*, Dec. 27, 2001, *available at* http://www.freedomforum.org/templates/document.asp?documentID=15516.

143. *Id.* At the time she was interviewed, she was married with children and teaching preschool in Missouri.

144. *Id.*

9

The Story of *Board of Regents of the University of Wisconsin System v. Southworth*: "Losing Battles, Winning Wars"

Linda S. Greene

Introduction

For centuries, our nation has been decorated by two shades of political color: one largely governed by traditional morality and conservative social mores, often casting a shadow over individual autonomy and freedom of choice; the other, however, subscribes to a contemporary school of progress and liberalism, free from governmental encroachment. This divisive dichotomy of political ideologies clashed in *Board of Regents of the University of Wisconsin System v. Southworth*,[1] a case where the U.S. Supreme Court upheld the right of the student government at the University of Wisconsin–Madison to distribute mandatory student fees to student organizations for extracurricular activities—even if students paying the mandatory fees objected to the viewpoints expressed by those organizations.[2] In doing so, the Supreme Court pointedly agreed with the objecting students that the funding scheme implicated First Amendment rights of freedom of speech and association,[3] but also recognized the compelling interest of the university in facilitating "dynamic discussion of philosophical, religious, scientific, social, and political subjects in [students'] extracurricular campus life outside the lecture hall."[4] As long as the student government distributed the mandatory fees in a viewpoint-neutral manner, the Supreme Court concluded, the objecting students were not entitled to a partial fee refund.

The legal antecedents of the *Southworth* decision lay at the convergence of three lines of precedent.[5] One line of cases involved compelled speech with the venerable decision prohibiting mandatory flag salutes in public schools at its head.[6] The other line addressed the use of compulsory bar and union dues in which the Court upheld compulsion but distinguished between the use of mandatory dues to speech activities "germane" to the organization and the funding of those that are not germane.[7] The third line of cases involved the application of First Amendment "public forum" decisions in the university context, holding that when a university creates a public forum it may not withhold access to that forum on the basis of the viewpoints students hold or express.[8] *Southworth*, therefore, provided an opportunity to test the application of these principles of compelled speech, compelled association, and viewpoint-neutrality in the context of mandatory student fees, as well as an opportunity to resolve conflicting decisions on this developing subject among federal and state courts.[9] It was also an opportunity to decide the case in the context of a university known as a hotbed of student activism, a school often referred to as the "Berkeley of the Midwest"—the University of Wisconsin–Madison.

The "*Berkeley* of the Midwest"

Set on the bucolic lakefront of Lake Mendota in Madison, Wisconsin, the University of Wisconsin–Madison, like the University of California–Berkeley, is one of the most prestigious universities in the world.[10] It was founded in 1848 and opened its doors to seventeen students in 1849 for pre-college preparatory courses.[11] The rest, as they say, is history[12] (and a rich and storied one at that). From those modest beginnings, the university has grown exponentially, amassing 41,480 students from every state in the union and over 120 countries.[13] With a budget of almost two billion dollars,[14] the University of Wisconsin–Madison awards more Ph.Ds per year than any other university in the country. Characterized by its liberal fervor, student activism and civic participation in this Big Ten institution quickly began to mushroom in the late 1960s. Although baby boomers' beliefs about the radicalism of the University of Wisconsin–Madison were linked to the 1971 antiwar Students for a Democratic Society bombing of Sterling Hall, in which a researcher was killed and several others injured,[15] the history of activism and protest at the University of Wisconsin–Madison long preceded those events. Like Berkeley, the University has long had a tradition of liberal activism, as one commentator suitably noted:

> The University of Wisconsin had for many decades attracted and encouraged an activist student body, which since the 1920s regularly included a sizable block of matriculants from eastern states. Many of these easterners were children of parents of varying leftist political persuasion and degrees of activism. These non-resident students, many of them Jewish, tended to be disproportionately active in campus politics and extracurricular affairs and more liberal-to-radical in their views than the great bulk of Wisconsin students. They helped give the University its worldly atmosphere, lively

extracurricular life, and activist reputation. They also played a leading part in developing and shaping the anti-war movement on campus in the latter sixties.[16]

Although much of the protest in Wisconsin was about the Vietnam war, the curriculum, and the academic opportunity for African–American students, a fair amount of discord also stemmed from the "drive for student power." Student skepticism about the legitimacy of adult authority led them to want an increased role in their university experience. As Cronon & Jenkins put it, "[students'] suspicion . . . led to a growing distrust of any authority, including that of the faculty, administrators, and regents charged with operating the University of Wisconsin. This fed the drive for student power and a determination to take charge of the educational process. . . ."[17]

In 1968, for example, a student survey showed that graduate students wanted "greater student influence over the curricular, grading policies, and University governance."[18] In that year, students formed myriad associations along academic departmental lines,[19] and some departments made formal efforts to include student input into their decision-making process.[20] African–American students went on strike for increased enrollment of African–American students, faculty, and administrators, as well as a black studies department.[21] Even a rancorous 24–day teachers' assistant strike included demands for their involvement in educational planning.[22] As a product of these incessant demonstrations, in 1973, the state legislature took a giant leap forward and explicitly authorized students to participate for the first time in institutional policy and governance. As active participants of academic and institutional governance, "[s]tudents in consultation with the chancellor . . . [now had] the responsibility for the disposition of those student fees which constitute substantial support for campus student activities. . . ."[23]

Prior to the 1973 legislation, the University of Wisconsin–Madison sat on committees that advised the Chancellor on the allocation of fees to support student health services, the student union, and recreational sports services and facilities.[24] After the passage of the legislation, university administrators created an advisory committee to make recommendations on the use of student fees predominantly composed of students appointed by student government, as well as an academic staff person and a faculty member, both appointed by the Chancellor. The committee was called the Student University Fund Allocation Committee (SUFAC). SUFAC continued to advise the chancellor on the allocation of funds to health service, recreational sports, and the student union, and also solicited requests from student groups who wanted funding to enhance services to students.[25] Over time, SUFAC entertained proposals for student advocacy and student political activity, and the funding of these proposals lead to conflict over the use of mandatory fees from students who disagreed with the aims of certain organizations. Ultimately, it was this ideological disagreement over the distribution of mandatory student fees that spawned the striking controversy that ultimately led to *Southworth*.

Enter *Southworth*

Scott Southworth, a Wisconsin native,[26] had an unusual background for a university student. He did not come to the University of Wisconsin–Madison right out of high school; instead, he joined the military at seventeen years of age.[27] After a four-year military stint, he continued his service in the Wisconsin Army National Guard. He came to the university (and later law school) as a mature student, a Christian, and a conservative Republican.[28] Accordingly, "[w]hen the young Christian conservative arrived on [the University of Wisconsin–Madison] campus in 1990 [as an undergraduate student], he signed up with the College Republicans and Campus Crusade for Christ."[29] Ultimately, he became the leader of the UW–Madison College Republicans, a self-described "leading conservative [group] on campus."[30] After Southworth and classmates, Keith Bannach and Amy Schoepke, enrolled in law school at the University of Wisconsin–Madison, they filed a lawsuit to vindicate their belief that they should not have to fund student associations that advocate for causes they abhor with their mandatory student tuition fees.[31]

> We filed the lawsuit because of our religious, political and ideological beliefs. We were all three conservative Christians, although we were not uniform in political or ideological viewpoints. I oppose the death penalty, for instance—Keith Bannach supported it. Regardless, we all held a fundamental view that no student, regardless of their beliefs, should be forced to fund someone else's advocacy—even if they agreed with it. I know that a veteran's organization was very upset with me because they received funding—although I am a member of the Wisconsin Army National Guard, I do not believe they should receive funding forcibly taken from other students.... I believe that no student—regardless of political, religious or ideological viewpoint—should be forced to fund the advocacy of any other private organization as a price to obtaining a degree from a public university. It rests squarely on the First Amendment....[32]

As chairman of the student government's finance committee, Southworth disbanded the committee so that no new money could be allocated to student groups.[33] When another committee was reformed to allocate students' fees, Southworth asked the legislature to pass a law that would permit students to direct their fees to the organization of their choice. Thereafter, he decided to transform his concern into a federal case.[34]

According to Southworth, he and the other two law students decided to do the work on a lawsuit they hoped would end up in the U.S. Supreme Court.[35] Southworth was inspired by a comment in Justice O'Connor's *Rosenberger* concurrence,[36] a case in which the Court ruled that the University of Virginia could not deny student fee sourced funding to a student newspaper that published a Christian message.[37] O'Connor may have literally invited the lawsuit when she suggested that mandatory student fees might be challenged on First Amendment grounds by students who disagreed with the message, citing the Court's union and bar dues cases—*Abood* and *Keller*.[38]

In 1994, Southworth contacted the Alliance Defense Fund (ADF), an organization founded by Christians "to defend religious liberty."[39] ADF recommended that they contact Jordan Lorence, a lawyer from the Washington D.C. area who was developing a reputation for taking on First Amendment cases for conservative and Christian causes.[40] Lorence agreed to take the case, and the students worked closely with him at every stage.[41]

On October 4, 1995, Lorence sent Michael Grebe, then president of the Board of Regents, a letter in which he argued that the mandatory student fee violated the rights of students who disagreed with the viewpoints of funded organizations.[42] He asked Grebe whether the "University would set up a system by which the students will not have to pay the portion of their mandatory student fee that goes to fund political and ideological groups on campus that espouse views the individual students do not want to fund." In his letter, Lorence acknowledged that many of the groups funded do provide educational benefits to students while others are much more controversial:

> These groups include the Lesbian, Gay, Bisexual Center, the UW Greens, the Wisconsin Public Interest Research Group (WISPIRG) and others. All of these groups take controversial stands on issues such as gay rights, the environment, social welfare legislation, etc. Scott Southworth disagrees with the points of view advocated by these groups because of his personal ideological and religious beliefs. He would not voluntarily contribute money to them and he does not want the University to compel him to fund them.[43]

Lorence argued that *Keller*, *Abood*, and O'Connor's concurrence in *Rosenberg* compelled his conclusion. He asked whether the University might allow Southworth and others to forego payment of the $7.99 of the fee that funded those groups. He ended the letter on a conciliatory note.

> If you think we are misunderstanding the constitutional principles in this situation, we want to know that. We are open to correction on this matter. However, I conclude from my reading of the relevant cases that the University has an affirmative duty under the U.S.

> Constitution to allow students to opt out of paying the segregated fee. I am also sending this letter to the University legal counsel and some other University officials. I look forward to your response in this matter.

Neither Grebe nor any other university official replied to the letter.[44]

The Lawsuit Begins

On April 11, 1996, while the Regents of the University of Wisconsin met in West Bend, Wisconsin, a process server served the board members with a summons and a complaint in the matter of *Southworth et al. v. Grebe*.[45] The Regents referred the matter to the Attorney General of the State of Wisconsin, James Doyle, formally requesting that his office provide legal representation.[46]

The complaint included four causes of action. The first alleged a violation of the plaintiffs' freedom of speech and association rights as a result of the Regents approval of student fee disbursement to fund groups that promote specific ideological and political points of views with which the plaintiffs disagree.[47] The absence of an opt-out process, noted the compliant, violated their rights.[48] The second cause of action identified the plaintiffs as "devout Christians" and stated that the mandatory fee burdened their free exercise of religion by compelling them to choose between attending the University of Wisconsin–Madison or adhere to their religious beliefs and practices.[49] The third cause of action alleged a violation of the Wisconsin Constitution provision prohibiting payment of public funds for private purposes because of the collection of mandatory fees to fund the activities of ideological and political groups.[50] And the fourth cause of action alleged that the Regents had exceeded their power to act for educational purposes by using the mandatory fee to fund groups promoting ideological or political beliefs.[51] The prayer for relief requested the court to stop funding private groups engaging in ideological or political advocacy.[52] As an alternative, the plaintiffs proposed that students "opt out" of the fee allocable to ideological and political activity.

The federal district court held that the mandatory fee violates the students' freedom of speech and association. The court cited the U.S. Supreme Court's decisions in *Abood v. Detroit Board of Education*[53] and *Keller v. State Bar of California*,[54] in which the Court struck down the organization's spending of the mandatory membership or service fees for the organization's political activities that are not germane to the organization's purpose. To apply these cases to the settings of student mandatory fees in a university, the district court relied on the California Supreme Court's decision involving a similar challenge in *Smith v. Regents of the University of California*.[55] In *Smith*, students from the

University of California–Berkeley challenged the allocation of their mandatory fees to student organizations that engaged in political or ideological activities.[56] The *Smith* court struck down the fee. The court reasoned that although the provision of mandatory fees to student groups was germane to the university's educational purpose, any benefit from subsidizing groups' ideological and political interests was outweighed by burdens on the dissenting students' First Amendment rights.[57]

Adhering to *Smith*, the district court in *Southworth* examined some of the targeted student groups in the University of Wisconsin–Madison, finding that the UW Greens, the International Socialist Organization, the LGB Campus Center, and the Ten Percent Society were primarily engaged in political and ideological activities, despite having some educational components.[58] The court thus concluded that the funding to these organizations violated the plaintiffs' First Amendment rights.[59] The court, then, rejected the defendant's argument that the fee is merely providing, in a viewpoint-neutral fashion, a public forum for the expression of diverse views. It said that these organizations' mostly off-campus "purely political and ideological activities," such as leading rallies and lobbying, are little to do with creation of fora for the exchange of ideas on the University of Wisconsin–Madison campus.[60] The court parenthetically rejected the defendant's allegation that the plaintiffs failed to show that the proceeds from the segregated fee were used for these political or ideological activities.[61] The court held that by subsidizing overhead expenses to student organizations, it subsidizes the entire effort of the particular group.[62]

The Seventh Circuit Affirms and Reverses the District Court

After an unsuccessful interlocutory appeal,[63] the University appealed to the U.S. Court of Appeals for the Seventh Circuit, which affirmed in part the decision of the district court.[64] The appellate court focused on the plaintiffs' objections and evidence with respect to funding for organizations engaged in political and ideological activities.[65] Reviewing the evidence below, the court noted that student fee funding supported a variety of activities including lobbying, the publication of voters' guides, political campaign activity, marches in opposition to legislative and gubernatorial decisions, opposition to abortion restrictions, opposition to legislative limitations on same sex marriage, and advocacy against the death penalty.[66]

The court approved some aspects of the district court's decision and rejected others. For example, the Seventh Circuit, like the district court, relied on *Abood* and *Keller* to conclude that the use of the mandatory student fee depended on the germaneness of the activity so funded.[67] In addition, relying on *Lehnert v. Ferris Faculty Association*,[68] the Seventh Circuit found limitations on the scope of those student fee funded activities germane to the Regents' interest in education.[69] Most importantly, the Seventh Circuit concluded that *Lehnert's* requirement that the scope of funding does not significantly add to the burden on the objecting individual's First Amendment right to be free from compelled speech precluded the funding of private group ideological and political activity with mandatory fees.[70]

> In sum, we conclude that the *Abood* and *Keller* analysis, as explained in *Lehnert*, governs the students' First Amendment challenge of the Regents' mandatory student fee policy. The Regents have failed to sustain their burden under this three-prong analysis; even if funding private political and ideological organizations is germane to the university's mission, the forced funding of such organizations significantly adds to the burdening of the students' free speech rights. Therefore, the Regents cannot use the allocable portion of objecting students' mandatory activity fees to fund organizations which engage in political or ideological activities, advocacy, or speech. We also hold that the 18 challenged private organizations engage in ideological and political activities and speech, and cannot be constitutionally funded with objecting students' fees.[71]

The Seventh Circuit characterized the requirement that plaintiffs' support the political and ideological speech as creating a "crisis of conscience"[72] and an "especially severe" compulsion in light of deeply held differences on the religious and political issues funded by the mandatory fees.[73] As to injunctive relief, the court agreed with the district court that the plaintiffs deserved a refund of their fees, but concluded that the order was overbroad in its reach to non-objecting students' fees.[74] As such, under the Seventh Circuit's holding, "the University cannot even temporarily collect from objecting students the portion of the fees which would fund organizations which engage in political and ideological activities, speech, or advocacy, whether or not the organization also provides some service in doing so."[75] "Funding of private organizations which engage in political and ideological activities," the court intoned, "is not germane to a university's educational mission, and even if it were, there is no vital interest in compelled funding, and the burden on the plaintiffs' First Amendment right to 'freedom of belief' outweighs any governmental interest."[76] Because the case excited much interest, the University asked the Seventh Circuit to revisit the panel decision en banc.[77]

Under en banc review, three judges dissented the court's prior ruling, resulting in two strong dissenting opinions from Judge Ilana D. Rovner and Judge Diane P. Woods. Judge Rovner, first of all, stated that *Abood* and *Keller* should be distinguished because the groups in those cases were themselves engaging in the speech[78] and "were funded *because of* their political and ideological positions, and *for the purpose of* furthering those positions,"[79] while the student government in *Southworth* was not engaging in political or ideological speech and its distribution of funds was viewpoint-neutral.[80] Judge Rovner also criticized the panel's holding that political and ideological speech as a whole is not germane to the educational mission; she pointed out that this view contradicts with the Supreme Court's reiteration of the importance of robust debate and free expression in universities.[81] Finally, she pointed out that the same funds are available to the objecting students to present opposing speech.[82]

Judge Wood's dissenting opinion commenced with relating her fear that the panel's decision "will spell the end, as a practical matter, to the long tradition of student-managed activities on [public universities'] campuses."[83] She warned that if the university was required to solicit and process the individual preferences from 40,196 students to reduce some amount of the semester fee from $165.75, it would most likely end up with elimination of forum altogether, resulting in undoing the very "tradition of thought and experiment" the Supreme Court vigorously sought to protect.[84] Judge Woods also stressed the difference between a compelled subsidy of speech itself and a compelled subsidy of a neutral forum for speech.[85] She squarely analogized the funding to federal taxpayers' compelled support of the National Mall in Washington, which can be used for expressing views that one feels objectionable, even for a mass gathered for the Pope.[86] The First Amendment, argued Judge Woods, does not require researchers in public universities to be funded based on each student's consent.[87]

The Amicus Briefs in the Supreme Court

That *Southworth* was an important case is summarily demonstrated by the broad interest of amici in the case. Student governments and organizations, university associations, states, labor organization and public interest organizations, as well as parties of the similar cases, submitted briefs supporting the petitioners. Of course, student government associations, who receive fees from students and use them for their own activities and distribute them to various organizations, filed briefs in support of the University of Wisconsin–Madison. The United Council of University of Wisconsin Students and various organizations of student government in the University of Wisconsin System, for example, argued that the mandatory fee should be viewed as a tax[88] and that its distribution should be treated as governmental speech. As such, they argued the scheme would be sustained under a rational basis test.[89] In addition, the United States Student Association, the Associated Students of Madison, and fifteen of USSA's other state and campus affiliates supported the University's claim, asserting that Southworth was really seeking to exclude a handful of student organizations from university-supported public forum because they disagreed with the messages of those organizations.[90] The University of California Student Association, which had experience with a student fee rebate system, argued that the plaintiffs in *Southworth* had no First Amendment right to opt out, but if the Court did sustain such an opt-out system, the Court should impose a pro rata refund-escrow system.[91]

Another important group of amici were public universities and their corresponding associations. These institutions had a strong interest in a court decision upholding a UW-like funding system. Among the public universities were those from New York, Arkansas, Colorado, Georgia, Hawaii, Iowa, Louisiana, Maryland, Massachusetts, Minnesota, Montana, North Dakota, Ohio, Oregon, and Tennessee.[92] The State of Oregon, which had successfully defended its system from similar challenges in the Ninth Circuit,[93] submitted a separate amicus brief, also supportive of the University of Wisconsin–Madison.[94] In addition, associations of universities and colleges, including the American Council on Education, representing over 4,000 colleges and universities, submitted a brief supporting the Big Ten university.[95]

Not surprisingly, the University of Wisconsin–Madison was also supported by a number of student organizations receiving funds, primarily the UW Lesbian, Gay, Bisexual and Transgender Campus Center ("LGBTCC"), the Lambda Legal Defense Fund, as well as fifty student groups from universities nationwide.[96] They argued the injury to nonconsenting members in the bar and union fee cases of *Keller* and *Abood* were distinguishable from *Southworth* because the fees go to a university fund which in turn supports a limited public forum that does not implicate the viewpoint of the non-consenting students.[97] LGBTCC and Lambda had also filed an amicus brief supporting the petitioner's writ of *certiorari*.[98] In the latter brief, they stressed that if not overruled, the Seventh Circuit's decision would "fall most heavily on small, fledging or unpopular groups like the LGBT Center—the very groups that provoke the exchange of viewpoints that universities cultivate for the benefit of all students."[99] "Small groups generally have few alternative resources to use as an expressive platform. The incantation that no First Amendment injury occurs as long as other avenues of speech remain open . . . is a fallacy that does not excuse closing down expressive avenues in a limited public forum that remain available to one's peers."[100] Like the prior organizations, associations for student press stressed the negative effect of the Seventh Circuit decisions on the student newspapers and other publications. They pointed out that most student presses could not survive without university funding and that virtually all of them engage in some kind of political or ideological commentaries.[101] After all the amicus briefs were filed, the U.S. Supreme Court came down with its salient decision.

The Supreme Court Decision

The Supreme Court unanimously reversed the judgment of the Seventh Circuit (except for the student referendum system that lets the students to decide which organization can or cannot receive the funding). Justice Kennedy wrote a majority opinion for six justices of the Court, with Justice Souter writing a concurring opinion joined by Justices Stevens and Breyer. The majority said that as long as the fund is distributed in a viewpoint-neutral manner, the university's distributions of mandatory fees to organizations that some students consider objectionable or offensive do not violate their First Amendment rights.

The majority reasoned that the precedents regarding public forums are instructive to this case and stated that the viewpoint-neutrality standard used in the public forum cases is controlling in this case.[102] The Court stated that this standard is sufficient to protect the interest of the opposing students.[103] Rejecting the germaneness test used in *Abood* and *Keller*, the Court stated that what speech is germane to a labor union was difficult to ascertain,[104] and it is even more so in "the public university setting, particularly where the State undertakes to stimulate the whole universe of speech and ideas."[105] The majority went on to say that "[t]o insist upon asking what speech is germane would be contrary to the very goal the University seeks to pursue,"[106] denying the lower courts' distinction between the student groups whose primary activities are political or ideological in nature and others. The Court, moreover, denied the distinction between on- and off-campus activities, explaining that "Universities possess significant interests in encouraging students to take advantage of the social, civic, cultural, and religious opportunities available in surrounding communities and throughout the country."[107] In addition, the Court denied the opt-out system as a constitutional requirement, reasoning that it could be so disruptive and expensive that the existence of the program to support extracurricular activities would be put at risk.[108] As for the referendum system by which the students decide which student groups do or do not receive the fund, the Court suggested that it is not a viewpoint-neutral measure and thus infringes the First Amendment right of the student, remanding the case for further examination.[109]

Justice Souter's concurring opinion, however, emphasized the autonomy of the university,[110] arguing that the majority opinion's "cast-iron viewpoint neutrality requirement" was not necessary.[111] Souter suggested that because the University is not required to make viewpoint-neutral choices on what to teach using the tuitions or the professors paid from tuition money can express a view which is offensive to others, the plaintiff students' challenge for the viewpoint-neutral allocation of the activity fee could not present any stronger argument.[112]

The Relitigation of Southworth

After the Supreme Court remanded the case to the Seventh Circuit to determine the constitutionality of the referendum system, the plaintiffs made two requests. They asked for permission to amend their complaint to raise a new claim that the fee allocation system was not viewpoint-neutral because it afforded the students government "unbridled discretion."[113] The plaintiffs additionally asked the court for permission to withdraw their stipulation that the fee allocation process was viewpoint-neutral.[114] They explained that they made the stipulation because they believed that the Supreme Court would extend *Abood* and *Keller* (which mandated refunds of non-germane ideological expenditures) to the educational setting.[115] In contrast, the Regents asked the Seventh Circuit to direct the district court to dismiss all claims that the funding of student activities violated the First Amendment.[116] Seizing on a brief phrase in the Supreme Court decision which could be read to leave open the question whether the stipulation would continue to control the case,[117] the panel noted that the Supreme Court's rejection of the refund holdings of *Abood* and *Keller* might represent a circumstance that might justify the withdrawal of the stipulation.[118] Thus, "[i]f the Stipulation is to continue to control the case, the University's program in its basic structure must be found consistent with the First Amendment."[119] The panel asked the district court to decide both issues, and indicated that they were both matters within the "sound discretion" of the district court to be overturned only if "the court has clearly and unmistakably abused its discretion."[120] And as the saying goes, the nose of the camel was under the tent, and the university's victory in *Southworth* was too quickly to become a hollow one. Prior to the time the district court considered the case on remand, the University of Wisconsin–Madison amended its policies in several respects to conform to the viewpoint-neutrality doctrine.

Upon remand to the federal district court, the issue at stake shifted once again toward ascertaining whether "the current system for compelling and distributing student fees to fund the political and ideological activities on campus" was constitutional.[121] The district court, allowing the plaintiffs to void their stipulation of viewpoint-neutrality, ruled that the operation of the segregated fee program was a violation of the First Amendment.[122] As if playing litigation roulette, the University appealed once again to the Seventh Circuit, making this the fourth time this case was presented before the court in five years.[123] On its final appeal, the University argued, among other things, that "the constitutional prohibition against granting government authorities unbridled discretion [did] not apply in the context of a student activity fee."[124] As a palliative to this concern, the Seventh Circuit agreed with the University, finding that many of its amended policies properly limited the discretion of student fees.[125] Although this marked the end of the litigation crusade (except for the contest over attorneys' fees to the plaintiffs),[126] the ideological battle was just beginning.

Battles Lost, Wars Won—The Evisceration of the **Southworth** *Victory.*

On its face, *Southworth*, in the U.S. Supreme Court, was a victory for the University of Wisconsin System. The decision set aside the rulings of the lower federal courts, which declared portions of the University student fee allocation system unconstitutional. One author, writing shortly after the decision, characterized the result in *Southworth* as a strategic miscalculation on the part of the right.[127]

> In *Southworth*, however, the religious right strangely did battle *against* the concept of the marketplace of ideas when it challenged a program designed to put more speech into the extracurricular academic marketplace. Rather than taking on the *Southworth* case, the right should have stopped while it was ahead in fighting perceived speech injustices on college campuses. With the right failing to appreciate the overwhelming power of the marketplace metaphor, the Court—ironically packed with appointees from conservative administrations—was able to hand a unanimous victory to one of the most liberal public universities in the country.[128]

Public interest groups, law professors, and university associations supportive of the University of Wisconsin–Madison hailed the decision as a victory.[129] The lead *Southworth* plaintiff, Scott H. Southworth, reluctantly agreed with that assessment.[130] At the time of the decision, some criticized the *Southworth* plaintiffs for their stipulation that the fee allocation process was viewpoint-neutral.[131] According to Donald Downs, a professor at the University of Wisconsin–Madison, Southworth and his colleagues made that concession because they wanted the Court to decide that any fee system that forced students to support speech to which they object was unconstitutional; in a sense, "... Southworth 'wanted to go for a home run, which was a riskier strategy ... It would have been a bigger victory if he won, but he lost' "[132] For his part, Southworth promised that he would "keep fighting the battle."[133] In an interview with the *Daily Cardinal*, the oldest student newspaper in the country, Southworth cautioned, "I'll pursue [this cause] even once my case is done ... I'm not going away. Ultimately I want a victory. I'm disappointed that we didn't get it today...."[134] Soldier Southworth continued, "To win a war, you have to fight a lot of different battles, and you're not going to win every battle. And it's of course, a loss, but we'll continue to fight and look at other avenues and hope for a victory at some point for the students."[135] Shortly after Southworth and the plaintiffs filed the lawsuit, the editors of the *Daily Cardinal* stated that the lawsuit ran "counter to the ideal of any academic institution to allow and encourage a varied voice in education" and predicted that "the case will not get far in the court system."[136] How wrong they were!

*Epilogue—*Rosenberger *Redux and the Establishment Clause*

Southworth did not address the provision of support for student religious activity, but it nevertheless partially relied upon *Rosenberger v. Rector and Visitors*[137] for the proposition that viewpoint-neutrality was essential to recognize the right of the university to provide for student participation in education activity and programming. *Rosenberger* and *Widmar* did address the question whether fear of an Establishment Clause violation would justify the denial of financial aid or facilities. But both decisions conclude that on the facts before the Court the provision of aid did not violate the Establishment Clause.[138] Both decisions also suggest that under other circumstances the provision of aid might raise more serious Establishment Clause questions. In *Widmar*, the court suggested that the dedication of a building for religious union might be distinguishable from the availability to all equally available groups.[139] And in *Rosenberger*, the court suggested that the payment of money to a printer for the print of a religious message might be distinguishable from "direct payments of money to a group that is engaged in religious activity."[140] The question, then, still remains whether the Establishment Clause imposes any check on the allocation of university resources for student religious activity after *Southworth*?

Two cases offer a preliminary view of this post-*Southworth* Establishment Clause conundrum. In *Linnemeier v. Indiana University Purdue University Fort Wayne*,[141] a 2001 case, Indiana residents and taxpayers, as well as members of the general assembly, challenged IUP Fort Wayne's decision to allow a student to direct a play with religious content. The play, called Corpus Christi, involved a young gay man who is surrounded by gay disciples named after the disciples in the New Testament of the Bible.[142] The plaintiffs characterized the play as an "undisguised attack on Christianity and the Founder of Christianity, Jesus Christ" and argued that the production of the play at a publicly-funded university violated the Establishment Clause.[143] The complainants detailed the extent to which the university supported the conduct of the play with, among other resources, the salary of the drama teacher, who students selected to direct the play.[144] On the other hand, the plaintiffs' uncontested factual allegations stated that the support was from the general fund and that all additional funding had been raised by the student director from non-public funds.[145] The case, decided in favor of some defendants on standing grounds[146] and in favor of others on capacity to be sued grounds,[147] raises the question whether university funds may be used to support instructional activity with religious advocacy content.

A second issue is related to university recognition and support of student groups. To what extent may the Establishment Clause trump religious-neutral requirements for student group recognition, such as non-discrimination requirements?[148] For instance, in *Christian Legal Society Chapter of University of California v. Kane*,[149] the University of California Hastings Law School's chapter of the Christian Legal Society, an association of Christian lawyers, law students, law professors, and judges, sued after the law school rejected the organization's application to become a registered student organization on the law school campus.[150] The defendant law school rejected the registration on the ground that the Hastings Christian Fellowship was not open to non-Christian students or gays and lesbians.[151] Applying the *Lemon v. Kurtzman* test to determine whether the Establishment Clause had been violated by the denial of recognition, the California federal district court concluded that Hastings' policies of non-discrimination had neither the purpose nor effect of inhibiting or advancing religion.[152] Nor did the policies promote excessive entanglement with religion.[153] This resolution, on Establishment Clause grounds, suggests universities may impose religious-neutral requirements on student groups and decline to recognize and support these groups if they do not comply.[154]

Southworth supporters have identified the pursuit of immunity from Establishment Clause based funding denials as the next battle ground.[155] The question has arisen in the context of the University of Wisconsin Roman Catholic Foundation, a student organization funded by the University of Wisconsin–Madison.[156] The funding, which rose from $47,000 to $147,000 over the last two years[157] has been criticized because of its amount and its possible use to buy religious materials for church services. It is unclear what limitations current precedent provides. Perhaps a viewpoint-neutral scheme may run afoul of the Establishment Clause. Are there any constraints on state support of student expression of religious viewpoints? And if those constraints are articulated in Establishment Clause terms, are they by definition not viewpoint-neutral? One possibility is that funding or support of religious student activity would be consistent with the First Amendment as long as that funding or support is the result of a viewpoint-neutral process. The other possibility is that support for such student expressive activity must be carefully structured in order to avoid the possibility of state endorsement of religious doctrine. This is an interesting possibility since *Widmar* and *Rosenberger* rejected Establishment Clause-based arguments as justifications for denial of access to university resources and financial support if the level of funding were excessive. But whatever one can make of the Supreme Court's "jumbled" Establishment Clause jurisprudence,[158] the possibility remains that the Clause may provide a check on the funding claims of student groups formed to promote religious beliefs or tenets. In this respect, there is a tension between First Amendment Establishment Clause concerns and First Amendment expressive association concerns. The other possibility is that religion neutral requirements may be imposed and enforced as long as that enforcement is not selective.[159]

In *Boy Scouts of America v. Dale*,[160] the Supreme Court concluded that the Boy Scouts claim of a First Amendment right of expressive association against homosexuality trumped New Jersey's public accomodation non-discrimination laws.[161] By extension under *Dale*, court may next see cases involving student organizations in which ideology and identity intersect and excluded individuals' claims of discrimination are pitted the student organizations' claims of expressive association.[162] Will courts conclude that university policies of nondiscrimination against students when groups rely on expressive association as a basis for their membership policies?[163] Put another way, will universities be able to enforce nondiscrimination policies against groups that claim an ideology-identity interest in controlling membership? These questions and many other remain unresolved in the wake of *Southworth*.

Conclusion

Southworth was an important case for various reasons. Although the Supreme Court rejected the right of students to be refunded their fees for activity at odds with their ideological or religious views, it did establish the principle that viewpoint-neutrality must be observed in the distribution of those fees. In this regard, *Southworth* extended prior cases on viewpoint-neutrality and public distribution of a mandatory fee. With this in mind, the Supreme Court decision vindicated the interests of universities in the collection of mandatory fees to provide students an avenue to express their diverse views. But on remand, the plaintiffs succeeded in transforming the question presented in the litigation from whether fees should be returned to non-consenting students to the question of whether viewpoint discrimination was possible under the system. Although on remand the final Seventh Circuit decision validated the eventual system put in place to control viewpoint discrimination, by this time the university made several policy changes that accounted for the district court's award to the plaintiffs of over a quarter of a million dollars in attorneys' fees. As a result, although *Southworth* was a battle won by the university, the result after remand cannot be characterized as a clear victory.

Southworth is also important because it was one battle in a war for the hearts, minds, and money of university students. *Southworth* grew out of a clash of ideology, the differences of viewpoint between Christian and conservative students and the liberal left. At the foundation of this clash, however, lie the great issues that form the cultural divide on campuses and in the broader society, namely religion and its relevance and presence in public life, abortion, the environment, gender, and sexual identity. Even though *Southworth* itself is over, the clash continues as new contests arise in the war for voice and power in student life. The case is also noteworthy because it arose out of a clash of ideology and principle among students, culminating to a "culture war."[164]

That culture war continues today. It continues in the contest of groups with divergent ideologies over funding,[165] in demands of religious groups for recognition, in funding for worship activities, and in the demand that aid once provided not be revoked or reduced. Thus, Southworth still represents a transcending decision that has already led to more litigation. Although the University of Wisconsin–Madison perceivably won the battle, there is still no clear answer over who will win this constitutional and ideological war.

EPILOGUE: Where Are They Now?

Jordan Lorence, the attorney for the *Southworth* plaintiffs, teaches constitutional law at Oak Brook College, an online college. He is still a First Amendment attorney with the Alliance Defense Fund.

Scott Harold Southworth is the elected District Attorney for Juneau County in Wisconsin. On March 1, 2006, he was named as a recipient of the prestigious General MacArthur Leadership Award, which recognizes twenty-seven of the best company-grade officers in the United States Army.

Judge John C. Shabaz is still one of two federal district court judges sitting in the Western District of Wisconsin.

Endnotes

1. 529 U.S. 217 (2000).

2. *Id.* at 234.

3. *Id.* at 230–31.

4. *Id.* at 232.

5. Patricia Brady, "Speech Outline Student Fees After *Southworth*", June 26–29, 2002, NACUA Annual Meeting.

6. W. Va. State Bd. of Educ. v. Barnette, 319 U.S. 624 (1943) (mandatory flag salute in public schools); *see also* Wooley v. Maynard, 430 U.S. 705 (1977) (mandatory display of license plate slogan "Live Free or Die").

7. For example in Abood v. Detroit Bd. of Educ., 431 U.S. 209 (1977), the Court rejected first amendment associational claims as to the use mandatory teacher union due for activity related to collective bargaining, contract administration, and grievances and any lobbying thereby associated with those activities but sustained them as to speech activities unrelated to the collective bargaining activities. *Id.* at 236. And in Keller v. State Bar of Cal., 496 U.S. 1 (1990), the Court concluded that the State Bar of California could impose mandatory dues to fund to regulate the legal profession and improve the quality of the legal services but could not impose mandatory fees the expression of political views or ideological causes not germane to those purposes. *Id.* at 16.

8. In Widmar v. Vincent, 454 U.S. 263 (1981), the Court held on First Amendment speech and free exercise grounds that a university could not deny a student religious group seeking to worship access to the use of university facilities. *Id.* at 276. In Lamb's Chapel v. Center Moriches Union Free Sch. Dist., 508 U.S. 384 (1993), the court held that the refusal to allow school property to be used to show a film with a religious message was unconstitutional viewpoint discrimination. *Id.* at 393. And in Rosenberger v. Rector and Visitors of the Univ. of Va., 515 U.S. 819 (1995), the court held that the refusal of a university to pay for expenses associated with a student newspaper that published a religious message was also unconstitutional viewpoint discrimination in violation of the First Amendment. *Id.* at 845–46.

9. The Ninth Circuit, the Fourth Circuit, the Fifth Circuit, and the Supreme Court of Washington had upheld a variety of first amendment challenges to the various mandatory fee schemes. *See* Rounds v. Oregon State Bd. of Higher Educ., 166 F.3d 1023 (9th Cir. 1999); Hays County Guardian v. Supple, 969 F.2d 111 (5th Cir. 1992), *cert. denied*, 506 U.S. 1087 (1993) (mandatory fees to support student newspaper); Kania v. Fordham, 702 F.2d 475 (4th Cir. 1983) (mandatory fees to support student newspaper); Good v. Associated Students of Univ. of Wash., 542 P.2d 762 (Wash. 1975) (en banc) (mandatory fees to support student educational activities). But in Smith v. The Regents of the Univ. of Cal., 844 P.2d 500 (Cal. 1993), the Supreme Court of California allowed the imposition of a mandatory fee but allowed dissenting students to seek a refund for the portion of the fee allocable to political and ideological student activity. And in Southworth v. Grebe, 151 F.3d 717 (7th Cir. 1998), the Seventh Circuit also recognized a right of dissenting students to a refund for the part of the mandatory fee that funded objectionable political or ideological expression. *Id.* at 735.

10. The American Association of Universities, a 60 member invitation only association of universities, is limited to the most prestigious academic institutions as measured by faculty members in scholarly societies such as the National Academy of Sciences, as well as research grants and research spending. http://www.aau.edu/aau/aboutaau.cfm.

11. E. D. Cronon & J. Jenkins, The University of Wisconsin 1 (1999).

12. M. Curti and V. Carstensen, The University of Wisconsin 1848–1925 (1949); E. D. Cronon and J. Jenkins, The University of Wisconsin: A History, 1925–1945, Volume III (1994); E.D. Cronon and J. Jenkins, The University of Wisconsin, A History, 1945–1971, Volume IV (1999).

13. Academic Planning and Analysis, Office of the Provost and the Office of Budget, Planning and Analysis, University of Wisconsin—Madison, Data Digest 2005–2006, at 2.

14. In 2004, the annual budget was $1,807,600,000. http://www.wisc.edu/about/facts.

15. D. Cronon & J. W. Fenkins, IV, The University of Wisconsin: A History, vol. 4, 1945–1971, 515–20 (1999).

16. *Id.* at 450.

17. *Id.* at 447.

18. *Id.* at 471.

19. *Id.* at 470–74.

20. *Id.* at 475–78.

21. *Id.* at 478–79.

22. *Id.* at 494–506. It is interesting to note that during the TAA strike and the black strike, a majority leader of the Wisconsin legislature introduced legislation to partial tuition payments for nonresident graduate students who were teaching assistants. That legislator was John C. Shabaz, who later became the United States federal district court judge who heard the *Southworth* case. *Id.* at 494–95.

23. Chapter 36.09(5), J. Solberg, Report of the Merger Implementation Study Committee, Annex E (1973), currently codified at Wis. Stats. 36.09(5) (2006).

24. Interview with Roger Howard, Former Associate Dean of Students October 19, 2006.

25. Proposals included services to returning veterans, increased hours for student campus information services, and tutoring.

26. Southworth is a native of New Lisbon Wisconsin. *See* Elizabeth Brixey, *High Court Rules for UW in Fee Case*, Wis. St. J., March 23, 2000, at 1A.

27. Biography—Scott Harold Southworth, 7–13–06 (correspondence on file with author).

28. July 13, 2006 email correspondence from Southworth to Linda Greene (on file with the author) [hereinafter July 13 email correspondence].

29. Ben Wildavsky, *Listen Up: Students want right not to speak*, U.S. News, Nov. 15, 1999, at 34. Southworth says he was also spurred by his religious convictions: "As Christians we are called to do the Lord's will. I was called to take a stand." Mike Leon, Campus Crusade in These Times, March 21, 1999, at 7.

30. *See* July 13 email correspondence, *supra* note 28.

31. *Id.*

32. *Id.* Southworth continued. "We filed the lawsuit because of our religious, political and ideological beliefs. We were all three conservative Christians, although we were not uniform in political or ideological viewpoints. I oppose the death penalty, for instance—Keith Bannach supported it. Regardless, we all held a fundamental view that no student, regardless of their beliefs, should be forced to fund someone else's advocacy—even if they agreed with it. I know that a veteran's organization was very upset with me because they received funding—although I am a member of the Wisconsin Army National Guard, I do not believe they should receive funding forcibly taken from other students." *Id.*

33. *Id.*

34. *Id.*

35. *Id.*

36. Rosenberger v. University of Va., 515 U.S. 819, 846 (1995) (O'Connor, J., concurring).

37. *Id.* at 837.

38. *Id.* at 851 (O'Connor, J., concurring).

39. For a detailed description of the Alliance Defense Fund, see http://www.alliancedefensefund.org/main/default.aspx. According to Scott Phillips of ADF, "We are an organization that provides resources that will keep the door open for the spreading of the Gospel through the legal definition and advocacy of religious freedoms, sanctity of life and family values." http://docket.medill.northwestern.edu/archives/000913.php.

40. http://www.thefire.org/index.php/person/3489.html.

41. *Id. See also supra* note 28.

42. October 4, 1995 letter from Jordan Lorence to Michael Grebe (on file with author). Lorence sent a copy of the letter to the General Counsel of the University of Wisconsin System Charles Stathas, the Chancellor of the University of Wisconsin Madison, David Ward, and to the President of the University System Katherine Lyall.

43. *Id.*

44. Author Interview with Patricia Brady, General Counsel, University of Wisconsin System, 7/7/06.

45. *Id. See* Complaint, Scott Harold Southworth et al. v. Michael W Grebe et al., No. 960292S, Western District of Wisconsin.

46. April 17, 1996 letter from Judith A Temby, Secretary of the Board of Regents to Attorney General James Doyle (on file with author). Doyle was elected Governor of the state of Wisconsin in 2002.

47. Complaint, p.3.

48. Complaint, p.4.

49. Complaint at p.5.

50. Complaint at p.6.

51. Complaint at pp. 6–7.

52. Complaint at p.7.

53. 431 U.S. 209 (1977).

54. 496 U.S. 1 (1990).

55. 844 P.2d 500 (Cal. 1993).

56. (Dist. Court) 25.

57. (Dist. Court) 35–36.

58. (Dist. Court) 26–28.

59. *Id.* at 30.

60. *Id.* at 30–34.

61. *Id.* at 33–34.

62. *Id.*

63. After the district court's declaratory judgment was given, the defendant appealed. Yet the district court had not addressed the plaintiff's request for the injunctive relief. The Seventh Circuit found that the district court's judgment was not a final under 29 U.S.C. § 1291 and dismissed the appeal. Southworth v. Grebe, 124 F.3d 205 (7th Cir. 1997).

64. Southworth v. Grebe, 151 F.3d 717 (7th Cir. 1998). After the Supreme Court decision, the constitutionality of the referendum was remanded to the Seventh Circuit. It remanded this issue to the district court, together with the plaintiff's request to leave for amend their argument that they can void their stipulation that the funding was provided in viewpoint-neutral manner. Southworth v. Board of Regents of the Univ. of Wis. Sys., 221 F.3d 1339 (7th Cir. 2000). Because the Supreme Court relied on the plaintiff's stipulation, its voiding might result in striking down of the actual funding process. At the district court, the parties stipulated to dismissal of the issue of the constitutionality of the referendum, which the University eliminated after the Supreme Court decision. *See* Southworth v. Board of Regents of the Univ. of Wis. Sys., 307 F.3d 566 (7th Cir. 2002). The district dismissed as moot the plaintiffs who had already graduated. Fry v. Board of Regents of the Univ. of Wis. Sys., 132 F.Supp.2d 740 (W.D. Wis. 2000). Then the district court granted the motion to void the plaintiff's stipulation of viewpoint neutrality, the motion for leave to amend their complaint, and the motion to add a new plaintiff. 302 F.3d at 570. The district court held a bench trial and ruled that the funding scheme was not viewpoint neutral because the student government has wide discretion. *Fry*, 132 F.Supp.2d at 748–50. The district court also struck down the fee system revised after the trial. Fry v. Board of Regents of the Univ. of Wis. Sys., 2001 WL 36082693 (W.D. Wis.2001). The Seventh Circuit, reversing the district court's judgment, found that the modified fee system satisfies viewpoint neutral requirement, 307 F.3d at 581–92, except for the allocation system for travel grants, *Id.* at 592, and the standard that allows consideration of the length of the time a student group had been in existence. *Id.* at 593–94.

65. 151 F.3d at 717. The Court reviewed evidence as to the of eighteen organizations that the record below showed the receipt of student fees and the use of those fees for political and ideological activities including "... WISPIRG; the Lesbian, Gay, Bisexual Campus Center; the Campus Women's Center; the UW Greens; the Madison AIDS Support Network; the International Socialist Organization; the Ten Percent Society; the Progressive Student Network; Amnesty International; United States Student Association; Community Action on Latin America; La Colectiva Cultural de Aztlan; the Militant Student Union of the University of Wisconsin; the Student Labor Action Coalition; Student Solidarity; Students of National Organization for Women; MADPAC; and Madison Treaty Rights Support Group. Reviewing the evidence in the light most favorable to the Regents, as we must, we conclude that the 18 organizations listed above both receive student fees and engage in political and ideological activities."

66. 151 F.3d at 721.

67. *Id.* at 732.

68. 500 U.S. 507 (1991).

69. Southworth v. Grebe, 151 F.3d 717, 724–25 (7th Cir. 1998).

70. *Id.*

71. *Southworth*, 151 F.3d at 733.

72. *Id.* at 731.

73. *Id.* at 729.

74. *Id.* at 733–34.

75. Id. at 733.

76. Id. at 727.

77. Southworth v. Grebe, 157 F.3d 1124 (7th Cir. 1998).

78. *Id.* at 1125–26 (Rovner, J., dissenting).

79. *Id.* at 1126 (emphasis added).

80. *Id.* at 1125–26.

81. *Id.* at 1126.

82. *Id.* at 1128.

83. *Id.* at 1127 (Wood, J., dissenting).

84. *Id.* at 1129 (quoting *Rosenberger*, 515 U.S. at 835).

85. *Id.* at 1128.

86. *Id.*

87. *Id.*

88. Brief of United Council of University of Wisconsin Students, Inc., as Amicus Curiae in Support of Petitioners, Board of Regents of the Univ. of Wis. Sys. v. Southworth, 529 U.S. 217 (2000) (98–1189) at 10–12. The Council described itself in the brief as "the statewide association of the student governments of the campuses of the University of Wisconsin System." *Id.* at 1.

89. *Id.* at 12–15.

90. Brief of Amici Curiae United States Student Association et al Urging Reversal at 17–18. "USSA is the nation's oldest and largest student organization, representing the student organization, representing the student governments of over 300 colleges and universities—both public and private—throughout the nation." *Id.* at 1.

91. University of California Student Association, Amicus Curiae Brief in Support of Petitioners at 17–28. UCCA is "a non-profit, unincorporated association governed by representatives of the graduate and undergraduate student government associations at each of the nine University of California campuses and Hastings College of the Law. It is financed almost exclusively by activity fee collected from students enrolled at the University of California campuses." *Id.* at 1.

92. Brief of States of New York et al. as Amicus Curiae in Support of Petitioner.

93. Rounds v. Oregon St. Bd. of Higher Educ., 166 F.3d 1032 (9th Cir. 1999) (the opposing students' petition for rehearing en banc is pending depending on this case).

94. Brief for the State of Oregon as Amicus Curiae Supporting Petitioner.

95. Brief of Amicus Curiae American Council on Education et al. in Support of Petitioners. The organizations that authored this brief are:

American Council on Education;

American Association of Community Colleges;

American Association of State Colleges and Universities;

American College Personnel Association;

Association of American Colleges and Universities;

Association of American Universities;

National Association of State Universities and Land–Grant Colleges;

National Association of Student Financial and Administrators;

NAWE: Advancing Women in Higher Education;

College Board.

96. Brief for the Lesbian, Gay, Bisexual and Transgender Campus Center at UW–Madison et al. as Amicus Curiae in Support of Petitioners. Those who joined the Center are 49 other student groups, the National Consortium of Directors of Lesbian, Gay, Bisexual and Transgender Resources in Higher Education, and Lambda Legal Defense and Education Fund. LGBT Center "is a Registered Student Organization at the University and one of the 18 groups whose funding through mandatory fees plaintiffs oppose. The LGBT

Campus Center provides educational programs and individual support services, including peer counseling and referrals to other resources, maintains a library and a research collection of documents; and works to ensure a pluralistic university environment that includes lesbians, gays, and bisexuals. It also fosters communication among students (including through a newsletter), works for positive relations among student groups, and serves as a safe space utilizable by all." (internal citation quotation marks omitted) *Id.* at 1.

97. Brief for the Lesbian, Gay, Bisexual and Transgender Campus Center at UW–Madison et al. as Amicus Curiae in Support of Petitioners, at 12.

98. Brief of the Lesbian, Gay Bisexual and Transgender Campus Center at the University of Wisconsin–Madison and Lambda Legal Defense and Education Fund as Amicus Curiae in Support of Petition for Writ of Certiorari.

99. *Id.* at 9.

100. *Id.* at 11.

101. Brief of the Student Press Law Center et al. as Amicus Curiae in Support of Petitioner at 7–13. The Associated College Press and College Media Advisers, Inc. joined this brief.

102. Board of Regents of the Univ. of Wis. Sys. v. Southworth, 529 U.S. 217, 229–30 (2000).

103. *Id.* at 230.

104. *Id.* at 231–32.

105. *Id.* at 232.

106. *Id.*

107. *Id.* at 234.

108. *Id.* at 232.

109. *Id.* at 235–36.

110. *Id.* at 237–38 (Souter, J., concurring).

111. *Id.* 236.

112. *Id.* at 243.

113. *City of Lakewood v. Plain Dealer Pub. Co.*, 486 U.S. 750 (1988).

114. *Southworth v. Board of Regents*, 307 F.3d 566, 570 (7th Cir. 2002).

115. Id. at 571–72.

116. Southworth v. Board of Regents, 221 F.3d 1339 (7th Cir. 2000).

117. Board of Regents of the Univ. of Wis. Sys. v. Southworth, 529 U.S. 217, 234 (2000).

118. *Southworth*, 221 F.3d 1339 (7th Cir. 2000).

119. 529 U.S. at 234.

120. *Id.* at *13 (quoting Graefenhain v. Pabst Brewing Co., 870 F.2d 1198, 1206 (7th Cir. 1989)).

121. Fry v. Board of Regents of the Univ. of Wis., 96–C–0292–S at 12 (W.D. Wis.).

122. *Id.*

123. Southworth v. Board of Regents of the Univ. of Wis., 307 F.3d 566, 568 (7th Cir. 2002).

124. *Id.* at 571.

125. *Id.* at 587–88.

126. On April 14, 2004, the district court awarded attorneys' fees to the plaintiffs in the amount of $211,697.86, Later, on August 4, 2004, the district court made a supplemental award of $41,057.83. Docket Sheet No 96 C 02–2S per Ryan Plender Deputy District Court Clerk.

127. Calvert, *Where the Right Went Wrong in Southworth: Underestimating the Power of the Marketplace*, 53 Me. L. Rev. 53 (2001).

128. *See id.* at 55; *see also* Schmidt, *Supreme Court Unanimously Endorses Constitutionality of Mandatory Fees, Chronicle of Higher Education*, Section Government and Politics, March 31, 2000, at A.29 (quoting Ivan Frishberg of U.S. Public Interest Research Group). "This decision is great news for the university, and for the students, and for the marketplace of ideas on campus." Robert O'Neil of the Thomas Jefferson Center for the Protection of Free Express who said that the "ruling 'totally vindicated, in all meaningful respect' those universities that have such fee systems in place."

129. *Id.* Southworth said the decision was "a loss" but vowed that "we will move on and keep fighting the battle".

130. *See* Schmidt, *supra* note 130, at A.29.

131. *Id.*

132. *Id.*

133. *Id.* K. Kail and D. Corcoran, U. Wisconsin: The *Southworth* Decision: Three Sides to the Story, Daily Cardinal, Mar. 23, 2000, 2000 WL 17589047.

134. *Id.*

135. *Id.*

136. *Daily Cardinal* Apr. 19–21, 1996, page 4. The *Daily Cardinal* is the nation's oldest student newspaper, in existence since 1892. http://www.dailycardinal.com/about.php.

137. 515 U.S. 819 (1995).

138. *Rosenberger*, 515 U.S.at 722–23; *Widmar*, 454 U.S. at 273–74.

139. *Widmar*, 454 U.S. at 272–73.

140. *Rosenberger*, 515 U.S. at 882 (Souter, J., dissenting).

141. 155 F.Supp.2d 1044 (N.D. Ind. 2001).

142. *Id.* at 1048.

143. *Id.*

144. *Id.*

145. *Id.* at 1049.

146. *Id.* at 1055–56.

147. *Id.* at 1056.

148. *See* Rubenfeld, *The First Amendment's Purpose*, 52 Stan L. Rev. 767, 814–16 (2001).

149. Christian Legal Society Chapter of University of California, Hastings College of the Law v. Kane, 2005 WL 850864 (N.D. Cal. 2005).

150. *Id.* at 1.

151. *Id.* at 2.

152. *Id.* at 3–4.

153. *Id.* at 4–5.

154. In another Christian Legal Society case concerning the Law School of University of Southern Illinois, the Law School revoked its recognition of that Christian Legal Society on the ground that the anti-homosexuality stance of CLS violated the University's affirmative action policies as well as federal and state antidiscrimination law. The federal district court denied the requested injunction, Christian Legal Soc'y Chptr. at S. Ill. Univ. Sch. of Law v. Walker, 2005 WL 1606448 (S.D. Ill. 2005), and the Christian Legal Society appealed, requesting an injunction pending appeal. The CLS contended that Boy Scouts of America v. Dale, 530 U.S. 640 (2000), which held that New Jersey could not enforce its policy against discrimination directed at homosexuals against the Boy Scouts, required the exemption of CLS from the University's nondiscrimination policies. The Seventh Circuit agreed granted the injunction pending appeal. Christian Legal Society v. Walker, No. 10 C 4070, slip. op. at 2–3 (7th Cir. 2005). When the Seventh Circuit decided the question whether the district court properly denied the preliminary injunction, the Seventh Circuit relied on *Dale* in reversing the district court. Christian Legal Society v. Walker, 453 F.3d 853, 863–864 (7th Cir. 2006). But on its remand to permit full consideration of the merits, the Seventh Circuit left open the possibility that the University of Southern Illinois might be able to justify the enforcement of its nondiscrimination policy against the Christian Legal Society, and that the Christian Legal Society might be able to resist that enforcement if it could show that the University had singled out the Christian Legal Society for enforcement of the nondiscrimination requirement while allowing other groups to violate the nondiscrimination policy. *Id.* at 866–867.

155. Correspondence from Donald Downs (on file with author).

156. Annie Laurie Gaylor, Letter from Freedom from Religion Foundation to John Wiley, February 26, 2006, http://www.ffrf.org/news/2006/wileyltr.php; *see* "Groups Battle Over UW Student Funding For Catholic Booklets," Channel 3000, March 1, 2006, http://www.channel3000.com/news/7591012/detail.html; Megan Twohey, "UW Chancellor gives OK to Catholic groups budget But Regents must. . . ." Milw. J. Sent., May 3, 2006 http://www.findarticles.com/p/articles/mi_qn4196/is_20060503/ai_n16345335; Andriy Pazuniak, *Wiley Hands UWRCF decision to Regents*, Badger Herald, May 3, 2006.

157. Megan Twohey, *UW Fee Handouts Again Stir Conflict*, Milw. J. Sent., April 30, 2006, *available at* http://www.jsoline.com/story/index.aspx?id= 419906 (noting that the Foundation received $44,000 in 2004 and $88,000 in 2005).

158. *See Rosenberger*, 515 U.S. at 819 (noting that "our establishment clause jurisprudence is in hopeless disarray"); *see also* Capitol Square Review and Adv. Bd. v. Pinette, 515 U.S. 753, 768, n.3 (1995) (noting the "chaos" in Establishment Clause doctrine).

159. Ultimately, UW–Madison decided not to recognize the UW Roman Catholic Foundation because the organization did not comply with the requirement that organizations "be controlled and directed by UW–Madison students." *See* Catholic Group loses Standing on UW Campus, Wis. State J., Sept. 23, 2006, at D1. In response, the UW Roman Catholic Foundation filed a religious discrimination complaint with the US Department of Justice. *Id.*

160. 530 U.S. 640 (2000).

161. *Id.* at 660.

162. For example, gays and lesbians might seek to exclude heterosexuals on the ground that the organization fosters identity as well as rights advocacy. Female Muslims might seek to exclude males on grounds that the preservation of their identity as respected Muslim women is inconsistent with the inclusion of non Muslims.

163. *See* Boy Scouts v. Dale, 530 U.S. 640 (2000); *see also* Christian Legal Society v. James Walker, 453 F.3d 853 (7th Cir. 2005). In this CLS case, two members of a Seventh Circuit panel granted an injunction pending appeal against the enforcement of Southern Illinois University sexual orientation nondiscrimination policy relying, *inter alia*, on *Boy Scouts*, and Hurley v. Irish–American Gay, Lesbian and Bisexual Group of Boston, 515 U.S. 557 (1995).

164. *See* Lawrence v. Texas, 539 U.S. 558, 602 (2003) (Scalia, J., dissenting).

165. For example, the conservative Foundation for Individual Rights and Education (FIRE) has as its mission to defend and sustain individual rights at America's increasingly repressive and partisan colleges and universities. It publishes several guides for students who seek to maintain conservative Christian values while attending secular universities and colleges. One is called FIRE's guide to First Year Orientation and Thought Reform on Campus, written by Jordan Lorence, counsel for the plaintiffs in *Southworth* and Harvey Silberglate, and FIRE's Guide to Student Fees and Legal Equality on campus. http://www.thefire.org/index.php/guides/. The guide proposed is to insure the fair distribution of funds. *Id.* In response to this effort to organize successors to the *Southworth* plaintiffs, the Campus Free Speech organization, which includes PIRG advisors, has continuing concerns about the effect of *Southworth* and is therefore developing a guide to student activity fee systems. They note the numerous legal, legislative, and administrative initiatives to stifle the voices of students by restricting access to student fees, limiting access to university facilities and censoring student publications. Ironically, both sides in the culture wars rely on the First Amendment for their claims. http://www.campusspeech.org.

10

The Story of *Keyishian v. Board of Regents*: Loyalty Oaths, Academic Freedom and Free Speech in the University Community

Robert M. O'Neil

When the Supreme Court first reviewed a constitutional challenge to New York's Feinberg Law, and the loyalty screen that law imposed on public employees, the Justices' response was clear and unambiguous: "[School] teachers may work for the school system upon the reasonable terms laid down by the proper authorities of New York. If they do not choose to work on such terms, they are at liberty to retain their beliefs and associations and go elsewhere."[1] The Court specifically addressed, and resoundingly rejected, claims that the oath required of New York public workers abridged their federal constitutional liberties. Anyone who seriously contemplated reopening the issue of the Feinberg Law's validity less than a decade and a half later might be seen as presumptuous or naïve or both. Yet that is precisely what a group of professors in Western New York did, and with remarkable success. The later case is the focus of this essay.[2]

In fact the constitutional climate had changed so dramatically during those years that a new challenge to New York's and other states' loyalty oaths seemed eminently logical and appropriate. Only a few years after the Adler decision, the Supreme Court had begun to question that notion that government could impose on public employees and other beneficiaries any conditions it wished. By 1958, Justice Brennan spoke for a bare majority in striking down California's requirement that honorably discharged veterans who sought a property tax exemption clearly designed to recognize their service had to prove their loyalty by disclaiming any possible subversive affiliation.[3] In that case, brought by Southern California ACLU Executive Director Lawrence Speiser on his own behalf, the Court first extended to individual rights and liberties the doctrine of "unconstitutional conditions," which had long been available to business corporations.

If an out-of-state company could not be subjected to unduly burdensome conditions as the price of doing business across state lines, it now seemed equally appropriate that a person who sought a government job or other benefit (such as Spieser's tax exemption) could not be forced to surrender freedom of expression or religion as the price of obtaining that benefit.[4] In essence, what government could not do by direct regulation and criminal penalties it could no longer do by indirect sanctions such as withholding or encumbering a benefit. Indeed, the Court noted, denial of a valuable benefit might be a far graver sanction than a small fine or suspended jail sentence. Thus Adler's notion that a state employee could be told to "go elsewhere" if he or she wished to "retain his beliefs and associations" was no longer constitutionally acceptable by the end of the 1950s.

There were other momentous changes during the decade that followed the Adler decision. Mere membership in the Communist Party could no longer be outlawed; nothing less than knowing, active membership with a specific intent to further an unlawful end would suffice for any government sanction against a Communist.[5] Starting in 1961, the Justices began to question directly the manner by which states might ensure the loyalty of those who worked for government or sought public employment. The first such case involved Florida's loyalty oath, which demanded that an applicant swear not only that he or she was not a member of the Communist Party, but that "I have not and will not lend my aid, support, advice, counsel or influence to the Communist Party." The Florida Supreme Court sustained this mandate against the constitutional challenge of a school teacher named Cramp.

Now, however, a unanimous Supreme Court would reverse, holding that the key language of Florida's oath was unacceptably vague under a series of cases that dated back to the 1920s (though none involving public employment).[6] Among "the vices inherent in an unconstitutionally vague statute" were the "risk of unfair prosecution and the potential deterrence of constitutionally protected conduct" among the "dangers to which all who are compelled to execute an unconstitutionally vague oath may be exposed." Although the teacher who brought the suit had conceded that he could "truthfully execute the oath"—that is, that he was personally loyal and trustworthy—the Court recognized that he had raised serious doubts about the validity of the law to which he was clearly subject, and thus had brought a wholly viable challenge.

Indeed, the Court went on to hypothesize situations in which Florida's loyalty screen might create an unconscionable dilemma for a loyal applicant—"Could a journalist who had ever defended the constitutional rights of the Communist Party take an oath that he had never lent the Party his 'support'?" Given such contingencies, the Court cautioned that "the compulsion of this oath provision might weigh most heavily upon those whose conscientious scruples were most sensitive." Finally, observed Justice Stewart with an eye looking back upon the now receding but still ominous McCarthy era: "It would be blinking reality not to acknowledge that there are some among us always ready to affix a Communist label upon those whose ideas they violently oppose. And experience teaches that prosecutors too are human."

Three years later the Supreme Court revisited the loyalty oath issue, this time in a case brought by a group of University of Washington faculty, staff and students led by Professor Lawrence Baggett. Although the language of Washington's oath was quite different from that of Florida, many of the same flaws tainted its key provisions. In addition to disclaiming membership in the Communist Party, a Washington state employee must swear that he or she is not a "subversive person"—specifically, that he or she is not one who "advocates, abets, advises or teaches any person to commit, or attempt to commit, or aid in the commission of any act intended to overthrow, destroy, or alter, or assist in the overthrow, destruction or alteration of, the constitutional form of government of the United States or of the State of Washington." The "subversive organization" to which an applicant may not belong was defined in similarly broad language.

To the seven Justices in the majority in the Baggett case, Washington's oath was no more acceptable under the Federal Constitution than had been that of Florida; the former "suffers from similar infirmities."[7] Specifically, "persons required to swear they understand this oath might quite reasonably conclude that any person who aids the Communist Party or teaches or advises known members of the Party is a subversive person because such teaching or advice may now or at some future date aid the activities of the Party." The majority opinion noted that "the susceptibility of the statutory language to require foreswearing of an undefined variety of 'guiltless knowing behavior' " was exactly what the Court had condemned three years earlier in the Cramp case, and compelled a similar rejection of Washington's loyalty screen. In addition, an earlier Washington oath that called on all state employees to "promote undivided allegiance to the government of the United States" suffered from severe vagueness; "it would not be unreasonable," observed the Justices, "for the serious-minded oath-taker to conclude that he should dispense with lectures voicing far-reaching criticism of any old or new policy followed by the Government of the United States."

Both the Cramp and Baggett Courts went to some lengths to assure the nation that they were not stripping states of power to exclude genuinely dangerous and subversive persons from positions of power and authority. The Baggett opinion concluded that "as in Cramp.... we do not question the power of a State to take proper measures safeguarding the public service from disloyal conduct." What was at issue, the Justices insisted, was not the goal but simply the means; any loyalty-security test must comport with federal requirements respecting free expression and due process. As a practical matter, it seemed unlikely that many of the loyalty oaths then on the books would pass muster, although the Supreme Court's consistent case-by-case approach left any possible generalization for another day.

That next day would occur in Western New York. The long-private University of Buffalo became a part of the State University of New York in 1962, and thus for the first time in its history faculty and staff were subject to New York state laws and regulations. Among those previsions were the loyalty-security standards of the Feinberg Law, which the Supreme Court had so confidently validated in the Adler case a decade earlier. A group of Buffalo professors resisted the Feinberg-mandated oath as a condition of continued employment once their university entered the public sector, and were warned that their appointments would not be renewed if they had not signed the requisite forms by the date of expiration. (Since none of the objecting faculty members was yet tenured, no issue arose of possible termination of those serving without term. Apparently none of Buffalo's tenured professors refused to sign the oath.)

The plight of the non-signers soon came to the attention of Richard Lipsitz, a practicing Western New York attorney who would later be described as "labor's advocate in Buffalo" because of the range and variety of union cases he had fought—and in most of which he had prevailed.[8] Since it had been decided about the time he began his labor practice, Lipsitz was keenly aware of the obstacle posed by the Adler precedent. But he was convinced that the climate had changed so markedly, as well as the outlook of a newer group of Justices who now dominated the Supreme Court, that reopening the issue was not only timely but promising. Thus he filed suit in the United States District Court for the Western District of New York, sitting in Buffalo, against the Regents of the State of New York, the Trustees of the State University of New York, the Chancellor of the SUNY System, the President of the campus at Buffalo, the New York Civil Service Commission and several other state officials who bore some responsibility for enforcement of the Feinberg Law.

Terminology on both sides of the case as it first appeared in court is revealing. Among the defendants, one might not expect to find "The Regents of the University of the State of New York" as well as the more predictable SUNY Trustees. That is because the former is an entity peculiar to New York State. Created in 1784, and thus predating the

Federal Constitution, the New York Regents have uniquely pervasive authority over all education in the state, not only the public sector but also every classroom in the private sector from a parochial kindergarten to a Columbia or Cornell doctoral seminar. Such education comprised, quite simply, the "University of the State of New York"—an entity not to be confused with others. The Regents' authority over private education exists not only on paper, but in practice, as the removal of several doctoral programs at Fordham and St. Johns Universities will attest, and as New York's highest court has several timed affirmed.[9] (The Regents actually possess even broader authority, including film censorship and other powers,[10] but any discussion of matters beyond higher education would be superfluous here).

The styling of the case on the plaintiff's side is even more intriguing. Although several of the non-signing professors bore names like Garver and Hochfield, both Assistant professors, the lead plaintiff was one Harry Keyishian, not only junior in rank to but also lower in the alphabet than his more senior colleagues. When Lispsitz was asked why Keyishian was chosen as the person whose name would forever identify a possibly major precedent, his response was simple and direct: "I just knew it would mean more to Harry than to any of the others." The lesson is important, though poorly understood even among lawyers: It is the plaintiff's attorney who determines what names will appear on the caption or heading of any court case. That is true not only on the plaintiff's side but also on the defendants' roster. Notably, a later suit brought against the University of Washington did not name as principal defendant the chairman of the Board of Regents (as did the Baggett loyalty oath suit) but rather the University's president, Charles Odegaard, who forever after believed (with some justification) that he had been the target of personal animus by the lawyer who brought the case. The point is that once the plaintiff's attorney makes such a selection, names on both sides tend to stick, barring a death or change in an ex official position.

The defendants promptly responded to the suit, addressing initially the question whether the constitutional claims were important enough to warrant the convening of a three-judge court. At that time and for over a decade thereafter, federal courts of three judges (typically one from the court of appeals and two from the district bench) were required when the constitutionality of a state law was drawn into question. The district judge before whom this issue came in the Keyishian case initially ruled that this requirement did not apply, so clearly was the law settled in favor of the Feinberg Law's validity.[11] But the federal Court of Appeals for the Second Circuit, sitting in New York City, saw the case quite differently—in part because the Adler Court had not addressed many of the claims that Keyishian and his colleagues now advanced.

Thus the higher court sent the case back to Buffalo, insisting that a three-judge court must be convened.[12] That action not only substantially raised the profile of the case, but assured that it would receive the careful attention of three federal judges. Even more important, this ruling ensured that the case would get to the U.S. Supreme Court, since at that time review of three-judge court decisions was virtually mandatory and not discretionary (as is the case today for virtually all lower court proceedings). Since the abolition of the three-judge court requirement—save for a few special situations like challenges to the Communications Decency Act and the McCain–Feingold Campaign Finance Law—whether a case ever gets on the Supreme Court docket is entirely up to the Justices. Many cases that went all the way up from three-judge courts under the old structure almost certainly would not have achieved such prominence in later times.

With the case now back in district court in Buffalo, Lipsitz had a chance to develop more fully his constitutional claims that state university teachers could not be forced to choose between keeping their jobs and avoiding a disavowal or disclaimer of vaguely defined political activity or affiliation. Although the Supreme Court had seemingly addressed those issues under the very law in question in the Adler case, Lipsitz now made two key points: First, that Adler had in fact not addressed all the constitutional issues he was now pressing, and second, that in any event the constitutional climate had changed dramatically in the intervening years.

While everyone awaited the three-judge court's ruling, a funny thing happened to the Feinberg Law. In June, 1965, the certificate requirement that had long been imposed under the law was suddenly rescinded by New York State civil service officials. Instead, each applicant for state employment was henceforth to be informed that the Feinberg Law and its provisions constituted part of his or her contract. The applicant was specifically to be warned of the disability or disqualification that would result from membership in any "subversive organization." Should any applicant have questions, he or she "may request a personal interview," noting that "refusal of a candidate to answer any question relevant to such inquiry by such officer shall be sufficient ground to refuse to make or recommend appointment." This change in procedure would become a pivotal source of divergence among the courts that would now consider the case.

In the first week of January, 1966, the three-judge court ruled resoundingly in the state's favor.[13] Even if the Feinberg Law's structure had been unchanged, its basic provisions would have been valid. To this panel, the Supreme Court had shown since Adler no diminished deference to the state's interest in the loyalty of its work force. Indeed, a couple of intervening decisions if anything served to reinforce that interest. As for Cramp and Baggett, it was true that the Justices had invalidated a couple of state loyalty oaths on the basis of imprecise language, but neither ruling "cast[s] any doubt upon the power of a state to act to prevent the incitement of violent overthrow on university campuses." Indeed, "Baggett made clear that narrowly drawn statutes aimed wholly at the control of subversive activities would be upheld as constitutional."[14]

The district court found the Speiser decision a bit harder to distinguish, but found in the changed structure of New York's loyalty system a means of doing just that. Conceding that the Feinberg certificate requirement "may have raised problems under Speiser," the new procedure neatly avoided such problems since not only were post-June, 1965 applicants no longer compelled to make such a declaration, but even pre-June employees were assured that they could not be terminated "solely by reason of" having refused to sign the oath. Moreover, "the candidate is given a chance to explain his doubts," and even though refusal to respond to an inquiry during such an interview might disqualify an applicant, "this seems reasonable, in light of the opportunity to explain."

Finally, responding to specific concerns the plaintiffs had raised, the three judge panel addressed the merits of the potentially chilling effect of the Feinberg Law's operative language on the university classroom: "Legitimate activities are not deterred ... Not [affected is] teaching Communist theory in a course in economic or political theory; only teaching that government shall or should 'be overthrown by force' is a basis for adverse consequences under these section." As for publishing or disseminating innocuous material that might be deemed subversive: "A distributor or editor of subversive literature must also advocate or embrace 'the duty, necessity or propriety of adopting the doctrine of violent overthrow,' before he can be disqualified for state employment."[15]

The state and university officials who had defended the Feinberg Law thus prevailed on every contested issue. The three-judge court had even considered several constitutional claims that had not figured prominently in the plaintiff's case, and rejected them as well—the remote possibility that such a statute could be deemed a "bill of attainder" or an "ex post facto law." The Supreme Court's recent blows at disclaimer type loyalty oaths, in the Cramp and Baggett cases, were not only distinguished in their narrow holdings; the broader premises of those two rulings were actually invoked to support the position of the three federal judges in the Buffalo case. While they might not have gone quite as far as to tell Keyishian and his colleagues that they were "at liberty to retain their beliefs and associations and go elsewhere," the tenor of their opinion implied virtually no change since the Adler ruling fourteen years earlier. The plaintiffs, predictably, appealed the decision to the Supreme Court just as soon as the ink had dried—or more precisely after the time had expired within which a rehearing might have been granted at the trial level. Things would seem quite different at the next level in the federal court system.

One anecdote from the summer of 1966 bears retelling. The case had now been comfortably docketed in the Supreme Court; being the judgment of a three-judge court that was not a matter of discretion but of mandate. Given the time of year at which the case was docketed, it could not be argued and decided before the Justices adjourned for the Term in June. That meant both sides would have ample time in which to prepare briefs and prepare for oral argument. In mid summer, Martin Meyerson arrived in Buffalo as the new President of the SUNY–Buffalo campus, succeeding Clifford Furnas (who had guided the institution through its metamorphosis from private to public university.) Meyerson, a seasoned city planner and scholar of urban design, headed the Joint Harvard–MIT Center for Urban Studies, and then served as Dean of the College of Environmental Design at the University of California–Berkeley—before taking on the daunting task of being Acting Chancellor in the immediate aftermath of the Free Speech Movement, the Sproul Hall sit-in and myriad other challenges.

President Meyerson had already established a widely admired commitment to academic freedom and free expression during his acting chancellorship at Berkeley. Thus it was hardly surprising that, on learning his new institution was the focal point of major loyalty-oath litigation, he wondered whether a new president might intervene in a helpful way. Specifically, during a summer, 1966 visit, he suggested to me the possibility of waiving any Feinberg Law requirements for the non-signers and thus striking a highly visible blow for academic freedom. During a visit to Buffalo and a meeting with President Meyerson preparatory to my joining his administration, I was horrified by such a prospect, though I deeply appreciated the laudable motive that occasioned the suggestion. I explained that given the Feinberg Law's new structure, it was probably no longer possible to moot the case in this way, even if it had been desirable to do so. But more to the point, getting the case dismissed would be the worst possible outcome at this stage—however beneficial and benign such an outcome might well have appeared to a non-lawyer.

There is in fact some fascinating history on this precise issue, which I shared with President Meyerson in the course of deterring his intervention. For many years, Maryland's Ober Law, the source of a loyalty oath similar to New York's, had been challenged by non-signers who were willing to risk the consequences, including non-payment of salary or stipend. (They were typically short-term visitors or lecturers for whom the risk was far lower than it would have been for long-term faculty or staff). Mysteriously, every time such a potential Ober Law-challenger refused to sign, officials in Annapolis waived the requirement for that person, and the paycheck somehow showed up on schedule in her or her bank account. Usually this happened even before a suit could even be filed, though in one or two cases the issue was already in court but was promptly dismissed when state lawyers made the judge aware of the waiver and thus the disappearance of any actual controversy.

Finally, just about the time the Keyishian case was on its way to the Supreme Court, Maryland authorities overlooked one such non-signer, a lecturer named Whitehill, and the Ober Law test that would take the issue to the Supreme Court was finally at a stage where waiver would not compel its dismissal. Given the inordinate difficulty of getting such cases beyond the judicial threshold, the fact that Keyishian now offered a "live one" seemed compelling. President Meyerson, reluctantly but appreciatively, agreed not to intervene and thus allow the Keyishian case to proceed to a Supreme Court hearing that, I assured him, would almost certainly strike a permanent blow to the Feinberg Law of far greater value than a dispensation to a small group of challengers.

With that delicate task accomplished, I returned to my faculty position at the School of Law (Boalt Hall) of the University of California–Berkeley, where I had been teaching since the fall of 1963. My major assignment for the summer of 1966 was to draft a brief for the American Association of University Professors to be filed in the Supreme Court. Since the parties were well represented, this was to be an amicus curiae or "friend of the court" brief. Theoretically, such a brief takes no position on either side of the merits, but simply advises the court on the principal issues from an objective and dispassionate perspective. Every so often, someone does bring to the Court such a neutral viewpoint—in that sense truly a "friend of the court." Yet most amicus curiae briefs present arguments for one side or the other in a pending case—and that was certainly the design for the AAUP brief to be filed in the Keyishian case.

The opportunity presented through such a brief was profound. Quite simply, the Keyishian case offered the first occasion for the Supreme Court to recognize and define academic freedom as a distinct constitutional liberty protected under the Bill of Rights. This concept had not been entirely overlooked by the Justices in the series of cases brought by university professors who sought protection against government threats, demands and investigations. By the summer of 1966, there were fragments—often in separate opinions—that gave encouragement to proponents of academic freedom.[16] What had not yet occurred, and what the Keyishian case promised, was an opportunity to establish academic freedom as a legal concept in its own right.

Actually the state of the law had come a considerable way in the fourteen years since the high Court ventured its callous view that professors and other public workers were "at liberty to maintain their beliefs and associations and go elsewhere." In that very case, which brought to the high Court the first challenge to New York's Feinberg Law, Justices Black and Douglas dissented, expressing intense disagreement with their colleagues. On three occasions during their passionate dissent, they specifically invoked academic freedom, insisting that in the climate of fear and anxiety that New York's loyalty-security system had created, "there can be no real academic freedom." They also charged that such a "system of spying and surveillance" as New York had imposed on its public sector "cannot go hand in hand with academic freedom."[17]

A few months later, Justice Felix Frankfurter (who, like Douglas, had been a university professor before joining the Court) added his support for the still embryonic concept of academic freedom. The case involved a rather different loyalty oath (this one from Oklahoma). The majority rather indifferently sustained state power to impose such conditions on public employees, and that disposed of the case. But Justice Frankfurter now joined Justices Black and Douglas, insisting for the first time that the academic profession presented a special claim: "[I]n view of the nature of the teacher's relation to the effective exercise of rights which are safeguarded by the Bill of Rights.... Inhibition of freedom of thought, and of action upon thought, in the case of teachers brings the safeguards of those amendments vividly into operation. Such unwarranted inhibition upon the free spirit of teachers [also] ... has an unmistakable tendency to chill that free play of the spirit which all teachers ought especially to cultivate."[18]

Another five years would pass before the Court had its next opportunity to address academic freedom claims. By now, Earl Warren had become Chief Justice, and although the Court's liberal wing would not have a working majority for another several years, the tide had begun to turn with regard to freedom of expression and related interests. The case that brought the issue to the fore involved demands by New Hampshire's red-baiting attorney general, Louis Wyman, for notes of lectures given at the University of New Hampshire by a prominent socialist, Paul Sweezy. The Court's rebuff to Wyman's demands invoked a rather narrow, almost technical, rationale—the absence of any evidence that the state legislature had empowered the attorney general to pursue such an inquiry.

The case might well have ended there. But Chief Justice Warren chose to expand upon the nature of the scholar's asserted interest. While Wyman's rogue inquiry would have been halted at the behest of any citizen, this case was special: "We believe that there unquestionably was an invasion of [Sweezy's] liberties in the area of academic freedom and political expression." The context was crucial: "The essentiality of freedom in the community of American universities is almost self-evident ..... Teachers and students must always remain free to inquire, to study and to evaluate, to gain new maturity and understanding; otherwise our civilization will stagnate and die.''[19] Thus for the first time—albeit beyond the narrow core ground on which the judgment rested—a Supreme Court majority had embraced academic freedom as an interest more clearly protected than the liberties of ordinary citizens.

Academic freedom was, not surprisingly, of even greater importance to Justice Frankfurter. In a concurring opinion, he made clear that he would have based a judgment in Sweezy's favor solely on that ground. Of paramount concern to him was the grave harm that could result from "government intrusion into the intellectual life of a university ... [given] ... the dependence of a free society on free universities." Moreover, he continued, "it matters little whether such intervention occurs avowedly or through action that inevitably tends to check the ardor and fearlessness of scholars." Thus, Frankfurter insisted, "political power must abstain from intrusion into this activity of [academic] freedom ... except for reasons that are exigent and obviously compelling.''[20] This latter standard was, incidentally, far more rigorous than the Court's expectation for demanding testimony from a recalcitrant citizen outside the academic profession.

To these cases might be added, by the summer of 1966, the two loyalty oath decisions that were reviewed earlier here, although in neither Cramp nor Baggett did the Justices make much of the academic interests of the plaintiffs. Indeed, neither case really posed such an opportunity, since the Cramp plaintiffs were public school teachers and the Baggett plaintiffs, led by a group of University of Washington professors, included some non-faculty staff members and even a group of concerned students. Thus as the Keyishian case appeared on the Supreme Court's docket for the Term that would begin in the fall of 1966, there were some encouraging signs but hardly an unambiguous affirmation of academic freedom as a core civil liberty of college professors.

The preparation of the AAUP's amicus curiae brief began in auspicious fashion. Having agreed in late spring to write the first draft of such a brief, I made a special trip to Buffalo on June 4, 1966. There I met with Richard Lipsitz and Buffalo Law Professor Saul Touster, who had long been active in faculty affairs, had chaired the faculty component of the presidential search committee—and whom I would join a year later as a fellow assistant to President Meyerson. The purpose of this congenial meeting was to make sure the AAUP brief would optimally complement the brief that Lipsitz would be filing on behalf of his clients, and would enhance the case against the validity of the Feinberg Law. Occasionally, a "friend of the court" is able to advance arguments that would be awkward for one of the parties to make, or can craft them differently. Moreover, the briefs filed by the parties often need to address technical arguments—in Keyishian, for example, the precise significance of the very recent and complex changes in New York's loyalty system, under which the certificate or oath was no longer required. Such an obligatory focus of the parties' briefs then leaves the amici free to step back and take a broader perspective on the central issues.

That was precisely the opportunity that filing such a brief presented to the AAUP. With Mr. Lipsitz' blessing, the brief augmented or complemented the brief being filed on behalf of the plaintiffs (now actually "appellants" in the Supreme Court), which would cover all the technical and operational issues. That left to AAUP the long-awaited opportunity to seek clear judicial recognition of academic freedom as a distinct and separate constitutional interest. To that end, the brief not only invoked the Supreme Court decisions (and separate opinions) that have just been reviewed here, but even more broadly addressed the underlying policy interests that AAUP had championed since its founding almost exactly a half century earlier. In short, there were reasons why academic freedom needed and deserved legal protection beyond the rights of citizens and of non-academic government workers. The relevant opinions of Chief Justice Warren, Justices Black, Douglas and Frankfurter had identified some—but by no means all—of those policy interests. The amicus brief to be filed in the Keyishian case now offered a unique opportunity to bring those interests directly to the attention of the nation's highest Court.

At this point a few words about the procedural posture of the Keyishian case may shed further light on the importance of the AAUP brief. Usually when a case goes up on appeal, there will have been a trial in the lower court, and that trial will have produced a record which is part of the appeal. In challenges to loyalty oaths and other government loyalty-security mandates, the challenger will usually have had an opportunity to explain just how the policy in issue affected his or her speech, affiliation and activity. Evidence of such a "chilling effect" evoked from witnesses under oath in a trial court can be quite compelling, and has often proved useful to sympathetic judges in higher courts.

But the Keyshian case represented a "facial challenge" to the Feinberg Law, and thus involved no trial or testimony. The judgment of the three-judge federal district court reflected the briefs and supporting papers filed by both parties, and oral arguments addressed to the court—but no statements from witnesses about the operation or effect of New York's loyalty screen. Thus the potential importance of an amicus curiae brief filed by the AAUP—setting forth the underlying academic freedom interests potentially affected by such state laws—became even more important here than would ordinarily have been the case even in a major constitutional controversy.

Four briefs were filed in September—one by Richard Lipsitz on behalf of the faculty challengers as plaintiffs and appellants, one by Ruth Iles, Assistant Attorney General of the State of New York, a third by Osmond K. Frankel for the American Civil Liberties Union (a longstanding and vigorous foe of loyalty oaths) and the fourth from the national AAUP, filed by Indiana University Law Professor Ralph Fuchs as General Counsel, joined by Professor Bernard Wolfman and by Senior Staff Counsel Herman Orentlicher. Curiously, there were no supporting briefs on New York's side of the case; usually when one state's laws are challenged in the Supreme Court, other states with shared interests or concerns are likely to file supporting briefs, though none appeared in the Keyishian case.

The oral argument of the case occurred on November 17, 1966, quite early in a Supreme Court Term that had begun, as always, on the first Monday in October. The nature of the questioning from the bench gave warning to the parties that this would be a close case—much closer, for example, than the two previous oath cases (Cramp had been unanimous, and Baggett was 7–2). Normally one would not have expected any ruling on a matter of such importance and difficulty until near the end of the Court's Term in June; save for a few major cases that turn out for some technical reason to be far simpler than anticipated, the Justices usually take the balance of the Term to complete work on such cases, and often announce judgments in the final week. Resolution is critical, however; any case that has not been decided by the end of the Term must be reargued the next year, since the Supreme Court never carries an argued case over through the summer.

Hardly anyone in the legal or academic community was prepared for a Keyishian ruling as early as January 23, 1967, the day on which it was announced. That day fell during the Court's first week back in session after its winter recess—a six-week period that for years had accommodated Justice Hugo Black's perennial Florida retreat reflecting his passionate commitment to tennis, maintained well into his 80s. The notion that a major case would come down so early—and less than two months after the oral argument—was surprising then, and to this day evades any easy explanation.

The early ruling was even more surprising when the votes were tallied. The Supreme Court had struck down the Feinberg Law, essentially overruling the Adler decision, by a 5–4 margin. Justice William J. Brennan, Jr., increasingly the Court's most eloquent champion of civil rights and liberties, wrote the majority opinion, which Justices Black, Douglas, Fortas and Chief Justice Warren joined. Justice Clark wrote a stinging dissent for himself and Justices Harlan, Stewart and White, near the end of which he accused the majority opinion of having "by its broadside swept away one of our most precious rights, namely, the right of self-preservation."[21]

Whether the majority's "broadside" justified so extreme a response remains a central issue in analysis of the Keyishian opinions. Justice Brennan did resolve virtually all of the contested issues in favor of the Feinberg Law's challengers. The recent change in procedure—the elimination of the certificate/oath requirement—which had been dispositive for the lower court, deterred the Supreme Court majority not the least. "The substance of the statutory and regulatory complex remains," insisted Justice Brennan in a two-sentence reply to this argument, "and from the outset appellants' basic claim has been that they are aggrieved by its application." Thus the central focus of analysis becomes that "basic claim" which brought the five-Justice majority to invalidate the entire New York loyalty structure.

Actually, two interacting themes pervaded the majority opinion—one, that Adler had not really addressed the issues now before the Court; and second, that when properly presented, the constitutional challenge was irrefutable and doomed the Feinberg Law. The first point was crucial because, to a greater degree than most of his colleagues, Justice Brennan was an ardent champion of stare decisis (legal precedent) who abhorred the notion of overruling a decision as recent as a decade and a half earlier. Thus he stressed that Adler had never really passed upon the central issues now posed in Keyishian. Specifically, even the older portions of the Feinberg Law had not been frontally challenged on vagueness grounds (and in one case, such a challenge had not been properly made in the lower courts, thus escaping Supreme Court review).

On that point, the majority could invoke the ruling of the federal appeals court which, in sending the case back down for review by a three-judge district panel, had insisted that "Adler ... refused to pass upon the constitutionality of [the challenged provisions]." Moreover, several of the most troubling sections of the law had not even been enacted until 1958, and thus obviously could not have been validated by the Adler ruling in 1952. Thus, concluded Justice Brennan with an obvious sigh of relief, "Adler is therefore not dispositive of the constitutional issues we must decide in this case." That left the Keyshian Court free to write on an essentially clean slate.

Actually, Justice Brennan's slate was not completely blank, since the Court had already addressed some closely analogous issues in ways that support the majority view in Keyishian. The vice of vagueness had resulted in reversal of convictions of accused subversives as far back as the 1930s, and the progressive narrowing of the punishable scope of Communist Party affiliation or activity in the 1950s. Cases like Speiser (the California veteran's property tax exemption oath case), and the two earlier loyalty oath cases, lent further support to the majority's view that New York could and should have been far more precise in warning its civil servants about political activities or affiliations that might jeopardize their jobs or occasion other sanctions. After reviewing the applicable precedents, Justice Brennan concluded: "We emphasize once again that 'precision of regulation must be the touchstone in an area so closely touching our most precious freedoms.' ... New York's complicated and intricate scheme plainly violates that standard.... The danger of [a] chilling effect upon the exercise of vital First Amendment rights must be guarded against by sensitive tools which clearly inform teachers what is being proscribed."

That specific reference to "teachers" immediately followed the majority's explicit recognition of academic freedom—more than a hint that university professors enjoyed greater protection than the general run of civil servants. With specific reliance on the Sweezy case, but going further, Justice Brennan set the tone for Keyishian's scope: "[A]cademic freedom ... is of transcendent value to all of us and not merely to the teachers concerned. That freedom is therefore a special concern of the First Amendment, which does not tolerate laws that cast a pall of orthodoxy over the classroom.... The classroom is particularly the marketplace of ideas. The Nation's future depends upon leaders trained through wide exposure to that robust exchange of ideas which discovers truth out of a multitude of tongues, [rather] than through any kind of authoritative selection."[22]

The majority's emphasis on academic freedom was especially welcome to the plaintiffs, all of them university teachers, and to the AAUP, which had filed an amicus curiae brief addressed directly to such concerns. When the dust settled, of course all New York state public employees received the same benefit from the judgment. Custodians and clerks were now as free of the Feinberg Law's constraints as were university professors; in that sense the scope of the ruling and its impact went well beyond its factual setting and much of its stated rationale. Yet the occupation of the plaintiffs/appellants should not be dismissed as irrelevant; who could be certain that the same result would have emerged—especially from so sharply divided a Court—had the sole challengers been clerks and custodians?

Given the force of the majority opinion, one might wonder how four dissenters (including at least two Justices who had often taken a more sympathetic view) ended up so far across the constitutional spectrum. For Justice Clark and his colleagues, the recent change in the New York loyalty/security procedure profoundly altered, and essentially mooted the case; the majority "does not explain how the statute can be applied to appellants under procedures which have been for almost two years a dead letter." On the merits, the Adler Court had addressed the central issues raised by the Keyishian plaintiffs, if not every dimension of the current challenge, and had resolved those issues correctly. For fifteen years, New York and other states had relied appropriately on Adler, the effective overruling of which prompted Justice Clark to lament that "no court has ever reached out so far to destroy so much with so little." Finally, the 1958 amendments concededly had not been validated by Adler. But for the dissenters, the post-Adler provisions were indistinguishable from federal loyalty-security regulations and laws of Pennsylvania and California that had received the Court's imprimatur only a few years earlier. (The majority's disinclination to take on this issue, the dissenters might have added, strongly implied that these precedents were now endangered if not completely abandoned.)

The Keyshian decision unambiguously ended the use of disclaimer-type loyalty oaths as a government security measure. Although the impetus for such intrusive measures had abated substantially with the end of the McCarthy era, many such measures would have remained on the books far longer—with at least nominal threat of enforcement—had the high Court not intervened so decisively. Perhaps most important of all, Keyishian firmly established academic freedom as an expressive interest entitled to a special level of solicitude by reason of the unique mission of the college and university in national life. Professor William W. VanAlstyne, a lifelong chronicler and champion of academic freedom, probably put it best. He drew an analogy between Keyishian and Justice Brennan's most influential of all opinions, recognizing a media privilege of fair comment on the activities of public officials (and later public figures), at the behest of the New York Times. Van Alstyne expressed his tribute this way: "Keyishian marks an important right of passage. What New York Times v. Sullivan had meant in respect to journalism in the United States ... Keyishian forcefully represents in respect to academic freedom."[23] Higher expectations one could hardly have had on that day in 1964 when Richard Lipsitz filed his suit in Buffalo's federal courthouse.

Two personal experiences provide an intriguing coda. On the very day in January, 1967, that the Keyshian decision was announced in Washington, my wife and I were quite by chance visiting in Buffalo, where we would soon move. During the day the triumphant plaintiffs and a few friends organized a victory party at the home of one of the prevailing professors. The party began in early evening, with much to celebrate. Suddenly our host rushed into the room, asked for quiet and announced to us all that on that very morning, the University of California Regents had dismissed Clark Kerr as President of the UC System, at the behest of newly installed Governor Ronald Reagan. Suddenly we realized that January 23 had brought for champions of academic freedom a unique mixture of good and bad news that we would never forget. The party soon dispersed. The next day's media carried President Kerr's wry and characteristically philosophical appraisal of these tumultuous events: "I left office just as I entered it—fired with enthusiasm!"

Several months later, while preparing to assume my post as Executive Assistant to President Martin Meyerson in Buffalo, I received a thick envelope of employment papers from the SUNY personnel office in Albany. Upon opening the envelope, I noted at once that the Feinberg Law apparatus lay atop the pile. The text of the law, and the ominous warnings to new employees of the State of New York, were unmistakable. I telephoned the appropriate person in Albany, explaining that I had just played a role in persuading the Supreme Court to invalidate the Feinberg Law. After checking with a superior, an obviously embarrassed personnel officer assured me that I should discard the loyalty-security papers, and proceed to the other forms. She also assured me that no future mailings would contain such materials. To my knowledge, I was the last applicant for New York State employment ever to encounter the Feinberg Law.

Endnotes

1. Adler v. Board of Educ., 342 U.S. 485, 492 (1952).

2. Keyishian v. Board of Regents, 385 U.S. 589 (1967).

3. Speiser v. Randall, 357 U.S. 513 (1958).

4. *See* William VanAlstyne, *The Demise of the Right–Privilege Distinction in Constitutional Law*, 83 Harv. L. Rev. 1429 (1968); Kathleen M. Sullivan, *Unconstitutional Conditions*, 102 Harv. L. Rev. 1415 (1989).

5. Scales v. United States, 367 U.S. 203 (1961), Noto v. United States, 367 U.S. 290 (1961).

6. Cramp v. Board of Public Instruction, 368 U.S. 278 (1961).

7. Baggett v. Bullitt, 377 U.S. 360 (1964). Justices Clark and Harlan dissented.

8. "Labor of Love: Richard Lipsitz Sr. Has Been Labor's Advocate for More than 50 Years," *Buffalo News*, May 7, 2003, p. B–6.

9. *See* http:usny.nysed.gov/aboutusny.html. *See also* www.rand.org/pubs/monograph_reports/MR1141/MR1141.chap2.pdf.

10. For an example of the Regents' authority over motion pictures, *see* Kingsley International Pictures v. Regents of the Univ. of the State of New York, 360 U.S. 684 (1959).

11. Keyishian v. Board of Regents, 233 F.Supp. 752 (W.D.N.Y. 1964).

12. Keyishian v. Board of Regents, 345 F.2d 236 (2d Cir. 1965).

13. Keyishian v. Board of Regents, 255 F.Supp. 981 (W.D.N.Y. 1966).

14. *Id.* at 986.

15. *Id.* at 992.

16. For example, in addition to the cases reviewed here, Shelton v. Tucker, 364 U.S. 479 (1960); Bates v. City of Little Rock, 361 U.S. 516 (1960); William VanAlstyne, *The Constitutional Rights of Teachers and Professors*, 1970 Duke L.J. 841.

17. Adler v. Board of Educ., 342 U.S. 485, 510–11 (1952).

18. Wieman v. Updegraff, 344 U.S. 183, 195 (1952).

19. Sweezy v. New Hampshire, 354 U.S. 234, 250 (1957).

20. *Id.* at 262.

21. Keyishian v. Board of Regents, 385 U.S. 589, 628 (1967).

22. Keyishian v. Board of Regents, 385 U.S. 589, 603 (1967).

23. William W. VanAlstyne, *Academic Freedom and the First Amendment in the Supreme Court of the United States*, in William W. VanAlstyne, ed., Freedom and Tenure in the Academy (Durham: Duke University Press, 1993), p. 114.

11

The Story of *Edwards v. Aguillard*: The Genesis of Creation–Science

Leslie C. Griffin[1]

The biblical "story begins, audaciously, with the creation of the world," of plants and animals, of all living creatures, and of man and woman.[2] The Book of Genesis contains two accounts of creation, one written by the Priestly author and a second by the Yahwist writer.[3] These stories recount that "God created humankind in his image, ... male and female he created them,"[4] and that the "LORD God formed man from the dirt of the ground, and breathed into his nostrils the breath of life; and the man became a living being."[5] While the Priestly author "presented a majestic God-centered scenario of creation," the Yahwist "presents a very different but equally profound story of origins ... centered more on human beings and familiar human experiences, and even its deity is conceived in more anthropomorphic terms."[6] The biblical text implies that creation occurred about 4000 B.C.E. The Genesis stories were influenced by other ancient epics of creation, including the Story of Atrahasis, from about 1700 B.C.E., the Enuma Elish, from 1125–1104 B.C.E., and the Epic of Gilgamesh, which contains stories that were current before 2000 B.C.E.[7] Atrahasis, for example, built a boat to save his family and livestock when the gods tried to destroy humanity with a flood.[8]

The Birth of Creation–Science

The constitutional story of creation-science is much younger, dating to the United States Supreme Court's 1987 decision, *Edwards v. Aguillard*,[9] and more directly to the publication of Charles Darwin's *Origin of Species* in 1859. According to Darwin's theory of evolution, "evolution is the inference that living things share common ancestors and have, in Darwin's words, 'descended with modification' from these ancestors."[10] According to Pulitzer Prize winning historian Edward Larson, "*Origin of Species* dealt a body blow to traditional Western religious thought. At a superficial level, Darwin's chronology for the origin of species differed on its face from that set forth in Genesis. Species evolved from pre-existing species over vast periods of time, he asserted; God did not separately create all of them in a few days.''[11] The story of creation-science arises from the conflict in American public schools between the Darwinian and the biblical accounts of origins. That story, which began with *Aguillard*'s ruling in 1987 that creation-science may not be required in the public school science curriculum to balance the teaching of evolution, is still unfolding twenty years later as federal courts now consider whether intelligent design [ID] is ''creationism re-labeled'' and therefore equally impermissible in the public school classroom.[12]

After the theory of evolution was increasingly taught in American science classes in the late nineteenth and early twentieth centuries, fundamentalist Christians organized to oppose its presence in the public school classroom.[13] Christian opposition to evolution achieved full strength in the 1920s, when Tennessee and other states passed legislation (sometimes called ''monkey laws'') criminalizing the teaching of evolution in the public schools. After a Tennessee jury convicted John Scopes of that crime in the famous Scopes trial, Scopes' conviction was reversed on a technicality,[14] thus ensuring that the anti-evolution laws remained on the books until 1968, when the United States Supreme Court invalidated an Arkansas statute outlawing the teaching of evolution in public schools in *Epperson v. Arkansas*.[15] The Court ruled that the Arkansas statute violated the Establishment Clause of the First Amendment because ''there can be no doubt that Arkansas has sought to prevent its teachers from discussing the theory of evolution because it is contrary to the belief of some that the Book of Genesis must be the exclusive source of doctrine as to the origin of man.''[16]

Post–*Epperson*, critics of evolution turned to a strategy different from barring evolution from classrooms, namely to balance the teaching of evolution with equal instruction about creation. That strategy raised an important constitutional question: what account(s) of creation could legally be taught in the public school classroom? Yale law student Wendell Bird addressed that issue in an influential 1978 note in the *Yale Law Journal*.[17] According to Bird, the exclusive teaching of evolution in public schools violated the Free Exercise rights of religious students. Exempting students from the evolution classroom was an insufficient remedy for the constitutional violation, Bird argued. Instead, it was more appropriate for the state to incorporate ''countervailing viewpoints'' (or balance) into the classroom.[18] Which viewpoints? Although Bird acknowledged that ''[p]resentation of *biblical* creation would contravene the establishment clause and thus could not be employed to neutralize a public school course,'' he recommended that ''*scientific* creationism'' was an appropriate classroom subject because it was science, not religion, and therefore not a violation of the Establishment Clause.[19] Bird cited research from the Institute for Creation Research (where he later worked as a lawyer), Henry Morris's *Scientific Creationism* (1974) and other works about the subject; he also called attention to the scientific, not religious, credentials of the authors involved in the field.[20]

Bird later explained that his motivation for writing the essay was not religious but was rooted in a desire for schools to present fair and balanced scientific information. Although he was a committed evolutionist in high school, where evolution was taught "as fact," once Bird learned of evidence challenging evolution, he decided that such material should be taught alongside evolution as a matter of fairness. After finishing law school, Bird clerked for federal judges and moved into legal practice, and did not lobby for the passage of legislation requiring the teaching of scientific creationism to balance evolution. Nonetheless, Bird's article received unusual interest and attention for a student law note. Bird recalls that his Yale essay became the most requested reprint from the journal, and that within a few years of its publication over half the states had pending statutes requiring the balanced treatment of evolution and creationism.[21]

In June 1980, for example, Louisiana State Senator Bill Keith introduced Senate Bill 956 in the Louisiana Legislature in order to

> "assure academic freedom by requiring the teaching of the theory of creation ex nihilo [i.e., out of nothing] in all public schools where the theory of evolution is taught." The bill defined the "theory of creation ex nihilo" as "the belief that the origin of the elements, the galaxy, the solar system, of life, of all the species of plants and animals, the origin of man, and the origin of all things and their processes and relationships were created ex nihilo and fixed by God."[22]

Although such language, with its invocation of God and creation ex nihilo, sounded more biblical than scientific, Senator Keith referred to his legislation as "scientific creationism."[23] A similar statute passed in Arkansas, home of the *Epperson* decision, on March 19, 1981. That Balanced Treatment for Creation–Science and Evolution–Science Act stated that "[p]ublic schools within this State shall give balanced treatment to creation-science and to evolution-science."[24]

A constitutional challenge to the Arkansas Act was filed on May 27, 1981, and on January 5, 1982, after an extensive trial with testimony by theologians, philosophers and scientists, a federal district court ruled that the Act violated the Establishment Clause. The definitions of creation-science in Section 4 persuaded the court that the statute was religious and not scientific. According to that section of the legislation:

> (a) "Creation-science" means the scientific evidences for creation and inferences from those scientific evidences. Creation-science in-

> cludes the scientific evidences and related inferences that indicate: (1) Sudden creation of the universe, energy, and life from nothing; (2) The insufficiency of mutation and natural selection in bringing about development of all living kinds from a single organism; (3) Changes only within fixed limits of originally created kinds of plants and animals; (4) Separate ancestry for man and apes; (5) Explanation of the earth's geology by catastrophism, including the occurrence of a worldwide flood; and (6) A relatively recent inception of the earth and living kinds.

Expert witnesses argued for the plaintiffs that the statutory definition of creation-science matched the contents of the Book of Genesis rather than any scientific theory. Hebrew Bible expert Father Bruce Vawter of DePaul University, for example, testified about Genesis and creation-science at the trial:

> On recross, [he] listed again the six elements of the Genesis account relevant to the case: ex nihilo, the use of the phrase "all living kinds," fixity of species, separate ancestry, the Noachic flood, and recent creation.
>
> "Are these in Genesis?"
>
> "Yes."
>
> "Are they in Act 590?"
>
> "Yes."
>
> "Are there any other views of origins that contain these elements, or these elements together in this way?"
>
> "No, there are none."[25]

Because of such testimony, Judge Overton concluded that "[s]ection 4(a) is unquestionably a statement of religion, with the exception of 4(a)(2) which is a negative thrust aimed at what the creationists understand to be the theory of evolution," and accordingly ruled that the Act violated the Establishment Clause.[26]

Back in Louisiana, a second draft of Senator Keith's bill contained language and definitions similar to Arkansas' Section 4. On May 28, 1981, however—the day after the complaint in *McLean* was filed—the legislature deleted the Genesis-like language and instead adopted the Balanced Treatment for Creation–Science and Evolution–Science Act, which provided:

> [P]ublic schools within [the] state shall give balanced treatment to creation-science and to evolution-science. Balanced treatment of these two models shall be given in classroom lectures taken as a whole for each course, in textbook materials taken as a whole for each course, in library materials taken as a whole for the sciences

> and taken as a whole for the humanities, and in other educational programs in public schools, to the extent that such lectures, textbooks, library materials, or educational programs deal in any way with the subject of the origin of man, life, the earth, or the universe. When creation or evolution is taught, each shall be taught as a theory, rather than as proven scientific fact.
>
> "Balanced treatment" means "providing whatever information and instruction in both creation and evolution models the classroom teacher determines is necessary and appropriate to provide insight into both theories in view of the textbooks and other instructional materials available for use in his classroom."
>
> "Creation-science" is defined as "the scientific evidences for creation and inferences from those scientific evidences." "Evolution-science" means "the scientific evidences for evolution and inferences from those scientific evidences."[27]

Now, with *McLean* in the background and the Louisiana Act in place, Louisiana lawyers and judges had to make decisions about the constitutionality of their statute.

The Litigation

Both sides struck simultaneously. The American Civil Liberties Union (ACLU), which had been involved in the Arkansas litigation, decided to file a similar lawsuit in Louisiana. ACLU lawyer Jack Novik asked Andrew Weltchek, of the New Orleans law firm Bachmann, Weltchek & Powers, to participate, and Weltchek quickly made contacts around the state with teachers, ministers and rabbis, working to achieve a "broad representation among religious people," and eventually signing up forty or so named plaintiffs.[28] The lead plaintiff was public high school teacher Donald Aguillard, who is now Superintendent of St. Mary Parish Schools, and author of a Louisiana State University Ph.D. dissertation entitled "An Analysis of Factors Influencing the Teaching of Biological Evolution in Louisiana Public Secondary Schools." On the state's side, Attorney General William J. Guste, Sr., called Wendell Bird and asked to meet with him immediately. Bird, who was then working at a San Diego law firm and the Institute for Creation Research, flew to Baton Rouge, and Guste named Bird a special assistant attorney general for the case.[29]

When the plaintiffs held a press conference (to which Weltchek brought bananas) announcing that their lawsuit challenging the Act would be filed the next day in the Eastern District of Louisiana, in New Orleans, the state surprised them by beating them to court with a lawsuit of its own in the Middle District, in Baton Rouge, presumably a location more favorable to the state's interests.[30] The state asked for an unusual declaratory judgment that the Balanced Treatment Act was constitutional. In December 1982, however, Judge Polozola dismissed that lawsuit, ruling that because the federal question asserted would arise only as a defense to enforcement of the Act, the Court lacked federal-question jurisdiction over the lawsuit.[31]

The state's declaratory judgment case delayed the decision in the plaintiffs' case in the Eastern District, which was the Establishment Clause challenge to the Balanced Treatment Act. In that lawsuit, the lawyers confronted a legal question that remained central to the case to its conclusion in the United States Supreme Court, namely whether the district court should hold a trial about the Act, as had occurred in Little Rock in *McLean*, or whether the case could be dismissed on summary judgment. From start to finish, the parties disagreed whether the Balanced Treatment Act's definition of creation-science was unconstitutional as a matter of law or a question of fact that required expert testimony and a jury's decision about the nature of creation-science. That simple yet complex question formed the narrative of the constitutional story of creation-science (and its successors): is it religion or science, and can the courts distinguish one from the other?

While Novik took over the practical management of the case for the ACLU, the New York law firm of Paul, Weiss, Rifkind, Wharton & Garrison, with a team led by partner Jay Topkis, was brought in to do the "heavy lifting."[32] Paul, Weiss "had people in the air taking depositions" and provided an "astonishing commitment of resources" to the lawsuit.[33] Burt Neuborne, who was then an ACLU lawyer and is now a law professor at New York University, recalls that "this was a rare situation where we had more resources than the bad guys—we were essentially outgunning the defendants in the case."[34] According to Neuborne:

> I think the case was won in large part because we outlawyered them at the trial level. You don't theorize yourself into an answer about what's science. I think the actual factual creation of the record was what persuaded the judge. We could not have done it in-house; we didn't have the resources or the temperament to dig into the factual issues and into building the factual record the way a private firm would. ACLU lawyers think theory down and this was a fact-up case.[35]

The plaintiffs' lawyers fondly remember Novik—who died in 1988 at age 42—as a mensch, a passionate and dedicated lawyer, who was the lead organizer on the legal team, and, in that capacity, "was a brilliant technician moving all the various chess pieces around."[36]

On the state's side, Wendell Bird created his own factual record, collecting witnesses to explain what he had argued in his law review note, namely that creation-science was science, and that there were plenty of scientific experts available to explain that point to the court. Bird was critical of the Arkansas litigation, in which theologians and philosophers had testified, and insisted that the emphasis must always be on creation-*science*. Years later, Bird insisted that he was representing the mainstream views of the people of Louisiana, and was "not a fanatic trying to tilt at a windmill." Indeed, he says he "bristles" when he is called a "creationist attorney," because his commitment has always been to the fair presentation of the scientific evidence in an unbiased manner.[37]

Law or fact, summary judgment or trial? Paul, Weiss lawyer Allan Blumstein recalls that he became involved in the case when Topkis was called out of town on other business, and that his "strategy both as a private and pro bono lawyer was get rid of the thing the easiest way possible, and summary judgment was the way out here. My view of the statute was that it was unconstitutional on its face, and Jay was gone, and I convinced the lawyers at the ACLU that we ought to move for summary judgment. It was not the easiest thing for them to agree to—the problem was you might lose—of course, you might win too."[38] Topkis agreed with Blumstein that their "gravest concern was to avoid a trial. We felt we just had to win the motion for summary judgment," because there was a "great risk" and "tremendous danger" in a jury trial: it is "awfully difficult to reverse a jury verdict, so we felt we desperately had to avoid a jury."[39] Topkis thought that the Skadden Arps law firm, which had represented McLean in Arkansas, had faced a risk in going to the jury in Little Rock, and that his team faced a similar risk in New Orleans. What if the jury had looked into the eyes of the creationists and believed them; could such a verdict be reversed?[40]

Judge Duplantier granted the plaintiffs' motion for summary judgment with a ruling that "[w]hatever 'science' may be, 'creation,' as the term is used in the statute, involves religion, and the teaching of 'creation-science' and 'creationism,' as contemplated by the statute, involves teaching 'tailored to the principles' of a particular religious sect or group of sects," in violation of *Epperson*.[41] Any trial testimony "could not affect the outcome" because there was "no legitimate secular reason" for the Balanced Treatment Act.[42] Judge Duplantier later defended his decision, remembering "in my judgment there never was any fact question. I don't think it's a question of fact really, as to whether creation is about religion. Just on the face of the statute it was clear."[43] The district court judge's perspective was shared by a panel of Fifth Circuit judges, who upheld the grant of summary judgment in an opinion by Judge Jolly holding "this particular case is a simple one, subject to a simple disposal: the Act violates the establishment clause of the first amendment because the purpose of the statute is to promote a religious belief.''[44]

Both Judge Duplantier and Judge Jolly focused on the *purpose* of the statute because *Lemon v. Kurtzman*, the Supreme Court's leading precedent on the Establishment Clause and public schools, required that ''the statute must have a secular legislative purpose'' in order to withstand a First Amendment challenge.[45] Because the panel was unanimous that the Balanced Act was ''a law respecting a particular religious belief,''[46] it could not survive *Lemon*'s scrutiny.

The state lost its motion for a rehearing en banc in the Fifth Circuit by the close vote of 8–7,[47] setting up an appeal to the Supreme Court. Topkis was grateful to get out of the Fifth Circuit alive, anticipating that his case faced a better audience in the Supreme Court.[48] Although he assigned the brief to associate Jerry Harper because of Harper's graceful writing style, he kept the oral argument for himself at the client's request.[49] Harper explained that he directed the brief's argument toward Justices Lewis Powell and Sandra Day O'Connor at the center of the Court, not at either Justice William Brennan (if he didn't have Brennan's vote, he didn't have any votes!) or Antonin Scalia (whose support was unexpected). He also did everything he could to let the Justices hear the voices of the legislators.[50] Both Harper and Topkis recalled Topkis' major contribution to the brief; in the ''finest word edit'' that Harper had ever seen, Harper's question whether the scientific evidence would show that man had walked hand-in-hand with animals was changed to ''hand-in-paw.''[51] After Justice Scalia asked him about Aristotle during the oral argument, Topkis was ''glad that he had taken a course in the humanities at Columbia College'' so that he ''was able to counter with St. Thomas and whoever else.''[52] Meanwhile, Bird hammered away at the same scientific point in his brief and in the oral argument. Attached to the brief were five affidavits from experts explaining the scientific evidence for creation.[53] At oral argument, Bird again insisted on the need for a trial that would include such evidence, arguing that the district and appeals courts were incorrect when they ''said, effectively by judicial notice we submit, creation science means X. It means religious doctrine including a creator. Not based on any factual evidence in the record, but just a priori.''[54]

In a 7–2 decision, with an opinion written by Justice William Brennan (joined by Justices Marshall, Blackmun, Powell, Stevens, O'Connor, and White), the Court agreed that summary judgment was appropriate because the Act failed the secular purpose test.[55] According to Justice Brennan, because a ''court's finding of improper purpose behind a statute is appropriately determined by the statute on its face, its legislative history, or its interpretation by a responsible administrative agency,'' a trial was unnecessary.[56] Post-enactment testimony about the meaning of creation-science by expert witnesses would not illuminate the actions of the Louisiana legislature in passing the bill. The majority concluded that the legislature's purpose in passing the Act was clear and not secular:

> In this case, the purpose of the Creationism Act was to restructure the science curriculum to conform with a particular religious viewpoint. Out of many possible science subjects taught in the public schools, the legislature chose to affect the teaching of the one scientific theory that historically has been opposed by certain religious sects. As in *Epperson*, the legislature passed the Act to give preference to those religious groups which have as one of their tenets the creation of humankind by a divine creator. The "overriding fact" that confronted the Court in *Epperson* was "that Arkansas' law selects from the body of knowledge a particular segment which it proscribes for the sole reason that it is deemed to conflict with ... a particular interpretation of the Book of Genesis by a particular religious group." [citations omitted] Similarly, the Creationism Act is designed *either* to promote the theory of creation science which embodies a particular religious tenet by requiring that creation science be taught whenever evolution is taught *or* to prohibit the teaching of a scientific theory disfavored by certain religious sects by forbidding the teaching of evolution when creation science is not also taught. The Establishment Clause, however, "forbids *alike* the preference of a religious doctrine *or* the prohibition of theory which is deemed antagonistic to a particular dogma." [citations omitted] Because the primary purpose of the Creationism Act is to advance a particular religious belief, the Act endorses religion in violation of the First Amendment.[57]

Justice Antonin Scalia, who had questioned Jay Topkis so vigorously at the oral argument, was joined by Chief Justice William Rehnquist in dissent. Justice Scalia accepted the state's argument that promoting the academic freedom of students was a legitimate secular purpose and accepted the findings of the legislature that there were two scientific theories with educational value for students.[58]

Edwards v. Aguillard is frequently cited both for its use of the secular purpose test to invalidate state legislation and for Justice Scalia's criticism of that standard and its application. *Aguillard* also raised particular questions about the application of the secular purpose test, namely whether judges should consider the statutory language only or if they appropriately focused on legislative history and the secular or religious commitments of individual legislators. Although such issues are significant for Establishment Clause jurisprudence, for the story of creation-science the recurring question is not about secular purpose, but on what is religious and what is scientific education.

The Story Continues

Although *Aguillard* closed the classroom door on creation-science, it left an open window for alternative theories to evolution with a sentence that said "teaching a variety of scientific theories about the origins of humankind to schoolchildren might be validly done with the clear secular intent of enhancing the effectiveness of science instruction."[59] Before creation-science developed, John Scopes had warned that " '[t]he fight will go on with other actors and other plays,' "[60] and, more recently and colloquially, Aguillard's attorney Andrew Weltchek observed "you can drive a stake through the heart of these people and they just keep coming and coming."[61] Post-*Aguillard*, the new actor, and the most recent challenger of Darwinian evolution, is Intelligent Design (ID), whose "main thrust ... is that intelligent agency, as an aspect of scientific theory-making, has more explanatory power in accounting for the specified, and sometimes irreducible, complexity of some physical systems, including biological entities, and/or the existence of the universe as a whole, than the blind forces of unguided and everlasting matter."[62] According to Professor Francis Beckwith,

> Although the *Edwards* Court sounded the death-knell for creationism as part of the science curriculum in public schools, it neither prohibited public schools from teaching alternatives to evolution, nor prevented schools from offering to their students theories that may be consistent with, and lend support to, a religious perspective. Both of these qualifications, combined with other factors, suggest that ID may be offered as part of a public school science curriculum or voluntarily by a teacher without violating the Establishment Clause, for, as we shall see, ID is an alternative to evolution that is consistent with, and lends support to, a number of philosophical and religious points of view. Unlike creationism, however, ID is not derived from a particular religion's special revelation, but is the result of arguments whose premises include empirical evidence, well-founded conceptual notions outside of the natural sciences, and conclusions that are supported by these premises.[63]

After a Dover, Pennsylvania school district passed a policy requiring students to hear a statement about intelligent design [ID] as an alternative to Darwin's theory of evolution, however, a federal judge ruled that the policy violated the Establishment Clause because ID is not science, but religion.[64] Like Judge Overton in Little Rock, and unlike Judge Duplantier in New Orleans, Judge Jones heard extensive testimony about the First Amendment challenge to the school's policy. He then concluded that ID "is nothing less than the progeny of creationism" or "creationism re-labeled."[65] Indeed, Judge Jones' words suggest that ID is the child of *Edwards v. Aguillard*: "The weight of the evidence clearly demonstrates, as noted, that the systemic change from 'creation' to 'intelligent design' occurred sometime in 1987, *after* the Supreme Court's important *Edwards* decision. This compelling evidence strongly supports Plaintiffs' assertion that ID is creationism re-labeled.''[66]

ID's critics had argued that, just as creation-science is religious because it implies a Creator, intelligent design is religious because it requires a Designer. Perhaps ID's supporters should heed the words of Wendell Bird, who acknowledged that although he used the creation-science label "because it was the language of the time," he is "not fully comfortable with the ID language, and would opt for something that was more secular," or scientific.[67] Secular language is more likely to fulfill a secular purpose.

The Story of Religion or Science?

Today we can reconsider the core dispute of *Edwards v. Aguillard*—how does a court determine if creation-science is religion or science?—through the perspectives of the case's advocates. For the ACLU and the Paul, Weiss attorneys, creation-science was by definition religious, and therefore any creation-science statute violated the Establishment Clause as a matter of law. According to Jerry Harper, for example,

> [t]here was nothing for trial. This was a law that said you had to assemble facts and inference in support of something then called creation-science and now called intelligent design. The question was whether or not on its face the statute directed the teaching of a religious belief in a classroom to the exclusion of a scientific theory. What was Wendell Bird going to prove at the trial, that God created the world, or there were facts that can be cited by scientists, or that there are facts that you could cite that question the theory of evolution? I'll concede that. What is it that you're going to try? Try that there are facts and evidence and experts who are prepared to say that the world was created as described in Genesis? Where does that get you as a legal matter? What is the outcome of that trial?[68]

"What was Wendell Bird going to prove at the trial?" Bird had the following answer to that question:

> It was very important to have a chance to go to trial and we felt very cheated that they wouldn't look into the evidence. We had lots of expert witnesses. In Arkansas several witnesses brought by the state were theologians, which didn't strike me as right way to handle the case and the scientists had published in creationist publications with religious views, which set them up for being cross-examined as to whether it was science.
>
> That religion would not be taught was part of the statute's express terminology. It is troubling that we didn't have our day in court. Were we to have an open-minded judge his decision would have said,

> religious views may not be taught as the statute says, scientific evidence may be taught. Was the statute Genesis in disguise? No, our exhibits and witnesses were about systematic gaps in the fossil records [and other scientific facts that contradict evolution] ... Scientific facts are not religious.[69]

Burt Neuborne disagreed: "The factual record was important for showing that [creation-science] was religious and for showing consensus on that point within the scientific community."[70]

Recent writers have provided an alternative argument that suggests that the defenders of the Balanced Act had it backwards. Perhaps evolution has become a religion whose classroom presence should be challenged under the Establishment Clause. According to University of California at Berkeley law professor Phillip E. Johnson, author of *Darwin on Trial*, and one of the leaders of the ID movement, evolution is another religion with its own myth of creation:

> The continual efforts to base a religion or ethical system upon evolution are not an aberration, and practically all the most prominent Darwinist writers have tried their hand at it. Darwinist evolution is an imaginative story about who we are and where we came from, which is to say it is a creation myth. As such it is an obvious starting point for speculation about how we ought to live and what we ought to value. A creationist appropriately starts with God's creation and God's will for man. A scientific naturalist just as appropriately starts with evolution and with man as a product of nature.
>
> In its mythological dimension, Darwinism is the story of humanity's liberation from the delusion that its destiny is controlled by a power higher than itself. Lacking scientific knowledge, humans at first attribute natural events like weather and disease to supernatural beings. As they learn to predict or control natural forces they put aside the lesser spirits, but a more highly evolved religion retains the notion of a rational Creator who rules the universe.
>
> At last the greatest scientific discovery of all is made, and modern humans learn that they are the products of a blind natural process that has no goal and cares nothing for them.[71]

Professor Johnson has also argued that the appropriate contrast is between creationism and naturalism, not between creationism and evolution. Evolution is naturalistic because it "involves no intervention or guidance by a creator outside the world of nature."[72] Although evolutionists believe that they are scientists who exclude creationist arguments because creationist arguments are not scientific, Johnson insists that naturalism is not a science, but a philosophical presupposition that "there is nothing outside of nature."[73] Thus creationism and naturalism are two competing philosophies of life, not one religion and one science.[74] On that account, both subjects—or neither—could be taught without violating the First Amendment.

In response, philosopher Robert Pennock has argued that Johnson confuses two types of naturalism, namely ontological naturalism (ON) and methodological naturalism (MN).[75] ON makes claims about what sorts of being do and do not exist, while MN is merely a method of inquiry. According to Pennock, Johnson pretends that evolution is ON, but it is MN.[76] If Pennock is correct, then courts may continue to distinguish evolution from creation-science and intelligent design.

So far the courts have rejected the argument that evolution is a religion, but that legal conclusion does not mark an end to my story.[77] Like Genesis, *Edwards v. Aguillard* was only the beginning of a bigger book, offering a first chapter about creation-science. Chapter Two, about intelligent design, is still being written, and there may be future chapters on naturalism, ON or MN. After all, anyone who has read the Book of Genesis knows that creation(-science) is only the beginning of the story!

Endnotes

1. I am grateful to Josh Thomas, Mon Yin Lung and Lesliediana Jones for excellent research assistance with this project.

2. John Collins, *Introduction to the Hebrew Bible* 11 (2004).

3. Genesis 1:1–2:4a; Genesis 2–3. The authors' names are based on the words they used to refer to God.

4. Genesis 1:27 (by the Priestly author).

5. Genesis 2:7 (by the Yahwist author).

6. Adele Berlin & Marac Zvi Brettler, eds., *The Jewish Study Bible* 15 n. 2.4–25 (2004).

7. Collins, *supra* note 2, at 30–37.

8. *Id.* at 31.

9. 482 U.S. 578 (1987).

10. Eugenie C. Scott, *Evolution vs. Creationism: An Introduction* 24–25 (2004).

11. Edward J. Larson, *Evolution: The Remarkable History of a Scientific Theory* 88–89 (2004).

12. *See* Kitzmiller v. Dover Area Sch. Dist., 400 F.Supp.2d 707 (M.D. Pa. 2005) (concluding that ID is the progeny of creationism and therefore unconstitutional).

13. Edward J. Larson, *Trial and Error: The American Controversy Over Creation and Evolution* (3d ed. 2003).

14. Scopes v. Tennessee, 289 S.W. 363 (Tenn. 1927).

15. 393 U.S. 97 (1968).

16. *Id.* at 107.

17. Note, *Freedom of Religion and Science Instruction in Public Schools*, 87 Yale L.J. 515 (1977–1978).

18. *Id.* at 550.

19. *Id.* at 553–554 (emphasis added).

20. *Id.* at 554–555, nn. 190–198.

21. Author's Interview of Wendell Bird, September 29, 2006.

22. *Aguillard*, 482 U.S. at 600 (1987) (Powell, J., concurring).

23. *Id.*

24. *See* Ark.Stat.Ann. § 80–1663, et seq. (1981 Supp.), invalidated by McLean v. Arkansas Bd. of Educ., 529 F.Supp. 1255 (E.D. Ark. 1982).

25. *See* Langdon Gilkey, *Creationism on Trial: Evolution and God at Little Rock* 87 (1985).

26. McLean v. Arkansas Bd. of Educ., 529 F.Supp. 1255 (E.D. Ark. 1982). *See also id.* at 1266 ("The idea of sudden creation from nothing, or *creatio ex nihilo*, is an inherently religious concept.").

27. La.Rev.Stat.Ann. § 17:286.1 *et seq.* (West 1982), cited in *Aguillard*, 482 U.S. at 598 (Powell, J., concurring).

28. Author's Interview of Andrew Weltchek, October 2, 2006.

29. Author's Interview of Wendell Bird, September 29, 2006.

30. Author's Interview of Andrew Weltchek, October 2, 2006.

31. Keith v. Louisiana Dep't. of Educ., 553 F.Supp. 295 (M.D. La. 1982).

32. Author's Interview of Burt Neuborne, September 20, 2006.

33. *Id.*

34. *Id.*

35. *Id.*

36. Author's Interview of Charles Sims and Elizabeth McNamara, September 25, 2006; *see also* Author's Interview of Jay Topkis, September 13, 2006 and Author's Interview of Andrew Weltchek, October 2, 2006.

37. Author's Interview of Wendell Bird, September 29, 2006.

38. Author's Interview of Allan Blumstein, September 27, 2006.

39. Author's Interview of Jay Topkis, September 13, 2006.

40. *Id.*

41. Aguillard v. Treen, 634 F.Supp. 426, 427 (E.D. La. 1985).

42. *Id.* at 427, 428.

43. Author's Interview of Judge Duplantier.

44. Aguillard v. Edwards, 765 F.2d 1251, 1253 (5th Cir. 1985).

45. Lemon v. Kurtzman, 403 U.S. 602, 612 (1971).

46. *Aguillard*, 765 F.2d at 1257.

47. Aguillard v. Edwards, 778 F.2d 225 (5th Cir. 1985).

48. Author's Interview of Jay Topkis, September 13, 2006.

49. *Id.*

50. Author's Interview of Jerry Harper, November 3, 2006.

51. *Id.* Author's Interview of Jay Topkis, September 13, 2006.

52. Author's Interview of Jay Topkis, September 13, 2006.

53. Brief of Appellants in the Supreme Court of the United States at A-7-A-40, Edwards v. Aguillard, 482 U.S. 578 (1987) (No. 85-1513).

54. Oral Argument, Edwards v. Aguillard, 482 U.S. 578 (1987) (No. 85-1513), 1986 U.S. TRANS LEXIS 9.

55. *Aguillard*, 482 U.S. at 600.

56. *Id.* at 594.

57. *Id.* at 593.

58. *Id.* at 626.

59. *Id.* at 594.

60. Peter Irons, *The Courage of Their Convictions: Sixteen Americans Who Fought Their Way to the Supreme Court* 215 (1990).

61. Author's Interview of Andrew Weltchek, October 2, 2006.

62. Francis Beckwith, *Public Education, Religious Establishment, and the Challenge of Intelligent Design*, 17 Notre Dame J. L. Ethics & Pub. Pol'y 461, 462 (2003).

63. Francis J. Beckwith, *Science and Religion Twenty Years after* McLean v. Arkansas*: Evolution, Public Education, and the New Challenge of Intelligent Design*, 26 Harv. J.L. & Pub. Pol'y 456 (2003).

64. Kitzmiller v. Dover Area Sch. Dist., 400 F.Supp.2d 707, 735 (M.D. Pa. 2005).

65. *Id.* at 722.

66. *Id.* at 722.

67. Author's Interview of Wendell Bird, September 29, 2006.

68. Author's Interview of Jerry Harper, November 3, 2006. *See also* Author's Interview of Burt Neuborne, September 20, 2006. ("I would have been shocked if we lost. I thought the issue was rather clear, once you fleshed out the facts, clear because both the doctrines of secular purpose or notions of what counted as religion, what counted as science, what the culture reviewed were categories that had some meaning.").

69. Author's Interview of Wendell Bird, September 29, 2006.

70. Author's Interview of Burt Neuborne, September 20, 2006.

71. Phillip Johnson, *Darwin on Trial* 133 (2d ed. 1993).

72. *Id.* at 64.

73. *See* Phillip E. Johnson, *Evolution as Dogma: The Establishment of Naturalism* in Intelligent Design Creationism and Its Critics: Philosophical, Theological, and Scientific Perspectives 66 (Robert T. Pennock, ed., 2001).

74. *See id.*

75. See Robert T. Pennock, *Naturalism, Evidence, and Creationism: The Case of Phillip Johnson*, in Intelligent Design Creationism and Its Critics: Philosophical, Theological, and Scientific Perspectives, *supra* note 73, at 77–97.

76. *Id.*

77. *See, e.g.*, Peloza v. Capistrano Unified Sch. Dist., 37 F.3d 517 (9th Cir. 1994) (concluding that evolution is not a religion, and rejecting the claim that the district established religion by requiring that evolution be taught).

12

The Story of *Santa Fe Independent School District v. Doe*: God and Football in Texas

Erwin Chemerinsky[1]

There is a deep divide in American society between those who believe that prayers are an essential part of school events and those who think that prayers have no place in public schools. This divide, of course, is not new. In 1962, in *Engel v. Vitale*,[2] the Supreme Court first declared prayer in public schools to be unconstitutional. The decision was immediately controversial and helped to fuel calls to impeach Chief Justice Earl Warren. Many schools simply ignored the Supreme Court's decisions banning prayer in schools and continued their long-standing practices.

In the 1990s, the battle lines were clearly drawn. On the one side, were those who believed that banning prayers violated the free speech and free exercise rights of students who wanted to pray. They saw no limit in the Establishment Clause on such religious observances at public school events. On the other side, were those, such as the American Civil Liberties Union, who were deeply committed to enforcing a wall separating church and state and to ensuring that prayer was kept out of public schools. Indeed, these opposing positions illustrate a classic constitutional conflict between the rights of the majority that want prayer as a part of schools and the rights of the minority that find such religious activities inherently coercive and an establishment of religion.

It was not surprising then that a major case about this arose in a small town in Texas and the context was football games. Some have observed that high school football seems itself to be a religion in many places in Texas.[3] Santa Fe, Texas fought all the way to the Supreme Court to protect the right of students to lead prayers at football games. The Supreme Court's rejection of such prayers, by a 6–3 decision, is an important reaffirmation of important First Amendment principles.[4] The story of the case reflects key aspects of the seemingly unbridgeable chasm over the role of religion in American public life and how this issue is being litigated.

The Place

Santa Fe Independent School District is located in the southern part of Texas. It has more than 4,000 students who attend two primary schools, one intermediate school, one junior high school, and one high school.[5] The town was incorporated in the late 1970s as a merger of the dairy towns of Arcadia, Algoa, and Alta Loma.[6] It is located on Texas Highway 6, along the Santa Fe railroad line and was named for it.[7] It is a mostly working class community and has many residents who work at nearby refineries and petrochemical plants.

Santa Fe is virtually all-white, with a few Latinos, but virtually no African–Americans.[8] It had only nine black residents in the 1990 census.[9] It is a town with a long history of racial tensions. It received some national attention in 1981 when the Klan held a rally there to protest Vietnamese shrimp fishers in the area.[10] In 1997, several local teenagers terrorized a busload of African American girls who were junior high school students who had come to Santa Fe for a basketball game.[11] The teenagers rocked the bus back and forth, yelled racial epithets, and brandished a piece of rope while making threats of hanging the girls.[12]

The emphasis on religion, and specifically on Christian religion, is quite apparent in the town. On the way into town, one sees billboards like, "Abortion Stops a Beating Heart" and "Pray Without Ceasing."[13] It is a town where churches outnumber restaurants.[14] As long as anyone can remember, prayers were a part of the schools in Santa Fe.

Bibles were regularly distributed in the public schools and students who did not take them faced ridicule.[15] Although it was contrary to official school policy to distribute religious material, for many years the school district had allowed Gideons International to hand out New Testament Bibles on school property.[16] In 1994, some parents complained about the practice and the school district ordered that the Bible distribution end. School Superintendent Richard Ownby, who had been in his position for 18 months, declared: "I'm told that they've been handing out Bibles here for years and years.... They passed them out at the intermediate school earlier in the year, and I don't recall getting a single call."[17]

The Litigation Begins

The decision by the plaintiffs to challenge prayers in the Santa Fe Independent School District stemmed from incidents that occurred in the years before the lawsuit was filed in 1995. In April, 1993, the plaintiff who came to be identified as Jane Doe II was in seventh grade at the public middle school. In her seventh grade Texas History class, her teacher, David Wilson, handed out fliers advertising a Baptist religious revival.[18] She asked her teacher if non-Baptists were invited to attend. Wilson then asked about her religious affiliation. When she said that "she was an adherent of the Church of Jesus Christ of Latter Day Saints (Mormon), Wilson launched into a diatribe about the non-Christian, cult-like nature of Mormonism, and its general evils."[19] Doe's mother complained to the school district and the teacher was reprimanded.

For many years, overtly Christian prayers were a part of graduations and football games. Prior to 1992, Santa Fe regularly had a clergy member deliver a prayer at its public school graduations. In that year, the Supreme Court, in *Lee v. Weisman*,[20] held that clergy delivered prayers at public school graduations violated the Establishment Clause of the First Amendment. Santa Fe then shifted to having students delivering the prayers. Not long after *Lee v. Weisman*, the United States Court of Appeals for the Fifth Circuit, which includes Texas, ruled that it did not violate the Establishment Clause for students to deliver nonsectarian, non-proselytizing invocations and benedictions for the purpose of solemnizing their graduation ceremonies.[21]

At Santa Fe High School, prayers were presented by students as "invocations" or "benedictions" at these events, and they usually were given by officers of the student council.[22] As the Fifth Circuit noted, the school district "maintained complete control over the programs and facilities during the reading of the prayers, including the ability to mute the microphone or remove the speaker. Furthermore, the text of the graduation invocations and benedictions was screened by [the school district] for content prior to the ceremony."[23]

The prayers were clearly and unequivocally sectarian. For example, the 1994 graduation benediction was: "Our most gracious heavenly Father: We thank you for bringing us to this, our graduation. We ask you to be with us as we start a new beginning to our lives. Father: We express our gratitude to all that have helped us over the past three years. Especially do we thank our parents, teachers, and friends who encouraged us, counseled us, and always extended a helping hand when needed. Please see us safely through this night and the tomorrows of our lives. In Jesus's name, Amen."[24]

In addition to the invocation and benediction, other student prayers were common at these events. For instance, the salutory speech in 1994 was unabashedly religious: "There is only one thing which we as Christians can truly rely [on]: the faithfulness and strength of a loving God. It is now that each of us must stand on a solid rock of Jesus Christ, stand up for those things on which we believe. Even if it is alone that we must stand. We, having done all, must continue to stand in faith remembering that Christ would have suffered and died for only one of us. So we begin the journey of life, not a life of mediocrity and compromise, but the possible life which Christ has promised, a life of abundance and joy, being confident of this very thing, that he who has begun a good work in you will complete it until the day of Jesus Christ. Thank You."[25]

In April, 1995, a lawsuit was filed in the United States District Court for the Southern District of Texas challenging the prayers at graduation and at school football games in Santa Fe. The plaintiffs asked to be listed as "Does" because of their concern over harassment and even violence.[26] In fact, despite the district court's order allowing the plaintiffs to proceed anonymously, those affiliated with the school district repeatedly tried to find out the plaintiffs' identities. This prompted the district court to issue an order threatening the "THE HARSHEST POSSIBLE CONTEMPT SANCTIONS" and/or "CRIMINAL LIABILITY" if they did not cease their investigations to learn the Does' identities.[27]

In May 1995, with graduation approaching, United States District Court Judge Samuel B. Kent issued a temporary restraining order. The district court said that "student-selected, student-given, nonsectarian, non-proselytizing invocations and benedictions would be permitted, and that such invocations and benedictions could take the form of a 'nondenominational prayer.' "[28] The court said that the school district could not be involved in choosing the students or in approving the content of the prayers. The court also tried to clarify what was permitted and what was not; the court explained that "generic prayers to the 'Almighty', or to 'God', or to 'Our Heavenly Father (or Mother)', or the like, will of course be permitted. Reference to any particular deity, by name, such as Mohammed, Jesus, Buddha, or the like, will likewise be permitted, as long as the general thrust of the prayer is non-proselytizing, as required by [*Clear Creek II*]."[29] The district court said that it would require the school district to clarify its policies by either banning all prayers or by establishing guidelines to allow non-sectarian and non-proselytizing prayer at school functions.

The school adopted a policy for its 1995 graduation to comply with the district court's order and the Fifth Circuit's ruling in *Clear Creek* allowing non-sectarian prayers at public school graduations. The School Board announced that it would permit the graduating senior class to vote by secret ballot as to whether an invocation and benediction should be a part of the graduation ceremony. If the students voted in favor of having a prayer, the class would then elect the student to do this from a list of students who had volunteered to be candidates.

The School Board Changes Its Policy

Following graduation, in July 1995, the School Board revised its policies concerning graduations. It followed the model that it had created for the spring 1995 graduation: students would decide by secret ballot whether to have invocations and benedictions and, if they voted in favor of them, there they would be an election to choose the student to present them. The policy had no limit on the content of the prayers. However, the policy had a provision that provided that:

> "If the District is enjoined by court order from the enforcement of this policy, then and only then will the following policy automatically become the applicable policy of the school district.... If so chosen, the class shall elect by secret ballot, from a list of student volunteers, students to deliver nonsectarian, nonproselytizing invocations and benedictions for the purpose of solemnizing their graduation ceremonies."[30]

In other words, the School Board would limit students to "nonsectarian, non-proselytizing invocations and benedictions" only if ordered by the court. The School Board did this despite the Fifth Circuit decision in *Clear Creek* that clearly held that such prayers had to be nonsectarian and nonproselytizing.[31] The Superintendent of the Santa Fe schools, Richard Ownby, declared at the time: "We don't tell them how to pray and we don't review the prayer. They just get up and pray. Our policy is to allow unrestricted prayer. By that I mean, it's not restricted to non-proselytizing, nonsectarian language."[32]

In October, 1995, the School Board adopted its first formal policy concerning prayers at football games. It followed the same model as it had chosen for graduations. As the Fifth Circuit noted, "[i]ts provisions were essentially identical to those of the July Policy on graduations."[33] The School Board policy provided for students to choose whether to have a prayer at football games and if they decided in favor of it, to elect a student to present it. The School Board policy also said that only if a court so ordered would the student be limited to a nonsectarian, non-proselytizing prayer.[34]

The School Board decided to proceed in this way so as to present this as a free speech issue: students were deciding what to say and who to say it. For the school to interfere would violate the free speech rights of the students. Kelly Frels, a Houston lawyer who was representing the School Board was instrumental in devising the policy and he declared at the time: "The policy represents the desire of the Santa Fe Independent School District board for a relationship between religion and public schools. We feel that what we have put together fits within the context of where the Constitution will allow the district to be. It says that once the school steps back and says that students may choose whether to have prayer, the question is 'Should the school then restrict what the students say? It's a free speech issue.' "[35]

The School District and its lawyers, from the inception of the policy, sought to recharacterize the issue as being about the free speech rights of students. Recent Supreme Court decisions had provided some basis for believing that this might succeed. In a series of cases, the Supreme Court had found that excluding religious speech was a violation of the First Amendment. For instance, in *Widmar v. Vincent*,[36] the Supreme Court declared unconstitutional a state university's policy of preventing student groups from using school facilities for religious worship or religious discussion. The Court stressed that this was an impermissible restriction on the expression of students to use a forum available for speech. Likewise, in *Lamb's Chapel v. Center Moriches Union School District*,[37] the Court declared unconstitutional a school district's policy of excluding religious groups from using school facilities during evenings and weekends. Again, the Court stressed that this discrimination against religious expression infringed freedom of speech under the First Amendment.

In June, 1995, just weeks before the Santa Fe School Board formulated its new policy, the Court once more ruled in favor of religious speech and against an Establishment Clause claim. In *Rosenberger v. Rector and Visitors of the University of Virginia*,[38] the Court declared unconstitutional a state university's refusal to give student activity funds to a Christian group that published an expressly religious magazine. The Court emphasized that the university violated freedom of speech by refusing to subsidize religious speech while paying for secular speech.

The Santa Fe School Board sought to similarly present their situation to the courts as a matter of free speech of students. Under the policy, it was for the students to decide whether to have an invocation and a benediction, who would deliver it, and what its content would be. The School Board put itself in the position of saying that if it tried to stop this it would be impermissibly restricting the speech rights of students.

The Decisions

The School District moved for summary judgment. The District Court, however, denied this motion and *sua sponte* granted summary judgment in favor of the plaintiffs who were challenging the policy. The court concluded that there was impermissible coercion, endorsement, and purposeful advancement of religion by the School District. The court said that the School District could be fairly said to have had "de facto policies" favoring the incidents because they "occurred amidst the

School District's repeated tolerance of similar activities and oftentimes with [its] awareness and explicit approval.''[39]

The court found that the policy as to graduations and football games allowing any prayer at the students choice violated the Fifth Circuit's command that prayers must be non-proselytizing and non-sectarian. The court said that the solution was to require that the School District follow the fall back provision contained within its graduation and football policies: students would be limited to a nonsectarian, non-proselytizing prayer. The district court concluded that it did not need to issue an injunction against the School District since it was simply ordering it to follow its own written policy, albeit its fall back policy.

In December 1996, the district court held a two-day trial on the issue of damages. The court ruled against the plaintiffs and denied them any damages or attorneys' fees. The court stressed that the plaintiffs could not prove that the School District was responsible for the violations of the First Amendment and under well-established law, a local government can be held liable only for its own policies or customs that violate the Constitution.[40]

Both the Does and the School District appealed. In a 2–1 decision, the Fifth Circuit ruled in favor of the Does and found that the School District policy violated the Establishment Clause of the First Amendment. The court rejected the School District's argument that allowing sectarian, proselytizing prayers was justified by the secular purpose of solemnizing the graduation and football ceremonies. In fact, the Fifth Circuit used strong language in rejecting this argument by the School District: ''Here we simply cannot fathom how permitting students to deliver sectarian and proselytizing prayers can possibly be interpreted as furthering a solemnizing effect. Such prayers would alter dramatically the tenor of the ceremony, shifting its focus—at least temporarily—away from the students and the secular purpose of the graduation ceremony to the religious content of the speaker's prayers. . . . In short, rather than solemnize a graduation, sectarian and proselytizing prayers would transform the character of the ceremony and conceivably even disrupt it.''[41]

The court concluded that the school's policy clearly had the effect of advancing religion. The court expressly rejected the School District's argument that the students' choice through election made the prayers permissible. The court stated: ''Indeed, if subjecting a prayer policy to a student vote were alone sufficient to ensure the policy's constitutionality, what would keep students from selecting a formal religious representative, such as the rabbi in *Lee*, to present a graduation prayer? Indeed, to take the argument one step further, there would be no reason to deny the students the authority to designate a formal religious representative to deliver a full-fledged, fire-and-brimstone, Bible- or Koran-quoting, sectarian sermonette (in the dress for a prolonged invocation or benediction) at graduation; for, by putting the ultimate choice to the students, the sermonette would not facially bear the government's imprimatur."[42]

The court reaffirmed its earlier decision in *Clear Creek*: prayers would be allowed at graduation so long as they were non-proselytizing and nonsectarian. Having done so, the court then analyzed the School District's policy as to football games. The Fifth Circuit concluded that even the fall back policy of allowing nonsectarian, non-proselytizing prayers violated the Establishment Clause in the context of high school football games. The court distinguished the "singular context and singularly serious nature of a graduation ceremony" from that of a football game.[43]

The Fifth Circuit affirmed the district court's conclusion that no money damages were appropriate, but reversed on the issue of attorneys' fees. The court concluded that the plaintiffs had substantially prevailed and were entitled to an award of fees.

Judge Jolly wrote a strong dissent. He began by lamenting: "Today, for the first time in our court's history, the majority expressly exerts control over the content of its citizens' prayers. And it does so notwithstanding that the Supreme Court has never required, suggested, hinted, or implied that the Constitution controls the content of citizens' prayers in any context."[44]

Judge Jolly accepted the School District's argument that restricting student prayers, while allowing secular student speech, was an infringement of expression protected by the First Amendment. He wrote: "When the government restricts sectarian and proselytizing religious speech, while embracing ecumenical religious speech, the government has engaged in illegitimate, viewpoint discrimination. That is why the Free Speech Clause is violated when the majority forces a nonsectarian, nonproselytizing requirement upon the speakers."[45] In other words, for Judge Jolly, limiting students to nonsectarian, non-proselytizing prayers was an impermissible content-based restriction on speech. He saw no prohibition in the Establishment Clause on prayers of any sort so long as they were the students' choice. He stressed that the School Board's policy was a permissible, neutral accommodation of religion.

Judge Jolly also expressly disagreed with the majority's holding that any prayers, even nonsectarian and non-proselytizing prayers, were impermissible at football games. He declared: "Of course, football games do not possess the solemnity of a graduation ceremony. But that fact has all the relevance to our First Amendment discussion today as the fact that a hog was slaughtered to make SFISD's football."[46] He accepted that there are good reasons for prayers at public school football games: "At sporting events, messages and/or invocations can promote, among other things, honest and fair play, clean competition, individual challenge to be one's best, importance of team work, and many more goals that the majority could conceive would it only pause to do so."[47]

The School District petitioned for rehearing en banc before the entire Fifth Circuit. The court denied this motion on April 7, 1999, but seven judges—unquestionably the more conservative judges on the Fifth Circuit—dissented and would have had the court hear the case en banc.[48] Judge Jolly wrote a dissent to the denial of en banc review, which was joined by the other dissenters, and which declared: "Every judge on this court must surely know that the policy announced by the majority of the panel—permitting students' ecumenical religious prayers or speech, but excluding all other religious prayers or speech by students—is unconstitutional."[49] He objected to the failure to grant en banc review and to clarify this muddled area of the law. He said: "When judges can pick and choose without the constraints imposed by precedent, the public is left stranded, vulnerable to liability, helplessly dependent on the panel it draws. We could fulfill our constitutional and professional duty to the public, vote this case en banc, and be of a single voice."[50]

The Exclusion of Prayer Gets Challenged

After the Fifth Circuit's decision, and as petitions for Supreme Court review were being prepared and pending, another lawsuit was filed by a student who wanted prayer at football games. In the spring of 1999, the students at Santa Fe High School voted to have a pre-game "message."[51] The students held a subsequent election and chose Stephanie Vega to deliver the message; Marian Ward finished second in the balloting. In August, with the football season approaching, Superintendent Ownby was asked what would happen if Vega delivered a prayer. Ownby said that the student would be punished "as if she had cursed."[52] This received a great deal of media attention and Vega resigned from being the student to deliver the message.

Ward took over the responsibility for doing this and heard rumors that she would be punished if she prayed, with possible punishments ranging from detention to expulsion to prison.[53] As a result, Ward's parents called an attorney, Kelly Coghlan. On September 2, 1999, he filed a suit in federal district court in Galveston, Texas and sought a temporary restraining order permitting Ward's ability to pray.[54] The football game was scheduled for September 3. Coghlan said that he saw this as a free speech issue and that "the ACLU should have been on my side."[55]

On Friday, September 3, Marian Ward was already in her band uniform ready to go to the game when she got word of the judge's decision. The district court judge assigned the case, Sim Lake, was obviously very sympathetic to her claim. At the hearing, Judge Lake asked Ward's lawyer to draft the order.[56] The School District told the judge that it agreed with Ward, but felt constrained by the Fifth Circuit's decision. Judge Lake obviously did not feel similarly constrained. Judge Lake's order, in part, stated: "If a student may select nonreligious solemnization, then neutrality requires that a student may also select a religious solemnization without government interference."[57] This, of course, directly contravened the Fifth Circuit's opinion that rejected any form of prayers at football games in Santa Fe. Judge Lake said that the school's guidelines favor "atheism over religion" and amounted to a "state-sponsored atheism."[58]

At the football game on September 3, Marian Ward received a loud ovation when she was introduced as a member of the band.[59] She was introduced by a speaker declaring over the loudspeaker: "Ladies and gentlemen, Marian Ward, a Santa Fe High School student, has been selected by her peers to deliver a message of her own choice. The Santa Fe Independent School District does not require, suggest, or endorse the conduct of Ms. Ward's choice of her pre-game message."[60]

Ms. Ward delivered her speech in a halting manner and ended her message, "In Jesus' name, Amen."[61] The crowd cheered in approval.[62] The football game then occurred and the Santa Fe team, the Indians, lost.[63]

Ward delivered a message before every home football game that season.[64] Her lawsuit was dismissed as moot after she graduated in the spring of 2000.

Members of Congress Weigh In

Meanwhile, in the fall of 1999, Representative Henry Bonilla, a Republican from San Antonio, led a group of thirteen Texas congressmen of both parties in proposing a House resolution calling on the Supreme Court to overrule the Fifth Circuit's decision and to allow prayer at football games.[65] They said that God and football are inseparable in Texas.[66]

They introduced a resolution declaring the "Sense of Congress Supporting Prayer at Public School Sporting Events."[67] The resolution begin by stating: "Whereas prayers at public school sporting events are entirely consistent with our American heritage of seeking Divine guidance and protection in all of our undertakings."

Several Representatives made strong statements in favor of the prayers at football games and condemning the Fifth Circuit's decision. Representative Bonilla, for example, said: "[W]e are very proud of a fall tradition we have in Texas.... A tradition has been threatened by a foolish decision in federal court."[68] Representative Trafficant, a Republican from Ohio, declared: "I keep hearing this First Amendment mumbo-jumbo.... The founders are rolling over in their graves.... This is absolutely ridiculous.... A nation without God is a nation without order. An American that restricts God gives license to the devil."[69]

The Supreme Court

The School Board voted 7–0 to seek review in the Supreme Court.[70] The Supreme Court granted the School District's petition for certiorari, but interestingly granted review only as to whether the Fifth Circuit erred in prohibiting even nonsectarian, non-proselytizing prayers at football games. The sole issue on which certiorari was granted was "[w]hether petitioner's policy permitting student-led, student-initiated prayer at football games violates the Establishment Clause." The Court did not grant review as to the constitutionality of student prayers at public school graduations even though there was a split of authority among the federal courts of appeals on this issue.[71] As of this writing in 2007, the Supreme Court still has not resolved whether student-delivered prayers at public school graduation ceremonies are permissible.

In a 6–3 decision, the Supreme Court held that the Santa Fe Independent School District's policy was unconstitutional and that student-delivered prayers at public school football games violated the Establishment Clause. Justice Stevens wrote the majority opinion, which was joined by Justices O'Connor, Kennedy, Souter, Ginsburg, and Breyer. Chief Justice Rehnquist and Justices Scalia and Thomas dissented.

Justice Stevens' majority opinion began by addressing the School District's claim that the prayers were private speech by students and thus protected expression under the First Amendment. He wrote: "[W]e are not persuaded that the pregame invocations should be regarded as 'private speech.' These invocations are authorized by a government policy and take place on government property at government-sponsored school-related events."[72] He noted that the school allows only one student to present the message and it is the same student for the entire year. Thus the place and event cannot be considered a public forum where all are allowed to express their views and where the government is prohibited from restricting the subject matter of the speech.

Nor could the School District avoid responsibility by claiming that it was just a choice by students and not the government. The Court noted that the government created the forum, determined who could speak, and set up the rules to encourage prayer at football games. Justice Stevens wrote: "In addition to involving the school in the selection of the speaker, the policy, by its terms, invites and encourages religious messages. The policy itself states that the purpose of the message is 'to solemnize the event.' A religious message is the most obvious method of solemnizing an event.''[73] The Court observed that there long had been prayers at football games in Santa Fe and was obviously mindful that the School District's policy was created to preserve that process.

The Court directly addressed the tension between the majority's desire for prayer and the minority who did not want it. Justice Stevens noted that ''the majoritarian process implemented by the District guarantees, by definition, that minority candidates will never prevail and that their views will be effectively silenced.''[74] The Court said that the rights of the minority, including their rights under the Establishment Clause, could not be put to the vote of the majority.

The Court then proceeded to explain the constitutional violation under any of the theories of the Establishment Clause. In recent years, the Justices have disagreed over the appropriate test for the Establishment Clause and there has not been a majority for any approach.[75] It is striking that without acknowledging that he was doing so, Justice Stevens proceeded to show that the Santa Fe policy was unconstitutional under any of these approaches.

The Court began by explaining that the reasonable observer would perceive the prayer as being endorsed by the School District. In recent years, some Justices have emphasized whether the government is ''symbolically endorsing'' religion is key under the Establishment Clause.[76] Justice Stevens noted that ''an objective Santa Fe High School student will unquestionably perceive the inevitable pre-game prayer as stamped with her school's seal of approval.''[77]

The Court also noted that the government's purpose was to advance religion. The Court long had held that the government violates the Establishment Clause if it lacks a secular purpose and if it acts with the primary purpose of advancing religion.[78] Justice Stevens noted the long history of prayer at Santa Fe football games and saw the new policy as being designed to continue the practice. He said that ''in light of the school's history of regular delivery of a student-led prayer at athletic events, it is reasonable to infer that the specific purpose of the policy was to preserve a popular 'state-sponsored religious practice.' ''[79]

Finally, the Court noted the inherently coercive nature of the prayers at the Santa Fe football games. In *Lee v. Weisman*, Justice Kennedy's majority opinion invalidating prayers at public school graduations focused on the coercion inherent to the practice.[80] The School District's brief to the Court stressed that football games are very different from graduation and that the absence of coercion makes the practice permissible.[81]

But the Court rejected this distinction and explained that like graduation, students are pressured, and sometimes required, to be at the football games. Justice Stevens explained: ''There are some students, however, such as cheerleaders, members of the band, and, of course, the team members themselves, for whom seasonal commitments mandate their attendance, sometimes for class credit. The District also minimizes the importance to many students of attending and participating in extracurricular activities as part of a complete educational experience."[82] The Court explained that many students feel great social pressure to be at the football games.

Moreover, the Court said that even if attendance were regarded as purely voluntary, those present would feel pressure to participate in a religious activity. The Court stated: "Even if we regard every high school student's decision to attend a home football game as purely voluntary, we are nevertheless persuaded that the delivery of a pregame prayer has the improper effect of coercing those present to participate in an act of religious worship."[83]

The Court flatly rejected the claim that preventing the prayers would violate free exercise of religion for those who wanted to pray.[84] The Court noted that students, of course, could still pray before, during, or after football games. The Court was just invalidating having a student deliver a prayer over the public loudspeaker before the games.

Chief Justice Rehnquist wrote the dissenting opinion, which was joined by Justices Scalia and Thomas. It reflected a radically different view of the Establishment Clause. Chief Justice Rehnquist's dissent saw the majority's opinion as reflecting impermissible hostility to religion. He began his opinion by declaring:

> "But even more disturbing than its holding is the tone of the Court's opinion; it bristles with hostility to all things religious in public life. Neither the holding nor the tone of the opinion is faithful to the meaning of the Establishment Clause, when it is recalled that George Washington himself, at the request of the very Congress which passed the Bill of Rights, proclaimed a day of 'public thanksgiving and prayer, to be observed by acknowledging with grateful hearts the many and signal favors of Almighty God.' "[85]

The dissent stressed that it was a choice by the students, via an election, to have a message before football games and to determine who would deliver it. Chief Justice Rehnquist thus declared that "any speech that may occur as a result of the election process here would be private, not government, speech. The elected student, not the government, would choose what to say."[86] The dissent accepted the School District's claim of a secular policy of solemnizing football games.[87] Chief Justice Rehnquist lamented: "Under the Court's logic, a public school that sponsors the singing of the national anthem before football games violates the Establishment Clause. Although the Court apparently believes that solemnizing football games is an illegitimate purpose, the voters in the school district seem to disagree. Nothing in the Establishment Clause prevents them from making this choice."[88]

The Significance of Santa Fe Independent School District v. Doe

On a doctrinal level, the case is important because six Justices strongly reaffirmed the ban on prayer at public school events. Even with the recent changes in the composition of the Court, there remain at least five Justices who take this view: Justices Stevens, Kennedy, Souter, Ginsburg, and Breyer.

Moreover, the case is important in making clear that the government cannot avoid the Establishment Clause by characterizing the issue as being about freedom of student speech. If the Court had decided differently, then prayer could be allowed on a daily basis in public school classrooms simply by having students vote to have it present and having a student deliver the prayer each day. Little would be left of the Court's restrictions on religion in public schools and at government events if the School District's position had prevailed.

Of course, that is exactly what the School District and its supporters, including the dissenting Justices, wanted. The case must be understood as reflecting a deep divide on the Supreme Court and in American society over the proper role of religion in government events, especially in public schools. School officials in Santa Fe were strongly committed to the presence of prayer at graduations and football games. By all accounts, they had the support of the majority of the parents and students. Some believe that this is crucial, if not decisive, in a democratic society. In his strong dissent in *Lee v. Weisman*, Justice Scalia concluded by declaring:

> "The reader has been told much in this case about the personal interest of Mr. Weisman and his daughter, and very little about the personal interests on the other side. They are not inconsequential. Church and state would not be such a difficult subject if religion were, as the Court apparently thinks it to be, some purely personal avocation that can be indulged entirely in secret, like pornography, in the privacy of one's room. For most believers it is not that, and has never been ... One can believe in the effectiveness of such public worship, or one can deprecate and deride it. But the longstanding American tradition of prayer at official ceremonies displays with unmistakable clarity that the Establishment Clause does not forbid the government to accommodate it."[89]

From this perspective, prayer at government events, including public school events, does not violate the Establishment Clause. In fact, the exclusion of prayer, as Chief Justice Rehnquist expressed in his dissent in *Santa Fe*, is seen as undue hostility to religion.

The plaintiffs who filed the suit challenging the prayer and the judges in the majority on the Fifth Circuit and the Supreme Court have a very different view of the Establishment Clause. Their view is that the First Amendment limits what the government may do to encourage or endorse religion. They see restrictions on religion at government events not as hostility to religion, but as protecting the ability of all to feel a part of their government. From this perspective, the Establishment Clause serves a fundamental purpose of inclusion in that it allows all in society, of every religion and of no religion, to feel that the government is theirs. When the government supports religion, inescapably those of different religious beliefs or those with none feel excluded. In a society that is overwhelmingly Christian, those of minority faiths feel marginalized and unwelcome.

From this perspective, the goal of inclusion is central, not incidental, to the Establishment Clause. Justice O'Connor explained: "Direct government action endorsing religion or a particular religion is invalid because it sends a message to nonadherents that they are outsiders, not full members of the political community, and an accompanying message to adherents that they are insiders, favored members of the political community."[90] Justice Stevens quoted this language in his majority opinion in *Santa Fe*.[91]

There seems no bridge between these two views of the Establishment Clause and the role for religion in American government. Prayers at football games may seem a trivial issue, but it is not in the context of the deep chasm between those who believe that public schools must be secular and those who would prefer the presence of religion there.

In recent years, the disagreement has intensified, not abated. Thus, *Santa Fe Independent School District v. Doe* is an important ruling, but certainly not the last on when religious activities in public schools violate the Establishment Clause.

Endnotes

1. I want to thank Tadhg Dooley for his excellent research assistance.

2. 370 U.S. 421 (1962).

3. *See* Steve Lash, *Justices Urged to Back Grid Prayer*, Houston Chronicle, October 20, 1989, at A29 (quoting Representative Henry Bonilla as saying that God and football are inseparable in Texas).

4. Santa Fe Independent School District v. Doe, 530 U.S. 290 (2000).

5. *Id.* at 294.

6. Claudia Kolker, *Pray*, Houston Press, September 14, 1995.

7. Pamela Colloff, *They Haven't Got a Prayer*, Texas Monthly, November 2000.

8. Kolker, *supra* note 6.

9. Colloff, *supra* note 7.

10. Kolker, *supra* note 6.

11. Colloff, *supra* note 7.

12. *Id.*

13. *Id.*

14. Kim Sue Lia Perkes, *In Santa Fe, A Struggle Over Prayer*, Austin American–Statesman, October 9, 1999, at A1.

15. Colloff, *supra* note 7.

16. Kevin Moran, *School Officials in Santa Fe to Halt Handing Out of Bibles*, Houston Chronicle, April 16, 1994, at A34.

17. *Id.*

18. These events are described in the Fifth Circuit's opinion, Doe v. Santa Fe Independent School District, 168 F.3d 806, 810 (5th Cir. 1999).

19. *Id.* at 810.

20. 505 U.S. 577 (1992).

21. Jones v. Clear Creek ISD, 977 F.2d 963 (5th Cir. 1992).

22. 168 F.3d at 810.

23. *Id.*

24. *Id.*

25. *Id.*

26. Interview with Anthony Griffin, Attorney for Plaintiffs. (Interview conducted by telephone on July 19, 2006).

27. 168 F.3d at 809 n.1 (emphasis in original).

28. *Id.* at 811.

29. *Id.*

30. 168 F.3d at 812.

31. Jones v. Clear Creek ISD, 977 F.2d 963 (5th Cir. 1992).

32. Kevin Moran, *Students to Vote on Prayers; School's New Policy Attacked by ACLU*, Houston Chronicle, July 26, 1995, at A1.

33. 168 F.3d at 812.

34. *Id.*

35. Kevin Moran, *Students to Vote on Prayers; School's New Policy Attacked by ACLU*, Houston Chronicle, July 26, 1995, at A1.

36. 454 U.S. 263 (1981).

37. 508 U.S. 384 (1993).

38. 515 U.S. 819 (1995).

39. Quoted at 168 F.3d at 813.

40. Monell v. Department of Social Services, 436 U.S. 658 (1978).

41. 168 F.3d at 816.

42. *Id.* at 818.

43. *Id.* at 823.

44. *Id.* at 824 (Jolly, J., dissenting).

45. *Id.* at 825.

46. *Id.* at 835.

47. *Id.*

48. Doe v. Sante Fe Indep. School Dist., 171 F.3d 1013 (5th Cir. 1999). The dissenting judges were Patrick E. Higginbotham, E. Grady Jolly, Edith H. Jones, Jerry E. Smith, Rhesa Hawkins Barksdale, Emilio M. Garza, and Harold R. DeMoss.

49. *Id.*

50. *Id.*

51. Victoria Loe Hicks, *New Football Matchup; Texas Town Energizes Debate Over School Prayer With Pre-Game Message*, The Dallas Morning News, November 7, 1999, at 1A.

52. *Id.*

53. *Id.*

54. Interview with Kelly Coghlan, Attorney for Marian Ward (Interview conducted by telephone on July 19, 2006).

55. *Id.*

56. *Id.*

57. District Court order, September 3, 1999.

58. Claudia Colker, *Girl Gets Blessing for Football Game Prayer*, Los Angeles Times, September 4, 1999, at A1.

59. Hicks, *supra* note 51.

60. *Id.*

61. Colker, *supra* note 58.

62. Chris Fletcher, *Pre-Game Prayer Earns Big Applause in Santa Fe*, The Austin-American Statesman, September 5, 1999, at B7.

63. Hicks, *supra* note 51.

64. Ward v. Santa Fe Independent School District, 393 F.3d 599, 601 (5th Cir. 2004).

65. Steve Lash, *Justices Urged to Back Grid Prayer*, Houston Chronicle, October 20, 1999, at A29.

66. *Id.*

67. H.Con.Res. 1999 (November 2, 1999), 145 Cong. Rec. 11325.

68. *Id.*

69. *Id.*

70. Pamela Coloff, *supra* note 7.

71. *Compare* Adler v. Duval County School Board, 250 F.3d 1330 (11th Cir. 2001) (unrestricted student message at graduation did not violate the Establishment Clause), *with* Cole v. Oroville Union High School Dist., 228 F.3d 1092 (9th Cir. 2000) (school district's refusal to allow student to deliver sectarian invocation at graduation was necessary to avoid an Establishment Clause violation).

72. 530 U.S. at 302.

73. *Id.* at 306.

74. *Id.* at 304.

75. For a description of the competing theories, *see* Erwin Chemerinsky, *Constitutional Law: Principles and Policies* 1192–98 (3d ed. 2006).

76. *See, e.g.*, Allegheny County v. Greater Pittsburgh ACLU, 492 U.S. 573, 627 (1989) (O'Connor, J., concurring in part and concurring in the judgment) (''As a theoretical matter, the endorsement test captures the essential command of the Establishment Clause, namely, that government must not [be] ... conveying a message that religion or a particular religion is favored or preferred.'').

77. 530 U.S. at 308.

78. *See, e.g.*, Lemon v. Kurtzman, 403 U.S. 602, 612 (1971); *see also* Wallace v. Jaffree, 472 U.S. 38, 56 (1985) (moment of silence for mediation or silent prayer violated the Establishment Clause because ''it was not motivated by any clearly secular purpose—indeed, the statute had no secular purpose''); Stone v. Graham, 449 U.S. 39, 41 (1980) (state law requiring the posting of Ten Commandments in public school classrooms was unconstitutional because the law ''has no secular legislative purpose'').

79. 530 U.S. at 309.

80. 505 U.S. at 592.

81. Brief for Petitioner at 39–44, Santa Fe Independent School District v. Doe, 530 U.S. 290 (2000) (No. 99–62).

82. 530 U.S. at 311.

83. *Id.* at 312.

84. *See* Brief for Petitioner, *supra* note 81, at 46.

85. 530 U.S. at 318 (Rehnquist, C.J., dissenting).

86. *Id.* at 321.

87. *Id.* at 322.

88. *Id.* at 322–23.

89. 505 U.S. at 645 (Scalia, J., dissenting).

90. Wallace v. Jaffree, 472 U.S. 38, 70 (1985) (O'Connor, J., concurring in the judgment).

91. 530 U.S. at 309–310.

13

The Story of *Pottawatomie County v. Lindsay Earls*: Drug Testing in the Public Schools

Robert M. Bloom[1]

The school setting can provide valuable civic lessons for students. In a case involving the right to be free from unreasonable searches in a school setting, a right guaranteed by the Fourth Amendment of the Federal Constitution, Justice John Paul Stevens said in a dissenting opinion:

> The schoolroom is the first opportunity most citizens have to experience the power of government. Through it passes every citizen ... The values they learn there, they take with them in life. One of our most cherished ideals is the one contained in the Fourth Amendment: that the government may not intrude on the personal privacy of its citizens without a warrant or compelling circumstance.[2]

Justice Ruth Bader Ginsburg expressed similar sentiments in her dissenting opinion in *Pottawatomie County v. Lindsay Earls*,[3] the subject of this chapter. She cites the language of the great jurist Justice Louis Brandeis in *Olmstead v. United States*: "Our government is the potent, the omnipresent teacher. For good or for ill, it teaches the whole people by its example."[4] She continues by stating that "wisdom should guide decision makers in the instant case: The government is nowhere more a teacher than when it runs a public school."[5]

This sentiment of these two Justices was not lost on Lindsay Earls during the fall of her sophomore year. Sixteen-year old Earls was sitting in choir, her first class of the day, when the Choir Director distributed the form[6] describing a new drug testing policy (the Policy).[7]

The teacher told the students to bring the form home, ask their parents to sign it, and return the form with a $4 processing fee. The form granted permission for urine drug testing of all students involved in competitive extracurricular activities, including choir. Lindsay was shocked. She thought the teacher was joking. She had never seen signs of drug use and couldn't believe the School Board would do something so unnecessary and invasive. This outrage started a four-year journey for Lindsay that ended with the Supreme Court decision in 2002 after her freshman year in college. Although the case was not always prominent in Lindsay's life, it shaped the woman she became and influenced the town she called home.

Tecumseh, Oklahoma, is a small, conservative, mainly Protestant town about forty minutes from Oklahoma City. With a population just over 6,000, Tecumseh is the kind of town where everyone knows everybody's business and news spreads quickly. According to the 2000 Census, the town is approximately 80% white; the next largest racial group is American Indian at 13%. The median household income in 2000 was $27,202. Ten percent of the town population has a college degree. There is some farming, but most residents work in Oklahoma City.

Tecumseh High School is a reflection of the town, with fewer than 200 students in each graduating class. Lindsay not only knew all of the students in her own class, but also those in the classes above and below her. Lindsay is a fifth generation Tecumseh graduate. She knew all the members of the School Board, and even called one of them "Grandma" due to connections with a childhood friend. Lindsay enjoyed high school and describes herself as pretty popular. She had a lot of friends and did well in school. She was a member of the show choir, the marching band, the Academic Team, and the National Honor Society. Until the suit was filed, Lindsay had never had a negative experience in Tecumseh schools.

Incidents of drug use were few and far between in Tecumseh before the school board enacted the policy. Prior to the enactment of the policy, Tecumseh drug prevention included utilizing dogs to sniff for drugs on school property, installing security cameras throughout the school, promoting anti-drug awareness educational campaigns, and conducting suspicion based searches of student lockers. These measures are still in place today. The school board had considered the idea of drug testing to deter drug use in years prior to the policy's enactment in October 1998. However, it was not until the spring of 1998 when a few drug related incidents prompted the school board to formally discuss enacting a drug testing policy. In her deposition, Dean Rogers, President of the Board of Education at the time, testified that a student called her to report that a marijuana cigarette was passed around during her English class. Rogers further testified that she was approached a couple of times at the grocery store by parents who had concerns about drug use. In addition, three teachers testified that they overheard students talking about using drugs in their classes. One student was found with drug paraphernalia in his car in the spring of 1998, and a bag of marijuana was found under a log on the edge of the school parking lot. However, evidence pertaining to drug use was limited to these few instances and a couple of incidents during the 1970s and 1980s. Lindsay was not aware of any immediate drug problem at the school at the time. Indeed, the results of a Tecumseh High School student survey of drug use at the time reported that less than five percent of the students had tried marijuana and a resounding 85% said that they never tried illegal drugs.

In August 1998, the school district held a meeting to discuss and vote on enacting a drug testing policy. Kay DeSomer, a parent of a student at Tecumseh High School, appeared and spoke of her son's drug problem and appealed to the board to enact a drug testing policy to help deter drug use. Initially, the school board discussed limiting the testing to student athletes, but decided to include all students engaged in competitive extracurricular activities, including the choir, band, academic team, Future Homemakers of America (FHA), and Future Farmers of America (FFA), because the board believed it was fairer to test all students in competition representing the school. The drug policy was enacted by the five-member school board in October 1998 with a unanimous vote even though the school board admitted that the students involved in FHA, FFA, Choir, Band, and Academic Team were not leaders of any drug culture in Tecumseh. Of note, Danny Jacobs, the Assistant Superintendent of Tecumseh schools, had recently transferred to Tecumseh from Purcell, another school district in Oklahoma that had enacted a similar drug testing policy that was popular in the district. However Purcell's policy only tested student athletes. During the first year of testing at Tecumseh, 1998–1999, 243 students were tested and there were three positive results. The next year, 1999–2000, there was one positive result from 266 tests.

The day Lindsay received the form describing the Policy, she brought it home to her parents and told them she thought it violated her rights. Her parents said they didn't know whether the school could do this and promised to investigate. Lindsay's father researched the issue, wrote letters to elected officials, and asked lawyers in town. When he didn't get any definitive answers he contacted the American Civil Liberties Union (ACLU). Meanwhile, Lindsay chose to sign the form because she wanted to continue participating in her extracurricular activities and needed them to achieve her goal to attend an Ivy League college. In January 1999, Lindsay and fifteen other students were selected to be tested. The assistant principle called her out of class in front of her peers and told her to report to the gymnasium for testing. Lindsay was then forced to urinate into a cup while three teachers stood outside the bathroom stall listening for "normal sounds of urination."[8] One of the teachers joked that the process was like engaging in "potty training."[9] Lindsay then had to give the cup to the teachers and watch as they held and inspected the sample to determine whether the urine was the proper color and temperature. Lindsay was embarrassed by the entire process and felt that her rights were violated. Although she was confident that she had never used drugs, she was nervous that she would have to endure the stigma that comes with a false positive result.

The ACLU took Lindsay's case, and in August 1999, the first week of Lindsay's junior year, her attorney, Graham Boyd, filed a suit challenging the Policy. Upon learning of the pendency of the law suit, the school board suspended the policy. Lindsay missed school the day the suit was filed. When she returned to English class late the next day, the room became completely silent upon her arrival. Her best friend told Lindsay that the students had been talking about her and speculating about her drug use despite her friend's efforts to defend her. For the next few weeks, people said nasty things about Lindsay and her family behind her back at school, on local talk radio, and in the local paper. They challenged her Christianity by insinuating that she must be a drug user and therefore not a good Christian. A supportive gesture occurred when several teachers called Lindsay's parents and offered a safe place at the school if Lindsay felt threatened or intimidated, but none off them publicly supported Lindsay's actions. The Principal of Tecumseh High School, James Blue, never talked with Lindsay about the suit. Mostly, the school administrators and teachers acted as though the suit was never filed.

The whirlwind of negative attention around Lindsay lasted only a few weeks. Then, in 2000, the District Court for the Western District of Oklahoma granted summary judgment to the school district, finding that "special needs" exist in the public school context, that the school had a legitimate interest and need for the Policy, and that the Policy was effective.[10] The School Board reinstated the Policy and again, Lindsay chose to participate in the drug testing in order to remain in choir and her other activities. Lindsay was tested once during her junior year, and then two or three times during her senior year. She never tested positive. Lindsay despised participating in the testing, but she enjoyed her activities and knew they were an important component of her education and were necessary to help her get into a college of her choice.

Lindsay decided to appeal to the Tenth Circuit Court of Appeals. The case was heard in January of her senior year at Tecumseh High School. On March 21, 2001, the Tenth Circuit reversed the District Court's decision, holding that the Policy violated the Fourth Amendment because the school failed to demonstrate a drug abuse problem.[11] Lindsay's last drug test was the day before this decision and she graduated from high school with no drug testing policy in effect. She was accepted to Dartmouth College and was the only student from Tecumseh High to go to an Ivy League school. In fact, only approximately half of Lindsay's class attended college, and only three or four of those went out of state. Many of her peers joined the military.

In November 2001 during Lindsay's freshman year at Dartmouth, the Supreme Court granted *certiorari*. In contrast to her experience in Tecumseh, Lindsay received a great deal of support and encouragement from her peers and professors at Dartmouth. Lindsay never actually told anyone outside of her roommate about the case. However, when the U.S. Supreme Court granted *certiorari*, students she had never met approached her and asked her about the case. The school paper published stories about the case and Lindsay was asked to speak in numerous classes about her experiences.

The Supreme Court heard oral arguments on March 19, 2002. Lindsay was nervous that morning, and surprised by the large number of young people outside the Court. She was overwhelmed by the size and grandiosity of the Courthouse building. Lindsay has described the entire experience as surreal, exciting, overwhelming, and nerve-wracking.[12] She remembers thinking that she couldn't believe that "this was all for me." One particularly shocking moment occurred during oral argument when Justice Kennedy implied that Lindsay used drugs. Justice Kennedy asked whether it would be constitutional for the school district to maintain two schools—a "druggie school" at which there were no drug tests or drug sniffing dogs, and another school with mandatory drug testing. Justice Kennedy told Mr. Boyd, Lindsay's lawyer, that no parent would send a child to the first school, that no one "other than perhaps your client wants to go there."[13] Mr. Boyd reminded Justice Kennedy that Lindsay was a student at Dartmouth College and had never failed a drug test.[14]

Because Lindsay took summer classes after her freshman year, she was on campus at Dartmouth the day the decision came down. The Supreme Court decided on June 27, 2002 that the Policy was constitutional. Graham Boyd called Lindsay at 9:30AM. She was devastated and cried for a long time before she called her parents. It was a really hard morning for her and she was particularly upset that Justice Thomas wrote the decision because she didn't think he was paying attention at the oral arguments and he didn't ask any questions. Lindsay said it looked like he was doing a crossword puzzle during the arguments.[15]

Tecumseh High School reinstituted the Policy after the Supreme Court decision. It is still in effect today. During the most recent school year, 2005–2006, approximately 900 students were tested with five positive results.

After the Supreme Court decided the case, Lindsay received countless emails from friends, professors, campus staff, and even people she had never previously met. She was surprised and pleased by the outpouring of support within the Dartmouth community because it was so different from the negative reaction she had received in Tecumseh. Even though Lindsay remains disappointed with the result, she has said that she would do it again.[16] However, Lindsay is upset that her younger sister, Casey, who is currently a sophomore at Tecumseh High School, must participate in drug testing.[17]

Today Lindsay works for the Indigenous Democratic Network, a Tulsa-based grassroots political organization devoted to recruiting and electing Native American candidates. She has plans to attend law school.[18]

Fourth Amendment Doctrine

The Fourth Amendment[19] is the reflection of our ancestors' concern with government officials acting with unlimited discretion to search whenever, wherever, and whomever they chose. Thus the Fourth Amendment to the Bill of Rights attempts to rein in the actions of governmental officials. It does this in two fundamental ways. First, it requires some justification for a government official to act. The precise justification language in the Fourth Amendment is "probable cause." Second, it requires this justification to be determined by a judicial official who issues a document called a warrant which lays out the particular scope of the government search.

The first question to be determined in the school context or any Fourth Amendment context is whether the action constitutes governmental action. The second question is whether the governmental action is a search or seizure. This is determined by whether there is a "reasonable expectation of privacy" or, stated differently, whether the expectation is one that society will accept.[20] The Fourth Amendment is applicable when there is government action that infringes upon a reasonable expectation of privacy. Once the Fourth Amendment is applicable, then one considers issues relative to justification and the need for warrants.

The Fourth Amendment is made up of two clauses joined by the conjunction "and."[21] The first clause forbids unreasonable searches and the second clause deals with the requirements of the warrant, including probable cause and specificity. For much of the history of the Fourth Amendment the two clauses were read together so the vague term unreasonable could be given meaning by the second warrant clause. Thus, in order for a search to be reasonable the government must have probable cause and a warrant specifically describing its scope.[22] In recent years, however, the trend has been for the Supreme Court to focus on the reasonableness clause without necessarily considering its relationship with the second clause. This reasonableness approach is especially applicable in the school setting as we will see in the landmark case, *New Jersey v. T.L.O.*[23]

The Court first turned exclusively to the reasonableness clause in cases when the probable cause standard utilized for criminal purposes, which focused on an individual or a particular location, would not work. For example, in a governmental search involving housing code violations, a health inspector is concerned about an area as opposed to an individual apartment. In *Camara v. Mun. Court of San Francisco*, the Court turned to the reasonableness clause of the Fourth Amendment and devised a balancing approach to this justification issue.[24] The Court stated that there exists "no ready test for determining reasonableness other than by balancing the need to search against the invasion which the search entails."[25] On one side of the balance, the Court weighed the governmental interest in or need to conduct the particular type of Fourth Amendment activity.[26] On the other side of the balance, the Court looked to the privacy intrusion that a particular search entailed.[27] Applying this approach, the Court upheld the administrative search in *Camara* due to the reasonableness of its administrative regulations rather than the existence of probable cause.[28]

Initially, warrants were required for these administrative searches unless some exigency was present.[29] Over time, however, the Court began dispensing with the warrant requirement for heavily regulated businesses where warrants would inhibit the inspections as long as the administrative regulations provided an adequate substitute for the particularity requirements of a warrant and thus limited the parameters of a search.[30] As we will see, the balancing approach has particular applicability in the school context.

The balancing approach also was utilized in the criminal context in the so-called stop and frisk case of *Terry v. Ohio*.[31] In *Terry*, the police officer did not have probable cause to believe a particular individual had committed a crime when the officer saw the individual casing a jewelry store and suspected the individual of preparing to commit a crime.[32] The police officers investigated by stopping and later frisking the individual, implicating the Fourth Amendment. Because probable cause did not apply here, the Court balanced the government interest in solving crime with the intrusion, which was somewhat less invasive than an arrest, and developed a standard of reasonable suspicion, a lesser standard than probable cause. It should be pointed out that although reasonable suspicion is different than probable cause it still requires individualized suspicion.

The Case of T.L.O.—Fourth Amendment in the Public Schools

Initially it was thought that government involvement for purposes of the Fourth Amendment was limited to law enforcement officers who were searching places or arresting individuals involved in criminal behavior. This notion was put to rest in *Camara*.[33] In finding that government health inspectors also were governed by the Fourth Amendment, the Court stated: "The basic purpose of this Amendment, as recognized in countless decisions of this court, is to safeguard the privacy and security of individuals against arbitrary invasions by governmental officials."[34] "It is surely anomalous to say that the individual and his private property are fully protected by the Fourth Amendment only when the individual is suspected of criminal behavior."[35]

In a school setting, the Fourth Amendment only applies to public schools, not private, because the school district represents action by a governmental entity. Historical even in the public school setting, the doctrine of *in loco parentis* was thought originally to exempt a teacher or a principal from being a government actor. In *Mercer v. State of Texas*[36] a principal found marijuana in the pockets of a pupil. The court did not consider this action to implicate the Fourth Amendment because the principal basically was acting as a parent. This authority to search the student was delegated, in effect, to the principal by the parents. The Court reasoned that the search by the principal was consistent with the authority of the pupil's parents. This concept of *in loco parentis* was disgarded in the seminal Fourth Amendment school case of *New Jersey v. T.L.O.*[37]

T.L.O., a 14–year–old freshman, and her classmate at Piscataway High School in Middlesex County, New Jersey, were caught by a teacher smoking in the school bathroom in violation of school rules. The two girls were brought to the principal's office where they met Assistant Vice Principal Choplick. Subsequent to questioning by Choplick, during which T.L.O. denied she had been smoking, Choplick brought T.L.O. to his private office where he demanded to see her purse. He opened the purse and found cigarettes and rolling paper. Because Choplick associated rolling paper with drug use based on his previous experiences, he did a further search of the purse and discovered a small amount of marijuana, a pipe, a number of empty plastic bags, a large quantity of one dollar bills, index cards that appeared to list students who owed T.L.O. money, and two letters that implicated T.L.O. in marijuana dealing. As a result of this discovery, the school called the police and delinquency charges were brought against T.L.O. T.L.O. sought to suppress the evidence claiming that Choplick's action constituted a violation of her Fourth Amendment rights.

The Court first analyzed whether this search was government action. In discounting *in loco parentis*, the Court observed that the school authorities are state actors for other constitutional guarantees such as due process and First Amendment concerns. Further, schools are regulated by compulsory education laws requiring school officials to follow publicly mandated educational and discipline policies. So, in essence, they are acting as representatives of the state, not as parents.[38]

Second, the Court resoundingly found that T.L.O. had a legitimate expectation of privacy that society would recognize. The State of New Jersey argued that because students are subject to all encompassing supervision they do not bother to bring unnecessary items to school. The Court discounted this argument. Even though the Court found no expectation of privacy in an earlier prison cell case because of the need to maintain order,[39] the Court refused to equate students with prisoners. "[The] prisoner and the schoolchild stand in wholly different circumstances, separated by the harsh facts of criminal conviction and incarceration."[40] The Court also observed that students not only bring items related to their school work, but also bring personal items such as keys, letters, diaries, and items for grooming and personal hygiene.

Once the Court concluded that the Fourth Amendment applied, it turned to the reasonableness clause and engaged in a balancing analysis similar to the one previously described in the *Camara* case. The majority of the Court concluded that the nature of the school setting, where there was a legitimate need to ensure an environment in which learning could take place, required some modification of the justification requirement for the search. Opting for a lesser standard than probable cause to justify Choplick's actions, the Court turned to the reasonableness clause of the Fourth Amendment. "The fundamental command of the Fourth Amendment is that searches and seizures be reasonable, and although 'both the concept of the probable cause and the requirement of a warrant bear on the reasonableness of a search ... in certain limited circumstances neither is required.' "[41]

The Court then applied the reasonableness balancing test discussed in *Camara*. On the government side, the Court weighed the need for school officials to establish discipline and maintain order in the school as well as the importance of the education and training of students. On the intrusion side, although the Court recognized Fourth Amendment applicability, it indicated that a student had a lesser privacy expectation in a school setting.[42] The Court concluded that the "niceties" of the probable cause standard would be too difficult for school officials to follow and opted for a reasonableness under all the circumstances standard in upholding Choplick's search.[43] With regard to a warrant, the Court concluded that it would be too difficult to impose such a standard in a school environment. "... [R]equiring a teacher to obtain a warrant before searching a child suspected of an infraction of school rules ... would unduly interfere with the maintenance of the swift and informal disciplinary procedures needed in the schools."[44]

Justice Blackmun, concurring, emphasized that generally the dictates of the second clause of the Fourth Amendment, probable cause and warrants, should be followed. However, the school setting presents "special needs" for flexibility justifying the reasonableness approach in this case.[45]

In his dissent, Justice Brennan urged a probable cause standard for the type of intrusive search conducted by Choplick.[46] He pointed out that the search of the pocketbook was a substantial intrusion similar to an arrest and therefore the balancing test utilized in *Terry*, which involved a lesser intrusion, was inappropriate. He argued that probable cause is a prerequisite for this type of search (non-administrative) given the relationship between the two clauses of the Fourth Amendment. He pointed out that the only time the Court has sanctioned a lesser standard is when the search is less intrusive.[47] He also pointed out that the probable clause standard had evolved into a "practical," "fluid," "flexible" concept and could be readily applied by teachers and certainly more easily than the "amorphous" "reasonableness under all the circumstances" standard adopted by the majority.[48] It is interesting to note that Justice Brennan did not think much of this balancing approach—he characterized it as "Rohrschach-like," allowing the Court to engage in "preordained" decision making.[49]

The precedent set by the *T.L.O.* decision, in which the Court utilized the balancing test of the reasonableness clause of the Fourth Amendment, has provided less privacy protection to school children. This approach to the Fourth Amendment as well as the Court's attitude to the privacy protection of students lays the groundwork for *Vernonia*[50] and *Earls*. It should be pointed out that the facts of *T.L.O.* did satisfy, at a minimum, individualized suspicion as there was justification to suspect T.L.O. of smoking in the lavatory.[51]

***Supreme Court Pivotal Precedent*: Vernonia Sch. Dist. v. Wayne Acton**

In 1991, James Acton, a seventh grader in Vernonia, Washington, decided he wanted to play football for his school. In order to participate in football he had to submit to a drug testing scheme that was adopted two years earlier by the Vernonia School District for all district-sponsored athletics. James' parents, Judy and Wayne, did not like this policy and refused to sign the permission form. At the time, James said, "I was like one of the smartest kids in class. I never got a referral (to the principal's office) and I thought that was probably enough for them to see I wasn't taking drugs. I didn't want to be forsaken from sports and decided I should do something."[52] James refused to take the drug test and was barred from playing football. With the help of the ACLU, James and his parents challenged the policy in federal court. They were unsuccessful in the district court, but successful in the Ninth Circuit Court of Appeals. In 1995, the Supreme Court granted *certiorari* and determined the constitutionality of the Vernonia School District drug testing policy.

The Court dealt with drug tests in a non-school setting prior to *Vernonia*. In *Skinner v. Ry. Labor Executives Ass'n*[53] the Court held that gathering and testing urine was a Fourth Amendment search. Obviously an individual would have a reasonable expectation of privacy in his/her urine. *Skinner* involved the testing of a railroad employee who had just been involved in an accident. The Court balanced the governmental interest, determining the cause of a railroad accident, against the nature of the privacy intrusion, which was somewhat lessened because railroad workers chose to work for a heavily regulated industry, and upheld the drug test. Employing this balancing analysis in *Nat'l Treasury Employees Union v. Von Raab*,[54] the Court allowed suspicionless drug testing for Custom Service workers involved in drug and firearm work who were seeking transfer or promotions. Both of these cases invoked the special needs doctrine mentioned earlier in Justice Blackmun's concurrence in *T.L.O.*

> We have recognized exceptions to ... [the warrant requirement] when "special needs, beyond the normal need for law enforcement, make the warrant and probable-cause requirement impracticable." When faced with such special needs, we have not hesitated to balance the governmental and privacy interests to assess the practicality of the warrant and probable-cause requirements in the particular context.[55]

Vernonia represents the first time the Court considered a bodily invasion, the testing of urine, that was not justified by work-related duties (*Von Raab*) or public safety concerns (*Skinner*). Citing *T.L.O.*, Justice Scalia, joined in the majority by Chief Justice Rehnquist and Justices Kennedy, Thomas, Ginsberg, and Breyer, pointed out that special needs exist in the school context.[56] He further pointed out that even though *T.L.O.* required some individualized suspicion, the Fourth Amendment does not always require this. The Court then opted to do a reasonableness balancing test and measured the nature and the immediacy of the government interest against the character of the intrusion on Fourth Amendment privacy interests.

On the intrusion side of the analysis, the Court used the *in loco parentis* doctrine to demonstrate that in general, because of the school's need for supervision and control, students have a lesser privacy expectation in the school environment than outside of it. To illustrate this point, the Court pointed out various required health screenings that occur in the school setting, such as hearing and vision tests as well as scoliosis screening. The Court found that "students within the school environment have a lesser expectation of privacy than members of the population generally."[57]

This lesser privacy expectation of pupils in general was coupled with the fact that the drug policy in *Vernonia* only affected athletes, who had even lesser privacy expectations than other students. By choosing to participate in athletics, students consent to preseason physicals, guarantee that they have adequate insurance and will maintain a certain grade point average, and agree to comply with rules of coaches and athletic directors relating to their conduct, dress, and training.[58] In addition, as the Court characterized it, school athletes are not as bashful as other pupils because they shower and dress together after games and practices.

The Court then considered the character of the intrusion of the drug test for urine and determined that the privacy interests compromised were "negligible."[59] When the urine was collected, the male students were fully clothed and only observed from behind while female students produced samples in an enclosed stall with a female monitor listening for tampering. The test was only for specific drugs and the results were only distributed to school personnel who needed to know. No information or positive test results were turned over to law enforcement.

The Court next analyzed the government interest and determined that the school's concern, "deterring drug use by our Nation's schoolchildren," was "important—indeed perhaps compelling."[60] The fact that the program was tailored to deal with the drug use of athletes who faced the possibility of immediate physical injury because of that drug use weighed heavily in the Court's analysis.[61] In addition, the Court pointed out that in *Vernonia* there was a clearly demonstrated problem and adopted the district court finding that "a large segment of the student body, particularly those involved in interscholastic athletics, were in a state of rebellion, that disciplinary actions had reached epidemic proportions and that the rebellion was being fueled by alcohol and drug abuses."[62]

As to the effectiveness of the method chosen, Justice Scalia indicated that it was self evident that such a program would work because it tested athletes, the very students who were the leaders of the drug culture.[63] Justice Scalia dismissed the necessity for individualized suspicion. He pointed out that parents are more willing to accept random testing of all athletes than specific testing of some students based on individualized suspicion because the latter type of program would transform the testing into a "badge of shame."[64] He also noted that requiring individualized suspicion would add to the myriad of responsibilities of teachers who already have a lot on their plates, and that with regard to determining individualized suspicion, teachers "are ill prepared and ... [it] is not readily compatible with their vocation."[65] Justice Scalia balanced the nature and immediacy of the government interest against the nature of the intrusion on students' privacy and concluded that the *Vernonia* policy was reasonable.[66]

In her concurrence, Justice Ginsburg emphasized that the policy was limited to athletes who voluntarily subjected themselves to closer school regulations and thus had reduced privacy expectations. Further, the potential for physical harm to athlete drug users was also an important factor to her on the government interest side. She was careful to limit the Court's decision on drug testing to athletes because she questioned whether such drug testing could be constitutionally imposed upon all students attending schools.[67]

Justice O'Connor, joined by Justices Stevens and Souter, dissented because she was concerned about the demise of individualized suspicion for this type of significant intrusion.[68] She highlighted the fact that *T.L.O.* involved individual suspicion and that in the Court's other cases, such as *Skinner*, which involved the chaotic scene of a railroad accident, it was not possible to develop individualized suspicion. Here, the school situation is quite different because individualized suspicion is easily ascertainable since students are under the constant scrutiny of school personnel. Such individualized scrutiny already exists for school disciplinary schemes. More fundamentally, individualized suspicion is more protective of students' privacy rights as it will invade the privacy of many fewer students. Justice O'Connor conceded that a suspicion-based system may not be as effective as the system before the Court, but wrote that we as a free society should pay that price for privacy protection.

Lindsay Goes to Court

Lindsay's case was filed in the U.S. District Court for the Western District of Oklahoma, located in Oklahoma City. She filed the case on August 18, 1999, some eight months after she was interrupted during a choral rehearsal and escorted by a school official to the girls' bathroom to urinate in a cup while a teacher waited outside. She asked for an injunction suspending the drug testing and declaratory relief to declare the drug policy unconstitutional in violation of the Fourth Amendment. Because the school board suspended the policy when it learned of plans to file the suit, there was no need for immediate injunctive relief. After the discovery process was completed, cross motions for summary judgment were filed and the case was resolved based on these motions for summary judgment.[69] In a summary judgment proceeding, the decision is based on application of law to undisputed facts.[70]

The court found the following pertinent undisputed facts:[71]

1) Tecumseh High Schools offered a range of student activity, including chorus, marching band, color guard, Future Farmers of

America and Future Homemakers of America. These are generally open to all students who wish to participate.

2) Tecumseh Schools also offer team sports that are limited to students on a competitive basis.

3) Most students participate in one or more of these activities and Lindsay Earls is a member of the show choir, the marching band, and the academic team.

4) On September 14, 1998, the school board adopted the Student Activities Drug Testing policy (the Policy) which requires all students who wish to participate in extracurricular activities to submit a written consent to suspicionless drug testing.

5) The Policy required students to undergo drug testing before participation, randomly while participating, and at any time while participating if there is reasonable suspicion. There is a $4.00 yearly fee charged to each student for the drug testing.[72]

6) The test detects amphetamines, marijuana, cocaine, opiates, barbiturates and benzodiazepines.

7) The Policy has only been applied to those extracurricular activities that involve some aspect of competition, and that are sanctioned by the Oklahoma Secondary Schools Activities Association.

8) The Policy involves the suspicionless drug testing of non-athletic extracurricular activity participants.

Unlike *Vernonia* where the drug problem with athletes was determined by the Court to be severe, the evidence in *Earls* as to the use of drugs is somewhat vague, uncertain, and sketchy.[73] Although the court recognized that "drugs were not a major problem," it found that it was undisputed that there was some drug use and that there was apparent acceptance of drug use, which made the problem sufficiently serious. The court specifically noted that "the evidence in this case does not show a drug problem of epidemic proportions or a student body in the state of rebellion."[74] It is interesting to note that Lindsay's attorney presented the school district's statement in the annual applications for funding from the Safe and Drug Free Schools and Communities program. In the statement the district indicated that although drugs were present they were "not a major problem at this time."[75] The court ironically characterized the statement as subjective and imprecise and then pointed out that although the statement says nothing concrete, it does indicate a problem.

The district court then utilized the balancing approach and identified a legitimate government concern in the generic notion of the importance of deterring drug use by all the nation's school children. With regard to the intrusion side, the court discounted the argument that athletes have less privacy expectations than other extracurricular activity participants. The court pointed out that "simply being a student in a public school is central to a lowered expectation of privacy.[76] It further decided that other competitive activities, although not as 'rigorous' " as athletics, still have rules and requirements for students participating. Major characteristics of the Tecumseh policy were similar to the Vernonia policy, including the nature of the intrusion, the method used to collect the urine, the limitation of the testing to certain students, and the fact that the results are only disclosed to those with need to know. The court also found that the consequences of refusing to consent would result in non-participation in the interscholastic competition but not the corresponding academic class.[77]

Lindsay's attorney argued that since some faculty members gave extra credit for competing in the activities subject to the Policy, these activities were not truly extracurricular because they had an academic component. The court discounted this by saying there was no evidence that any grades were lowered for refusing to consent. If other classmates can get extra credit, however, isn't a nonparticipant's grade lowered in comparison to participating students' grades?

The last piece of the balancing analysis was whether the policy is effective. Once again, the court discounted the reasoning in *Vernonia* that relied on evidence that had isolated the athletes as the leaders and source of the drug problem. Here, the court did not feel it was necessary to resolve whether children like Lindsay, who participate in extracurricular activities, were role models or likely to do drugs. It concluded that the test was effective because "it can scarcely be disputed that the drug problem among the student body is effectively addressed by making sure that the large number of students participating in competitive, extracurricular activities do not use drugs."[78]

Court of Appeals

Lindsay appealed the district court opinion to the United States Court of Appeals for the Tenth Circuit.[79] In a 2–1 decision the court found the Tecumseh policy to be unconstitutional when it employed the balancing test and weighed the government's interest against the intrusion on students' privacy rights. On the government interest side, the court considered the nature of the drug problem and the policy's efficacy in addressing this problem. On the intrusion side, the court considered both the students' expectation of privacy when participating in extracurricular activities as well the character of the intrusion, specifically the method used to conduct the test. The court looked to the Supreme Court precedent in *Vernonia* and found enough distinguishing factors to change the outcomc of the balancing test.

On the intrusion side of the equation, the court found that the way the test was administered as well as the lesser privacy expectations of students participating in extracurricular activities was similar to *Vernonia*. However, on the government interest side of the equation, the court did not find the drug problem in Tecumseh to be as serious as *Vernonia*'s "epidemic" and "immediate crisis".[80] The court was unimpressed with using drug testing as a means of providing a solution to the minimal drug problem. In addition, unlike the athletes in *Vernonia*, the court had a hard time imagining that members of Tecumseh's academic team or Future Homemakers of America needed special protection from physical harm associated with participation in these activities. Furthermore, the testing of students in Tecumseh who had no measurable drug problem was substantially less effective than the testing of athletes in *Vernonia* who were at the heart of the drug problem. "[W]e see little efficacy in a drug testing policy which tests students among whom there is no measurable drug problem."[81] The court suggested a common sense method to evaluate the constitutionality of random suspicionless drug tests. First, the school must demonstrate that there is a drug problem within the school district and then demonstrate that the testing policy in question actually will reach those students who present the problem.[82]

The dissent reached a different conclusion when applying the balancing test and focused on the drug problem nationwide in public schools and adolescents' susceptibility to the problem. Judge Ebel cited a study that indicated that among children between ages 12–17, 18.7% used marijuana, 2.4% used cocaine, 5.7% used hallucinogens, and 9.1% used inhalants.[83] The dissent urged the school district to take the case to the Supreme Court so as to resolve the split between the circuits.[84] On June 11, 2001, the Board of Education agreed unanimously to petition the United States Supreme Court to hear the case. Board member Tony O'Rorke commented on the vote and said: "We do this for a reason and that is for the kids in the district ... Why stop now ... It's been a huge issue to us ... It's not just for Tecumseh, but for the state of Oklahoma."[85]

The Supreme Court

As we follow the case to the Supreme Court, we can see that Lindsay's case is distinguishable from James Acton's case in several ways. First, the drug problem in Vernonia was significant and the athletes were identified as the ringleaders and source of the problem. In Tecumseh, the drug problem was minimal and there was no evidence that the students who participated in extracurricular activities were the source of that minimal problem. The athletes in Vernonia had a lower expectation of privacy because they showered together and agreed to adhere to state-wide regulations, including submitting to physicals, maintaining certain grades, and following specific disciplinary standards. Thus, the testing was a lesser intrusion on their privacy. The extracurricular activity students in Tecumseh only had to maintain academic standards set by the state and follow some rules set by the specific activity's advisor.[86] In addition, most students participate in some extracurricular activity because involvement in these activities is an integral part of the education experience and participation essentially has become a requirement in order to be competitive in applying to colleges. Finally, there is a significant safety concern in athletics that just does not exist in other extracurricular activities. Interestingly, this did not stop the school board from arguing that FHA members could get hurt by sharp cutlery or band members by a bass drum.[87] In her dissent, Justice Ginsburg responded in this humorous way. "Notwithstanding nightmarish images of out-of-control flatware, livestock run amok, and colliding tubas disturbing the peace and quiet of Tecumseh, the great majority of students the School District seeks to test in truth are engaged in activities that are not safety sensitive to an unusual degree."[88]

Linda M. Meoli, an attorney with The Education Law Center, Inc. in Oklahoma City, argued this case in the lower courts, and represented the school district at the Supreme Court. During her oral argument she maintained that the case was a minor logical extension of *Vernonia*.[89] She equated the choice to participate in athletics (*Vernonia*) with the choice to participate in extracurricular activities (*Earls*) because the voluntary nature of these activities separates the students involved in these activities from the rest of the school population. Meoli also emphasized that the purpose of the program was not to punish the students, but to deter the use of drugs.

Paul Clement, now Solicitor General, argued for the United States as amicus curiae. In his argument he emphasized the existence of a drug problem nationwide, citing that "over half of all 12th graders have tried illegal drugs by the time they graduate from high school."[90] He stressed that it was essential to reach children when they are young before drugs became a habit. To highlight the importance of this need he referred to federal statutes that carry stricter penalties for selling drugs to minors or near schools than for selling to adults.[91]

Graham A Boyd, the founder and director of the ACLU's Drug Policy Litigation Project, argued for Lindsay Earls. To support his argument to require individualized suspicion, he distinguished the facts of *Earls* from *Vernonia*. He emphasized the safety aspects in *Vernonia* (protecting athletes from the heightened risk of injury while playing under the influence of drugs), whereas in *Earls* everyone conceded that safety was not a reason for the drug policy. Further, the drug problem in *Vernonia* had reached crisis proportions because discipline was out of control, while in *Earls* the problem was minimal and to the extent it existed, the school had addressed it already with the use of dogs, security cameras, and disciplinary measures when there was some level of justification. Boyd stressed that the existence of a drug problem throughout the nation is not a valid reason alone to implement a drug testing policy in an individual school district without evidence of a major drug problem.

Justice Thomas, who gave Lindsay the impression that he was not paying attention throughout the oral arguments, wrote the opinion for a majority of five Justices finding the policy constitutional.[92] He was joined by Chief Justice Rehnquist and Justices Scalia, Kennedy and Breyer. Justice Breyer also wrote a concurring opinion.[93] Justice Thomas began the Court's opinion by stating that he will analyze the issue based upon the "reasonableness" clause of the Fourth Amendment, "which is the touchstone of the constitutionality of a governmental search."[94] Although some level of individualized suspicion is preferred, the Court has dispensed with both the need for a warrant and for individualized suspicion when a special need beyond the normal necessities of law enforcement exists. From the Court's decision in *T.L.O.*, we know that the school context present such a special need. Here, reasonableness is determined by weighing the governmental interest against the nature of the intrusion. Justice Thomas continued and used the *Vernonia* balancing test to determine the constitutionality of Tecumseh's policy.

On the intrusion side, Justice Thomas recognized that because the state is responsible for maintaining discipline, health, and safety of school children, students have lower privacy expectations in a school setting. He rejected the argument that the holding of *Vernonia* was based on the special role of the athlete. Instead, Justice Thomas reasoned that it was the school's custodial responsibility and authority, not the characteristics of athletics, that was the Court's prime justification in *Vernonia*.[95] Justice Thomas, moved by Attorney Meoli's argument, highlighted the point that students subject themselves to some intrusion because of the voluntary aspect of participation in extracurricular activities. With regard to the character of the intrusion, Justice Thomas found that the method used to obtain the urine sample and the distribution of the results were even less invasive than in *Vernonia*.[96]

On the government interest side of the equation, Justice Thomas, rather than looking at an individual school or district, accepted the generic argument that deterring drug use among our nation's youth was an immediate enough concern to justify the policy. "Indeed, the nationwide drug epidemic makes the war against drugs a pressing concern in every school."[97] He pointed out that it was not necessary to show a pervasive drug problem among the particular district's students like what existed in *Vernonia*. Justice Thomas suggested that this type of showing would be difficult to quantify. Accordingly, the Court rejected the Court of Appeals holding that required a demonstration that there was a substantial drug problem among the particular students where the testing was to be done and that the test would involve a sufficient number of students who had the problem.

With regard to the efficacy of the policy in addressing the government's concern, the Court held that the *Vernonia* decision did not require the school to test the group most likely to use drugs and that because Tecumseh's policy was a reasonably effective way to deter and prevent drug use, it met the efficacy requirement. The Court reached this conclusion without any analysis. Justice Thomas also expanded and generalized the particular safety concerns discussed in *Vernonia* and held that drug use was a health risk to all children, not just athletes. "We know all too well that drug use carries a variety of health risks for children, including death from overdose."[98] It is interesting to note that this generalization argument negates the concern for safety to others rationale that was implicit in *Vernonia*.

In his concurrence, Justice Breyer added a couple of points not otherwise mentioned. He further emphasized the government interest at stake here by pointing out that today's schools are called upon to do considerably more than schools in the past. "Today's public expects its schools not simply to teach the fundamentals, but 'to shoulder the burden of feeding students breakfast and lunch, offering before and after school child care services, and providing medical and psychological services' all in a school environment that is safe and encourages learning."[99] He also addressed the efficacy of the program and stressed that Tecumseh's policy neutralizes peer pressure, which he considered the main factor leading to children taking drugs. "It offers the adolescent a non-threatening reason to decline his friend's drug use invitations, namely, that he intends to play baseball, participate in debate, join the band, or engage in any one of half a dozen useful, interesting and important activities."[100] Justice Breyer also suggested that the best way to resolve issues of intrusiveness was by airing opinions in a public forum, which was done in this case. In distinguishing the Tecumseh policy from one which would involve testing the entire student body, Justice Breyer pointed out the voluntary consensual nature of participation in extracurricular activities, and suggested that one can avoid testing by choosing not to participate.

Justice Ginsburg, joined in her dissent by Justices O'Connor, Souter, and Stevens, the three Justices who previously dissented in *Vernonia*, found *Earls* to be distinguishable from *Vernonia*.[101] She looked to the reasonableness of the search under all the circumstances and cited the Court's decision in *Chandler v. Miller*[102] for the proposition that suspicionless searches should be a "closely guarded category."[103] Justice Ginsburg found significant differences between *Vernonia* and *Earls*.

First, there was no epidemic of drug use or disciplinary problems in *Earls*. Second, Vernonia's policy was limited to athletes whereas Tecumseh's policy had a much broader scope because it involved all participants in extracurricular activities. Third, the immediate safety concerns for athletes are different than those for students who participate in the choir, band, or on the academic team, as Lindsay did. Fourth, Vernonia's policy was directed at students with heavy involvement in drugs use, while in Tecumseh there was no nexus between the group of students subject to testing and any drug use at the school. In fact, there were strong indications that they were less involved in the drug culture than students not participating in extracurricular activities.[104] In their depositions, numerous teachers testified that the students participating in extracurricular activities in Tecumseh were less likely to use drugs.[105] Further, extracurricular activities serve important education goals, service all kinds of students, and although they are voluntary, they are an essential part of a student's education and play a crucial role in getting into college. When Justice Ginsburg added each of the above factors into the balancing analysis, she concluded that the search authorized by the Policy was unreasonable, and therefore violated the Fourth Amendment.

Testing for Everyone

Does the *Earls* decision give the green light to school districts to implement drug testing for the entire student population? The *Earls* decision was 5–4. In his concurrence, Justice Breyer (the crucial fifth vote) noted that students had the choice to opt out of participating in extracurricular activities to avoid the drug testing. However, because school attendance is mandatory, students facing a school-wide drug testing policy would not have the option to avoid testing by choosing not to attend school. Therefore it is unlikely that Justice Breyer would find a school-wide testing program constitutional. "Students who participate in competitive extracurricular activities voluntarily subject themselves to many of the same intrusions on their privacy as do athletes."[106] For this reason, the courts could find that the involuntary nature of attending public school increased the students' privacy interests enough to tip the "balancing test" scales against testing all students.[107]

A further issue to be considered with a school-wide drug testing policy is the consequence of failing the drug test. Being penalized by not being allowed to participate in the particular extracurricular activity is certainly less severe than suspension from school. The costlier consequences of an all-student drug testing policy also add weight to the privacy intrusion side of the scale[108].

Another grey area is just how much of a drug problem must be demonstrated by a school district to justify implementing a drug testing policy. Although the problem in Tecumseh was substantially less severe than what existed in Vernonia, there was still some semblance of a drug problem. The majority in *Earls* was unclear as to just how much a problem must be demonstrated in order to justify implementing a testing program. Some of the language of the decision seems to hold that the generic problem of drug use among the nation's youth constitutes a significant government concern. On the other hand, there is at least some language that indicates that drug use in Tecumseh was increasing and that this factor played a role in the Court's decision. Some lower courts have adopted the generic approach that "drug and alcohol abuse in public schools is a serious social problem today in every part of the country" and thus is a sufficient justification for any school district to commence testing even without any showing that "there is a demonstrable problem with substance abuse among its own students."[109] State courts also may apply provisions of their own state constitutions. In 2003, the New Jersey Supreme Court applied its own state constitution and found that the demonstration of a significant drug problem within a school district was an important factor that justified the challenged policy and therefore the court held that the policy was constitutional.[110]

Since the *Earls* decision, Justice O'Connor, who dissented in both *Vernonia* and *Earls*, has been replaced by Justice Alito. Although Justice Alito did not decide any school drug testing cases while serving as a judge on the Third Circuit, he did invalidate a drug testing program for maintenance workers employed by a transportation authority.[111] In doing the balance, he found on the intrusion side that the workers, unlike the railroad workers in *Skinner*, did not have a diminished expectation of privacy as there were not pervasive regulations involving this job. On the government interest side of the balance, he did not find a substantial risk of harm to others. This case demonstrates the flexibility and subjectivity in the balancing standard and it is therefore hard to draw any insights from it for the school setting.

The additions to the U.S. Supreme Court of Chief Justice Roberts and Justice Alito certainly will affect Fourth Amendment jurisprudence. In *Samson v. California*,[112] a case involving the unjustified search of a parolee, both Chief Justice Roberts and Justice Alito joined with the majority opinion written by Justice Thomas in allowing such searches. The Court upheld the search after applying the balancing test that we have been discussing. In *Hudson v. Michigan*, both Chief Justice Roberts and Justice Alito joined Justices Scalia and Thomas in holding that a knock-and-announce violation did not require suppression of all evidence.[113] In one other case involving the Fourth Amendment in which Justice Alito did not take part, Chief Justice Roberts joined with Justices Scalia and Thomas and ruled in favor of the government.[114]

Do Student Drug Testing Policies Work?

The short answer to this decisive question is that we are not really sure. The *Earls* decision is emblematic of the controversy associated with student drug testing. Studies show that substance abuse among 7th to 12th graders is declining with regard to marijuana, cocaine, heroin, ecstasy, methamphetamines, and LSD. But the use of inhalants and prescription medication is on the rise.[115] According to the 2005 *Monitoring the Future Study* completed by the Institute for Social Research at the University of Michigan, the use of illicit drugs among 8th, 10th, and 12th graders has declined by 35%, 23% and 10%, respectively, since peak usage years in the mid 1990s.[116] However, despite some evidence of a decline in drug use, adolescent drug abuse has remained a major concern throughout the country and there is much debate over the effectiveness of drug testing in combating this problem.

Opponents of student drug testing argue that testing students does not deter drug abuse, and rather, may increase drug use in some cases. Because extracurricular students already are less likely to use drugs, testing these students does not deter others from using drugs, and on the contrary, may discourage those who could most benefit from more structured extracurricular activities from participating. Extracurricular students are more likely to stay in school, earn higher grades, and set and achieve higher educational goals.[117] This indicates that testing students who are the least likely to use illegal drugs does not effectively address the school district's goal to prevent drug use among its students.

Opponents also argue that these policies are expensive and the money would be better spent on other forms of deterrence, such as increased educational programming and after-school activities. The typical cost of a drug test per student is $42,[118] and the estimated annual cost to school districts per year is anywhere from $1,500 to $36,500.[119]

Supporters of student drug testing argue that drug testing gives students another reason to "just say no." Danny Jacobs, Assistant Superintendent of the Tecumseh Schools, said that he got letters from students when the policy was in abeyance during the case, asking him to reinstate the policy so that they could use the drug testing as an excuse to say no to peer pressure.[120] White House Drug Czar John Walters commented "It'll give a kid a suit of armor."[121] Peer pressure is an interesting factor when considering student drug testing policies. In a survey of student athletes conducted by the U.S. Department of Education, 25% and 60% of the students admitted to using marijuana and alcohol respectively.[122] The same students, however, said that if there was a mandatory drug testing policy, only 9% would continue using marijuana and only 12% would continue using alcohol.[123]

Both sides of the debate agree that there have been few organized empirical studies conducted to determine the efficacy of drug testing in combating drug abuse. The Office of Safe and Drug–Free Schools within the U.S. Department of Education is about to conduct the first large scale evaluation of mandatory random student drug testing policies. This year, a preference will be given to those schools applying to receive federal grants that agree to participate in the study.[124] Half of the schools in the study will start random student drug testing and the other half will delay for a year. After a year, follow-up surveys will be distributed to compare drug use among the schools.[125]

Legal Status of Student Drug Testing Today— State Constitutional Challenges

In 1977, in response to Supreme Court decisions that cut back on individual protections, Justice Brennan wrote a seminal article urging states to apply their own constitutional principles to expand individual rights.[126] In the last thirty years, many states followed Justice Brennan's suggestion and interpreted their own state laws to provide greater individual protections than those provided by the Bill of Rights. This phenomenon is called the "new federalism."[127] Certainly school drug testing, a local and state issue, might be an ideal opportunity for the application of state law. In sharp contrast to the lack of empirical evidence presented in *Earls*, a review of the states that have addressed this issue utilizing their own laws does provide some indication that most of the states want to see a discernable drug problem.

In a 2003 case, the Pennsylvania Supreme Court applied its own state constitution and pointed to the reasoning in *Vernonia* for support when it held that the challenged policy would "pass constitutional scrutiny only if the District makes some actual showing of the specific need for the policy and an explanation of its basis for believing that the policy would address that need."[128] The court needed to see a greater demonstration of a drug problem than *Earls* had required. In addition, it needed to see that the method chosen would actually test the drug users like in *Vernonia*, or at the least, a showing that the policy would directly address the existing demonstrated drug problem.

The Supreme Court of New Jersey, by a close 4–3 decision, turned to *Earls* for guidance, although not for absolute precedent, and held an extracurricular testing policy reasonable under the New Jersey Constitution.[129] The court deviated from the *Earls* decision by requiring that "schools will have to base their intended programs on a meticulously established record."[130] In this case there was significant evidence of a drug problem including: the testimony of the school principal that she was personally aware of two students snorting heroin on campus; the fact that during one school year, thirty students were drug tested under the existing suspicion-based policy and twenty-seven (ninety percent) tested positive; and the results of a survey of the students that showed that over 33% of tenth through twelfth graders had used marijuana, 13% of seniors had tried cocaine, 12% of juniors had used hallucinogens, and 21% of freshmen had tried inhalants.[131]

The Texas Court of Appeals, in applying its state constitution, relied on *Earls* as precedent when it found a random drug testing policy constitutional because the language of the Texas Constitution did not afford greater protection than the Fourth Amendment.[132] Prior to the *Earls* decision, Indiana[133] and Oregon[134] upheld extracurricular testing utilizing their own state constitutional principles. It is interesting to note that unlike *Earls*, in both the Indiana and Oregon cases, there was a record of demonstrated drug abuse among the students. In Indiana, the school district enacted its policy after a survey revealed that students in the district were using drugs more than other students in the state. In addition, during one school year there were five expulsions and five suspensions of students for drug usage.[135] Similarly, in New Jersey a survey showed that the school's students were using drugs at a higher rate than other students in the state.[136] In an Oregon case, there was a documented epidemic of drug use among the school's athletes similar to that in *Vernonia*.[137] Over 80% of the student athletes reported using alcohol, more than 62% reported that they had either driven drunk or been in the car with a drunk driver, and 25% had tried anywhere from two to seven different types of drugs.[138] In each of these cases there was a well-documented drug abuse problem among the students in the schools. This is a sharp contrast to the lack of empirical evidence presented in *Earls*.

Conclusion

The case of Lindsay Earls represents a significant expansion on suspicionless drug testing in schools. Despite the many factual differences with *Vernonia*, the Court through the application of the balancing test extended the opportunities for drug testing to extracurricular activities. In doing the balance by weighing governmental interest with the intrusion on the individual, the Justices cannot help but bring their own ideological perspectives with regard to drug use in the schools.

You might recall that Justice Brennan referred to the balancing as "Rohrschach-like." Although the balancing approach looks as though it is steeped in an analytical foundation, it is nothing more than a Justice's attitude toward the so-called drug war.

Irrespective of the debate surrounding the efficacy of random student drug testing policies, and the uncertainty over how far the *Earls* decision will allow school boards to go in enacting their policies, the number of schools adopting these policies is increasing. As of June 2006, approximately 13% of the nation's high schools had adopted random student drug testing policies.[139] Although it is difficult to determine how quickly these policies are expanding, the number of mandatory or voluntary drug testing programs is increasing in Alaska, Arkansas, California, Connecticut, Florida, Georgia, Indiana, Kentucky, Mississippi, New Jersey, North Carolina, Oklahoma, Oregon, Pennsylvania, and Texas.[140] Tom Angell, campaign director for Students for Sensible Drug Policy, hears from students and parents who oppose testing and estimates that one school board per week adopts a new testing policy.[141]

Since *Earls* the Bush Administration has made student drug testing of middle and high school students a priority.[142] Federal funding for drug testing policies has increased from $2 million in 2003 to more than $7 million in 2005, and the White House is pushing for $15 million to fund these policies next year.[143] The number of public schools receiving federal funding to subsidize drug testing policies in 2005–2006 jumped from 79 the previous year, to 373.[144] However, the number of schools with testing policies is still a small percentage of the approximately 28,000 public schools in the country.[145] This may be because schools are uncertain about how their policies will fare under state constitutional challenges or they simple have more important items on their agenda like reducing class size or shoring up the science curriculum. It seems that battles in the state courts ultimately will determine the future of student drug testing policies as courts can choose to follow the Supreme Court's precedent in *Earls*, or can interpret their state constitutions to grant their student citizens greater privacy rights.

Postscript

In a recent interview, David Earls, Lindsay's father, stated that he has no regrets over the lawsuit and would do it again even knowing its outcome. "I am angry for parents and kids subjected to it (mandatory drug testing). As a parent, I had something taken away from me that I felt was a God-given right. I should be making the decision for my kids, not them."[146] Lindsay is confident the ruling one day will be overturned.[147] This opportunity may come in the near future if the Court is forced to define just how far the *Earls* decision reaches as school boards adopt policies that test ever expanding groups of students. In the fall, Nettle Creek School District in Hagerstown, Indiana, will put in effect a policy that may force the Court to revisit its decision in *Earls*. The policy will test not only all extracurricular activity participants and student drivers, but also any student who wishes to attend any school dance or class party.[148]

With at least the strong possibility of a school wide drug testing program meeting the Fourth Amendment requirements, pragmatic political and economic concerns will enter the equation. First, drug testing is expensive. In times of tight school budgets with user fees and reduction of teaching staff, it is hard to imagine a school board including drug testing as part of its budget or passing it on to parents who already have been assessed additional costs. This is coupled with the fundamental question of just how effective these programs are at deterring drug use among students. Danny Jacobs, Assistant Superintendent of Tecumseh Schools, insisted that the policy has been "incredibly effective."[149] There is no empirical evidence to support this statement, however. Many experts including the National Education Association and the American Academy of Pediatrics have suggested that drug education is much more effective than drug testing.[150] Since there is no clear cut evidence of the effectiveness of drug testing, should we allow such a policy to undermine the sacred privacy interest of school children? How are they to learn of the special freedoms that this country has symbolized when their schools, by their actions, are demonstrating that the individual privacy traditionally protected by the Fourth Amendment simply does not matter?

Endnotes

1. I wish to thank Jennifer Dolle and Hillary Massey, my research assistants, for their superb work. I also wish to thank Lindsay Earls for her cooperation in sharing her story with us.

2. New Jersey v. T.L.O., 469 U.S. 325, 385–6 (1985).

3. Pottawatomie County v. Earls, 536 U.S. 822, 854 (2002) (Ginsburg, J., dissenting) (citing Olmstead v. United States, 277 U.S. 438, 485 (1928)).

4. *Id.*

5. *Id.* at 855 (Ginsburg, J., dissenting).

6. Tecumseh Public School District Student Drug Testing Consent Form

Statement of Purpose and Intent

Participation in school sponsored extra-curricular activities at the Tecumseh School District is a privilege. Activity Students carry a responsibility to themselves, their fellow students, their parents, and their school to set the highest possible examples of conduct, which includes avoiding the use or possession of illegal drugs.

Drug use of any kind is in incompatible with participation in extra-curricular activities on behalf of the Tecumseh Public School District. For the safety, health, and well being of the student of the Tecumseh Public School District, the Tecumseh Public School District has adopted the attached Activity Student Drug Testing Policy and the Student Drug Testing Consent for use by all participating students at the middle school and high school levels.

Participation in Extra–Curricular Activities

Each Activity Student shall be provided with a copy of the Activity Student Drug Testing Policy and Student Drug Testing Consent which shall be read, signed and dated by the student, parent or custodial guardian, and coach/sponsor before such student shall be eligible to practice or participate in any interscholastic activities. The consent shall be to provide a urine sample: a) as part of their annual physical or for eligibility for participation; b) as chosen by the random selection basis; and c) at any time requested based on reasonable suspicion to be tested for illegal or performance-enhancing drugs. No student shall be allowed to practice or participate in any activity governed by the policy unless the student has returned the properly signed Student Drug Testing Consent.

Student's Last Name First Name MI

I understand after having read the "Student Activity Drug Testing Policy" and "Student Drug Testing Consent," that, out of care for my safety and health, the Tecumseh Public School District enforces the rules applying to the consumption or possession of illegal and performance-enhancing drugs. As a member of a Tecumseh extra-curricular interscholastic activity, I realize that the personal decision that I make daily in regard to the consumption or possession of illegal or performance-enhancing drugs may affect my health and well-being as well as the possible endangerment of those around me and reflect upon any organization with which I am associated. If I choose to violate school policy regarding the use or possession of illegal or performance-enhancing drugs any time while I am involved in in-season or off-season activities, I understand upon determination of that violation I will be subject to the restrictions on my participation as outlined in the Policy.

Signature of Student Date

We have read and understood the Tecumseh Public School District "Activity Student Drug Testing Policy" and "Student Drug Testing Consent." We desire that the student named above participate in the extracurricular interscholastic programs of the Tecumseh Public School District and we hereby voluntarily agree to be subject to its terms. We accept the method of obtaining urine samples, testing and analysis of such specimens, and all other aspects of the program. We further agree and consent to the disclosure of the sampling, testing and results as provided in this program.

Signature of Parent or Custodial Guardian Date

7. Form presented on website believed to be the form Lindsay received.

8. *Earls*, 536 U.S. at 832.

9. Joint Appendix to the Supreme Court, Dec. 31, 2001, at 17a (Complaint for Declaratory and Injunctive Relief filed Aug. 18, 1999), Pottawatomie County v. Earls, 536 U.S. 822 (2002) (No. 01–332).

10. Earls v. Board of Educ., Tecumseh Pub. Sch. Dist., 115 F.Supp.2d 1281 (W.D. Okla. 2000).

11. Earls v. Board of Educ., Tecumseh Pub. Sch. Dist., 242 F.3d 1264 (10th Cir. 2001).

12. Telephone Interview by Robert Bloom and Hillary Massey with Lindsay Earls (April 11, 2006).

13. Transcript of Oral Argument at Supreme Court, March 19, 2002, Pottawatomie County v. Earls, 536 U.S. 822 (2002) (No. 01–332), 2002 WL 485032, at *55–56.

14. Kennedy's comments are reminiscent of a comment by a parent who attended the school board meeting that adopted the policy: "[I]f you don't take them [drugs] you don't have anything to worry about." Amy Greene, *Students' Suit Stirs Tecumseh: National Spotlight Hard to Avoid*, The Daily Oklahoman, Aug. 25, 1999, at 1.

15. Telephone Interview by Robert Bloom and Hillary Massey with Lindsay Earls (April 11, 2006).

16. *Id.*

17. *Id.*

18. Background information on Tecumseh, incidents of student drug use, the Policy enacting process, and testing results is drawn from the record in the case before the United States Supreme Court (including the Joint Appendix filed by the parties on Dec. 21, 2001); a telephone interview with Lindsay Earls on Apr. 11, 2006; a telephone interview by Jennifer Dolle with Danny Jacobs, Assistant Superintendent of Tecumseh Public Schools on July 11, 2006; and statistics from the 2000 U.S. Census.

19. U.S. Const. amend. IV.

20. Katz v. United States, 389 U.S. 347, 360 (1967).

21. The Fourth Amendment reads: The right of the people to be secure in their persons, houses, papers, and effects, against unreasonable searches and seizures, shall not be violated, and no warrants shall issue, but upon probable cause, supported by oath or affirmation, and particularly describing the place to be searched, and the persons or things to be seized.

22. According to the Supreme Court, probable cause exists when "the facts and circumstances within their [the officers'] knowledge and of which they had reasonably trustworthy information were sufficient to warrant a prudent man in believing that the [suspect] had committed or was committing an offense." *See* Beck v. Ohio, 379 U.S. 89, 91 (1964).

23. 469 U.S. 325 (1985).

24. *See* 387 U.S. 523, 536–37 (1967).

25. *Id.*

26. *See id.* at 535.

27. *See id.* at 538–39.

28. *See id.* at 538 ("Having concluded that the area inspection is a 'reasonable' search of private property within the meaning of the Fourth Amendment, it is obvious that 'probable cause' to issue a warrant to inspect must exist if reasonable legislative or administrative standards for conducting an area inspection are satisfied with respect to a particular dwelling.").

29. *See, e.g., id.* at 535.

30. *See, e.g.*, Donovan v. Dewey, 452 U.S. 594, 602–03 (1981) (upholding warrantless inspections required by the Mine Safety and Health Act). *See also* United States v. Biswell, 406 U.S. 311 (1972) (upholding warrantless inspections required by the Gun Control Act of 1968).

31. 392 U.S. 1 (1968).

32. Because no crime was yet committed, traditional criminal probable cause simply would not work.

33. 387 U.S. 523 (1967).

34. *Id.* at 528.

35. *Id.* at 530.

36. 450 S.W.2d 715 (Tex. Civ. App. 1970).

37. 469 U.S. 325 (1985). T.L.O. is the initials of the plaintiff, who was a minor.

38. Ingraham v. Wright, 430 U.S. 651 (1977) (noting in a corporal punishment case that the authority of teachers derives from a school's need to maintain group discipline and provide a proper education, rather than deriving from parental delegation).

39. Hudson v. Palmer, 468 U.S. 517 (1984).

40. *T.L.O.*, 469 U.S. at 338.

41. *Id.* at 340 (citing Almeida–Sanchez v. United States, 413 U.S. 266 (1973)).

42. In their concurrence, Justices Powell and O'Connor pointed out that because of the close relationship students develop with teachers by spending many hours together, the students have a lesser privacy expectation in this setting and therefore are entitled to less protection. 469 U.S. at 348–50.

43. *T.L.O.*, 469 U.S. at 343.

44. *Id.* at 340.

45. *Id.* at 351–52 (Blackmun, J., concurring).

46. *Id.* at 358 (Brennan, J., dissenting).

47. *Id.* at 355 (citing Terry v. Ohio, 392 U.S. 1 (1968)).

48. *T.L.O.*, 469 U.S. at 364–65 (Brennan, J., dissenting). Justice Brennan referred to the case of Illinois v. Gates, 462 U.S. 213 (1983), in which the Court moved from the so-called two prong test used to establish the veracity of informants to a more flexible, easily applicable standard looking at the totality of the circumstances. *Id.*

49. *T.L.O.*, 469 U.S. at 358 (Brennan, J., dissenting).

50. Vernonia Sch. Dist. v. Acton, 515 U.S. 646 (1995).

51. *T.L.O.*, 469 U.S. at 342 n.8. The Court did not decide, however, whether individualized suspicion was an essential element of the reasonableness standard. *Id.*

52. Harry Lenhart, ACLU Faces of Liberty Project, *available at*: http://acluor.convio.net/site/PageServer?pagename=Res_faces_acton.

53. 489 U.S. 602 (1989).

54. 489 U.S. 656 (1989).

55. *Skinner*, 489 U.S. at 619 (citing Griffin v. Wisconsin, 483 U.S. 868 (1987)).

56. *Vernonia*, 515 U.S. at 653.

57. *Id.* at 657 (citing New Jersey v. T.L.O., 469 U.S. 325 (1985)).

58. *Id.*

59. *Id.* at 658.

60. *Id.* at 661.

61. *Id.* at 662.

62. *Id.* at 662–63.

63. *Id.* at 663.

64. *Id.*

65. *Id.* at 664.

66. *Id.* at 664–65.

67. *Id.* at 666 (Ginsburg, J., concurring).

68. *Id.* at 667–68 (O'Connor, J., dissenting).

69. *Earls*, 115 F.Supp.2d 1281 (W.D. Okla. 2000).

70. Summary judgment is appropriate "if the pleadings, depositions, answers to interrogatories, and admissions on file, together with affidavits, if any, show that there is no genuine issue as to any material fact and that the moving party is entitled to judgment as a matter of law." Fed. R. Civ. P. 56(c).

71. *Earls*, 115 F.Supp.2d at 1282–83.

72. The cost of the drug test rose to $5 per student the second year of testing.

73. Three teachers and a school board president testified at deposition that they had heard students speaking openly about using drugs. Two teachers said they had seen students who appeared to be under the influence of drugs. A drug dog once found a marijuana cigarette near the boundary of the school parking lot. Joint Appendix to the Supreme Court, Dec. 21, 2001, at 103, 116, Pottawatomie County v. Earls, 536 U.S. 822 (2002) (No. 01–332).

74. *Earls*, 115 F.Supp.2d at 1287.

75. *Id.*

76. *Id.* at 1289.

77. For example, Future Farmers of America enroll in an agriculture course and Lindsay enrolled in a vocal music class to be in the school chorus.

78. *Earls*, 115 F.Supp.2d at 1295.

79. *Earls*, 242 F.3d 1264.

80. *Id.* at 1272.

81. *Id.* at 1276–77.

82. *Id.* at 1278.

83. *Earls*, 242 F.3d at 1280 (Ebel, J., dissenting), citing from Substance Abuse and Mental Health Services Administration, 1999 *National Household Survey on Drug Abuse*, *available at*: http://www.oas.samhsa.gov/nhsda/2kdetailedtabs/Vol_1_Part_1/sect1v1.htm#1.1a.

84. *Earls*, 242 F.3d at 1287 (Ebel, J., dissenting). With its decision that the policy in *Earls* was unconstitutional because the school board did not provide evidence of a drug problem in schools or that the policy would test these students using drugs, the 10th Circuit departed from precedent set by the 7th and 8th Circuits in prior decisions. In Todd v. Rush County Sch. Dist., 133 F.3d 984 (7th Cir. 1998), Joy v. Penn–Harris–Madison Sch. Corp., 212 F.3d 1052 (7th Cir. 2000), and Miller v. Wilkes, 172 F.3d 574 (8th Cir. 1999), the 7th and 8th Circuits upheld policies even without evidence of drug use in the school district. These courts based their decisions on a different interpretation of *Vernonia* than the 10th Circuit. The 10th Circuit read *Vernonia* to require some showing of a drug problem among the students tested. In contrast, the 7th and 8th Circuits cited *Vernonia* for the proposition that deterrence of drug use among children is a legitimate government interest and that a school district did not need to wait for a certain number of students to start using drugs before they enact a policy.

85. Tippi Heidebrecht, *Board Continues Fighting to Test Students for Drugs, Members Agree in Tecumseh to take Issue to Supreme Court*, The Daily Oklahoman, June 12, 2001.

86. Joint Appendix to the Supreme Court, Dec. 21, 2001, at 45, Pottawatomie County v. Earls, 536 U.S. 822 (2002) (No. 01–332).

87. Brief of Petitioners to the Supreme Court, Dec. 21, 2001, at 43, Pottawatomie County v. Earls, 536 U.S. 822 (2002) (No. 01–332).

88. *Earls*, 536 U.S. at 852 (Ginsburg, J., dissenting).

89. Transcript of Oral Argument, Pottawatomie County v. Earls, 536 U.S. 822 (2002) (No. 01–332), 2002 WL 485032, at *3.

90. Transcript of Oral Argument, Pottawatomie County v. Earls, 536 U.S. 822 (2002) (No. 01–332), 2002 WL 485032, at *21.

91. *Id.* at *28.

92. *Earls*, 536 U.S. at 822.

93. *Id.* at 838 (Breyer, J., concurring).

94. *Id.* at 828.

95. *Id.* at 831.

96. *Id.* at 832.

97. *Id.* at 834.

98. *Id.* at 837.

99. *Id.* at 840 (Breyer, J., concurring) (citing Brief for National School Boards Association, et al., as Amici Curiae at 3–4).

100. *Id.* at 840–41 (Breyer, J., concurring).

101. *Id.* at 844 (Ginsburg, J., dissenting).

102. 520 U.S. 305 (1997). In this case, the Court held that Georgia's requirement that candidates for public office pass a drug test violated the Fourth Amendment.

103. *Earls*, 536 U.S. at 854 (Ginsburg, J., dissenting).

104. "Nationwide, students who participate in extracurricular activities are significantly less likely to develop substance abuse problems than are their less involved peers." *Earls*, 536 U.S. at 853 (citing N. Zill, C. Nord, and L. Loomis, *Adolescent Time Use, Risky, Behavior, and Outcomes* 52 (1995)).

105. Joint Appendix to the Supreme Court, Dec. 21, 2001, at 101, 116, 120 (testimony of: Dean Rogers (Pres. of Bd. of Educ.), Sheila Evans (FHA teacher and coach), Danny Sterling (FFA teacher and coach)), Pottawatomie County v. Earls, 536 U.S. 822 (2002) (No. 01–332).

106. *Earls*, 536 U.S. at 831. (Breyer J, concurring).

107. Indeed in 2001, a district court in Texas held that a policy that tested all students was unconstitutional in part because the students' privacy interests were greater when all students were subjected to testing and the voluntary aspect was not present. Tannahill v. Lockney, 133 F.Supp.2d 919, 929 (N.D.Tex. 2001).

108. Consequences of requiring counseling or informing parents would be less severe than suspension and might reduce the weight of the privacy intrusion side of the scale.

109. Miller v. Wilkes, 172 F.3d 574 (8th Cir. 1999). *See* Wayne R. LaFave, *Search and Seizure* Vol. 5, § 10.11 (4th ed. 2004).

110. Joye v. Hunterdon Cent. Reg'l High Sch. Bd. of Educ., 826 A.2d 624 (N.J. 2003).

111. Bolden v. Southeastern Pennsylvania Transp. Auth., 953 F.2d 807 (3d Cir. 1991).

112. 126 S.Ct. 2193 (2006).

113. *See* Hudson v. Michigan, 126 S.Ct. 2159 (2006).

114. Georgia v. Randolph, 547 U.S. 103 (2006).

115. The Partnership for a Drug–Free America, *The Partnership Attitude Tracking Study 2005*, May 16, 2006, *available at*: http://www.rwjf.org/files/research/Full_Teen_Report5–16–06.pdf.

116. Monitoring the Future Study, University of Michigan Institute for Social Research, April 2006, *available at*: http://monitoringthefuture.org/pubs/monographs/overview2005.pdf.

117. Brief of Amici Curiae American Academy of Pediatrics et al. Supporting Respondents at 8, Pottawatomie County v. Earls, 536 U.S. 822 (2002) (No. 01–332).

118. Donna Leinwand, *More Schools Test for Drugs*, USA Today, July 12, 2006, 2006 WLNR 11982050.

119. R. Dupont, T. Campbell & J Mazza, *Elements of a Successful School–Based Drug Testing Policy*, U.S. Dept. of Educ., July 22, 2002, at 8.

120. Telephone Interview by Jennifer Dolle with Danny Jacobs, Assistant Superintendent Tecumseh Public Schools (July 11, 2006).

121. Leinwand, *More Schools, supra* note 115.

122. Dupont et al., *supra* note 116, at 3.

123. *Id.*

124. Michael Doyle, *Federal Funds Boosted for School Drug Testing*, McClatchy Newspapers, June 2, 2006, *available at*: http://www.shns.com (Click "Search" and enter key word "drug" and start and end date of June 2, 2006).

125. *Id.*

126. "State courts cannot rest when they have afforded their citizens full protection of the federal Constitution. State constitutions, too, are a part of individual liberties, their protection often extending beyond those required by Supreme Court's interpretation of federal law." William J. Brennan Jr., *State Constitutions and the Protection of Individual Rights*, 90 Harv. L. Rev. 489, 491 (1977).

127. Phrase from Charles H. Whitebread & Christopher Solbogin, Criminal Procedure 1030–1032 (4th ed. 2000).

128. Theodore v. Delaware Valley Sch. Dist., 836 A.2d 76, 92 (Pa. 2003).

129. *Joye*, 826 A.2d at 655.

130. *Id.* at 653.

131. *Id.* at 628.

132. Marble Falls Indep. Sch. Dist. v. Shell, No. 03–02–00652–CV, 2003 WL 1738417 (Tex. App. 2003).

133. Linke v. Northwestern Sch. Corp., 763 N.E.2d 972 (Ind. 2002); Penn–Harris–Madison Sch. Corp. v. Joy, 768 N.E.2d 940 (Ind. App. 2002).

134. Weber v. Oakridge Sch. Dist., 56 P.3d 504 (Or. App. 2002).

135. *Linke*, 763 N.E.2d at 975–76.

136. *Joy*, 768 N.E.2d at 942.

137. *Weber*, 56 P.3d at 508.

138. *Id.*

139. Doyle, *supra* note 123. Further, a 2003 study completed by the University of Michigan polled 894 schools nationwide and determined that 13.8% of the schools drug tested students based on suspicion, 5.3% tested student athletes, and 2.4% tested all extracurricular activity participants. The remainder of the schools did not drug test students. R. Yamaguchi, L. Johnston, & P. O'Malley, *Drug Testing in Schools: Policies, Practices, and Association with Student Drug Use*, Youth, Education and Society Occasional Paper, University of Michigan Institute for Social Research, 2003, page 11.

140. Joseph R. McKinney, *The Effectiveness and Legality of Random Student Drug Testing Programs Revisited*, 205 Ed. Law Rep. 19, 20 (2006).

141. Donna Leinwand, *Principal: Drug Testing Students Works*, USA Today, July 12, 2006, 2006 WLNR 11982078. Students for Sensible Drug Policy is a grassroots network of students pushing for sensible drug policies. *See* http://www.ssdp.org.\

142. Leinwand, *More Schools, supra* note 117.

143. Doyle, *supra* note 123.

144. Leinwand, *More Schools, supra* note 117.

145. *Id.*

146. Ann Weaver, *Woman Turns Case into Career: High School Activist's Supreme Court Challenge to Be Featured in Series*, The Oklahoman, October 13, 2005, at 11A.

147. Telephone Interview by Robert Bloom and Hillary Massey with Lindsay Earls (April 11, 2006).

148. Leinwand, *More Schools, supra* note 117.

149. Telephone interview by Jennifer Dolle with Danny Jacobs, Assistant Superintendent Tecumseh Public Schools (July 11, 2006).

150. "Experience teaches that whether a particular prevention approach will work depends critically on the perceptions and responses of its adolescent subjects, and involuntary, school-based urine testing regimes of the sort at issue—because they are experienced as intensely intrusive and distrustful—are especially unlikely to work as intended." Brief of Amici Curiae American Academy of Pediatrics, National Education Association et al. Supporting Respondents at 4, Pottawatomie County v. Earls, 536 U.S. 822 (2002) (No. 01–332).

*

Contributors

Michael A. Olivas is the William B. Bates Distinguished Chair in Law at the University of Houston Law Center and Director of the Institute for Higher Education Law and Governance at UH. From 1983–1987, he also chaired the UH graduate program in Higher Education. From 1990–95, he served as Associate Dean of the Law Center; he once again served in 2001–2004. He was named Bates Professor of Law in 1996, and Bates Distinguished Chair in 2002. In 2001, he was selected for the Esther Farfel Award, as the Outstanding Professor at the University of Houston. Before joining the faculty at the University of Houston in 1982, Professor Olivas held teaching and research positions at the Ohio State University and Howard University; he served as Director of Research for the League of United Latin American Citizens (LULAC) in Washington, D.C. from 1979–1982. In 1989–90, he was a Visiting Professor of Law at the University of Wisconsin, and Special Counsel to then-Chancellor Donna Shalala. In 1997, he held the Mason Ladd Distinguished Visiting Chair at the University of Iowa College of Law. He is the author or co-author of eight books, including The Dilemma of Access (Howard University Press, 1979), Latino College Students (Teachers College Press, 1986), Prepaid College Tuition Programs (College Board, 1993) and The Law and Higher Education (3rd ed., Carolina Academic Press, 2006). His most recent book, Colored Men and Hombres Aqui, was published in 2006. He has served on the editorial board of more than 20 scholarly journals. He has been elected to membership in the American Law Institute and the National Academy of Education, the only person to have been selected to both honor academies. He served as General Counsel to the American Association of University Professors (AAUP) from 1994–98. He has been designated as a NACUA Fellow by the National Association of College and University Attorneys.

Ronna Greff Schneider is Professor of Law at the University of Cincinnati College of Law where she teaches courses focusing on Constitutional Law, Education Law, and the First Amendment. She is the author of Education Law: First Amendment, Due Process, and Discrimination Litigation (Thomson West 2004). She has written on civil rights issues, including a book chapter, *Hate Speech in the United States: Recent Legal Developments*, in Striking A Balance: Hate Speech, Freedom of Expression and Non–Discrimination 269 (Sandy Colliver, ed.,

Article 19, International Centre Against Censorship and the Human Rights Centre, University of Essex, UK 1992). She clerked for the Honorable Frank H. Freedman of the federal district court in Massachusetts. She has twice served as the Chair of the Association of American Law Schools Section on Law and Education.

Professor Leland Ware was appointed in 2000 as the first holder of the Louis L. Redding Chair for the Study of Law and Public Policy at the University of Delaware. Before his present appointment, he was a professor of law at St. Louis University School of Law from 1987 to 2000. He was a visiting professor at Boston College Law School in 1992 and at the Ruhr University in Bochum, Germany, in 1997. Professor Ware was University Counsel at Howard University from 1984 to 1987. For the five years prior to his position at Howard, he was a Trial Attorney with the U.S. Department of Justice, Civil Division, in Washington, D.C. He had previously practiced with a private firm in Atlanta, Georgia, and with the U.S. Department of Health, Education and Welfare. Professor Ware has authored more than eighty articles in academic journals and other publications on various aspects of civil rights law. He is a co-author, with Robert Cottrol and Raymond Diamond, of Brown v. Board of Education: Caste, Culture and the Constitution (2003). He has lectured and made other presentations to numerous audiences in the United Sates and Europe. Professor Ware serves on the editorial board of the Fair Housing/ Fair Lending Reporter. He is a member of the Board of Directors of WHYY Inc., Philadelphia and Delaware's Public Broadcasting (radio and television) affiliate. At the University of Delaware, Professor Ware teaches courses in Civil Rights Law, Administrative Law and Employment Law. Professor Ware is a graduate of Fisk University and Boston College Law School.

Michael Heise, Professor of Law at Cornell Law School, specializes in empirical legal scholarship and bridging empirical methodologies, legal theory, and policy analysis. He writes in public and private law areas, including civil justice reform, punitive damages, education policy, criminal sentencing, and judicial decisionmaking. Professor Heise's teaching areas include torts, empirical methods for lawyers, constitutional law, education law, and law and social science. His scholarly publications include numerous contributions to education law, with an emphasis on issues relating to school choice, desegregation, school finance, and equal educational opportunity. Professor Heise has co-edited the Journal of Empirical Legal Studies since 2005.

Wendy Parker is Professor of Law at Wake Forest University School of Law. She joined the Wake Forest faculty in 2003 from the University of Cincinnati College of Law, where she twice won the Goldman Prize for Excellence in Teaching. She writes in the area of civil rights, focusing on school desegregation and remedies for racial and ethnic discrimination. She teaches Civil Procedure, Civil Rights Remedies, Remedies, and Torts. Before teaching, Professor Parker litigated school desegregation cases for the Lawyers' Committee for Civil Rights as a Skadden Fellow and for the U.S. Department of Justice as a Trial Attorney. She graduated magna cum laude from The University of Texas at Austin and with honors from The University of Texas School of Law. She also served as a law clerk to Judge Jerre S. Williams of the Court of Appeals for the Fifth Circuit.

Laura Rothstein is Professor of Law and Distinguished University Scholar, University of Louisville, Louis D. Brandeis School of Law. She joined the University of Louisville as Professor of Law and Dean in 2000, serving as dean until 2005. She has written and lectured extensively on disability discrimination, with emphasis on disability issues in higher education, particularly legal education. She has served in a number of leadership positions on disability and diversity issues in legal education, including chairing the AALS Special Committee on Disability Issues (1988–1990). From 1980 to 1986, she served as Faculty Editor of the Journal of College and University Law, the law journal published by the National Association of College and University Attorneys. Before coming to the University of Louisville, Professor Rothstein was a Law Foundation Professor of Law at the University of Houston Law Center, where she served as Associate Dean for Graduate Legal Studies (2004–2005) and Associate Dean for Student Affairs (1987–1993). Since 1976, she has served on the faculties at five law schools. She earned her bachelor's degree from the University of Kansas and her doctor of jurisprudence from Georgetown University Law Center. She acknowledges with appreciation the research support provided by the University of Louisville and the Louis D. Brandeis School of Law.

Rachel F. Moran is the Robert D. and Leslie-Kay Raven Professor of Law at the University of California School of Law (Boalt Hall) and Director of the Institute for the Study of Social Change at the University of California at Berkeley. She is the co-author of the fourth edition of Educational Policy and the Law (with Mark G. Yudof, David L.Kirp, and Betsy Levin), co-editor of a forthcoming book on Race Law Stories (with Devon Carbado), and author of Interracial Intimacy: The Regulation of Race and Romance. She has published numerous articles on educational equity, including *Undone by Law: The Uncertain Legacy of Lau v. Nichols*, 16 Berkeley La Raza Law Journal 1 (2005); *Brown's Legacy: The Evolution of Educational Equity*, 66 University of Pittsburgh Law Review 155 (2004); *Bilingual Education, Immigration, and the Culture of Disinvestment*, 2 Iowa Journal of Gender, Race, and Justice 163 (1999); *The Politics of Discretion: Federal Intervention in Bilingual Education*, 76 California Law Review 1249 (1988); and *Bilingual Education as a Status Conflict*, 75 California Law Review 321 (1987).

Professor Moran is grateful to Roger Rice, Edward H. Steinman, Stephen D. Sugarman, Ling-chi Wang, and Judge Raymond Williamson, who enriched the story of *Lau v. Nichols* by sharing their recollections of the case. She also appreciates the invaluable research assistance that she received from Bernice Espinoza and Arthur Liou as well as helpful feedback from her colleagues Stephen D. Sugarman and Goodwin Liu. Finally, she is grateful to Dr. Gary Orfield, who called to her attention relevant information on the Nixon administration's support for bilingual programs, which appeared in the Watergate hearings.

Rosemary C. Salomone is the Kenneth Wang Professor of Law at St. John's University School of Law. Previously, she served on the faculty of the Harvard Graduate School of Education in the Administration, Planning, and Social Policy Program and in the Institute for Educational Management. She is a former trustee of the State University of New York and former chair of the Education and the Law Committee of the Association of the Bar of the City of New York and the Section on Education Law of the Association of American Law Schools. She has held the Bretzfelder fellowship in Constitutional Law at Columbia University as well as a fellowship from the Open Society Institute. She is the author of Same, Different, Equal: Rethinking Single–Sex Schooling (Yale University Press); Visions of Schooling: Conscience, Community, and Common Education (Yale University Press); and Equal Education under Law: Legal Rights and Federal Policy in the Post–"Brown Era" (St. Martin's Press). She is currently writing on a book on language, identity, and schooling. She gratefully acknowledges the support of the Faculty Research Program at St. John's University School of Law and the Kenneth Wang endowment.

Robert M. O'Neil, director of the Thomas Jefferson Center for the Protection of Free Expression and an authority on the First Amendment, teaches constitutional law of free speech and press, and church and state. He came to Virginia in 1985 to become the University of Virginia's sixth president, a position he held until 1990. After his law school graduation, O'Neil clerked for U.S. Supreme Court Justice William J. Brennan, Jr. In 1963 he began his law faculty career, first as a teacher at the University of California–Berkeley and then as a teacher-administrator. His posts included provost of the University of Cincinnati, vice-president of Indiana University, and president of the statewide University of Wisconsin system. He has served as the president of the Virginia Council for Open Government, chairman of the Council for America's First Freedom, director of the Commonwealth Fund and the James River Corporation, and chair of the American Association of University Professors Committee on Academic Freedom and Tenure. He is currently director of the Ford Foundation's Difficult Dialogues program, chair of the American Association of University Professors' Special

Committee on Academic Freedom and National Security in Time of Crisis, and is a consultant to the Association of Governing Boards on issues of Board Accountability. He has served as a trustee for the Teachers Insurance & Annuity Association (TIAA) and as a trustee for the Carnegie Foundation for the Advancement of Teaching. He has also chaired the National Association of State Universities and Land–Grant Colleges, a commission on the future of Virginia's judicial system, and a commission of the Markle Foundation on media coverage of presidential elections.

Linda Greene is the Evjue Bascom Professor of Law at the University of Wisconsin Madison. She teaches constitutional law, civil rights law, and civil procedure. She was Associate Vice Chancellor of the University of Wisconsin Madison from 1999–2005. A graduate of the University of California Berkeley Law School, she was a Staff Attorney to the NAACP Legal Defense Fund in New York where she specialized in housing discrimination, employment discrimination, and death penalty issues. She was also a Civil and Constitutional Rights Attorney with the City of Los Angeles, as well as Counsel to the United States Senate Judiciary Committee where she specialized in Judicial Confirmations, federal courts, constitutional law, and civil rights. She has been a tenured professor at the University of Oregon and a visiting professor at Harvard and Georgetown Law Schools. She teaches abroad in Germany, Japan, and Thailand.

Anne Proffitt Dupre, J. Alton Hosch Professor of Law at the University of Georgia, teaches education law, children and the law, and contracts. She is the co-author of the casebook Children and the Law (2d ed. LexisNexis) (with Gardner) and has published extensively on education law and policy, including *The Spirit of Serrano: Past, Present, and Future* in the Journal of Education Finance (with Dayton); *School Finance Litigation: Who's Winning the War* in the Vanderbilt Law Review (with Dayton); *Education Transformation: The Lesson from Argentina* in the Vanderbilt Journal of Transnational Law; *A Study in Double Standards: Discipline and the Disabled Student* in the Washington Law Review; *Disability, Deference, and the Integrity of the Academic Enterprise* in the Georgia Law Review; and *Should Students Have Constitutional Rights? Keeping Order in the Public Schools* in the George Washington University Law Review. Dupre is currently writing a book titled School Speech for Harvard University Press. She is Senior Fellow at the UGA Institute of Higher Education and the co-director of the Education Law Consortium. Dupre has been honored by law students with the Faculty Book Award for Excellence in Teaching and the John C. O'Byrne Award for Significant Contributions Furthering Faculty–Student Relations. She has received several campus-wide honors, including the UGA Teaching Academy, UGA International Fellow and the UGA Lilly Teaching Fellowship. In May 2007 she was selected to be a UGA Senior Teaching Fellow. Dupre served as judicial law clerk to U.S. Supreme Court Justice Harry A. Blackmun following her clerkship with Judge J.L. Edmondson of the Eleventh Circuit U.S. Court of Appeals. She practiced law with the Washington, D.C., firm of Shaw, Pittman, Potts & Trowbridge. Dupre earned a bachelor's degree from the University of Rhode Island and a law degree from UGA, where she graduated first in her class and served as editor-in-chief of the Georgia Law Review.

Leslie Griffin holds the Larry & Joanne Doherty Chair in Legal Ethics at the University of Houston Law Center. She is author most recently of *Law and Religion: Cases and Materials* (Foundation Press, 2007). She has written numerous articles about the First Amendment and the ethics of the legal profession.

Erwin Chemerinsky is the Alston & Bird Professor of Law and Political Science, Duke University. Before joining the Duke faculty in 2004, he taught for 21 years at the University of Southern California, where he was the Sydney M. Irmas Professor of Public Interest Law, Legal Ethics, and Political Science. He is the author of four books and over 100 law review articles on issues of constitutional law and federal court jurisdiction. He also frequently argues appellate cases, including having argued several in the United States Supreme Court. Beginning in 2007 he assumed the inaugural deanship of the School of Law at the University of California, Irvine.

Robert M. Bloom is the Robert Popeo Scholar and Professor of Law at the Boston College Law School. His research interest focuses on the police practice aspect of criminal procedure. He has written extensively in this area with a focus on the fourth amendment. His books include: "Searches, Seizures, and Warrants" (Praeger 2003) "Ratting" (Praeger 2002). He is the co-author (with Professor Mark Brodin) "Criminal Procedure: The Constitution and The Police" now in its fifth edition (Aspen Press 2007). He recently wrote an article (with William Dunn) published in the William and Mary Bill of Rights Journal (Fall 2006) focusing on the Fourth Amendment implications of President Bush's use of the National Security Agency. He has also taught at Boston University Law School, Temple University Law school program in Rome, Italy, and at Kwansei Gakuin University School of Law in Nishinomiya, Japan. He has taught comparative criminal procedure in Italy and introduction to American law in Japan. He has lectured on the American Jury System in Italy, Japan, and Tomsk, Russia. Prior to entering law school teaching, he was a Reginald Heber Smith Fellow assigned initially to Savannah, Georgia and then to Somerville, Massachusetts. In this capacity he represented juvenile and school children who were wrongly academically classified.

Acknowledgments

We thank the dozen authors whose work we highlight here. All of them were a joy to work with, and everyone came through with his or her promised best work, in timely fashion. We thank Paul Caron, John Bloomquist and Ryan Pfeiffer from Foundation Press, Jessica L. Contreras and Deborah Y. Jones from the University of Houston Law Center and Connie Miller from the University of Cincinnati College of Law. We also thank the Harold C. Schott Foundation for its support of this project.

†